THE PRINTED PAGE IS EVERYMAN'S UNIVERSITY

THE CIVILIZATION OF THE AMERICAN INDIAN

ALSO TRANSLATED AND EDITED BY

ALFRED BARNABY THOMAS

Forgotten Frontiers: A Study of the Spanish Indian
Policy of Don Juan Bautista de Anza, Governor of
New Mexico, 1777-1787 (Norman, University of
Oklahoma Press, 1932)

After Coronado

SPANISH EXPLORATION NORTHEAST
OF NEW MEXICO, 1696-1727

Documents from the Archives of Spain
Mexico and New Mexico

TRANSLATED AND EDITED BY

ALFRED BARNABY THOMAS

WITH A HISTORICAL INTRODUCTION

NORMAN
UNIVERSITY OF OKLAHOMA PRESS
1935

SET UP AND PRINTED AT NORMAN, OKLAHOMA, U. S. A., BY THE UNIVERSITY OF
OKLAHOMA PRESS, PUBLISHING DIVISION OF THE UNIVERSITY
FIRST EDITION APRIL 15, 1935

TO
MURIEL

PREFACE

S PAIN in the West usually means California, Arizona, New Mexico, and Texas. Spanish activities north of New Mexico are less familiar. However, touching the vast area of present Utah, Colorado, Kansas and Nebraska, the characteristic process of Spanish expansion in North America left records of exploration, accounts of tribal rivalries, the location and range of important Indian groups, and detailed the initial steps of the international struggle between Spain and France for the trans-Mississippi West.

The range of these activities covers the 280 years between Coronado (1541) and the end of Spanish rule in North America (1821). No comprehensive attempt has been made heretofore to investigate either the nature or extent of Spanish influence beyond New Mexico during these centuries. After Coronado and Oñate, a significant period of Spanish expansion into this area fell between the years, 1696-1727. The documentary record of these decades here presented, so far as it is available, portrays the chief features of this little known field of Western history.

It is a pleasure to acknowledge my debt herein to Professor Herbert E. Bolton under whose direction this investigation was initiated. From his Collection on Mexicana he supplied me with copies of the source materials that form the principal part of this study and has constantly evinced an encouraging interest in its progress during the past ten years. In the search for materials, I have greatly appreciated the aid of a Native Sons of the Golden West Fellowship, University of California, and a Fellowship on the John Simon Guggenheim Memorial Foundation, both of which provided opportunity for investigation in the Archivo General de Indias, Seville. A grant from the American Council of Learned Societies and a subsidy from the Research Council of the University of Oklahoma, for both of which I am grateful, made possible study in the archives of Mexico and the securing of transcripts and photostats. The kindly interest of Mr. P. A. F. Walter, president of the New Mexico Historical Society, facilitated the gathering of materials from the Spanish Archives of New Mexico, Santa Fé. With no wish to avoid responsibility for errors that may appear herein, I thank Mr. Marvin E. Butterfield, whose expert knowledge of the Spanish language and Mexican usage aided the revision of my translation. To the Civil Works Administration whose enlightened educational program furnished me invaluable assistance, I am indebted.

ALFRED BARNABY THOMAS

Norman, May 1, 1934

CONTENTS

	PAGE
PREFACE	vii
HISTORICAL INTRODUCTION	1
I. SPANISH EXPLORATION NORTHEAST OF NEW MEXICO, 1541-1680	5
II. SPANISH EXPEDITIONS NORTHEAST OF NEW MEXICO, 1696-1727	12
A. Early Reports of Frenchmen in the Northeast	12
B. The Flight of the Pueblo Indians: Expedition of Vargas, 1696	14
C. The Return of the Pueblo Indians: Expedition of Ulibarri, 1706	16
D. Campaign Against the Apaches: Expedition of Hurtado, 1715	22
E. Campaign against the Comanches: Expedition of Valverde, 1719	26
F. The Search for the French: The Villasur Expedition to the Platte River, 1720	33
III. PLANS TO OCCUPY EL CUARTELEJO, 1720-1727	39

DOCUMENTS RELATING TO THE NORTHEASTERN FRONTIER OF NEW MEXICO, 1696-1727

I. THE EXPEDITION OF JUAN DE ARCHULETA TO EL CUARTELEJO, 1664-1680 (*ca.*)	53
II. GOVERNOR VARGAS' DIARY OF CAMPAIGN IN PURSUIT OF THE REBELLIOUS PICURÍES, 1696	53
III. THE DIARY OF JUAN DE ULIBARRI TO EL CUARTELEJO, 1706	59
A. Governor Cuerbó Reports the Return of the Picuríes, 1706	77

IV. COUNCIL OF WAR AND DIARY OF JUAN PÁEZ HURTADO
AGAINST THE FARONES, 1715   80

    A. *Council of War, Santa Fé, July 20, 1715*

       1. TESTIMONY OF DON GERÓNIMO, SANTA FÉ, JULY 20, 1715   80
       2. TESTIMONY OF DON LORENZO, SANTA FÉ, JULY 22, 1715   82
       3. ORDER OF MOGOLLÓN, SANTA FÉ, JULY 22, 1715   82
       4. ORDER FOR COUNCIL OF WAR, SANTA FÉ, JULY 22, 1715   83
       5. COUNCIL OF WAR, SANTA FÉ, JULY 23, 1715   84

    B. *Appointment of Hurtado, Santa Fé, August 20, 1715*   86

    C. *Order to Hurtado, Santa Fé August 26, 1715*   86

    D. *List of Soldiers with Hurtado, Santa Fé,
August 28, 1715*   87
    E. *List of Settlers with Hurtado, Santa Fé,
August 28, 1715*   88
    F. *List of Pueblo Indians with Hurtado, Santa Fé,
August 28, 1715*   89
    G. *Hurtado's Review of Forces and Equipment,
Picuríes Pueblo, August 30, 1715*   90

V. DIARY OF THE CAMPAIGN OF JUAN PÁEZ HURTADO, 1715   94

VI. COUNCIL OF WAR AND DIARY OF THE CAMPAIGN OF
GOVERNOR VALVERDE, 1719   99

    A. *Order for Council of War, Santa Fé, August 13, 1719*   99

    B. *Council of War, Santa Fé, August 19, 1719*   100

VII. DIARY OF THE CAMPAIGN OF GOVERNOR VALVERDE, 1719   110

VIII. A PORTION OF THE DIARY OF VILLASUR, 1720   133

IX. PROCEEDINGS CONCERNING DESIGNS OF THE FRENCH, 1719-1727   137

    A. *Plans for the Occupation of El Cuartelejo, 1719-1727*   137

       1. CRUZ TO VALERO [TAOS, 1719]   137
       2. ORDER OF VALERO, MÉXICO, AUGUST 1, 1719   138
       3. VALERO TO CRUZ, MÉXICO, SEPTEMBER 3, 1719   139
       4. DURÁN TO VALERO, MADRID, JANUARY 30, 1719   139
       5. ORDER OF VALERO, MÉXICO, JULY 13, 1719   140

6. VALVERDE TO VALERO, SANTA FÉ, NOVEMBER 30, 1719   141
7. CRUZ TO VALERO, PARRAL, DECEMBER 11, 1719   146
8. REVOLLEDO TO VALERO, MÉXICO, DECEMBER 29, 1719   149
9. CRUZ TO VALERO, PARRAL, NOVEMBER 30, 1719   151
10. ORDER FOR COUNCIL OF WAR, MÉXICO, JANUARY 10, 1720   154
11. VALVERDE TO VALERO, SANTA FÉ, MAY 27, 1720   154
12. COUNCIL OF WAR, SANTA FÉ, JUNE 2, 1720   156
13. VALVERDE TO VALERO, SANTA FÉ, JUNE 15, 1720   160
14. VALVERDE TO VALERO, SANTA FÉ, OCTOBER 8, 1720   162
15. VALERO TO SAINZ, MÉXICO, NOVEMBER 3, 1720   167
16. SAINZ TO VALERO, MÉXICO, NOVEMBER 4, 1720   167
17. REVOLLEDO TO VALERO, MÉXICO, NOVEMBER 12, 1720   169
18. ORDER OF VALERO [MÉXICO, NOVEMBER 12, 1720]   170
19. DECLARATION OF MARTÍNEZ, MÉXICO, NOVEMBER 13, 1720   170
20. DECLARATION OF GARDUÑO, MÉXICO, NOVEMBER 15, 1720   172
21. DECLARATION OF TAMARIZ, MÉXICO, NOVEMBER 15, 1720   174
22. REVOLLEDO TO VALERO, MÉXICO, DECEMBER 9, 1720   175
23. MARTÍNEZ TO VALERO [MÉXICO, 1720]   177
24. MARTÍNEZ TO VALERO, MÉXICO, 1723   187
25. REVOLLEDO TO CASA FUERTE, MÉXICO, SEPT. 22, 1723   189
26. DECLARATION OF AVILES, MÉXICO, SEPTEMBER 25, 1723   191
27. REVOLLEDO TO CASA FUERTE, MÉXICO, JULY 11, 1724   191
28. ROSALES TO CASA FUERTE, MÉXICO, SEPTEMBER 25, 1723   192
29. REVOLLEDO TO CASA FUERTE, MÉXICO, OCTOBER 11, 1723   192
30. REVOLLEDO TO CASA FUERTE, MÉXICO, APRIL 10, 1724   192
31. ORDER FOR COUNCIL OF WAR, SANTA FÉ, 1723   193
32. DECREE FOR COUNCIL OF WAR, SANTA FÉ, NOV. 8, 1723   193
33. COUNCIL OF WAR, SANTA FÉ, NOVEMBER 9, 1723   195
34. DIARY OF BUSTAMANTE, NOVEMBER 17-27, 1724   197
35. BUSTAMANTE TO CASA FUERTE, SANTA FÉ, JAN. 10, 1724   201
36. REPLY OF THE FISCAL, MÉXICO, APRIL 2, 1724   203
37. REVOLLEDO TO CASA FUERTE, MÉXICO, JULY 12, 1724   205
38. BUSTAMANTE TO CASA FUERTE, SANTA FÉ, MAY 30, 1724   208
39. REPLY OF THE FISCAL, MÉXICO, OCTOBER 20, 1724   209
40. ORDER OF CASA FUERTE, MÉXICO, OCTOBER 21, 1724   209
41. RIVERA TO CASA FUERTE, PRESIDIO DEL PASO DEL RÍO
     DEL NORTE, SEPTEMBER 26, 1727   209
42. REPLY OF THE FISCAL, MÉXICO, DECEMBER 14, 1726   217
43. REVOLLEDO TO CASA FUERTE, MÉXICO, MARCH 31, 1727   218
44. ORDER OF CASA FUERTE, MÉXICO, APRIL 1, 1727   219

X. Proceedings of the Trial of Governor Valverde, 1726-1727 219

   A. *Writ of Rivera, El Paso, May 13, 1726* 220
   B. *Notification to Valverde, El Paso, May 13, 1726* 221
   C. *Valverde to Rivera [Santa Fé, 1726]* 222
   D. *Writ of Rivera, Santa Fé, June 7, 1726* 224
   E. *Testimony of Aguilar, Santa Fé, July 1, 1726* 226
   F. *Testimony of Tamariz, Santa Fé, July 2, 1726* 228
   G. *Confession of Valverde, Santa Fé, July 5, 1726* 230
   H. *Council of War Ordering a Presidio at La Jicarilla* 234
   I. *Council of War: The Punishment of Valverde*
      [México], 1727 239
   J. *Reply of the Fiscal, México, November 23, 1726* 240
   K. *Revolledo to Casa Fuerte, México, May 29, 1727* 241

XI. Investigation of Illegal Trading between French
      Louisiana and New Mexico, 1723 245

   A. *Order for Council of War, Santa Fé, April 19, 1724* 245
   B. *Council of War, Santa Fé, April 21–May 4, 1724* 246
     1. DECLARATION OF CASSADOS, SANTA FÉ, APRIL 21, 1724 246
     2. DECLARATION OF HURTADO, SANTA FÉ, APRIL 21, 1724 247
     3. DECLARATION OF VIJIL, SANTA FÉ, APRIL 21, 1724 248
     4. DECLARATION OF A. AGUILAR, SANTA FÉ, APRIL 21, 1724 249
     5. DECLARATION OF A. AGUILAR, JR., SANTA FÉ,
       APRIL 21, 1724 250
     6. DECLARATION OF TAMARIZ, SANTA FÉ, APRIL 22, 1724 250
     7. DECLARATION OF VEGA, SANTA FÉ, APRIL 22, 1724 252
     8. DECLARATION OF QUIROS, SANTA FÉ, APRIL 23, 1724 252
     9. DECLARATION OF ROYVAL, SANTA FÉ, APRIL 23, 1724 253
     10. DECLARATION OF ALVA, SANTA FÉ, APRIL 23, 1724 253
   C. *Edict of Bustamante, Santa Fé, May 2, 1724* 255
   D. *Bustamante to Casa Fuerte, Santa Fé, April 30, 1727* 256
   E. *Revolledo to Casa Fuerte, México, August 19, 1727* 259
   F. *Revolledo to Casa Fuerte, México, November 21, 1727* 260

EDITORIAL NOTES 261

BIBLIOGRAPHY 285

INDEX 293

HISTORICAL INTRODUCTION

HISTORICAL INTRODUCTION

WITH rare exceptions, writers fit the history of the West into the mould of the "Westward Movement." This provincial interpretation, however widely accepted, is out of joint with the three-century record of Spanish expansion northward into the Southwest. There Spaniards founded towns and cities, planted significant institutions, made important discoveries, and left invaluable records. The current practice is to brush aside this accumulated data and initiate the study of the West with the exploits of Clark, Lewis, Pike, or Austin. No attempt is offered here to unravel all the resulting confusion of thought. However, neglecting Spain's work, writers have left a two-and-a-half-century gap in plains exploration between Coronado and Pike.

Pike was not a pioneer explorer. In the vanguard of the Anglo-American movement, he entered areas already crisscrossed and named by the successors of Coronado. Every landmark, stream, and mountain range of importance honored Spanish saint or deity long before Pike began his dubious meanderings. Governor Anza had crossed the main range of the Rockies, explored Estes Park, and mounted Ute Pass in full view of the Peak, a quarter of a century before Pike christened the pile. The Arkansas bore at least two Spanish names dating from the early eighteenth century. The Canadian was the Río Colorado; the Red, the Río Rojo; the North Platte, the San Lorenzo; the South Platte, the Río de Jesús María; the Platte itself, the Río Chato; the Purgatoire, the Río de las Animas; while the Huerfano, San Carlos, Cimarron, Tucumcari, Sierra Blanca, Sangre de Cristo, Sierra de la Jicarilla, Sierra del Almagre, and an infinity of lesser streams and ranges bear testimony to an indefatigable Spanish activity north and east of New Mexico.

Throughout this vast area as far as the Platte the Spaniards had designated the more important Indian tribes: Comanches, Apaches, Cuartelejos, Faraones, Jicarillas, Flechas, Calchufines, Palomas, and other Apache bands; the Pananas (Pawnees), Utas (Utes), the Kansa. Responsible for this extensive exploratory activity and carrying on the tradition of Coronado were a host of Spanish conquerors, soldiers,

1

traders, padres, and adventurers: Humana, Leyba, Oñate, Záldivar, Baca, Salas, Archuleta, Vargas, Ulibarri, Hurtado, Valverde, Villazur, Bustamante, Menindueta, Anza, Vial, Escalante. Behind them in turn was the whole machinery of Spanish expansion: the governor, the viceroy, the king, the Church. All participated in planning or approving expeditions, projecting presidios and looking forward to expanding New Mexico northward. At the end of this long development in which Coronado is the first, appear Pike, Wilkinson, Long, Fowler. Trailing the footsteps of the French, they but continued a tradition of western exploration already several centuries old.

The years 1696-1727 encompassed an outstanding period of Spanish activity northeast of New Mexico. Spain's interest in that salient antedated the occupation of the province itself and was a reason for that conquest. The Spanish authorities of the late sixteenth century firmly believed that beyond the Pueblos was the undiscovered strait of Ánian. New Mexico surely would be a base for new expeditions to make that elusive seaway Spanish. After the Conquest, acquaintance with Pueblo legends that pointed an origin in the northwest stimulated a curiosity undeterred by the failure of seventeenth century California expeditions to discover the western end of the strait. Pueblos, captured and spirited away to unknown northern regions, told stories on their return of populous cities, great rivers, and lakes hidden in the fastness of the mountains. Indians themselves appearing in the frontier towns astonished the Spaniards with tales of a northern king who wore a crown. Late seventeenth century expeditions that pushed eastward only whetted Spanish avidity to explore *más allá*. The arrival of the eighteenth century made imperative the solution of this "northern mystery."

In the main, two factors propelled the Spaniards forward. On the one hand, disturbances among the Indians beyond the border dislocated local New Mexican arrangements with the savages there; on the other, this New Mexican advance had a vital connection with the larger expansion movements of New Spain in the later seventeenth century. In the West the hundred years of Jesuit progress along the Mexican Pacific littoral begat after 1680 the inspired work of Father Kino in Sonora, Lower Arizona, and Lower California. New Mexico itself, was a scene of vigorous Spanish efforts to reconquer the Pueblos after their revolt of 1680. Sixteen years later Vargas, by a major feat of conquest, succeeded in reëstablishing Spanish power there.

Contemporaneous with these events the Spaniards advanced into Texas at the end of the century. The slow and natural processes of the growth of New Spain had by that year carried Spaniards to the lower Río Grande. The sudden descent of La Salle in 1686 upon the Texas coast impelled a long northeastward thrust of Spanish power to block French plans for the occupation of the Mississippi. Though the specific expedition of La Salle was shortly in pieces, its genesis was of such magnitude that the Spanish mind, accustomed to think in terms of continents, sensed the threat to the Gulf, the mines of northern Mexico, and the safety of Florida. By sea and by land from Mexico and from Florida, Spanish expeditions swarmed toward the Texas coast. León's discovery in 1689 of La Salle's ruined post on the Garcitas River was warrant enough for the viceroy to direct the occupation of this vast province. In the following two years missions were founded in eastern Texas on the Nechas River. In 1693, however, with no French actually menacing Texas and the missions made unsafe by hostile Indians, the authorities abandoned the enterprise. Meanwhile, Vargas' success in the adjoining province left New Mexico as Spain's lone rampart beyond the Río Grande. Frenchmen soon renewed their pressure west of the Mississippi River. The resulting Franco-Spanish hostilities northeast of Santa Fé, linked with those on the Texas-Louisiana-Florida borders, gave to New Mexico's frontier at this early date the international character of all the "Spanish borderlands."

Beyond that far-flung line of the "Spanish borderlands" was the constant danger of Indian invasion. Continental in extent, it was bound inextricably with Spain's defense against the French and the English. In New Mexico, the danger was accentuated. Spain's control there meant assuming as her enemies those of the Pueblos. As the French in Canada befriended the Algonquins and found the Iroquois on their flank, so the Spaniards in New Mexico had to face the vast Apache tribe that encircled the Pueblo settlements. The ever-present chance of an alliance between the Pueblos and these border enemies questioned Spain's hold of the province.

The Apaches at the beginning of the eighteenth century who bedeviled the region along its northern and eastern borders were the Navajos to the northwest and the Faraones on the east. Directly to the northeast of Santa Fé were certain friendly groups of Apaches: the Jicarillas and the Carlanas or Sierra Blancas who lived in northeastern New Mexico and south of the Arkansas River; beyond that stream were the Cuartelejo and Paloma Apaches.

The peace of these inoffensive Indians was suddenly disturbed by the invasion of the Comanches. In alliance with the Utes, these invaders

3

reached the northern frontier of New Mexico at the beginning of the eighteenth century. They soon shoved their attacks into New Mexico and made the tenancy of the province even more precarious. The full force of this Comanche-Ute attack first fell, between 1696-1727, upon the northeastern sector. There, to defend themselves and the friendly Apaches, the Spaniards dispatched expeditions of significant proportions.

Combined Apache and Comanche attacks made the Spanish fear a weakened province, an easy prey to the French. This fear had considerable foundation in the fact that along the Platte River beyond the Cuartelejos were the powerful Pawnee tribes in firm alliance with the French. Pawnees had entered New Mexico in the seventeenth century as captives ransomed from the Apaches. In point of fact, however, there is no known record of a Pawnee attack upon the province itself. Yet as early as 1706 Pawnees and French were making raids upon the Cuartelejos far down in present eastern Colorado. The possibility that these combined forces would extend their forays and invade the province was an important factor in the frontier situation in the northeast.

Finally, missionary interest in the various Indian groups bordering on the north and the east drew Spanish attention thither. The natural zeal of the padres was stimulated by the Indians over the border. Observing the protection afforded the Pueblos from their enemies, the Jicarilla, in particular, sought baptism in the hope that Spain would shelter them from Comanches, Utes, and Faraones. Constantly, these Apaches, promising obedience, begged missionaries and soldiers from the fathers at Taos and the governors in Santa Fé. The latter consistently urged these wails upon the viceroy as proof of the Jicarilla hunger for Christianity.

With these powerful factors operating on the northeastern frontier of New Mexico between the years 1696-1727 it is not difficult to understand why Spanish influence spread beyond the northern frontiers. The advance assumed a variety of forms. Punitive expeditions moved forward to curb the power of the Utes, Comanches, and Faraones. A reconnaissance party explored far away to the Platte River to learn the exact location of reported French posts there. Plans were laid to include the Jicarillas, Sierra Blancas, and Cuartelejos in a widespread Apache-Spanish alliance. To buttress this project, further plans were made to establish a presidio and mission at El Cuartelejo, beyond the Arkansas River in present eastern Colorado, an undertaking modified shortly in favor of a closer site among the Jicarillas. In addition, these defensive

4

activities coincided with the actual reoccupation of Texas itself and arrangements there on the northern and eastern borders of that province for Indian alliances, presidios and missions.

Broadly viewed, Spanish expansion northeast of New Mexico in the early eighteenth century has a distinctive international flavor. More, illuminating the principles of her border Indian policy and the development of her frontier defense in western North America, her activities in this salient contribute to an understanding of the history of exploration in the trans-Mississippi West.

I. SPANISH EXPLORATION NORTHEAST OF NEW MEXICO, 1541-1680

Coronado, the pioneer, symbolizes the northward movement of Spain's frontiers in western America. With emphasis focused upon his contribution to the Pueblo civilization of New Mexico, his journey on the plains is too often viewed as the last futile act of a disappointed man. This conception has obscured the magnificent achievement of his whole undertaking. His Odyssey to Quivira initiated on the plains a long procession of Spanish explorers. Their history furnishes the needed perspective with which to view the activity of the Anglo-American—i.e., the last phase of western plains exploration.

Leaving Pecos in the spring of 1541, the line of his march moved to the southeast. His first meeting with the plains Indians, undoubtedly the Apache, was with a group called Querechos, signifying Buffalo Eaters. Beyond them still to the southeast he found in the headwaters of the Brazos, the frontiers of the great Teya nation. Indian-like, they turned him northward toward their neighbors. Pursuing the new direction of the Seven Cities, his small command traveled forty-two days across the panhandles of Texas and Oklahoma. Beyond the Arkansas River they reached, in the Kansas of today, the Indians of Quivira, who now give their name to the whole northeastern region.

"All that there is at Quivira," so one of his followers wrote, "is a very brutish people, without any decency whatever in their home nor in anything. These are of straw, like the Tarascan settlements; in some villages there are as many as two hundred houses; they have corn and beans and melons; they do not have cotton or fowls, nor do they make bread which is cooked, except under the ashes. Francisco Vázquez went twenty-five leagues through these settlements, to where he ob-

5

tained an account of what was beyond, and they said that the plains came to an end, and that down the river there are people who do not plant, but live wholly by hunting..... We went back by a more direct route, because in going by the way we went we traveled three hundred and thirty leagues, and it is not more than two hundred by that by which we returned. Quivira is in the fortieth degree and the river in the thirty-sixth."[1] Probably the return course lay southwest from present Kansas along the approximate Santa Fé trail of a later day. Thus, while Coronado found no great cities, his exploit disclosed a vast area northeast of New Mexico, ranged by Indians who thereafter intrigued Spanish curiosity.

For forty years interest waned in the far north. Events within Mexico itself fixed attention there. A serious rebellion, the Mixton war, supervened; deep silver mines poured out their wealth; new settlements sprang up. Inevitably the frontier crept forward. In 1580, with Santa Bárbara established on the Conchos River in New Vizcaya, a permanent base for expansion up the Río Grande was at hand. The initial movements leading to colonization of New Mexico were the expeditions of Rodríguez and Espejo in 1581-83.[2] Their reports of silver and settled Pueblos revived hopes of a new Mexico. At once powerful individuals petitioned king and viceroy for permission to conquer the north. While the authorities debated, impatient souls on the frontier set off. Sosa, the first of these, reached Taos, but the viceroy had him arrested and returned to Mexico.[3] Three years later another entourage, under Francisco Levya de Bonilla and Antonio Gutiérrez de Humaña, defied the authorities and lost their lives. Near present San Ildefonso these adventurers spent nearly a year. Then, like Coronado, they turned northeastward to reach a large Indian settlement on the present Arkansas River. From there during the next twelve days they traveled northward an undetermined distance to another stream, possibly the Platte. Later, murder and massacre on the plains overtook all but the guide, one Josephe, who escaped to New Mexico to tell the story.[4]

[1] G. P. Winship, "Journey of Coronado," Bureau of Ethnology, *Fourteenth Annual Report*, Pt. I, p. 585.

[2] H. E. Bolton, *Spanish Exploration in the Southwest, 1542-1706*, pp. 135-60; J. L. Mecham, "The Second Spanish Expedition to New Mexico," *New Mexico Historical Review*, I (1926), 265-91; "Antonio de Espejo and His Journey to New Mexico," *Southwestern Historical Quarterly*, XXX (1926), 114-38; G. P. Hammond and A. Reys, eds., *The Rodríguez Expedition, Gallegos' Relación; Expedition in New Mexico Made by Antonio de Espejo, 1582-1583, as Revealed in the Journal of Diego Pérez de Luxán*, Quivira Society Publications, Vol. I (Los Angeles, 1929).

[3] Dorothy Hull, "Sosa's Expedition," *Old Santa Fé Magazine*, October, 1916, pp. 307-32.

[4] Herbert E. Bolton, *Spanish Exploration in the Southwest, 1542*, pp. 201, n. 1; 258, 261.

6

By 1595 the persistent reports of frontiersmen, missionaries, and the raids of Drake and Cavendish in the Pacific, accompanied by reported English threats to fortify the western mouth of the strait of Anian, prodded the authorities into action. The award to colonize New Mexico went to Don Juan de Oñate, of old and distinguished family. Three years later he set out leading a carefully equipped colony from Santa Bárbara, the outpost of New Vizcaya. On the Río Grande he took possession and, moving slowly up the river, established at the pueblo of Caypa, now San Juan, the first capital of the province.[5]

Exploration began at once, Oñate himself hunting for treasures he hoped would rival those of Mexico. In 1599, the thread of exploration to the eastern plains fell first to Vicente de Saldívar Mendoza. Dispatched for a supply of buffalo fat his party met some distance beyond Pecos a band of Indians they called Vaqueros, undoubtedly Apaches, who begged Spanish aid against their enemies, the Jumanos.[6] Further, about one hundred and thirty miles, near the present Texas-New Mexico line, a second roving band was met not far from the Canadian River of today just "coming from trading with the Picuríes and Taos, populous pueblos of this New Mexico, where they sell meat, hides, tallow, suet, and salt in exchange for cotton blankets, pottery, maize, and some small green stones which they use." Nearby in a ranchería, probably of Apaches, Saldívar found "fifty tents made of tanned hides, very bright red and white in color and bell-shaped, with flaps and openings, and built as skillfully as those of Italy and so large that in the most ordinary ones four different mattresses and beds were easily accommodated." To drag the tent poles, supplies of meat and pinole or maize, the Indians used medium-sized dogs. Harnessed round their breasts and haunches and snarling at one another, they kept pace with their masters, who followed the roaming buffalo.[7]

Oñate himself was the next to throw light on the east. "The Apaches of whom we have also seen some," he wrote in March, 1599, "are innumerable, and although I heard that they lived in rancherías, a few days ago I ascertained that they live like these [Indians] in pueblos, one of which, eighteen leagues from here, contains fifteen plazas."[8] Later in 1601, having explored the west, he turned plainward. Leading a large party through Pecos he found, as did his predecessors, a group

[5] George P. Hammond, *Juan de Oñate and the Founding of New Mexico* (Santa Fé, 1927).

[6] The Jumanos lived in southeast Texas. See editorial note No. 22.

[7] Bolton, *Spanish Exploration*. . . . , pp. 223-32.

[8] *Ibid.*, p. 218.

7

of Indians whom he called Apachi. Reaching the Canadian, he followed that stream to the present boundary of Oklahoma and Texas. There he turned northeastward. On this route the party encountered a ranchería of Indians, called Escanjaques. "To them the governor and the religious went with more than thirty armed horsemen to reconnoiter the people and the ranchería, and they all drawn up in regular order in front of their ranchos, began to raise the palms of their hands towards the sun, which is the sign of peace among them. Assuring them that peace was what we wanted, all the people, women, youths, and small children, came to where we were; and they consented to our visiting their houses which all consisted of branches an estado and a half long, placed in a circle, some of them being so wide that they were ninety feet in diameter. Most of them were covered with tanned hides, which made them resemble tents. They were not people who sowed or reaped, but lived solely on the cattle. They were ruled and governed by chiefs, and like communities which are freed from subjection to any lord, they obeyed their chiefs but little."[9]

Friendly, the Escanjaques guided the explorers to the Arkansas River. Beyond they refused to go, stating that their enemies lived there. Undaunted, Oñate pushed on and visited the Quiviras, whose grass huts identify them with the later known Wichitas. Giving up further exploration, the Spaniards retraced their steps to Santa Fé, but had to defeat the Escanjaques, now hostile.[10] Writing in 1626, Zarate Salmerón, a father who labored in New Mexico, distinguished the Quiviras and Escanjaques from the Apaches Vaqueros. More specifically, he reported that the Quiviras, having learned of the defeat of their enemies, the Escanjaques, sent "from Quivira an Indian ambassador of high standing and gravity. He brought six hundred servants with bows and arrows, who served him..... At last he arrived and gave his message inviting the Spaniards with his friendship and lands to help him fight against their enemies, the Ayjaos."[11] The identity of the Escanjaques and Ayjaos is confirmed by Father Posadas, a later custodian of the New Mexican missions, who wrote in 1687 that the Aijados

[9] Ibid., pp. 252-58. The circles mentioned in this account may have some relation to those of rocks that can still be seen in the Panhandle of Oklahoma in the vicinity of Guymon. See W. K. Moorehead, "Recent Explorations in Northwest Texas," American Anthropologist (New Series), XXIII, 1-11, for a description of these circular groups of stones.

[10] Bolton, Spanish Exploration...., pp. 258-65.

[11] Gerónimo de Zarate Salmerón, "Relación....," trans. C. C. Lummis, The Land of Sunshine, XII, 47 (hereafter cited Zarate Salmerón, "Relación").

8

[Ayjaos] accompanied Oñate into the land of the Quiviras and proposed to burn their houses, but forbidden this act, attacked the Spaniards.[12]

While Quivira unfolded itself in the northeast, the vast area directly north of New Mexico, known as Teguayo, came within the range of Spanish interest. Though the earliest known use of this term Teguayo, or Tatago, appears in Peñalosa's proposal in 1678 to explore that land, Oñate gives us the first intimation of the Indians there. On his return from Quivira in 1601, he entertained the delegation from Quivira seeking aid against the Escanjaques. The "Indian ambassador of high standing and gravity" then told the captain-general that if he sought gold he had gone in the wrong direction. The proper way he advised was "through Taos and through the lands of the great Captain Quima through those places." Oñate promised to follow his advice and forthwith named twelve soldiers for the expedition, but shortly changed his mind. Later Zarate Salmerón criticized this neglect. "Here," he said, "was lost a very great opportunity and we can say it will be long before the lost chance will be recovered."[13] However, within three years Father Perea had the honor of leading the first known expedition north of New Mexico.[14] "To the nation of the Apaches of Quinia and Manases went the Father Fray Bartolomé Romero, reader of theology, and Fray Francisco Muñoz, preacher, And since it was the first expedition to that bellicose nation of warriors, Don Francisco de Sylva, governor of these provinces, went along, escorting them with twenty soldiers. Although this precaution was not necessary, because on their part [the Apaches'] opposition was lacking and with exceeding pleasure they besought the Holy Baptism."[15] The details of the expedition are too meager to indicate where or how far the expedition proceeded to the north.

Beyond the Quima Apaches, the next group of northern Indians to appear in Spanish seventeenth century records were the Utes. How early the Spaniards were acquainted with them is not clear. Oñate in 1604-06, on his Colorado River expedition, learned from the Indians there that the source of that stream rose one hundred and sixty leagues

[12] Fray Alonzo de Posadas, "Informe a S. M. sobre las tierras de Nuevo Mexico, Quivira y Teguayo," in Cesáreo Fernández Duro, *Don Diego de Peñalosa* (Madrid, 1882), p. 63 (hereafter cited Posadas, "Informe").

[13] Zarate Salmerón, "Relación," in Lummis, *op. cit.,* p. 47.

[14] Benavides, however, mentions the Quinias on the side of the north (*Memorial,* p. 41).

[15] "Fray Estevan de Perea's Relación," L. B. Bloom, ed., *New Mexico Historical Review,* VIII, 226.

to the northwest.[16] Twenty years later, Zarate Salmerón wrote that "if one goes from New Mexico for this exploration one has to go by way of Zama [Chama] traveling northwest so Indians of New Mexico told me when I got my information from them...." From the Pueblo Indians, Zarate also learned that some strangers had entered New Mexico, but later had returned to their own lands, "not by the road they had come, but by way of the river Zama, upstream, traveling to the northwest, according to the direction they showed me.

"113. When I said to these Hemex that if there were guides I would very gladly go to discover this nation, for the much love I bear it, and inasmuch as I know the tongue, and that by this means it would be easy to convert them to the true knowledge and bosom of the Church, they replied that to go straight to the Lagoon of Copalla there was no need of a guide. [One only had to] go out by way of the river Zama; and that, past the nation of the Apache Indians of Nabajú, there is a very great river which flows to that lagoon, and that the river suffices for a guide. And that all was plain with good grasses and fields between the north and northwest; that it was fertile land, good and level, and that there are many nations—the province of Quazula, the *qusutas,* and further inland another nation settled. That they have ladders of sonte to go up to the houses; that they knew all these things from the Apache Indians and others who have seen all that world."[17] There is no information at present to make a satisfactory analysis of the various details given above, but possibly we have here in the word *"qusutas"* the first reference to the Utas, as the Utes were called by the Spaniards.[18] Later in the century, the Utes were well known and were understood to live northwest beyond the Hopi. At this early time they had established friendly relations with the Spaniards, who prized their valor. Indeed, wrote Father Posadas, the Utes were equal to the Apaches in constancy of arms and were never known to turn their backs in combat, but, like the ancient Spartans, conquered or died.[19]

Beyond the Utes, the Spaniards acquired before 1680 some fragments of information concerning Teguayo itself from Indians who had escaped captivity there. The general location of the region was placed at sixty leagues northeast of the Utes. "This region," remarked Posadas, "is known in the old Mexican [Aztec] traditions as Copala, and many

16 Bolton, *Spanish Exploration....*, p. 275.

17 Zarate Salmerón, "Relación," in Lummis, *op. cit.,* XII, 183.

18 This suggestion was first made by Lummis, *ibid.,* p. 183.

19 Posadas, "Informe," in Duro, *op. cit,* p. 63.

10

writers and geographers confound it with Quivira, but this is not so, as Teguayo is to the west and Quivira to the east." From Teguayo to Quivira, Posadas estimated, was a very great distance though the two were connected and came together at about fifty leagues north of Santa Fé. The basis of his belief was that buffalo were known in Teguayo, having reached there from Quivira. He concluded, too, that the inhabitants could pass back and forth likewise.[20]

Of the Teguayan inhabitants, the Spaniards knew nothing, except that the region had many people and different tribes. One captive who escaped from the land, Don Juanillo of Jémez, reported that during his two years' captivity he saw there multitudes who spoke different tongues, some of which were known in New Mexico. He also observed there a large lake, on the shores of which dwelt many people. Furthermore, he related, certain governors of New Mexico promised him they would make a journey to the region under his guidance. The most that came of the proposals, however, were the two unsuccessful petitions of Captain Francisco Lújan to make the expedition.[21] Beyond these details of the northwest, the Spaniards so far as known did not add to their knowledge until almost a century had passed, when the Domínguez and Escalante expedition, making use of the Rivera diary, attempted to reach Monterrey by striking northwest of Santa Fé.

With the turn of the half-century, the pointer of Spanish interest again swung to the northeast.[22] Pueblo unrest, a feature of seventeenth century New Mexico, broke forth some time after 1664 in Taos, whence some families fled eastward to the plains of Cíbola and became the slaves of the Apaches. The Spanish governor shortly dispatched an expedition of twenty soldiers with Indian allies commanded by Juan de Archuleta to bring them back. Arrived among the Apaches of present eastern Colorado, Archuleta found the Pueblos living in some small

20 *Ibid.*, p. 63.

21 *Ibid.*, pp. 65-66.

22 In the half-century after Oñate's eastward expedition, at least four journeys were made into the plains of New Mexico. Baca advanced, so it is reported, three hundred leagues eastward to a large river which Posadas identifies as the Mississippi. There Indian hostility forced his return (Posadas, "Informe," in Duro, *op. cit.*, p. 60). Likewise, between 1629 and 1654, the proselyting expeditions by Father Salas among the Jumanos, and the pearling forays along the Nueces River by Martin, Castillo, and Guadalajara, opened up the area southeast of Santa Fé (Posadas, in Duro, *op. cit.*, pp. 56-59). It has been definitely proved that Peñalosa's claim that he made an extensive journey into the plains east of New Mexico has no foundation in fact (C. W. Hackett, "New Light on Don Diego de Peñalosa: Proof that he never made an expedition from Santa Fé to Quivira and the Mississippi River in 1662," *Mississippi Valley Historical Review,* VI, 313-35).

structures observed later in 1706, whence derives the name of El Cuartelejo, thereafter applied to the region as well as to the Apaches themselves. Archuleta also observed among these fugitives copper and tin,
which he was informed came from Quivira where the Pueblos and
Apaches visited. Further, records Father Escalante, who chronicled the
event in the eighteenth century, the Spaniards learned that the Pawnees
were beyond the Cuartelejos and were already trading with the
French.[23] Archuleta successfully brought back his charges, but the
meager details give no indication of his route to and from El Cuartelejo.

Further expansion into the north was suddenly cut short by the
disastrous Pueblo Revolt of 1680. Driven from the Upper Río Grande,
the Spaniards fled back to El Paso.[24] From here attempts went forward
to occupy the lost province, a northward movement paralleled at the
moment by the Jesuit expansion into Sonora and lower Arizona and,
on the east, by an advance into eastern Texas to dislodge La Salle.[25]
While Spain found it convenient to abandon the Texas establishments
in 1693, the thorough subjection of the Pueblo region progressed under
Don Diego de Vargas, 1692-96. New Mexico, thus brought back into
the empire, became once more the base for Spanish expansion northward into the unexplored reaches of Quivira.

II. SPANISH EXPEDITIONS NORTHEAST OF
NEW MEXICO, 1696-1727

A. Early Reports of Frenchmen in the Northeast

In the years between 1696-1727, the northeastern frontier of New
Mexico became the scene of an important phase of Franco-Spanish conflict in the trans-Mississippi West. While the French in 1696, to be
sure, offered no real threat to Spain's possessions, the actual landing of

23 "Letter of Escalante," in Ralph E. Twitchell, *Spanish Archives of New Mexico*,
II, 78, item 53.

24 An important branch of Spanish plains explorations from El Paso east to the Jumano country took place after the retreat to El Paso (Bolton, *Spanish Exploration....*, pp.
311-44). Cf. also Bolton, "The Jumano Indians in Texas, 1650-1771," *Texas State Historical Association Quarterly*, XV, 71-74.

25 Herbert E. Bolton, ed., *Kino's Historical Memoir of Pimería Alta* (Cleveland,
1919); William Edward Dunn, *Spanish and French Rivalry in the Gulf Region of the
United States, 1678-1702* (Austin, 1917); Irving A. Leonard, "Don Andrés de Arriola
and the Occupation of Pensacola Bay," *New Spain and the Anglo-American West*,
I, 81-106.

La Salle on the Texas coast was too recent for authorities to disregard New Mexican reports of these Europeans. On the other hand, the French were roaming over vast areas west of the Mississippi. By 1678 the Pawnees were sufficiently well known to be placed correctly on Father Hennepin's map. By 1694 Canadian traders were among the Osage and Missouri tribes.[26] While some ten years later (1706) a Spanish expedition was to find evidence of French visitors and trinkets among Apaches in present eastern Colorado.[27]

As early as 1695 Vargas reported to the viceroy the first news of these Europeans. Some Chipaynes Apaches visiting the Picuríes pueblo told a story of white and blond men who had destroyed a very large tribe of Conejero Apaches who lived beyond the Chipaynes.[28] In Mexico the fiscal, in January of 1696, in a council of war stated more definitely that Luís Gramillo, an Apache, had information that many French were coming toward the Plains of Cíbola. Again, in October, two Apache chiefs visiting in Taos stated that six tribes on the east had reports that "some white men came to the banks of a lake to make war on the Quiviras, had gone away and returned later for the same purpose." None of the white people, however, had been seen by those Apache informants. Nevertheless, Vargas requested of México two pieces of artillery to repel any attack, but was refused.[29]

In the next year, 1697, fresh news arrived of French progress westward. The Navajos, accustomed to make long journeys to Quivira, frequently fought the French and Pawnees, in alliance at that time, and brought the spoil to trade in New Mexico. On one occasion in 1694 they returned with some captive children whom they beheaded after the Spaniards had refused to ransom them. The atrocity so shocked the Spanish king that he ordered thereafter the use of royal

[26] Bolton and Marshall, *Colonization of North America*, p. 100. See also *Calendar of Manuscripts in Paris Archives and Libraries Relating to the History of the Mississippi Valley to 1803*, ed. by N. M. Miller Surrey (Washington: Carnegie Institution of Washington, Department of Historical Research, 1926), item for years 1702-03, I (1581-1739), 84.

[27] "Diary of Ulibarri, *infra*, p. 67; and "Declaration of Garduño," p. 173.

[28] These Apaches were Faraones who ranged the plains east of New Mexico. See "Declaration of Don Gerónimo," *infra*, p. 80. The Conejeros were Jicarilla Apaches who lived northeast of Santa Fé. See "Diary of Ulibarri," *infra*, p. 63.

[29] "Reply of the Fiscal, January 3, 1696," in *Reconquista del Reyno de la Nuebo Mexico, por d^n Diego de Vargas Zapata, Anno de 1694*, Archivo General y Público de la Nación (México), Sección de Historia, Tomo 30, fol. 459 (MS copy in Bolton Collection). See also Frederick W. Hodge, "French Intrusion toward New Mexico in 1695," *New Mexico Historical Review*, IV, 72-76.

funds to save such unfortunates.[30] Three years later, in 1697, the Navajos made another of their customary expeditions to the east. The French and Pawnees, however, destroyed, so it was reported, four thousand of the invaders. In 1698 the Navajos returned for vengeance and annihilated three Pawnee rancherías and a fortified place. Returning in 1699, they appeared at the Spanish fair laden with spoil: slaves, jewels, carbines, cannons, powder flasks, gamellas, sword belts, waistcoats, shoes, and even small pots of brass. They then related to the astonished Spaniards the defeat of the year before and praised the French for their valor, their dexterity in shooting, and their readiness in reënforcing their allies.[31] Reports of the French continued thereafter to drift into New Mexico. In Taos in 1700 the Apaches related the French had destroyed a Jumano pueblo, a circumstance that occasioned much worry in Santa Fé. Two years later, in July, 1702, an expedition was sent eastward against the Faraones. And in the same month, doubtless with this expedition, fifty-six Pecos Indians killed a "Francisco" [Frenchman?] among the Jumanos.[32] No defensive measures, however, were taken until twenty years later when the French advance from the Mississippi seemed at last to offer a real threat both to New Mexico and Texas.

B. *The Flight of the Pueblo Indians: Expedition of Vargas, 1696*[33]

The first known expedition northeast of Santa Fé, after the Reconquest came as a result of a revolt of certain Pueblo groups in the fall

[30] A. F. Bandelier, "Expedition of Pedro de Villasur from Santa Fé, New Mexico, to the Banks of the Platte River," *Contributions to the History of the Southwestern Portion of the United States* (Cambridge, 1890), p. 185, n. 4, notes the presence of Pawnees in New Mexico earlier in the seventeenth century. The Pawnees were known in New Mexico as the Genízaros.

[31] Padre Juan Amando Niel, "Apuntamientos que a las Memorias del Padre Fray Gerónimo de Zarate hizo, no tan solo sestando practico del terreno que se cita, si no es que llevaba en la mano las memorias para cortejarlas con el," in "Relación de Nuevo Mexico," *Documentos para la Historia de México* (Tercera serie, México, 1856), pp. 108-11. Bandelier, *op. cit.,* p. 181, n. 2, cites: "Relación Anónima de la Reconquista del Nuevo Mexico" (Archives at México, MS), which may be the source on which Padre Amando Niel bases this part of his "Apuntamientos." Compare the above list of captured articles with those which the Cuartelejos had in their possession taken from the Pawnee in 1706 (*infra*, p. 67).

[32] "Este Cuaderno se cree ser obra de un Religioso de la Provincia del Santa Evangelio," in "Relaciones de Nuevo Mexico," *Documentos para la Historia de México* (Tercera serie, Mexico, 1856), p. 180; Bandelier, *op. cit.,* p. 181, n. 3. This 1702 expedition doubtless went to the southeast of Santa Fé against the Faraones. However, see the discussion of Jumano-Apache relations in editorial note No. 22. ("Este Cuaderno se cree ser obra de un Religioso," etc., hereafter cited, "Este Cuaderno . . . . de un Religioso.")

[33] "Diary of Vargas," *infra*, pp. 53-59. Also see editorial note No. 3.

14

of 1696. This movement originated among some Taos and Picuríes Indians who refused to submit to Vargas, and fled eastward with their possessions and families. Vargas followed in hot pursuit. When his command reached the Picuríes pueblo, he found it empty, but learned from neighboring Indians that the fugitives had left three days before, driving before them loaded horses, ewes, and goats. Crossing the mountains east of the Pueblos on October 23, Vargas dispatched a scouting expedition which shortly hauled in a Taos Indian. Forced to guide the party, the captive took the Spaniards to an abandoned camp of thirty-one Apache lodges some five leagues to the east. Pueblos and Apaches retreated with such haste on Vargas' approach that he found their trail strewn with *tipi* poles and other evidences of headlong flight. Pursuing rapidly, the Spaniards soon came upon the fugitives in a ravine. They captured with little difficulty a chief and some followers and forty loaded horses. Others succeeded in escaping though a few met death in the attempt. Further pursuit was abandoned, but on the two days following Pueblo men, women, and children dribbled into the Spanish camp to surrender. Vargas welcomed them and humanely ordered his men to share provisions with the unfortunates. From these the commander learned further that the Picuríes chief, Don Lorenzo, and some others had fled eastward with the Apaches. Erecting a tall cross to commemorate the victory, the cavalcade began their return to Pecos through a driving blizzard:

"On the seventh day of the month of November, 1696, I, the governor and captain-general, arrived at this village of Pecos with the commanders and some of the officers of the army to send relief to the army force which I left at the foot of the mountain of this village at a distance of eight leagues. Having been on the march since the twenty-eighth up to this day in the fury of snowstorms and driving hurricanes which obliged me to stay two days unable to move from the spot, I as well as all the people ran great risk in going on foot because the snow was so deep, the frost and winds moreover making a tempest. Every day dawned upon many horses dead and others in like manner benumbed by it and frozen, so that they were almost gone. When the count was taken we had lost more than two hundred horses and five mules belonging to the soldiers and my own; the Indian allies lost more, the Pecos as well as the Tiguas of Tezuque who came on the campaign. We went through most of the places in a melting snow, serving roasted corn to the people for food and also the flesh of the horses that died. The delays of the campaign were due to the accidents caused

15

by the storm....." In Santa Fé the recaptured Pueblos, eighty-four in number, counting the suckling babes, Vargas divided as servants among the soldiers and citizens who had accompanied him.

While this expedition accomplished its purpose in the main, it adds little to our knowledge of the northeast. The Apaches mentioned in the pursuit cannot be identified. However, ten years later the Spaniards learned that Don Lorenzo, the Picuríes chief, and his fleeing kinsmen were the slaves of the Cuartelejo Apaches in present eastern Colorado. The distance traveled on the expedition Vargas later stated to be eighty-four leagues. Doubtless this was the entire distance going and coming so that the expedition probably reached only into northeastern New Mexico.[34]

C. The Return of the Pueblo Indians: Expedition of Ulibarri, 1706[35]

The next known expedition to penetrate the northeast was that of Juan de Ulibarri, dispatched to return the fleeing Picuríes of 1696 to New Mexico. Apparently, early in 1706 their chief, Don Lorenzo, had sent a messenger from El Cuartelejo to pray forgiveness and ask for aid. Governor Cuerbó approved the petition in a council of war which named Ulibarri for the undertaking. In the diary of this commander we get our first real insight into the Indian area northeast of New Mexico, a century before Pike.

In Santa Fé in the early days of July, Ulibarri assembled twenty presidials, twelve settlers, and one hundred Indians, the latter according to custom, recruited from the various pueblos. Two of the individuals are interesting. One, an Indian scout and fighter, José Naranjo, had served with distinction under Vargas. The other was a Frenchman, Juan de l'Archévèque, a survivor of La Salle's expedition. Generally credited with a hand in the murder of his chief, this renegade seized by León's expedition into east Texas in 1690 eventually found his way into New Mexico, where he married and became a trader. Both he and Naranjo later died in the massacre of the Villasur expedition at the forks of the Platte River in 1720.[36]

July 13 saw the expedition on its way to Taos. At the Picuríes pueblo the inhabitants gratefully loaded the force with supplies of cotton and woolen blankets and provided horses for the return of their kinsmen. At Taos the command learned that the Utes and Comanches were

[34] Col. R. E. Twitchell, *Old Santa Fé* (Santa Fé, 1925), p. 147, states that Vargas reached the Panhandle of present Oklahoma.

[35] "Diary of Ulibarri," *infra*, pp. 59-77. Cf. editorial note No. 6.

[36] For some details concerning Archévèque see editorial note No. 24.

16

planning an attack. Ulibarri reported the news to Cuerbó and awaited instructions, gathering more supplies meanwhile. Receiving no word by the twentieth of July, and the attack not materializing, the Spaniards set out for El Cuartelejo.

Following the San Fernando Creek, which flows down from the mountains to water Taos cornfields, the expedition reached the summit late at night. The next morning, leaving camp on Ciéneguilla Creek, still so called, they made their descent over fallen timber, through a series of delightful valleys, and finally, mounting to a flowery pass, prepared to descend to the plains, where they could see faintly the Apache trails below. Descending rapidly, they crossed two streams and camped on the latter, the Río de Magdalena, some forty miles from Taos and east of the present site of Cimarron. Here they met friendly Jicarilla Indians, Conejeros, Ochos, and Río Colorados, who warned Ulibarri that other hostile groups, Penxayes, Flechas de Palo, Lemitas, and Nemantinas, blocked the way eastward.[37] Rewarding these informants, the commander distributed gifts of tobacco, knives, pinole, and corn biscuits among them.

Undoubtedly influenced by the news, the command turned sharply to the left. For four days, from the twenty-second to the twenty-sixth, they traveled northward, naming ponds, streams, and springs. At the last camp, named Ojo de Naranjo after the chief scout, Ulibarri found himself among more friendly Ajaches. Their head chief, El Coxo, or in Apache, Ysdalnisdael, made a speech, a welcome to their lands and assurances that on the return they would find supplies of dried grapes in their rancherías where as good people they cultivated grain, maize, corn, frijoles, and pumpkins. Responding to the friendly advances, Ulibarri left his tired horses in their care and gave them pleasing gifts.

The command now turned to ascend the sierra that separated the headwaters of the Purgatoire from those of the Canadian River.[38] Twenty-two leagues through the rough foothills brought them to a canyon, to which the commander gave his own name. The stream therein, called the Río de Santiago, emptied into another, the Santa Ana. There Ulibarri found Apaches, the Penxayes, whose fields

[37] With regard to these Apache groups who lived in northeastern New Mexico and southern Colorado of today, see editorial note No. 13. With the exception of the Conejeros, who are mentioned in Vargas' report to the viceroy in 1695 (*supra*, p. 13) this is the first known reference to these Apache bands. Ulibarri found the Penxayes living in present southern Colorado.

[38] This range was known at this time as the Sierra de Jicarilla or Sierra Blanca ("Declaration of Martínez," *infra*, p. 171, and that of Garduño, *infra*, p. 173).

17

along the banks grew corn, frijoles, and pumpkins. The Penxayes fled to the hilltops upon the sudden appearance of the Spaniards, but presents shortly reassured them. Doubtless, the position here on the Santa Ana was on the present Purgatoire, near Trinidad of today. Possibly, Ulibarri's canyon was that now called Lorencito Canyon, whose stream Ulibarri noted flowed from south to north and emptied into the Santa Ana, which flowed "northeast like all the rest."[39]

The next stage of their journey took the expedition directly north over the broken foothills of the Rockies to the Arkansas. Leaving the Santa Ana where they came upon it, their first march of ten leagues brought them to a spring, Ojo de Jediondo (Stinking Spring), doubtless one of the several that today bear the name of Stinking Spring or Stinking Arroyo in that region.[40] Pushing on through the rough country and crossing several small streams, the command encountered in the next two days more Apaches who lived throughout the region, at the moment fleeing to join their kinsmen for a battle with the Utes and Comanches. In return for tobacco, pinole, and biscuits, the Penxayes provided quantities of cherries. Soon after meeting the last of the Indians, and after a journey of some forty leagues from the Santa Ana, the command reached the Arkansas, or as it was then known, the Río Napestle:

"We .... arrived on the great river which all the tribes call the Napestle, and I, remembering the name of the señor governor and captain-general, in honor of his Christian zeal, gave the river the name of his saint, calling it the Río Grande de San Francisco. It runs from north to east..... The plain on our side is a strand of a long league of level and extremely fertile land as shown by the many prunes, cherries and wild grapes on it..... It is more than four times as large as the Río del Norte and bathes the best and broadest valley discovered in New Spain....." The spot where Ulibarri reached the Arkansas was opposite the present site of Pueblo, Colorado.

On Friday, July 30, the expedition turned sharply eastward toward its destination, El Cuartelejo. A four-league march the first day brought them to the Río de San Buenaventura, present Fountain Creek. Beyond this stream they followed the faintly marked buffalo trails. Soon lost however, Ulibarri dispatched his men to look for water. Success attended their search, but the next day their Indian guide again missed

[39] This phrase establishes that Ulibarri was in present southern Colorado, where the streams run northeast.

[40] Stinking Spring and Stinking Arroyo are indicated on geologic maps of this region. See editorial note No. 17.

18

the trail. Another search brought the party by good luck upon a dry arroyo, at the head of which they presently found an Apache water hole. From this point, some miles north of the Arkansas, Ulibarri sent out scouts to search for water before the expedition again moved. Traveling generally to the east, the scouts shortly stumbled upon one of the outlying rancherías of El Cuartelejo itself, located evidently in the branches of present Horse Creek in either western Kiowa or southern Lincoln county. The Cuartelejo Apaches who welcomed the scouts returned to guide the command.

Their next journey took them twenty-five miles to the east to another and larger ranchería where more friendly Apaches gave the soldiers bison meat and corn. Here, also, Ulibarri received other Cuartelejos and some Picuríes arrived to present the respects of Don Lorenzo. Cordial relations soon established, Ulibarri pushed on. From this ranchería, named by Ulibarri Nuestra Señora de los Angeles de Porciuncula, the entourage arrived the next morning after a short march at the Ojo de Santa Rita, a spring in a pleasant dale. From there they climbed a prominence where many Apaches welcomed the travelers to El Cuartelejo. "The Apaches," writes Ulibarri, "came without weapons, very happy and elated. They brought us much buffalo meat, roasting ears of Indian corn, tamales, plums, and other things to eat. .... From out of the huts or little houses came Don Lorenzo and the rest of the Picuríes Indians, men and women who were with him. There we alighted a second time and embraced him and gave them to understand why we were coming, having been sent by our governor and captain-general." The party finally halted in the principal center of the rancherías, located on the Río de Penas, where Ulibarri in a picturesque ceremony took possession of El Cuartelejo for his king.

Here on this arroyo, the Spaniards established their camp, where the rabble plagued them miserably with their comings and goings. When the chiefs themselves came to visit the commander, Ulibarri warned them not to interfere with his mission. Surprisingly, they assented. In return Ulibarri assured them peace, friendship, and the aid of the Spanish king. Urging at once a practical demonstration, the Apaches invited the command to join them in a raid on the French and Pawnees. However, with an eye to business and his mind on the snows soon to fall in the Santa Fé mountains, Ulibarri promised to come another year. This and the promise of a gun satisfied his hosts.

The mention of the French, hints of whom he had already heard among the Indians, stirred Ulibarri to press for details. The Apaches

19

frankly told their latest exploit. Apparently, some time before Ulbarri's arrival, the Pawnees, accompanied by some French, set out to attack El Cuartelejo, aware that the Apache braves were away hunting buffalo. The Cuartelejos, however, learning of their approach, retreated, where-upon the enemy fled. At once the Apaches dispatched a party to follow. In a little wood along a stream the spies caught up with a white man and woman whom they murdered. The bald head of the man they let alone, but scalped the woman, and carried off a red cap, some powder, and a gun. Archévèque at once recognized the weapon as French. Upset by the interest the Spaniards showed in the incident, the Apaches altered their story, swearing they had killed only a Pawnee chief. Later Ulibarri learned that the three carbines and other weapons they had also came from the same source. Bartolomé Garduño further testified in 1720 that the Cuartelejos had captured from the Pawnees, "some fowling pieces, clothes, small short swords, and French iron axes .... and a foot of a gilded silver chalice which they sold [him] for two yards of sackcloth, and two French guns for two horses."[41] From these Apaches, Ulibarri also learned that the Pawnees frequently sold Apache women and children into slavery among the French as the Apache themselves sold Pawnee captives in New Mexico. The location of the French, however, Ulibarri was unable to determine from the meager details supplied by the Cuartelejos.

The next day, August 5, Ulibarri dispatched three parties to visit the neighboring rancherías of Adidasde, Nanahe, and Sanasesli, where Don Lorenzo explained the Picuríes were held captive. In the latter they found the son of Don Luís Tupatú, the Picuríes chief who had succeeded Popé in command of the Pueblo Revolt of 1680. The Apache chief there, Isdelpain, welcomed Naranjo, regretted Ulibarri's not coming in person, readily turned over Tupatú and eighteen others, and promised to bring the rest, some Santa Clarans, when they returned from hunting buffalo. In the meantime, Ulibarri made good use of his time. The careful notes of this intelligent Spaniard supply the first and only known detailed account of El Cuartelejo and the character of Indian and Spanish ideas of the trans-Mississippi country in the early eighteenth century.

Noting the Cuartelejos' regard for the Christian faith, Ulibarri asked them what "reason they had for wearing crosses, medallions, and rosaries without knowing what they wore." With simple naïveté, the Apaches explained that "for many years they had traded and had

41 "Declaration of Bartolomé Garduño," *infra*, pp. 172-74.

20

commerce with the Spaniards and that they knew they [the Spaniards] wore crosses and rosaries and images of the saints...." and ".... that when they fight.... the Pawnees and the Jumano and become tired they remember the Great Captain of the Spaniards who is in the heavens and then their weariness leaves them and they feel refreshed."

After remarking the fertility of the soil at El Cuartelejo that produced crops of maize, watermelons, pumpkins, wheat, and kidney beans, Ulibarri commented at length upon the location of the neighboring tribes, important rivers and Apache names thereof. Finally, he closed his survey with details that indicated the proximity of the French to that region.[42]

On Wednesday, the eleventh, the round-up parties were back and Ulibarri prepared to return. His last act was to cement Spanish-Apache friendship by appointing a representative of Spanish authority in El Cuartelejo. For the honor he chose a fine looking Apache, Indatiyuhe, the chief in fact of all the Cuartelejos, to whom he gave a baton of authority. Turning to the assembled Apaches, he commanded them to erect a high cross in the center of their land and to worship it. While he bade the chiefs farewell, the Apache women and children took affectionate leave of their erstwhile captives, loading them high with presents of meat and corn.

"I brought back," wrote Ulibarri, "sixty-two persons, small and grown, of the Picuríes who were living as apostates, slaves of the devil, and as captives of the barbarity of the Apache. Among them were two of the most noteworthy Indians of the entire kingdom and provinces: they are Don Lorenzo and Don Juan Tupatú, his nephew. I assisted them with particular care in their sustenance, loaning them riding horses until they arrived at their pueblo."

The journey over the same route to Santa Fé was accomplished with business-like efficiency. They reached the Napestle on the seventeenth; five days later they rested their weary and footsore horses along the green stretches of the Purgatoire. On the twenty-sixth, over the divide, they were among the Jicarillas, friendly as before, who returned their horses and told Ulibarri of an attack suffered from the Comanches and Utes. Leaving more presents behind, the expedition pushed on across the mountains and reached the Picuríes pueblo on the thirty-first. There the Spanish father, Ximénez, absolved the long-absent fugitives while

[42] The passages in Ulibarri's diary (*infra*, pp. 72-73) from which the above accounts are taken are among the most significant details known of the region northeast of Santa Fé at this early time. See also editorial note No. 25. For location of El Cuartelejo, see editorial note No. 79.

the pueblo gave the day over to rejoicing. Two days later, in Santa Fé, the commander reported in person to Governor Cuerbó the success of the undertaking.

Ulibarri's expedition marks another extension of Spanish activities into the northeast. Besides yielding invaluable data regarding the location of Indian tribes and their relation with one another and the Spaniards, this diary sounds the first important note of French activity near the Rockies. The arrival of these traders at this distant point and at such an early date is a fact hitherto unsuspected. Doubtless, the expedition had considerable local importance in further cementing Pueblo-Spanish relations so soon after the Reconquest. The undertaking, certainly, is a striking evidence of kindness and sacrifice, so infrequently attributed to Spaniards in behalf of their subject people.

D. Campaign Against the Apaches: Expedition of Hurtado, 1714[43]

Pueblo flights to the plains after 1706 are unrecorded. Spanish activities in the north, however, continued with increasing vigor, induced by raiding Navajos, eastern Apaches, and Utes and Comanches. Never completely buttressed against these incursions, it is to their credit that the Spanish pioneers never adopted the doubtful expedient of their Anglo-Saxon successors: extermination. As a means of protection, the New Mexicans dispatched against their foes punitive expeditions and welcomed alliances with the Cuartelejo and Jicarilla Apaches for mutual defense. The years between 1702 and 1719 are filled with accounts, some brief, others detailed, of these terrific assaults upon Spanish and Pueblo New Mexico.

The Navajos early in the century were the chief offenders. In 1702 they broke their peace of some years standing, and against them Governor Cuberó led one hundred men and one hundred fifty Indian allies. A Navajo chief, however, hastening to make amends at Taos, ended that campaign.[44] Three years later, in 1705, with the Navajos again on the warpath, Governor Francisco Cuerbó dispatched a large force against them under his maestro de campo, Roque de Madrid. This officer struck north, crossed the Río Grande near Taos, and swung off to the northwest, for forty-six leagues along the Piedra de Carmeno, Sierra del Cobre, Río de Chama, and the Arroyo del Belduque. The Navajos took refuge on a high peñol, but suffered several defeats so severe that they soon sought peace. Victorious, the expedition dropped

---

[43] "Council of War and Diary .... of Hurtado against the Faraon Apaches," 1715, *infra,* pp. 80-98.

[44] "Este Cuaderno .... de un Religioso," *loc. cit.,* p. 180.

back to the pueblo of Sia on the nineteenth of August.[45] Towards the end of 1708, the Navajos renewed their forays, which lasted well into the year 1710. Only by invading and laying waste their lands were the Spaniards able to enforce submission.[46] Four years later they renewed hostilities. Madrid with a command of three hundred including soldiers, settlers, and Indian allies again ravaged their country; details are lacking.[47]

Against the Apaches on the east, the first known punitive expedition of which a detailed record is available, is that of Don Juan Paez Hurtado in 1715. The Faraones, whom he pursued, had long bedeviled the province from Albuquerque to Taos. Presumably, some of the Indians met with by the explorers on their journeys toward Quivira in the preceding centuries were Faraones. The earliest known reference to this tribe under their Egyptian name is in the 1692 report of Governor Don Diego de Vargas.[48] There is no known record of an expedition against them, however, until July, 1702, when Governor Cuberó campaigned successfully among their rancherías.[49] Again, in 1704, Vargas, then governor for a second time, died while pursuing these harriers along the eastern slope of the Sandia mountains.[50] Nine years later, in 1712, Governor Don Juan Ignacio Flores Mogollón marched against the same marauders;[51] while less than two years after, in 1714, Don Antonio Valverde Cosio chased them eastward.[52] His efforts apparently had little effect, for back once more in the spring of 1715, they made another audacious attack on the Picuríes and Taos Pueblos. This raid brought on the punitive expedition here considered. Though no victory resulted, the record of the undertaking has the unique value of detailing the exact procedure of organizing a campaign for this frontier service on the New Mexico borders in the early eighteenth century.

To plan the campaign and to secure information regarding the habits of the Faraones, Governor Mogollón called a council of war and sent for Don Gerónimo, the Taos chief, and Don Lorenzo, the lieutenant-

45 *Ibid.*, p. 187.
46 "Este Cuaderno .... de un Religioso," *loc. cit.*, p. 197.
47 *Ibid.*, p. 205.
48 Twitchell, *Spanish Archives of New Mexico*, II, 78, item 53. Bandelier, *op. cit.*, p. 183, n. 2, states the lair of the Faraones was in the Sierra de Sandia and in the Sierra de los Ladrones.
49 "Este Cuaderno .... de un Religioso," p. 180. Cf. also *supra*, p. 13, n. 28.
50 *Ibid.*, p. 187 (Twitchell, *Spanish Archives of New Mexico*, II, 127-33, item 99, has a translation of this account).
51 *Ibid.*, p. 201.
52 *Ibid.*, p. 206. Bandelier, *op. cit.*, p. 183, n. 2, refers to the original documents of these expeditions of 1714 and 1715.

governor and chief at Picuríes. The people of these pueblos frequently pursued the Faraones to retrieve their stolen horses, women, and children. Before the governor, they identified these Apaches as the Chipaynes, Limitas, Faraones, Trementinas, or in the Taos language, Sejines.[53] Leaving the periodic fairs held in the border towns and pueblos, the Faraones customarily raided the horseherds of La Cañada, Taos, and those of the Jicarilla Indians. The latter, so the chiefs stated, had seen droves of New Mexican horses and mules on the plains rancherías. The nearest of these was ten days marching to the east where there were thirty wooden dwelling places on a river. To that point water was plentiful, but beyond, it failed under a sweltering sun. The Pueblos believed that the best time to campaign was about the middle of August, when the Faraones were reaping, for afterwards until the following April or May they hunted buffalo for hides, or Pueblos—for corn! Don Gerónimo advised against taking the Pecos and Queres Indians as allies as some of the former were known to be friendly to the Faraones, while the latter always found means to warn the enemy.[54] The Tiguas, Picuríes, and Taos tribes were the only ones, they felt, worthy of confidence.

On July 20, in the midst of the proceedings, news arrived that the Faraones had again raided the Picuríes pueblo. The governor sent Hurtado to aid, but heard shortly that the Picuríes had overtaken their enemies and retrieved their stolen horses. The next day the council convened again to listen to the opinions of the principal officers of the presidios at Santa Fé and those of experienced settlers. In general, all were agreed that the Faraones should be punished, but differed as to the choice of time and allies. Lieutenant Francisco Montes Vigil believed the month of September most suitable, since he felt that the Faraones could not possibly reap in August maize sown late in April. As to Indian assistance, Joseph Domínguez urged taking fifty Pecos Indians, in spite of the Pueblo objections. All agreed to this proposal except Felix Martínez, the presidio captain, who pointed out that the Pecos pueblo itself could not afford the warriors for in case of a Faraon invasion, the presidio at Santa Fé, likewise weakened, could not send aid.[55]

The council over, the governor in view of the opinions decided upon the procedure of the campaign. He set the date in September because

53 These important identifications are in the declaration of Don Gerónimo, *infra,* p. 80.

54 Declaration of Don Gerónimo, *infra,* p. 81.

55 "Council of War," *infra,* pp. 83-85.

24

an impending *visita* demanded his attention in New Mexico; selected the Picuríes pueblo as the assembling point; put Hurtado in command, but deferred drawing up the latter's instructions until his return. A month later, back in Santa Fé, Mogollón proceeded with the work. At his direction, Hurtado mustered forty soldiers from the presidio and twenty settlers, and departed for Picuríes. With him he carried his instructions to review in Picuríes the whole command and remit a list of those actually participating in the campaign. He was further ordered to proceed by stages to conserve the strength of the horseherd, to avoid molesting friendly Indians met on the way, and to spare, if a battle occurred, the Faraon women and children, who were to be handed over to the governor himself. Finally, all gambling was forbidden.[56]

On the thirtieth of August, Hurtado, having arrived at the pueblo, reviewed his small troop and submitted the report demanded by the governor. Under his command were thirty-six soldiers, fifty-two settlers, and one hundred forty-nine Indians; in all, two hundred thirty-eight. The soldiers and settlers took with them thirty-six mules and two hundred thirty-nine horses. One of the Spaniards had eleven horses; the least anyone had was two, while eight out of the fifty-seven had anywhere from four to six animals apiece. Curiously, there is nothing to indicate any mounts or pack animals for the Indians. These allies, dispatched by their respective alcalde mayores, were drawn from the Pueblos of Pecos, San Juan, Nambé, Ildefonso, Santa Clara, Pujuque, Tesuque, Taos, and Picuríes and supervised by Captain Joseph Naranjo, the scout. Seventy-six of these allies had guns; the arms of the rest are not indicated.[57]

Advised by the Picuríes to go by way of the Mora River rather than through La Jicarilla, Hurtado crossed the summit on August 30 and followed that stream some distance. On this journey he incorporated a band of thirty Jicarillas and one Cuartelejo, the latter to act as guide. After twenty leagues along the river, the expedition turned to the southeast and reached the Canadian, then called the Río Colorado from its red terrain.

From the fifth to the fourteenth of September they continued along the Canadian for ten days. On the eighth, Naranjo found Apache trails, though they yielded nothing. Thereafter, they crossed and recrossed the river, finding thereby sufficient pasture and water in pools,

56 "Order to General Hurtado," *infra*, pp. 86-87.
57 "Troop Review of General Hurtado," *infra*, pp. 90-93.

springs, and arroyos filled by sudden showers. Having journeyed in this manner some one hundred and fifty miles from Santa Fé, they left the Río Colorado to search for a Chipaynes ranchería at the suggestion of the guide. Their detour proved barren. A new guide, a Picuríes, then took the command somewhat north of the stream where Picuríes themselves went in pursuit of Faraones. There Hurtado found pasture, water, and the tracks of many Apache horses. Giving up further advance, the commander concluded that the Faraones had heard of the expedition contemplated against them while trading at Pecos and had "absented themselves from the Río Colorado where they have their rancherías." The return journey was likewise eventless, the command reaching New Mexico on September 30.[58]

Doubtless the visita required of Mogollón affected the choice of the time of the departure and therefore the success of the expedition. The record of the attempt, however, does reveal the successive steps followed in organizing such campaigns and establishes that Faraon rancherías were located about one hundred and fifty miles east of Santa Fé on the present Canadian River.[59]

E. Campaign Against the Comanches: Expedition of Valverde, 1719[60]

In the northeast raids of the Utes and Comanches next forced the Spaniards into that area. Unknown in the seventeenth century in New Mexico, the Comanches had their original home with the Shoshone in southern Wyoming. Their separation from the parent stock took place, according to ethnologists, at the beginning of the eighteenth century.[61] They appear for the first time in the early eighteenth century in historical records of New Mexico in company with the Utes. The circumstances of their relations with the Utes previous to this date are unknown, though doubtless the proximity of the two northwest of Santa Fé accounts for the friendly relations that marked their association in the early eighteenth century.[62]

The first recorded hostility of the Utes toward the province after the Reconquest is in 1704.[63] Two years later, in 1706, the Utes and Coman-

[58] "Diary of General Hurtado," *infra*, p. 98.

[59] For other references to Indian occupation of this area, see *ante*, pp. 7-8 and editorial note No. 43.

[60] "Council of War" and "Diary of Valverde's Campaign against the Utes and Comanches," *infra*, pp. 99-110, 110-33.

[61] F. W. Hodge, *Handbook of American Indians*, Pt. I, "Comanche."

[62] In the later seventeenth century the Utes were generally recognized as friends of the Spaniards of New Mexico (Posadas, "Informe," in Duro, *op. cit.*, p. 63).

[63] "Diary of Ulibarri," *infra*, pp. 61, 76.

ches are mentioned by Ulibarri, who in July of that year reported to Governor Cuerbó an expected attack on Taos by these enemies. On his return from El Cuartelejo, Ulibarri learned that the Comanches had in fact descended upon the Jicarilla and Carlana rancherías in northeastern New Mexico. During the rule of the Marqués de la Peñuela, 1707-12, the Utes and Comanches came to New Mexico to seek peace. The treaty that accorded them this privilege is the earliest known between the Spaniards and Comanches. The document, however, has not come to light. Under the cloak of this peace, nevertheless, the Comanches continued to steal goods and animals from the province.[64] Some years later, in 1716, these enemies raided Taos and other nearby settlements. Retribution was swift. Thirty leagues north of Santa Fé, Captain Serna killed some and captured the rest of the marauders, who were later sold in New Vizcaya.[65] Within two years the Comanches reappeared in the northeast, driving the Jicarillas upon the Spaniards in New Mexico. Their piteous supplications for protection fell upon the ear of Father Juan de la Cruz at Taos, who urged upon Viceroy Valero, early in 1719, the opportunity to convert these heathen.[66] A few months later, in July, the Comanches returned and murdered some inhabitants of Taos and Cochití. Governor Valverde now took a hand and called a council of war to prepare an expedition into the Comanche country.[67]

Coinciding with these increasingly frequent invasions, the threat of a French attack on both New Mexico and Texas was arousing the fear of the Spanish authorities. Reports from Captain Ramón of French designs in Texas reached Viceroy Valero about the time of the arrival of Father de la Cruz' communication regarding the Jicarilla prayer for baptism and protection. Valero at once commanded Valverde to aid this padre of the Apaches with a view of using them as a buffer against the French and ordered the governor to reconnoiter the French position beyond New Mexico.[68] Acknowledging receipt of the orders, Valverde replied that he would dispatch the reconnaissance expedition the following spring as the season was too late for an attempt that year.

[64] Twitchell, *Spanish Archives of New Mexico*, II, 133, item 104, relative to the reported conspiracy of Utes and Apaches with the Pueblo Indians. The reference to the peace accorded the Comanche is in the testimony of Captain Serna, *infra*, p. 105.

[65] *Ibid.*, p. 184, item 279; Hon. Amado Chaves, *The Defeat of the Comanches in 1716* (Santa Fé, 1906), *Publication No. 8 of the New Mexico Historical Society*.

[66] "Father Cruz to Valero," Taos (n.d.), *infra*, pp. 137-38.

[67] "Council of War .... against the Utes," *infra*, pp. 99-110.

[68] "Order of Valero," México, August 1, 1719, *infra*, pp. 138-39.

27

He felt, however, that the contemplated campaign against the Comanches would produce information concerning the French.[69]

On August 13, the governor held a council of war in Santa Fé to decide upon plans for the Comanche undertaking. The members of the junta included the Utes in the declaration of war since both tribes, according to reports from Taos and Cochití, had participated in the murders there. These hostilities marked an important departure in the traditional friendship between the Spaniards and the Utes.[70]

On the fifteenth of September, Governor Valverde mustered sixty troops from the presidio and marched to Taos.[71] There, he opened his ranks to volunteers and the command quickly grew to over six hundred, including the original presidials, forty-five settlers, and four hundred sixty-five Indian allies, later augmented in La Jicarilla by one hundred ninety-six Apaches. So poor were the settlers that Valverde himself had to furnish them with leather jackets, guns, powder, shot, and seventy-five horses. How many animals were taken along is unknown. Besides these seventy-five, the soldiers undoubtedly possessed both horses and mules. The Pueblo Indians had six hundred eighty beasts, and the Apaches from Jicarilla added one hundred three, making an imposing known total of over eight hundred fifty animals. A drove of sheep, great quantities of pinole, chocolate, tobacco, and presents for the friendly Indians to be met en route completed the supplies of the expedition. The governor himself took several casks of wine, "a small keg of very rich spirituous brandy," some glasses, and rich melon preserves for important saints' days. To replenish their larder from time to time, hunting of fine fat turkeys, bears, deer, and buffalo supplanted the more serious pursuit of Indians.

The marching procedure was that customarily adopted by the Spaniards on frontier expeditions. The main body comprised two parts, the Spanish presidials and settlers in one group and the Indians in the other. On the march these divisions were separated by the pack animals, while spies flanked the whole line to guard against ambush and to search for trails. In the small group of soldiers acting as vanguard, the governor usually traveled; a second similar group protected the rear. At night the Indians and Spaniards made two distinct camps, even keeping the horses in different herds.

[69] "Confession of Valverde," *infra*, pp. 230-34.

[70] "Council of War .... against the Utes," *infra*, p. 99.

[71] The following account is based upon the diary of Governor Valverde, *infra*, pp. 110-33.

Leaving Taos on the twentieth, the expedition turned east into the mountains. Passing up San Fernando Creek, they camped on the summit of La Ciéneguilla Creek and on the following day descended to a stream at the foot of the range to halt near present Cimarron, New Mexico. There Valverde encountered the Jicarillas. Among them the expedition moved slowly during the next week. Welcoming the Spaniards on every side, the Apaches complained bitterly of the Utes and Comanches. At the Spanish camp on the twenty-first, a former village, they told how their enemies had killed sixty people there, burned a house and heaps of corn, and carried off many women and children. Naturally anxious to join the expedition for revenge, one hundred seven savages offered their services. Valverde, glad of re-enforcements, accepted them.

Of the life of these Apaches, Valverde fortunately leaves valuable notes. Near the site of their camp on the twenty-first, at the foot of the mountains, one of the officers found a small adobe house surrounded by planted fields. Some five miles to the east along a small stream the Spaniards found nine other adobe houses, one surmounted with a cross, while nearby were fields of yellow corn, beans, and squash. Another five leagues beyond was the site of the village and cornfields destroyed by the Comanches. Near this, intact, were seven terraced houses built by the Apaches. Some of these, the governor wrote, had already gathered in their crops of corn and had heaped it up in rows like walls, about eighteen inches high, or hung long ropes of it up to dry. Others not yet finished their reaping; their corn lay about unhusked. They had also built ditches and canals to irrigate their fields. Chief Carlana, who was with the party, counted twenty-seven tipis about the lands where the Apaches lived while harvesting.[72] This evidence of the stability of the Jicarilla was collected apparently to substantiate a later report of Valverde's regarding their possibilities as converts and allies: "Thus," he wrote to the viceroy, "I found them very close to embracing our holy faith, and as I have informed your Excellency on other occasions, they only lack priests to instruct and convert them. They work hard, gather much Indian corn, squashes and kidney beans, lay out ditches to irrigate their crops, and have always and at present maintain friendship with us."[73]

[72] The details above are gleaned from the diary of Valverde, *infra*, pp. 111-16. It is interesting to note that the irrigation ditches flat-roofed houses, and the agricultural activities of these Apaches indicate a level of Indian culture hitherto unknown in this part of New Mexico.

[73] "Valverde to Valero," Santa Fé, November 30, 1719, *infra*, p. 142.

Leaving these friendly people, the governor proceeded eastward to the Río Colorado, the present Canadian, which he reached near present Dillon. Here, joined by twenty more Apaches, he prepared to cross the divide to the Río de las Animas,[74] or the Purgatoire of today. The march over the summit was bitterly cold, though the command reached the Las Animas without mishap. Here more Apaches, sixty-nine in number under Chief Carlana, joined the camp and danced that night, smeared with bright colored paint, before the governor's tent.

Setting out from Las Animas on the twenty-eighth, the expedition turned northward along the foothills toward the Arkansas River. This region, the former hunting grounds of the Apaches, supplied deer, bear, and fine fat turkeys. The thirtieth found the command moving northward, with mountains rising high on the left. They soon crossed a branch of the upper waters of the present Huerfano and, definitely in the enemy country, traveled by night. Here they found their first traces of the enemy leading away from a deserted Carlana ranchería. They did not follow the lead, but pushed steadily northward. On October 2 they reached the main stream of the Huerfano, called Chiopo by the Apaches and San Antonio by Valverde. Crossing this, the command drew near the pine-covered slopes of the present Wet Mountains. Following the San Carlos of today, lined with plum and cherry trees, they reached on October 4 a point below the Arkansas River, some distance southeast of present Pueblo, Colorado.

Here the expedition turned eastward from the foothills to follow the Río Napestle. The scarcity of wood now forced the use of dung plentifully supplied by the vast herds of moving buffalo. Their journey on the seventh brought them to an abandoned Comanche camp of sixty fires whose departing trail was marked by dragging tent poles. Again on the fourteenth, some twenty-one leagues from the foothills, they found another deserted enemy camp of over two hundred fires. Valverde estimated fully one thousand Indians had been there. Two leagues further the tent-pole trail swung to the northeast. Here Valverde concluded that the expedition, some distance south of the Arkansas, was four or five days from El Cuartelejo. Undecided whether to advance there, he consulted the Apache chief, Carlana, and his scout, Naranjo. Both warned that scarcity of water after the passage of the fleeing multitude made further pursuit inadvisable. Calling the command into a general council of war, the governor stated his willingness

[74] The command was probably near Trinidad of today. Valverde's application of this name to the stream is the earliest known instance of its use. See editorial note No. 68.

30

to go on and left the decision to the members. The soldiers and settlers voted to return, fearing the snows soon to fall in the mountains behind them and the possible loss of their horses.

The same day, the fourteenth, while the command was resting and hunting buffalo for meat, ten Cuartelejo Apaches reached camp to advise Valverde that their people were coming to visit the expedition. After some indecision, the governor decided to set out to meet them on the Arkansas. Reaching the stream, east of present La Junta, bordered there with poplar groves, Valverde dispatched two Taos Indians to welcome the savages and assure them friendship. At the same time, anticipating a shortage of provisions incident upon entertaining the Apaches, he dispatched a messenger to Taos for supplies to be sent him on the road.

On the twenty-first, the Apache horde of Cuartelejos, Palomas, and Calchufines arrived. They camped on the opposite side of the river, some two hundred tipis, numbering in all, Valverde estimated, more than a thousand souls, warriors, women and children. On Valverde's welcoming them with a visit to their camp, the governor learned that one of their number, a Paloma, had a gunshot wound received in a battle with the French. Alert to fulfill the viceroy's order, he summoned the Indian to his tent. There the latter related that recently he and others of his tribe had been attacked far in from El Cuartelejo by the French, Pawnees, and Jumanos.[75] Only night saved them and, weak in numbers, they had fled, leaving their lands in the possession of the Pawnees. Further questioning elicited the information that the French had "built two pueblos, each of which is as large as that of Taos. In them they lived together with the Pawnee and Jumano Indians whom they have given large guns and have taught to shoot. With one of these they had wounded him. They also carry some small guns suspended from their belts.... [and] have done them much damage in taking away their lands and that each day they are coming closer. This is the reason that moved the Apaches to come establishing themselves on this lower part of the river, to be able to live in safety from their enemies." Valverde later noted that the Apaches knew of French settlements on a very large river, called in New Mexico the Río Jesús María, two towns on its northern bank being recently established.[76] From the

[75] Valverde intimates elsewhere that the Río Jesús María, the present South Platte, separated Apache lands from those of the Pawnees (infra, p. 163). With this definition of boundaries, the Palomas apparently lived in present northeastern Colorado. Regarding this reference to the Jumanos, see editorial note No. 22.

[76] "Valverde to Valero," Santa Fé, November 30, 1719, infra, p. 144.

31

older settlements on the Mississippi, the Apaches also stated, the French brought arms and everything necessary to supply the new ones.

This important information, one of the objects of his expedition, acquired, Valverde prepared to return. In vain the Apaches urged him to await the arrival of other bands that were hurrying to meet the Spaniards. Salving their disappointment with presents, Valverde offered them the aid and protection of his king against the French and their allies and promised to return to destroy their villages. Delighted, the Apaches bade the expedition a cordial and noisy farewell.

It is interesting to speculate upon Valverde's return route. Two facts shed a little light on the subject. One is Valverde's report to the viceroy that they withdrew by a different route from that followed out to the plains;[77] the other is the tantalizing fragment which concludes the diary: "The governor set out with his command from the spot, the march being made all along the Río Napestle on which they had been going....."[78] One might infer from this statement that they followed the Arkansas as far as the present Huerfano and then took the route along that river across, possibly, present Sangre de Cristo Pass to Taos. In any event, the expedition reached Santa Fé some time between the fifteenth and thirtieth of November, having traveled in all three hundred leagues.

Recounting his experiences in the northeast to the viceroy, Valverde suggested measures he thought appropriate to protect New Mexico from possible French aggression. "Thus, most excellent Lord, having solicited news of the French by all means, from these Indians, I found it to agree with that which was known by Captain Naranjo, with whom I counseled, and with those who went with me on this expedition. Having informed myself of the country, [I judge] this villa would be two hundred leagues more or less distant from the settlements of the French. The purpose of the enemy appears, accordingly. to penetrate little by little into the land. This country is very suitable for doing this because of its abundant game, meat, streams, and plains..... This information being of such service to his majesty that it may be of moment to the important measures your Excellency is now considering for protection from these enemies so that they may not gather on the boundaries of this kingdom, which though far removed, is the bulwark of New Spain, obliges me to dispatch the present mail so that with the knowledge of this report, your Excellency

[77] *Ibid., infra*, p. 143.
[78] "Diary of Valverde," *infra*, p. 133.

may order that which I ought to do. I am prepared for the time being as I mentioned in my former letter, to attend to the matter personally, or my lieutenant-general will do so, that is, the making of a reconnaissance of the enemy in order to report to your Excellency in regard to everything the most certain knowledge, if in the interim I have no new superior order." Besides the plans for the reconnaissance, Valverde asked of authorities in Mexico munitions of war, gun carriages for his stone mortars, and men able to manage them and train the soldiers of New Mexico in European methods.[79]

Valverde's expedition to the northeast was an event in the history of this New Mexican frontier. Besides adding valuable details to our knowledge of intertribal relationships in that area, it represents an additional step in Spanish expansion beyond the province begun by Vargas, Ulibarri, and Hurtado. Finally, though not achieving its immediate purpose, it was positive evidence regarding the French advance for the viceroy and his council, planning at the moment a post at El Cuartelejo as part of the general Texas-New Mexico frontier defense against the French.

F. The Search for the French: The Villasur Expedition to the Platte River, 1720

French northeast of New Mexico was a matter of grave import to Viceroy Valero. To him early in the year the king had communicated the news that the duke regent of France and the king of England had declared war upon Spain. With the announcement the sovereign sent instructions to prevent English and French ships from putting in at any port whatsoever, commanding immediate seizure of the vessel, confiscation of the goods, and internment of the crews. The English, particularly, known to be outfitting two frigate to attack Chile, Peru, and the Manila galleon off the Mexican coast, were to be guarded against with great care.[80] Upon the heels of this actual outbreak of hostilities came the alarming report of Governor Juan de la Cruz of New Vizcaya, at Parral, that French soldiers to the number of six thousand were but seventy leagues from Santa Fé.[81] Valverde's subsequent account of the French, while allaying the immediate fears of the viceroy for the north, nevertheless, impelled him to vigorous action.[82]

[79] "Valverde to Valero," Santa Fé, November 30, 1719, infra, p. 145.
[80] "Durán to Valero," Madrid, January 30, 1719, infra, p. 140.
[81] "Governor Cruz to Valero," Parral, December 11, 1719, infra, pp. 146-48.
[82] "Valverde to Valero," Santa Fé, November 30, 1719, infra, pp. 141-45.

Following a council of war held on January 2, 1720, he directed Valverde on the tenth to establish a presidio of twenty to twenty-five soldiers and two or three missionaries in El Cuartelejo to hold back a possible French intrusion; secondly, to direct the conversion of the Apaches and induce them to cultivate the land so that they might present a barrier far to the east.[83] At the same time, to erect a perfectly united front, Valero informed the Marqués de San Miguel, heading the Texas establishments, of the Apache alliance and directed him to attempt a similar arrangement with the northern Indians of Texas. Finally, affirming the earlier order to Valverde, the viceroy commanded a reconnaissance to locate the French in the northeast.

Governor Valverde replied to the viceroy's communication on May 27. For the reconnaissance, he reported that preparations were in process under the direction of his lieutenant-general, Don Pedro de Villasur. Concerning the foundation of the post at El Cuartelejo, however, he felt that the council had erred, himself supposing that the order ought to apply to La Jicarilla. The former location, he pointed out, was over one hundred and thirty leagues to the northeast, while the latter was but forty away in the same direction. Moreover, he noted, the Jicarilla Indians inclined to Christianity. More fully to present the matter, Valverde proceeded to call a council of war in the province wherein experienced New Mexicans might express an opinion on the relative merits of the two places.[84]

The gist of the council's opinion found expression in that of José Naranjo, whose experience embraced four expeditions into the northeast. The place was inappropriate, he affirmed, since it had practically no wood, lacked sufficient water and all other conveniences, for even the Apaches themselves found it necessary to leave after harvesting their crops. More than that, he doubted even fifty men sufficient to garrison this Apache settlement, surrounded as it was by so many different, hostile tribes. Its great distance from Santa Fé rendered in an emergency assistance a practical impossibility. Finally, he felt that La Jicarilla offered ideal conditions. It was but forty leagues away, the land excellent, timber and water available, and the Apaches numerous and friendly.[85] The governor added his indorsement, praying that fifty men be assigned to the projected presidio so that the Apaches there could be adequately brought into the fold of the Church and be pro-

[83] Bandelier, *op. cit.*, p. 186, n. 2, states that the viceroy's letter was dated the tenth of January, 1720.

[84] "Valverde to Valero," Santa Fé, May 27, 1720, *infra*, pp. 155-56.

[85] "Council of War," Santa Fé, June 2, 1720, *infra*, pp. 156-60.

tected from the Utes and Comanches as well as the Faraones on the east.[86] About two weeks later, on June 15, Valverde again urged on the viceroy the establishment at La Jicarilla and announced his lieutenant-general, Villasur, about to depart on the reconnaissance of the French in the northeast.[87] Unquestionably, Valverde took a sound position. He knew what local conditions were and the danger to a presidio so far away as El Cuartelejo. Expansion into La Jicarilla, on the other hand, was a logical advance, both because of its proximity and the assured friendliness of the Indians there.[88]

In Mexico City a second council of war, on September 17, duly impressed with the superior claim of La Jicarilla, recommended the establishment of a presidio there; and the viceroy dispatched the necessary orders to Valverde for the purpose. Moreover, he commanded, in accordance with the opinion of the council, the fathers should arrange a perpetual alliance with the Apaches, and took steps for the recruiting of soldiers and the dispatching of skilled artisans asked for by Valverde.[89] In the meantime, Villasur had been marching into the northeast seeking the French.

A glance at the expansion of French traders westward from the Mississippi River before 1720 will reveal the actual situation of these European rivals of the Spaniards and provide a setting for Villasur's exploit. Reference has already been made to the earliest notices of the French approach toward New Mexico from the Illinois country before 1700. After this date other traders coming from Louisiana supplemented this expansion along the Red and Arkansas rivers. As early as 1703 twenty Canadians left the Illinois country in search of New Mexico to trade and investigate the mines thought to be there.[90] In 1706, Ulibarri encountered evidences of French commerce and trade and even heard of a white man and woman who had been killed.[91]

[86] *Ibid., infra*, pp. 159-60.

[87] "Valverde to Valero," Santa Fé, June 15, 1720, *infra*, pp. 160-62.

[88] "Council of War," Santa Fé, June 2, 1720, *infra*, pp. 156-60. This council of war has been termed farcical (W. E. Dunn, "Spanish Reaction against the French Advance toward New Mexico, 1717-1727," *Mississippi Valley Historical Review*, II, 354). That writer, however, simply failed to grasp the plain wisdom of the reasons put forth by the members of the council against the establishment of a post so far away as El Cuartelejo. Indeed, the viceregal government recognized the weight of the argument of these men who had first-hand knowledge of the country to the extent of deferring to their opinions and ordering the presidio placed at La Jicarilla ("Council of War," México, September 26, 1720, *infra*, pp. 234-39).

[89] "Valero to Valverde," México, September 26, 1720, *infra*, p. 238.

[90] Bolton and Marshall, *Colonization of North America*, p. 282.

[91] "Diary of Ulibarri," *infra*, pp. 67, 70.

Between 1706 and 1719 this French advance went on apace. In the north, the Missouri River is reported to have been explored three hundred to four hundred leagues in 1708 by Canadians. In the south, five years later, 1713, St. Denis from Louisiana founded Natchitoches on the Red River and prepared to extend French trade to Old Mexico. The next year this Frenchman startled the Spaniards with his appearance at San Juan Bautista, a presidio on the Río Grande.[92]

Thus awakened to the growing French danger, the authorities in Mexico in 1715 moved to occupy Texas. From their post on the Red River the French now turned up that stream and along the Arkansas. In the year that St. Denis reached the Río Grande, 1714, some Indians reported in New Mexico that a number of French traders, allied with the Jumanos, had attacked El Cuartelejo.[93] Hurtado's entrada along the Canadian, however, in 1715 reported nothing of these invaders. Yet four years later the voyageurs had carried their advance to the Cadadachos where they had established a post; on the Red River itself Du Rivage had proceeded some distance. Meanwhile, La Harpe moving up the Arkansas had proposed a post among the Toucaras, at the mouth of the Canadian, to trade with New Mexico. Du Tisné, coming from Missouri, in this same year went through the Osage to the Arkansas, established an alliance with a Pawnee group on that stream, ran up the French flag over the villages, and traded in Spanish horses.[94]

Contemporaneous with this thrust toward New Mexico, St. Denis and several others dared to make a second journey to the Spanish Río Grande settlements. Thus, reports of this adventurous Frenchman and the advices emanating from New Mexico inspired Viceroy Valero to command, late in 1718, a reconnaissance of the French position beyond the latter province.[95] Valverde's expedition of the following year, 1719, produced, as already noted, news of a Pawnee-French alliance menacing the Apaches in the northeast. Such is the background of French expansion and Spanish worries behind the Villasur expedition of 1720.

Villasur left Santa Fé late in June or early in July. Accompanying him were forty-two soldiers, seasoned by the expeditions of Ulibarri, Hurtado, and Valverde, three settlers, sixty Indian allies,[96] and a priest, Father Juan Mínguez. Juan de l'Archévèque went as interpreter;

[92] Bolton and Marshall, *Colonization of North America*, pp. 282-84.

[93] "Este Cuaderno .... de un Religioso," *loc. cit.,* p. 295. See also Twitchell, *Spanish Archives of New Mexico,* II, 175, item 226.

[94] Bolton and Marshall, *Colonization of North America,* pp. 283-84.

[95] "Confession of Valverde," *infra,* p. 231.

[96] "Martínez to Valero," *infra,* p. 182, supplies the number of Indians and settlers.

Naranjo acted as chief scout. Well provisioned for the journey, Villasur carried in addition a quantity of maize, short swords, knives, sombreros, and half a muleload of tobacco to reward the Indian guides and placate the tribes met.[97] For his own use he had several silver platters, cups, spoons, a silver candlestick, an inkhorn, writing paper, quills, and a saltcellar.[98]

The route followed was always to the northeast from Santa Fé. Undoubtedly, they passed over the well known terrain of the Valverde and Ulibarri expeditions. Doubtless, too, the Jicarillas and Carlanas guided the party through their lands as they had the previous expeditions. They crossed the Arkansas River on rafts and made their way to El Cuartelejo, where they rested.[99] From here the command reached on August 6, the present South Platte River, then called the Río Jesús María.

On that date, having traveled three hundred leagues without encountering a sign of the French, Villasur held a council of war, which, after some debate, decided to seek the Pawnees and learn from them, if possible, where the French were.[100] The next day, with the command across the Jesús María, Villasur sent Naranjo ahead with some scouts. The party shortly returned to report a band of Pawnees holding a war dance some eight leagues ahead. The Spaniards now crossed a second stream, the North Platte, named the San Lorenzo, that had just merged with the Jesús María. From their camp Villasur next sent a Pawnee captive, the personal servant of Captain Serna, to win the confidence of his kinsmen. However, at a ford where the envoy found a Pawnee village of many people, tomahawks greeted him, and he fled back to camp. The following day, the tenth, the expedition moved up opposite the village[101] and camped on "the banks of a very full flowing stream which has an island in the middle of it where there is a very large settlement of Indians of the Pawnee nation."[102]

Twenty-five or thirty savages came to the edge of the water to talk peace. Villasur seized upon their request for the interpreter to send him

97 Archévèque took along ten horses and six pack mules (Bandelier, *op. cit.,* p. 194).
98 "Declaration of Aguilar," Santa Fé, April 21, 1724, *infra,* p. 249.
99 "Declaration of Manuel Teniente de Alva," Santa Fé, April 21, 1724,*infra,*pp.254-55.
100 "Diary of Villasur," *infra,* p. 134. Their location at the moment was a few miles west of the junction of the present North and South Platte rivers.
101 "Diary of Villasur," *infra,* p. 137. This spot, about eight leagues from the junction of the Platte, was between the present towns of Maxwell and Brady, Nebraska.
102 "Martínez to Valero," México (n.d.), *infra,* p. 183. There is an island opposite these two towns mentioned above.

across with the customary presents. He did not return, but called across the stream, stating that the Indians though well disposed would not let him go and that of "Spaniards" (French) among the Pawnees he knew nothing. However, some of those Indians visiting Villasur's camp the next day spoke of a white man. Villasur now directed Archévèque to write a note in French for the Pawnees to take back. The only reply the Indians made was to return the following day bearing an old linen flag and a paper covered with illegible writing.

Vexed with the lack of results, Villasur urged on a council of war a proposal to cross and secure the desired information. His officers, more cautious, interpreted the detention of the interpreter as a warning, a position considerably strengthened by the fact that the Pawnees had just seized some Spanish Indians bathing in the river. In the end the officers prevailed, the expedition fell back, recrossed the San Lorenzo, and halted on its southern banks about four o'clock in the afternoon of August 13. That night the horseherd pastured, Indian sentinels were placed to guard the camp. Soon after nightfall unmistakable signs of a stalking party were heard. The guard reported a barking dog and noises, seemingly made by people crossing the river. Villasur warned the sentinels and sent a party of Indians along the river who, however, shortly reported that all was well.[103]

Suddenly at daybreak, while the Spaniards were roping their horses and preparing their packs, a band of Pawnees and French attacked with deadly effect. Taken completely by surprise, the horse guard lost valuable time recovering their animals. Finally, rounded up, they charged the enemy. Their attempt was useless. The Indians riding in a circle poured a murderous fire upon the disorganized camp. Villasur and his body servant, both unarmed, were killed before the commander's own tent. Archévèque died in the first volley while his personal servant, Santiago Giravalle, suffering from seven wounds, miraculously escaped and fled when he could no longer aid his master.[104] Eventually twelve other Spaniards extricated themselves from the carnage and took flight in the wake of the forty-eight panic-stricken Indian allies. Left dead and dying in the tall grass were Villasur, the chaplain, Mínguez, five corporals, nineteen soldiers, L'Archévèque, Captain Christóval de la Serna, four of his servants, the hardy frontiersman, Naranjo,

[103] The above account is based principally upon the statements of Rael de Aguilar and Phelipe Tamariz, eyewitnesses of these events (infra, pp. 226-30).

[104] Bandelier, op. cit., p. 202, n. 2.

and eleven Indians. The Pawnees, so the survivors later reported, suffered greatly and lost so many that they were unable to pursue.[105]

At El Cuartelejo, the Apaches received the remnants of the command with tenderness, nursed their wounds and offered their poor supplies. Eventually, on September 6 following, the survivors brought the sad news to Valverde.[106] The blow was crushing. Besides the thirty-two widows and many orphans, the New Mexican settlements now found themselves terribly weakened by the loss of at least a third of their best soldiers. With a heavy heart Valverde sent the news to the viceroy by Tamariz, an eyewitness, so that the authorities could question him further. Eulogizing Villasur, whom he said preferred death rather than to return without fulfilling his mission, the governor charged heretical Huguenots with the disaster. He begged for thirty presidials to replace those lost, recorded his fears of a French invasion, and insisted that the weakened condition of the province would render him unable to repel the Utes, Comanches, and Faraones, who were again riding the frontiers.[107]

III. Plans To Occupy El Cuartelejo, 1720-1727

In Mexico news of Villasur's destruction created alarm and spurred the viceroy's program for defense. The war declared in 1719 was by August of 1720 over. The French had returned Pensacola in Florida and had surrendered the captured posts in Texas. The reconnaissance of Villasur, accordingly, far from being an act of war, was an entirely legal activity. Thus the fiscal who heard Valverde's messenger and read the reports labeled the attack a flagrant violation of the truce, recommended war supplies sent to New Mexico and that the presidio provided for be established to repel invasion.[108]

The viceroy referred the fiscal's opinion to Dr. Olivan Revolledo, the auditor of war, with the request that the interview Tamariz, Valverde's messenger, a former governor of New Mexico, Martínez, and one

105 The site of the battle was on the south side of the North Platte River, near the present town of North Platte, Nebraska. With regard to Father Mínguez and the battle, see Twitchell, *Spanish Archives of New Mexico*, II, 170, item 194; and p. 184, item 280a. For a discussion of the location of the battle, cf. editorial note No. 152.

106 Tamariz reported the event to Valverde (Bandelier, *op. cit.*, p. 195, n. 3).

107 "Valverde to Valero," Santa Fé, October 8, 1720, *infra*, pp. 162-67. See Martínez's interesting prediction of the probable effects of the defeat upon the province of New Mexico ("Martínez to Valero," México [n.d.], *infra*, p. 185).

108 "Sainz to Valero," México, November 4, 1720, *infra*, pp. 167-69.

Garduño, a former soldier at Santa Fé, and recommend a course of action for the council already summoned. Moreover, the gravity of the loss in New Mexico was enhanced by the recent rebellion of the Julimes Indians at the junction of the Conchos and Río Grande, so that the possibility of French aid to these rebels was a further matter for consideration.[109]

From Martínez, Revolledo learned that La Jicarilla was fifteen leagues to the northeast; the Napestle sixty leagues beyond, and El Cuartelejo fifty leagues from the river. This latter statement was evidently a guess as Martínez testified that he had never been beyond the Napestle. The Río Jesús María itself he believed was fifty leagues from El Cuartelejo, where he knew the Pawnees lived. The other Indians in the area he knew to be the Canceres, French allies who lived east of the Sierra Blanca, while the Carlana were between the Napestle and La Jicarilla. He doubted the French could invade New Mexico since they had no cavalry. Finally, he estimated that inasmuch as the Julimes were fully four hundred forty leagues south of the Jesús María, the Pawnees and French could extend them no aid.[110] Guarduño's information differed in no essential detail from that of Martínez beyond his statement that Santa Fé was two hundred leagues from El Cuartelejo whence he had journeyed twelve years previously.[111] Felipe Tamariz added the most important information, but unfortunately his contribution has not appeared. He stated that he had lost the diary of the journey on the battlefield, but in Santa Fé while events were still fresh he had composed another, which, on his arrival in Mexico City, he had turned over to the viceroy.[112]

On December 9, Auditor Revolledo returned his recommendation to Viceroy Valero. Recognizing the seriousness of the loss of forty-five presidials, the possibility of invasion either by hostile tribes or by the Pawnees and French, should they find and make use of the lost diary, he urged that the soldiers be replaced with troops instructed in the art of European warfare and that the presidios already recommended be established in La Jicarilla. Dismissing the possibility of Pawnee and French aid to the revolting Julimes, he recommended that the king be fully informed of the tragic breach of the truce. Finally, he urged that the Marqués de San Miguel commanding in Texas seize all Pawnees

[109]"Dr. Olivan Rebolledo to Valero," México, November 12, 1720, *infra*, pp. 169-70.
[110] "Declaration of Martínez," México, November 13, 1720, *infra*, pp. 170-72.
[111] "Declaration of Garduño," México, November 15, 1720, *infra*, pp. 172-74.
[112] "Declaration of Tamariz," México, November 15, 1720, *infra*, pp. 174-75.

in his province and assure the Texas Indians that the king would extend to them the same protection from their northern enemies that he was giving the Cuartelejos, Sierra Blancas, and Jicarilla Apaches on the frontiers of New Mexico.[113]

These well-planned measures for the defense of New Mexico did not materialize. Lack of soldiers prevented immediate action while a frontier inspection in progress at the moment suggested to the viceroy that the Visitor Don Antonio Cobián Busto should probe further into the causes of Villasur's defeat and pass upon the advisability of a post at La Jicarilla. It was not until October 22, 1722, that Cobián Busto began the investigation in New Mexico.[114] Shortly thereafter he gave up his office. The matter was next turned over to his successor, Visitor Don Pedro de Rivera. This official began the frontier inspection anew on July 24, 1724.[115] Two years later, June 28, 1726, he reached Santa Fé to consider the propositions originally assigned to Cobián Busto.[116]

Taking up first the question of responsibility of Valverde for the defeat of Villasur, Rivera at the direction of the viceroy preferred charges against the governor based essentially upon two counts: first, that Valverde had entrusted the investigation to Villasur instead of making it himself; secondly, that even if he established a lawful reason for delegating the duty, he was negligent in selecting a lieutenant inexperienced in the military affairs of those countries. Early in July, Rivera received the testimony of the living eyewitnesses,[117] with Valverde's own version of his actions, and forwarded the proceedings to the authorities in México for final disposition.[118] There Auditor Revolledo disagreed sharply with the fiscal, who would have absolved Valverde.[119] Submitting his own conclusions to the viceroy on May 29, 1727, Revolledo's analysis of the testimony elicited unanswerable arguments of Villasur's incompetence and thus established the responsibility of Valverde.

113 "Dr. Olivan Revolledo to Valero," México, December 9, 1720, infra, pp. 175-77.

114 "Writ of Rivera," infra, pp. 220, 225. For a reference to Cobián Busto's visit to New Mexico, see Twitchell, Spanish Archives of New Mexico, II, 192, item 318.

115 Pedro de Rivera, Diario y derrotero de lo caminado, visto, y observado en el discurso de la vista general de Precidios, situado en las Provincias Ynternas de Nueva Espana (Guatemala, 1736), fol. 1.

116 "Trial of Valverde," infra, pp. 219 ff.

117 "Testimony of Aguilar," infra, pp. 226-28; "Testimony of Tamariz," infra, pp. 228-30. The details provided by these witnesses concerning the massacre have been utilized above in telling the story of the massacre, so that they need not be repeated.

118 "Council of War," México, 1727, infra, pp. 239 ff.

119 "Reply of the Fiscal," infra, pp. 240-41.

41

In the first place, the auditor contended, if Villasur had been competent he would not have wished to cross the river to the Pawnee pueblo without first making sure of their friendship, particularly as their suspicious attitude was evident; secondly, still uncertain of their temper he sent the interpreter to ask the Pawnees about the French, at the time at war with the Spaniards; thirdly, since the Pawnees had captured one of the Spanish Indians, the commander, having retreated thereupon and made camp, ought to have set out the most trusted sentinels and not Indians; fourthly, the Spaniards being in enemy country, Villasur ought to have posted Spanish pickets to observe the movement of the enemy; fifthly, since a noise made by swimmers in the river was heard in the silence of the night and was believed to have been made by the enemy, Villasur ought to have augmented his care with sentinels about the camp itself; sixthly, since a barking dog gave them advice of the enemy, the camp ought to have been aroused by Villasur, and the squad in charge of the horseherd ordered that night back into camp, instead of in the morning. The law in the case, Revolledo concluded, was that the governor was under obligations to select a man as fit, as vigorous, as prudent, and as expert as himself. Having failed to do so, Revolledo recommended as a sufficient punishment that Valverde pay fifty pesos for charity masses for the souls of the dead soldiers and one hundred fifty pesos for aiding in the purchase of chalice and ornaments for the missions at Junta de los Ríos.[120] The viceroy, reviewing the case, agreed with the auditor and commanded Governor Bustamante to carry out the sentence.[121] Doubtless Valverde's long record saved him more severe punishment. Indeed, for all practical purposes, the fine undoubtedly assuaged the feelings of the widows and other relatives of the dead who had demanded his punishment.

The question of a presidio in La Jicarilla proposed by Valverde in place of the one commanded at El Cuartelejo had before Rivera's arrival again forced itself on the attention of the authorities in Mexico City. At Santa Fé on November 8, 1723, Captain Carlana appeared at the head of a delegation lamenting the outrages of the Comanches and prayed Governor Bustamante to aid them. In return they promised to obey the king, to settle in pueblos like the Indians of New Mexico, be baptized and instructed by missionaries and governed by an alcalde. To choose suitable sites for the pueblos, they invited Bustamante to visit La Jicarilla.[122]

120 "Dr. Olivan Revolledo to Casa Fuerte," México, May 29, 1727, *infra,* pp. 241-44.
121 "Order for Council of War," México, (n.d.), *infra,* p. 245.
122 "Decree of Bustamante," Santa Fé, November 8, 1723, *infra,* pp. 193-95.

Foregoing a campaign planned against the Faraones, a council of war in Santa Fé decided to accept the Jicarilla offer in the hope that their example would stimulate other eastern Apaches likewise to settle down,[123] and thus form a secure barrier against French invasion. After notifying Viceroy Casafuerte of the action, the governor set out for La Jicarilla on November 17 accompanied by fifty presidials and Father Camargo. Doubtless, they proceeded over the usual route from Santa Fé to Taos and thence over the range by way of San Fernando Creek. Arrived on the twenty-fifth in La Jicarilla, the command camped in the valley of the Río de Guadaloupe, possibly Cimarron Creek. There, Carlana, six other chiefs, and fifty young warriors welcomed the expedition. Bustamante assured the band of his protection, the acceptance of their allegiance, and asked to be taken to the rest of the rancherías. Proceeding five leagues along the river, they reached the ranchería of Chief Churlique. These Apaches likewise promised to accept Christianity and Spanish rule, and Bustamante assured them aid against the Comanches when they had settled in pueblos. Passing on next to the ranchería of Captain Coxo, four leagues beyond, the governor received the usual welcome. Many of these Indians here were apostates, but they vociferously promised to return to the fold, and Bustamante on his part promised protection and tools with which to cultivate the land. Satisfied with the spirit of the Jicarillas, Bustamante here took possession of the land. Then presenting a horse and some flour to each of the various chiefs, he retraced his steps to Santa Fé.[124]

Writing Viceroy Casafuerte on January 10, 1724, Bustamante reported the results of his entrada into La Jicarilla. He urged anew the necessity for a presidio there of fifty soldiers not only to keep out the French but to drive away the Comanches. Such a post he thought ought to be provided with a church, its ornaments and jewels, and supplies for a year: tools, and hoes for cultivation, and hatchets for building houses.[125] In Mexico, the project still found favor. The fiscal to whom the matter was referred found precise justification for the undertaking in the royal laws, recommended that the superior prelate of the custody of New Mexico select the missionaries and provide their supplies, and finally that Bustamante direct the settling of the Indians and furnish them with their tools. Regarding soldiers, he suggested

[123] "Council of War," Santa Fé, November 9, 1723, *infra*, pp. 195-97. See also Twitchell, *Spanish Archives of New Mexico*, II, 193, item 324.

[124] "Diary of Bustamante," *infra*, pp. 197-201.

[125] "Bustamante to Casa Fuerte," Santa Fé, January 10, 1724, *infra*, pp. 201-03.

that they could be taken from other presidios in old Mexico and be commanded by an officer from Santa Fé.[126]

The auditor next passed upon the matter. He reviewed the history of the earlier proposals and the authority given at various times to establish the post. Agreeing with the fiscal in all particulars but that of the garrison, he thought that fifty men from Santa Fé should be sent because of their experience in local affairs and that these should be replaced by twenty-five men each from the presidios at Conchos and Casas Grandes. Finally, he added if it were expedient later to colonize La Jicarilla, provincials from New Mexico itself might be allotted there lands, water and haciendas.[127]

Meanwhile, Viceroy Casafuerte had written Bustamante to encourage the Indians while he considered what should be done for them.[128] Replying on May 3, 1724, the governor announced that in fulfillment of this order he had met with a second delegation from La Jicarilla which had come begging aid against their old enemies. Delaying for the second time a projected Faraon campaign, he had pursued the Utes and Comanches and had successfully retrieved sixty-four captured Jicarillas, women and children. However, the Jicarillas, still frightened, were contemplating joining forces with the Navajos.[129] The governor's fears that such an event would make their conversion immeasurably harder were shared in Mexico. The fiscal recommended accordingly, on October 20, 1724, that Bustamante offer the Jicarillas lands close to the pueblos in New Mexico and furnish them supplies from the royal treasury for the first and second years.[130] However, the execution of this wise proposal received still another setback for the viceroy on the next day, October 21, referred the whole matter to Visitor Rivera, who, as already noted, did not reach Santa Fé until June of 1726.[131]

Rivera, fresh from his survey of the Mexican border posts, viewed the project in relation to the needs of the entire northern frontier of New Spain. Consequently, he discounted certain New Mexican considerations and eventually concluded that there was no pressing need for a presidio in La Jicarilla. Reviewing the findings of the various councils of war, the different proposals for the location of the presidio, Rivera flatly stated that the Jicarillas had sought baptism and armed protection

[126] "Reply of the Fiscal," México, April 2, 1724, infra, pp. 203-05.
[127] "Dr. Olivan Revolledo to Casafuerte," México, July 12, 1724, infra, pp. 205-07.
[128] Mentioned in "Bustamante to Casafuerte," Santa Fé, May 3, 1724, infra, p. 208.
[129] Ibid, infra, 208-09.
[130] "Reply of the Fiscal," México, October 20, 1724, infra, p. 209.
[131] "Order of Casafuerte," México, October 21, 1724, infra, 209.

as a device to save themselves from the Comanches. He did recognize that they were harried and could only seek refuge in New Mexico. He saw no difficulty, therefore, in adopting the fiscal's proposal that they be invited to settle within the province near Taos. There, he felt, by doubling the population they would effectively bar any French aggression. On the other hand, he pointed out, the uselessness of a presidio in La Jicarilla itself was apparent when attention was paid to the vast unoccupied areas within the empire. Between Santa Fé and Zuñi, he observed, little was occupied; about Taos was an abundance of land and few settlers; between Chihuahua and El Paso were ninety-four leagues and the only settlements were Carrizal and Ojo Caliente and two haciendas near Chihuahua. With so much unprotected land closer than La Jicarilla and El Cuartelejo, it was pointless for the government to populate other regions which had so little immediate value. If every time a presidio were suggested, he concluded, it had to be founded because the laws approved, the treasury of Midas would not suffice to establish presidios from "Durango to New Mexico and from here to the Californias and from there to Los Adaes .... and no one will be astonished if I consider this expense useless."[132]

In Mexico, Rivera's recommendations were accepted and thus the proposal for extending the empire northeast of New Mexico received its deathblow.[133] The final upshot of the matter was simply the viceroy's order to Bustamante to encourage the Jicarillas to locate their homes near Taos.[134] Logical and convincing as the reasoning of Rivera was, his conclusions, viewed with much hindsight, admit a fundamental defect. In 1720 the all-important consideration controlling the decisions of the Spanish authorities was a strategic one—the occupation of the territory northeast of Santa Fé to prevent French ingress into New Mexico. In 1726 the question was essentially whether Spaniards ought to occupy the region, not primarily to guard against French aggression, but to protect the Jicarilla Indians there from the onslaughts of the Comanches, Utes, and Faraones. Rivera's decision, therefore, was apparently oblivious to the fact that the Jicarillas were in effect a buffer in the northeast between the Utes and Comanches, and Spanish New Mexico. For that reason the post did have a real significance for the maintenance of the province. Later governors in fact lamented the disappearance of the Jicarillas and the use of their lands by the Coman-

132 "Rivera to Casafuerte," El Paso, September 26, 1726, *infra*, pp. 209-17.
133 "Dr. Olivan Revolledo to Casafuerte," México, March 31, 1727, *infra*, pp. 218-19.
134 "Order of Casafuerte," México, April 1, 1727, *infra*, p. 219.

ches as a raiding base against the Pueblos and Spanish towns, but this contingency did not impress, if it occurred to, Rivera in 1726.[135]

Presumably following Viceroy Casafuerte's order to invite the Jicarillas to New Mexico, Bustamante in 1727 visited these Apaches.[136] In any event, they came to live near Pecos and about twelve miles north of Taos, where a mission was established among them in 1733. Soon after, however, according to one report, the greater part fled somewhere beyond the frontier, though the faithful remnants joined the Taos against the Comanches.[137] Another and perhaps more reliable source asserts that the few originally from La Jicarilla remained near Taos and Pecos. For this account we are indebted to Governor Codallos, who in 1748 urged anew the project of a presidio against the Comanches and the French in those lands "where were located in times past, the Indians of the Jicarilla nation, (a branch of the Apaches) who were numerous and had houses, palisade huts and other shelters. Thence the pagan Comanches despoiled them, killing most of them. The few that remained have established and maintained themselves in peace nearby the Pueblos of Taos and Pecos, with their families. The former site of the Jicarillas is the pass for shutting off the aforesaid populous nation of the Comanches and the French, if they tried to make any entrance to this said kingdom."[138]

Apache reports of the French continued to reach New Mexico after Rivera left the province. But with peace established between the mother countries, Governor Bustamante did no more than forward to the viceroy accounts that he heard and offer to investigate the rumors. On April 30, 1727, he wrote Casafuerte that the alcalde mayor of Taos had informed him of the reported arrival of six French in El Cuartelejo, others being settled on the Río de Chinali.[139] Likewise, when Brigadier Rivera was in Santa Fé in 1726, a group of Apaches, Escalchufines, and Palomas fled into New Mexico before the Comanches among whom, from the Indians' description of their pursuers, Bustamante concluded,

135 A possible explanation of Rivera's action may be that as a Spaniard he failed to grasp the importance of the Indian attacks—an American problem. Had the French been as close, he would doubtless have supported the presidio, for France and Frenchmen were realities to the continental Spanish mind.

136 Twitchell, *Spanish Archives of New Mexico,* II, 196, item 347.

137 Joseph Antonio Villa-Señor, *Teatro Americano,* Segunda Parte (México, 1748), p. 420.

138 "Opinion of Governor Codallos y Rabal," Charles F. Lummis, trans., *Land of Sunshine,* VIII, 129. Bandelier, *op. cit.,* p. 189, n. 1, refers to part of this document in the original.

139 "Bustamante to Casafuerte," Santa Fé, April 30, 1727, *infra,* pp. 256-59.

were French.[140] Some time later a Comanche woman captive specified details unmistakably marking the white men as French. They wore, she said, white clothes, some with red coats, hats banded with silver, and carried equipment of tents and weapons. They prepared their food of meat and bread, she added, by cooking it in copper kettles and pounding chocolate in jugs. Moreover, at a short distance from El Cuartelejo on the Río de Chinali, this captive observed, these white people had built some walled houses.[141]

On still another occasion, the governor reported a Taos chief and some of his men out hunting were invited in La Jicarilla to see a Frenchman three days distant from there, other Frenchmen being at El Cuartelejo whence they had gone with a force of Palomas, Cuartelejos, and Sierra Blancas against the Comanches. Finally, concluded Bustamante, the Apaches believed these Frenchmen had won over the greater part of the Indians on the plains. Accordingly, he proposed a foray to El Cuartelejo and Chinali. Viceroy Casafuerte, however, merely instructed Bustamante in his reply that further news should be gathered, but that the French were, he felt, at El Cuartelejo only to trade their dry goods, muskets and arms, or to aid one tribe against another as was their practice.[142]

After 1727 the French, with exception of an intrusion in the middle of the century, were no longer a serious threat to New Mexico.[143] The real problem in the northeast became one of defense against the Ute and Comanche invasion. Some time after that date, with the Jicarilla erased, and the Apaches quite generally driven from the northeast, the Utes and Comanches turned upon one another to wage a war of extermination. Late in the century after 1763, when Indian attack on all the northern provinces of New Spain became acute, Charles III took extensive measures to meet the menace by erecting the Commandancy-General of the Interior Provinces. The execution of the royal policy in New Mexico was placed in the hands of Governor Juan Bautista de Anza, who successfully established in 1786 a peace with the Utes, Navajos, and Comanches, and used these Indians, now reconciled with one another, against the Apaches.[144] This peace on the northern border

---

140 *Ibid., infra,* pp. 256-57.

141 *Ibid., infra,* p. 257.

142 "Revolledo to Casafuerte," México, November 26, 1727, *infra,* p. 260.

143 Herbert E. Bolton, "French Intrusions into New Mexico, 1749-1752," *The Pacific Ocean in History* (New York, 1917), pp. 389-407.

144 Alfred B. Thomas, *Forgotten Frontiers: A Study of the Spanish Indian Policy of Juan Bautista de Anza, Governor of New Mexico, 1777-1787* (Norman, 1932), *passim.*

lasted a quarter of a century. The advent of Anglo-Saxon traders after 1800 into the West, however, dissolved these barriers thrown about New Mexico and reproduced anew an international conflict on the northern frontier, the features of which resembled strongly the Franco-Indian-Spanish struggle of a century before.

Spanish activities northeast of New Mexico in the early eighteenth century were an important part of the process of Spanish expansion in western North America. The pioneer explorations of Archuleta, Vargas, Ulibarri, Hurtado, Valverde, Villasur, and Bustamante, following those of Oñate and Coronado, opened the first chapter in early western American exploration in areas now identified with Texas, Oklahoma, Colorado and western Nebraska. Leaving records rich in contemporary information, these pioneers opened trails widened by eighteenth century Spaniards and Frenchmen and plotted the background for Pike, Long, Wilkinson, the more often-chronicled Anglo-Americans.

The varied interests of the New Mexicans in this salient throw a reflected light on adjoining Indian civilizations. During the sixty-odd years, 1664-1727, Spaniards established the existence and range of certain Apache groups. The notes on Jicarilla customs, their habits, crops, use of irrigation, flat-roofed adobe houses, all indicate a level of Indian culture hitherto unsuspected in northeastern New Mexico. The study of the records considered here illustrate the mode by which immediate elements of pueblo culture were carried into the areas touching New Mexico on the north and east.

Here may be seen the origins of the Comanche entry into the Southwest and the beginning of the Apache, Ute, and Comanche tribal conflict. Ulibarri's entrada in 1706 into this area substantiates the Ute-Comanche displacement of the Apaches from their ancient homelands. In the twenty years following, Valverde, Rivera, and Bustamante supply the details of the Jicarilla retreat from this quarter. Similarly, these same writings chart the movements of the Comanches before their advent into Texas in the middle of the eighteenth century.

International politics emphasized this Spanish-Indian border conflict. That French traders had reached the foothills of the Rocky Mountains by 1706, though not generally known, is implicit in the present record. With control of the intervening Apache Indians as the prize, the victory, after Villasur's defeat, rested with the French. The triumph was an empty one, for they found themselves blocked out of New Mexico by the intruding Comanches. Finally, the history of this three-

48

cornered conflict is the precursor of that which came a century later when Spain had to face on this same frontier the young United States.

Upon New Mexico itself this two-century conflict had definite effects. The campaigning against Comanches, Utes, and Apaches exemplifies the ceaseless defensive struggle waged by the Spaniards across all New Mexico's frontiers. The history of this remarkable defense of the pueblo Southwest might amply demonstrate that Spanish blood alone saved from utter obliteration a large part of this distinctive and picturesque civilization. Naturally, Spain's defense of the pueblo limited there her own cultural growth. The hostility of Comanches, Utes, and Apaches make obvious the reason why Spanish power never took root in the Arkansas valley. The marvel is that Spain successfully retained possession of New Mexico flung so far across the northern border of New Spain.

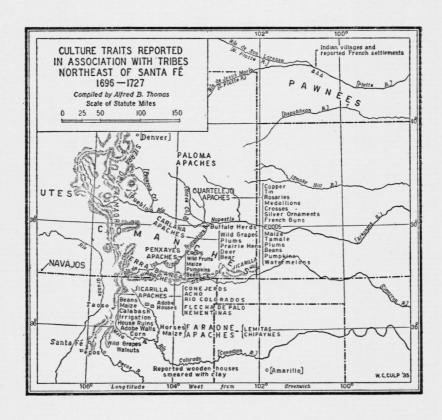

CULTURE TRAITS REPORTED
IN ASSOCIATION WITH TRIBES
NORTHEAST OF SANTA FÉ
1696 — 1727

Compiled by Alfred B. Thomas
Scale of Statute Miles

0   25   50   100   150

Indian villages and
reported French settlements

PAWNEES

Rio de San Lorenzo
[N. Platte R.]

Rio de Jesus Maria
[S. Platte R.]

[Platte R.]

[Republican R.]

40°

[Denver]

PALOMA
APACHES

UTES

QUARTELEJO
APACHES

[Smoky Hill R.]

Copper
Tin
Rosaries
Medallions
Crosses
Silver Ornaments
French Guns

[Arkansas R.]

CARLANA
APACHES

COMANCHES

Napestle

Buffalo Herds

FOODS

Wild Grapes
Plums
Prairie Hens
Deer
Bear

Maize
Tamale
Plums
Beans
Pumpkins
Watermelons

38°

NAVAJOS

PENXAYES
APACHES

SIERRA BLANCA

CROPS
Wild Fruits
Maize
Pumpkins
Beans

JICARILLA

Rio Grande

JICARILLA
APACHES

CONEJEROS
ACHO
RIO COLORADOS
FLECHA DE PALO
NEMENTINAS

[Taos]

Beans
Maize
Calabash
Irrigation
House Ruins
Adobe Walls
Corn

Adobe
Houses

36°

36°

Santa Fé

Wild Grapes
Walnuts

Pecos

Pecos R.

Horses
Maize

FARAONE
APACHES

LEMITAS
CHIPAYNES

Cimarron R.

Colorado

[Canadian R.]

Reported wooden houses
smeared with clay

o [Amarillo]

W. C. CULP '35

106°   Longtitude   104°   West   from   102°   Greenwich   100°

102°   100°

DOCUMENTS RELATING TO THE NORTHEASTERN FRONTIER OF NEW MEXICO
1696-1727

PUBLISHER'S NOTE: The spellings, accents and capitalization in the documents that follow are those which appear in the documents from which the Editor has made his translations, and, consequently, frequently will appear inconsistent. The Editor has sought to preserve as closely as translation permits, the style and feeling of the original documents. The superior figures in the documents refer to the Editorial Notes, to be found at the end of Part Two.

DOCUMENTS RELATING TO THE NORTHEASTERN FRONTIER OF NEW MEXICO, 1696-1727

PART TWO

I. The Expedition of Juan de Archuleta to El Cuartelejo 1664-1680 (*ca.*)[1]

ABOUT the middle of the past century some families of Christian Indians of the pueblo and nation of Taos revolted and fled to the plains of Cibola and fortified themselves in a spot, which since then on this account they call El Cuartelejo. They remained there until D. Juan de Archuleta, by order of the governor, went with twenty soldiers and a force of Indian auxiliaries and brought them back to their pueblo. He found in the possession of these rebellious Taos kettles and other pieces of copper and tin.[2] Having asked them where they had acquired these, they answered from the Quivira pueblos, to which they had made a journey from El Cuartelejo. This caused great surprise and content to all the Spaniards and religious of the kingdom, as they believed that these and the rest of the pieces and kettles were made in La Quivira. From this, they inferred it to be a kingdom very civilized and wealthy. From El Cuartelejo, by that route, one goes to the Pawnees, and today it is evident certainly that there are no other pueblos except these mentioned. With them the French at that time were trading. More than this, in all the pueblos from the Jumanos to the north or northeast that the English have discovered, we do not know that any have been found with the advancement and richness that is imagined of Gran Quivira.

II. Governor Vargas' Diary of his Campaign in Pursuit of the Rebellious Picuríes, 1696[3]

[*Marginal note:* The governor and captain-general arrives at the village of Picuríes and finds on the road the spies who say they have seen no one.] On the twenty-second of the month of October, of this date and year, I, the governor and captain-general, arrived at this village

53

of Picuríes, and with the camp following, encountered on the road the spies whom yesterday I dispatched to reconnoiter. They notified me that there were no people in the village, and I saw that there was none. In witness whereof I signed this with my secretary.

Before me

DIEGO DE VARGAS   DOMINGO DE LA BARREDA,
ZAPATA LUJAN PONCE DE LEON   [rubric]
    [rubric]   Secretary of Government and War.[4]

[Marginal note: Information given by a Tano Indian who was taken by the Pecos who went to reconnoiter the country.] On the said day, month and year at about six in the evening, the Pecos who had been scouring the country came in with a prisoner, an Indian of the Tanos nation from the town, who says he is named Miguel. Being questioned through Mattias Lujan where the people of Picuríes are, he says that they are moving on the plains with the Tanos and Teguas, having set out three days ago. Asked how long since Don Lorenzo went, he maintains that he and his people left with the others, taking many loaded horses; that the Picuríes took more horses than the Teguas [Tiguas] and Thanos; that the Teguas are herding many ewes and goats, but no oxen or cattle at all. Examined concerning which way they are going, he specifies the river road.[5] Asked if it is a good trail, he replied that it may be good on horseback up to the summit; that as far as that there are some hills, and afterwards it is a good road. It being inquired where he heard the Picuríes say they were going, he answers that they were headed toward the place where the bulls run.

[Marginal note: The governor and captain-general sets out in pursuit of the enemy down the river. He made camp at a distance of eight leagues.] On the twenty-third of the month of October, of said date and year, I, the governor and captain-general, as a result of the preceding declaration, set out with the camp today, from the pueblo of Picuríes in pursuit of the rebels referred to in the testimony. I followed the road which comes down the river of this pueblo to the east; the river on the right hand. I found the footpath between the two sierras like a canyon in some places and wholly mountainous, and filled with stones which are in those hills. Having traveled apparently about five long leagues, I found the ranchería which the enemy had attacked first. Further on about two leagues it was recognized that the enemy had been there, because they took the trail from there along the stream.

Having covered from here one long league, I made camp. I, the governor and captain-general, passed the night in the spot with the camp.

[*Marginal note:* The governor and captain-general sends spies out following the river road, with orders to go as far as they can, and if they find the enemy, to return and report.] On the said day, month and year, I, governor and captain-general, before night fell sent out spies to follow the path and river and go as far as they could, since by the fires that the enemy would have to light, on account of the severity of the cold, they might discover them. Having thus ascertained where they might be, they were to return to give me notice, so that at the moment of their arrival, I could set out with a small party and destroy the foe.

[*Marginal note:* The governor and captain-general goes with the army about nine leagues and halts.] On the twenty-fourth of the month of October of this day and year, I, the governor and captain-general, having gone about two leagues from this mountain ridge, came upon the walls of a ruined farm which betokened a delay, but we could not see the trail of the fugitives well on account of its having rained. Being very undecided whether to discontinue the pursuit on account of the great advantage they had, I determined to spend all the day searching out the places where they had their huts; and at a little more than a league I hit upon the way where they had been going. Five leagues from there, coming from behind a ridge on the right, we found traces near a watering hole formed by the river and the slope. In this place, they left a stone grinder. The trail was not old, and in order to cover all the ground possible in the pursuit, I went on after sunset after the cavalry arrived. Having made about two leagues, we saw where the enemy had been in a hollow. It being already late and having tired out four horses, on account of the darkness, I was obliged to spend the night in their neighborhood.

[*Marginal note:* The governor and captain-general goes in pursuit of the enemy.] On the twenty-fifth of October, this date and year, I, the governor and captain-general, saw the fire left by the enemy at the place where I passed the night, and the fresh trail of their party. I sent ahead under my orders adjutant Juan Ruis, a captain, and an ensign, and several soldiers. If the enemy should be discovered, they were not to go near them, but to wait and send me word. I, having pursued the march apparently seven or eight leagues, met this captain, ensign, and adjutant who had gone out together with the lieutenant-general of the cavalry, coming with an Indian prisoner. Through Mattias Lujan, he testified that he was a Taos and that he left the Picuríes, the fugitive

55

enemy, this morning at a camp of thirty-one lodges of Apaches; that they had slept in the bed of a river flowing down from two mountain ridges which are about five long leagues from this place; that he had sought a daughter he had among the fugitives from the Picuríes and, as she was not willing to give herself up, he was returning to his village of Taos.

Upon this report, I called a halt at this spot to rest the horses. After a siesta of about two hours, and changing mount, I set out from there, putting the Indian ahead as guide, although the trail was very fresh. Thus I reached the bed of the river at about eleven at night, finding there two fires left by the fleeing enemy. Coming up to them and reconnoitering, we encountered no one. Continuing for about an hour on the upper part of the ridge, we made out a warning signal fire lit by some spy of the enemy who then went down below towards the river. At him the commander, Juan de Ulibarri, discharged an arquebus, instantly killing him: there were no more warning signals that night. Pressing on cautiously as was necessary, because having lost the trail among the rocks and declivities, the Indian prisoner vowed he could not pick up a trace, as did also the officers and commanders aforesaid and the friendly Indians. I was forced to camp the rest of the night at this spot.

[*Marginal note:* The governor and captain-general goes on and routs the enemy.] On the twenty-sixth of the month of October of this date and year at sunrise, I, the governor and captain-general, found myself with the command following the mesa of the river bed. About half a league along the mountain, I came out on a plain, on which having rapidly covered about three leagues, we found a small hole and the fires that the enemy had made last night when they had news of my arrival at this river bed. We judged they had fled and scattered by the trails and tent poles they had left. I kept on along the trail in the direction of their flight, and having hurried over more than four leagues by changing horses, we reached an open region of the country without any trail at all.

I separated our force, with my position on a part of this ground, while my lieutenant and two other soldiers took the direction of a ravine. We discovered some fugitive Indians who were going along the other bank to escape and seeking for means to cross. With great difficulty we found a way among the rocks by breaking through the chaparral and trees there. Thus surmounting the slope, we captured some people of the rabble and five of the enemies' horses, loaded with their

56

goods and supplies which they left behind. We recognized that it was the Indian Don Antonio, their governor, who immediately took to flight on a swift horse. Because the lieutenant-general of the cavalry, with some other soldiers, had gone ahead and was coming back down the said path to join me, he met him fleeing with six rebels. One of the soldiers gave the Indian a lance thrust and another wounded one of them with a shot. In this ravine an Indian began shooting arrows; they killed him, together with Don Antonio. They later took prisoner another Indian who was identified by the wife of Don Antonio, who was among the crowd of women prisoners, and by all the other women as the one who came to their village to rouse the people and who was the cause of all their troubles. In view of this, and of his being taken in open war, I ordered him shot, after having been prepared by the Father Chaplain Fray Diego de Chavarria, who had great difficulty therein on account of his obstinate nature.

Having gathered together the command, I halted in the lower part of the ravine and glen on a level spot near it for the celebration which took place. It was found we had gained from the enemy forty animals and some provisions with some clothing, and counted up some fifty persons, women and children of all ages. After sunset there wandered into camp a young brave with twenty more women and children, swearing that they came to put themselves under our protection. I made much of them, announcing that it would please me greatly if they would all come back.

[*Marginal note:* The governor and captain-general sets out from this place, leaving a cross planted there in memory of the triumph.] On the twenty-seventh of the month of October of this date and year, a number of other women and strays of the natives, having come into the camp, claimed they came to join their people and that Don Lorenzo, their governor, had gone with the rest, following the Apaches who had moved ahead, as soon as they heard us. I, the governor and captain-general, made much of them and told them if they had left any others near there they must go after them, and advise them I was going to sleep that night with their people, who were with me, at the watering place lying opposite the place, whence they had scattered on account of the warning given them by the Apaches that I was coming among them. I ordered all the soldiers of the camp who had some of the provisions they had taken from the enemy to divide equally with them so that I might give it to the people. As a memorial of this triumph, I ordered a high cross be set at this spot. Having assisted in its elevation,

I mounted and set out from this place with the army, arriving at the aforesaid watering hole at three in the afternoon of this day.

[*Marginal note:* The governor and captain-general continues the retreat; more people from the rebels come in.] On the twenty-eighth of the month of October of this date and year, I, the governor and captain-general, because of a heavy snow and windstorm in a strange country, gave orders that the army should halt. Ten other persons of the rebels, for whom I also ordered supplies, had drifted in the night before. Pushing on till about two in the afternoon, I was forced to rest on account of the heavy snow. Thus being closed in by the darkness of the storm, I missed the place to which we were journeying. I remained with the army to spend the night without water on the plain.

[*Marginal note:* The governor and captain-general arrives at the village of Pecos on the seventh of November; he notes the storm and loss of horses on this account.] On the seventh of the month of November, 1696, I, the governor and captain-general, reached this village of Pecos, with the commanders and some officers of the army. From here I sent relief to the army which I left at the foot of the mountain of this village at a distance of eight leagues. I had been on the march since the twenty-eighth day up to this day in the fury of snowstorms and driving blizzards which obliged me to stay two days, unable to move from the spot. I, as well as all the people, ran great risk in going on foot because the snow was so deep, the cold and winds, moreover, making a storm. Every day dawned upon many dead horses. Others, benumbed and frozen, were almost gone. Even in the short distance of four or five leagues, when the count was taken, we had lost more than two hundred horses and five mules belonging to the soldiers and to me. The friendly Indians lost more, the Pecos as well as the Teguas [Tiguas] and those of Tezuque. Those who came on this campaign went through most of the places in a sleeting snow. Toasted corn was served to the people for food, also the flesh of the horses that died. The delays of the campaign were due to the accidents caused by the storm.

[*Marginal note:* The governor and captain-general arrives at the villa of Santa Fé with the army and parcels out the eighty-four prisoners.] On the ninth of the month of November, I, the governor and captain-general, reached this town of Santa Fé. There I found news of the Indians of San Ildephonso and of the village of Jacona and most of those of Nambé. Those who were missing were declared to be returning. They were all in their village subdued. I had account, likewise, from the superior judge of the post of Bernalillo that the Indians

58

of Cochití were about to make peace. They are divided, some on the mountains, others in the village on their mesa, and others in the bed of the river. He assured me that the Queres of the Rock of Ácoma also desired peace, according to the information brought to the pueblo of Zía by the Zuñi Indian. He had been there to report that they had driven the rebels of the village of Santo Domingo from the rock, and the Xémes who went up to the mountain lying in front of the Rock of Ácoma.

In this villa of Santa Fé nothing especial had happened and they were all rejoicing over my good fortune and that of the people who went on the above mentioned campaign. Moved by pity, I had Lieutenant-Captain Don Alphonso de Aguilar, assisted by my secretary of government and war, divide the prisoners. This they did, the number being eighty-four persons, counting the suckling babes of the women, and the boys and girls of all ages, and five married braves. In justification of the distribution, I explained to the Indians that because of their desertion of our holy religion and their royal vassalage, it was to save their lives by maintaining them that I gave them out as servants to the soldiers and citizens who went out on the campaign, as I also impressed on the settlers that for this purpose they were allotted to them in this town, and not to be taken outside into the country or anywhere else.

In witness of all the aforementioned, I signed this with my secretary of government and war.

Don Diego de Vargas Zapata
Lujan Ponce de León
    [rubric]
Before me,
Domingo de la Barredo
    [rubric]
Secretary of Government and War.

III. The Diary of Juan de Ulibarri to El Cuartelejo, 1706[6]

Year of 1706   No. 4
                        New Mexico
The diary and itinerary of the journey which Sergeant-Major Juan de Ulibarri made at the order of his Excellency, the Governor and Captain-General of this kingdom, Don Francisco Cuerbó y Valdés, Knight of the Order of Santiago, to the unknown land of the plains

for the ransom of the Christian Indians of the Picuríes nation; and the discovery of the new province of San Luís and the large settlement of Santo Domingo of El Cuartelejo, which is inhabited by innumerable tribes of pagan Indians, who are peaceful, and obedient to his majesty, the king, etc.

With testimonials and certificates of this undertaking.

CUERBÓ   Expediente No. 4

J^E LAFARTA
[rubric]   pages 24
CUBERÓ[7]
[rubric]

See the letter

The campaign having been arranged for, the troops assembled and equipped with all necessary rations as well as with powder and balls needed for their defense, I, General Juan de Ulibarri, sergeant-major of this kingdom, received the troops and orders from General Don Francisco Cuerbó y Valdés, Knight of the Order of Santiago, governor and captain-general at the present time of the kingdom and province of New Mexico, and warden of its forces and presidios, by order of his majesty. I received at the same time the enlistment roll of the soldiers and settlers, and found that it comprised forty men of war: the twenty-eight military men and the twelve settlers of the militia. [*Marginal note:* Forty men, twenty-eight military and twelve militia.] These were joined by some groups of friendly Indians of different tribes who came from the pueblos and missions of this kingdom. They amounted to one hundred Indians.

Today, Tuesday, July 13, we set out from this villa of Santa Fé, and on this same day, having marched seven leagues, reached the valley and spot of La Cañada. We camped on the banks of the Río del Norte, where we finished assembling everything that was prepared for this campaign. From there we continued on Wednesday, the fourteenth, to the pueblo of San Juan of the Tegua [Tigua] tribe. Thence I set out, after adding to our command the Reverend Padre Fray Pedro de Matha, [*Marginal note:* chaplain] chaplain, chosen by his most reverend prelate, and arrived on this day at the pueblo and mission of San Lorenzo of the Picuríes tribe. The few Indians who lived there came to me, the sergeant-major, and told me that they were exceedingly gratified and hoped, with the assistance of God and the Spaniards, to see in their pueblos, restored to their kinsmen, those who were now in captivity and oppressed by the barbarous heathen Apache tribes of the plains and Cuartelejo. To help them in some manner, they were bringing them some cotton and woolen blankets, and other things for their use, together with as many horses as they could collect, under the charge of Don Antonio, the Indian chief of this pueblo, and present governor. There were also going at the same time two well known interpreters and the Indian guide, whom Don Lorenzo, the Indian chief of this tribe [sent] with a message and a petition to the Governor and Captain-General Don Francisco Cuerbó y Valdéz, of the Order of Santiago. After everything that was necessary had been prepared with great pleasure and rejoicing on the part of all, the reverend father chaplain, Fray Pedro de Matha, told me he was ill and for this just cause and reason he decided not to go on this campaign. Because of this he wrote to his prelate, and I, the sergeant-major, to the governor and captain-general so that his council might decide with these reports what is most important to the service of both majesties——[*Marginal note:* The chaplain is excused.] Thursday, the fifteenth, we set out from the pueblo and mission of San Lorenzo of the Picuríes (up to which the day before we had marched to the north seven leagues), and on this day having traveled in the same direction eight leagues, arrived at the valley, pueblo and mission of San Gerónimo de los Taos. After we had been welcomed by the Reverend Father Fray Francisco Ximénez, its minister, and the rest of the Indians, the inhabitants who came to see me, the Governor Don Juan Pacheco, and the rest of the chiefs then informed me that they were very certain that the infidel enemies of the Ute and Comanche tribe were about to come to make an attack upon this pueblo, which information they wished to send to the governor and captain-general, and knowing I was going with other Spaniards, they delayed doing so until my arrival.[8] These important matters moved me to give an account of everything to the governor and captain-general. I waited meanwhile in the pueblo for his reply and for the final decision of the father chaplain. Friday sixteenth, Saturday seventeenth and Sunday eighteenth, I remained there for these reasons, constrained as well to order ground a little pinole and cornmeal to be equipped in everything. On this day [Sunday] at six o'clock in the evening, Captain Don Felix Martínez, alcalde mayor of the said pueblo and its jurisdiction, arrived at the pueblo of Taos bringing in his company [*Marginal note:* Another chaplain.] the Reverend Father Fray Domingo de Aranz, who was coming to go on the campaign as chaplain at the order of his most Reverend Prelate, to whom he then wrote. While awaiting the reply, we also spent Monday, the nineteenth, in the pueblo of Taos. When evening of this day arrived, I decided to set out on Tuesday, the twentieth.

Having placed myself under the protection of the most glorious Apostle, our patron saint, Santiago, and the very serene Queen of the Angels, the most holy Mary of the glorious name Carmel, we crossed on this day part of the mountains at their highest summit. We went down a canyon its entire length and along a river which they call Don Fernando.[9] The terrain is very broken, mountainous, narrow and full of many precipices, so that it was necessary for this reason to proceed in groups, and lead the horses over by short cuts. Before leaving the pueblo of Taos, I had given notice of my departure to the governor and captain-general, to whom I sent a general muster roll that I called in that pueblo and thus finished with what appeared to me most important. We happily succeeded in crossing the first part of the mountain and descended to a very delightful valley which they call La Cieneguilla,[10] eight leagues distant from the pueblo. We marched to the east. There are on the road many marshes and miry places.

Wednesday, the twenty-first, we set out from this spot and again climbed the mountain. We arrived at another canyon, very rough and mountainous, which I ordered called La Palotada, because there was much fallen timber in it. [*Marginal note:* Canyon named.] Having crossed this, we discovered exceedingly beautiful valleys. In the first there is a very large pond which I named La Laguna de Santa Tomas de Villa Nueva. I called the second valley, La Valle del Espiritu Santo. This extends until it rises to a pass to which I gave the name of Puerto Florido because of its pleasing appearance. [*Marginal note:* Lake named.] The latter drops to another valley, which I called El Valle de San Cayetano. [*Marginal note:* Valley *idem.*] This ends in a little pool which I called Santa Cruz because there was painted on a poplar tree a small holy cross which appeared to be very old. [*Marginal note:* Pass *idem.*] From there we ascended the last summit, which was very rough and mountainous. [*Marginal note:* Pond *idem.*] From this slope the plains can be made out and the unknown land with its trails. After we had quite descended the mountains, we reached, at the foot of it, a river which is very pleasant with groves of poplar and other trees. To this I gave the name of Río de San Francisco Xabier [for him] under whose protection I was marching across unknown land, barbarously inhabited by innumerable heathens. [*Marginal note:* River *idem.*]

Crossing the river we arrived at another, very pleasant and larger.

62

This I named Río de Santa María Magdalena.[11] [*Marginal note:* River *idem.*] We had marched ten leagues in the same direction to the east. To this region the first heathen Indians of the Conexeros, Acho, and Río Colorado[12] came down. They had been previously with some of those in the pueblo of Taos and had told me then in that pueblo, as they did now in this spot, that all the tribes were very happy that we Spaniards were coming into their lands and among their rancherías without doing them any injury. But that it would be well to guard ourselves from other nations who were on the road in the distance, particularly from those called the Penxayes, Flecha de Palo, Lemitas, and Nementina.[13] These had always been very bad thieves and had even injured them. I answered them that I esteemed very highly their information and advice, but that I was trusting in our God who was the creator of everything and who was to keep us free from the greatest dangers. After presenting them with much tobacco, knives, pinole, corn, biscuits, and having given them suitable presents, I said goodbye to them and they went away satisfied.

Thursday, the twenty-second. After marching to the north eight leagues, we crossed another large stream which I called the Río de la Santíssima Cruz. These other small streams unite with it and the largest, the Río de San Nicolas de Tolentino. From this one, we crossed to another which I found very swollen, so much so that it detained me. I was forced to make a bridge of large trunks of poplars which grow thickly on this stream, which I named Río de San Blas. Although I tried to ford or cross it on this bridge, I did not succeed because [the banks] were miry and boggy. [*Marginal note:* River *idem.*] Of this sort was the road on this entire day, as well as on the two days following, notwithstanding that I had sent out a reconnaissance party on the river above and below. Sergeant Bartolomé Sánchez discovered a ford on the river above, which although very bad we considered the best and thus we crossed, naming the ford after the sergeant. The little stream above, very miry and marshy, I ordered called El Arroyo de las Ansias, because of the many troubles I had in cutting through it.

Having succeeded in setting out from this spot with fortune, on Friday, the twenty-third, we marched eight leagues to the north. Crossing the Río de Santo Catalina, we halted at the spring of Naranjo. Other heathen Indians of La Xicarilla,[14] Flechas de Palo, and Carlanas tribes came down to this place from the Sierra Blanca, under the leadership of different chiefs. The head chief was a lame man whom they called Ysdalnisdael. They showed a great deal of friendship toward us, saying that in the name of all the Indians of their tribe and of Chief Ucase, they were coming to give me many manifestations of gratitude for having entered their land without doing them any injury; that they were all very happy; and that on my return I would find them together in the rancherías of the Jicarillas. There they would give me raisins which they always preserved for the most worthy Spaniards, and that not only they were supplying them but also all the tribes that were living along the banks of all the streams I had seen and others that I had failed to cross, and others that I will meet further on; that they were very good people; they had not stolen anything from anyone, but occupied themselves with their maize and corn fields which they harvest, because they are busy with the sowing of corn, frijoles, and pumpkins. I, making use of this confidence, left with them some worn-out horses to keep for me, and having presented them with tobacco, knives, and biscuits, they went away very happy, carrying away the good presents which I gave them.

Saturday, the twenty-fourth. We set out from this spot, marched ten leagues to the north and went over the stream of San Gil. We ascended to the pass of Buena Vista, crossed the ponds of San Pedro, passed on our right, the ridge of La Jicarilla,[15] and came to a halt on the Río de San Christobal, which is a very pleasant stream with a good poplar grove and shrubbery.

Sunday, the twenty-fifth. We set out from the said spot, and traveling twelve leagues to the north, crossed over a small pass and at a short distance descended into a very broad, high and deep canyon with good flatlands, to which I gave the name of Canyon of Ulibarri. A fairly large pleasant stream runs its entire length, bordered with poplar groves, many prunes, a fruit resembling a cherry, with wild grapes. (There are these same fruits on the rest of the streams.) Having marched some twelve leagues entirely through this canyon, we arrived at the Río de Santa Ana,[16] which runs to the northeast (like all the rest, except that of this river of Santiago, which runs from south to north; on the banks of this [the Santa Ana] the heathen Apaches of the tribe called Penxayes have much land planted to corn, frijoles, and pumpkins. These with some fear came down to the foot of our mesa on this canyon to talk with me, the sergeant-major. Having assured them of good treatment and friendship, I permitted no injury to be done to their fields, which pleased them highly and made them sure of our friendship.

Monday, the twenty-sixth. We set out from the said Río de Santa

64

Ana and at a short distance ascended the hill of Nombre de Dios. We climbed it with considerable difficulty and trouble because it was very rough and cut off by precipices. Having succeeded in crossing it with good fortune, we continued marching in the same direction to the north, ten leagues, crossed the stream of Santa Rosa, and had to stop at the Ojo de Jediondo[17] because we did not know the road. The Indian who was guiding us had already lost the way. We left the good for the bad until we improved our sense of direction of the place by retracing our steps.

Tuesday, the twenty-seventh. We set out from this spot, Ojo de Jediondo, and at a short distance discovered the stream of Las Piletas, which is very pleasant. After crossing the Río de San Pantaleón and that of Jesús María, we came to the stream of San Valentine, having gone in the same direction to the north eight leagues.

Wednesday, the twenty-eighth. We set out from the said spot of San Valentine, and at a distance of two leagues we overtook an Apache Indian who had with him two women and three little boys. He said he was of the same tribe as the Penxayes and that he was going to join all the rest who live along those rivers and streams in order to defend themselves together from the Utes and Comanches, who were coming to attack them according to the information of the rest of his tribe. After I had wished them a good journey and had given them all some pinole, tobacco, and biscuits, they lost fear and were content. We continued our route to the north, discovering on our right in the distance two little hills very much alike, sharp and pointed. I called them Las Tetas de Domínguez. After we had marched twelve leagues, we arrived on the Río de San Juan Baptista.[18]

Thursday, the twenty-ninth. We set out from the Río de San Juan Baptista and following the same line to the north twelve leagues we crossed the arroyos of San Diego and San Antonio. Therein we found an Indian woman with a little girl gathering cherries. She said she was of the same tribe as the Penxaye and gave us the same information as had the Indian of the day before. Assured that we would do her no injury, given some pinole and biscuits, she was very happy. We arrived at the large river which all the tribes call the Napestle.[19] Having recalled the name of the señor governor and captain-general, I named it after his saint, calling it Río Grande de San Francisco because of the memorable glory of his Christian zeal. It runs from north to east. It is much more than four times as large as the Río del Norte and bathes the best and broadest valley discovered in New Spain. It has many poplar trees and throughout the upper part most beautiful open stretches. The plain on our side is a strand of a long league of level land and extremely fertile as is shown by the many plums, cherries, and wild grapes which there are on it. I was particularly surprised to observe that the time taken to cross it was about the equivalent of thirty-three Credos recited very slowly. Having crossed happily from one side to the other, we passed the night.

Friday, the thirtieth. We set out from the said river of San Francisco and went northeast four leagues and came to a stop on the Río de San Buenaventura[20] in order to lessen the journey, for our Indian guide advised us that we would undergo much suffering because there was no water and, if any, very little and that far ahead, and that the trail was only open land.

Saturday, the thirty-first. We set out from this spot of San Buenaventura and marched to the east guided by the Indian.[21] He took his direction from hummocks of grass placed a short distance apart on the trail by the Apaches, who lose even themselves there. In this way they had marked out the course. All of this was of no use to us, for, although the Indian took especial care, we became lost entirely. The Indians, according to their shallow natures, were overcome with fear to such extreme despondency that they almost wept. I, the sergeant-major, used all possible measures and placed myself under the patronage of Our Lady the Virgin Mary, conqueress of this kingdom and of the Glorious Patriarch, San Ignacio de Loyola, because of its being his happy day. It was the good fortune that two scouts who searched the land found water very far above from where we were. The news of this filled the whole camp with joy, and many thanks were given to God and his most holy Mother because of whose good will I ordered that spring be named El Ojo de Nuestra Señora del Buen Suceso. After I had the Indian guide come before me, he said that he had become lost because what he was following appeared to him to be the best road, but that henceforth he would not mistake the way. Realizing that the animals were very badly tired out, I left eighteen mules and horses in this spot to pick up on the return, in spite of the contingency and risk that they might be carried off.

Sunday, August 1. We set out from the spot and the spring of Nuestra Señora del Buen Suceso and, while marching in the same direction to the east, the Indian guide again lost the way. I, with the experience of the preceding day, scattered the whole command, even those who were going in my company. We discovered a sand bank and a dry

66

arroyo with many poplars. Some went up and others down so that we came upon the spring. All the others joined us there by following the tracks. The Indian guide recognized it to be the stopping place of the Apaches. We halted on it this day, as well as the following, which was Monday the second of the present month. At night, about ten o'clock, the horseherd of the Indians went into a stampede. The sentinels who were guarding the camp, hearing the noise and seeing confusion, shouted out, "To arms, to arms." Informed, I mounted a horse and, having arranged the camp in good order, went to the horseherd where it was learned that there was no invasion of Indian enemies, but only that a horse in the herd had become untied. Thus this disturbance passed.

I determined on that day, Monday, the second, to dispatch Ensign of the Militia Ambrosio Fresqui, Captain Joseph Naranjo, the Indian guide, and two of the pueblo of Taos to look for the stream before the command should become lost a third time. After these had set out, it happened thus that they became lost and, wandering, arrived at the first ranchería which the Apaches called Tachichichi, where after talking with its chiefs and the rest of the Apaches, the Ensign Fresqui returned bringing the chief and other Apaches. The Indians and Captain Naranjo remained in the said ranchería, and the Indians entertained and feasted them a great deal as I did the chief and Apaches who remained in the camp this night.

[*Marginal note:* News of the French.] Among the many things we asked him and he asked us, he told us that it must have been four days ago that on the large ranchería they had scalped a white man whom they had killed. They had taken from him a large gun, a kettle, a red-lined cap, [and] the powder which he carried. At the same time, they had killed a woman who was going with this white man. From what they heard us say they now considered them French. The poor woman was pregnant; the hair was hers and not that of the man, who was bald. Upon arriving at the ranchería, they said they would show me the spoils referred to. With these and other good explanations, they were given to understand our mission, and the end to which it was destined. We left the spot of San Ignacio, as I thus called it. The river valleys are quite large and pleasant and of much fertility. There are in their streams many delicious fish, such as catfish, spotted fish, and many mussels, and also other species of fish.

Tuesday, the third. We set out from the spot of San Ygnacio. From there to the spring of Nuestra Señora del Buen Suceso there are eight leagues. Accompanied by the chief of the Apaches, we marched partly

67

to the south and partly to the east some ten leagues and reached the outlet of San Miguel, which is just before the ranchería of Tachichichi. From this place all the Apaches came out to meet us, bringing out to us from it much bison meat and roasting ears of Indian corn, rejoicing, showing pleasure upon seeing us in their country. In this manner we arrived at the ranchería, and in a little while some Apaches of the large ranchería came and with them three Picuríes; the two of those who were with Don Lorenzo, and one of those I had sent previously to advise Don Lorenzo. On his behalf he sent me many acknowledgments and remembrances, saying that everyone was very happy, both the Picuríes who were with him as well as the Apaches, and the rest of the people in whom I could put trust.

The whole day was spent in talking of peace and of the good relations which we were desirous of entering into with the Apaches and dwelling upon the enmity which they have with the barbarous tribes of the Pawnees and Jumanos.[22] At the same time they gave me the same information of having killed four days ago a white man whom they called French and a woman, all of which agreed with the same story told before. They assured me that they would not evade showing the large gun and the rest of the spoils. I ordered this ranchería called Nuestra Señora de los Angeles Porsiuncula.

Wednesday, the fourth. We set out from the Ranchería de Porsiuncula and, at a short distance, arrived at the Ojo de Santa Rita, which is in a very pleasant dale. From the bottom of this we ascended to the ridge where many chiefs of the settlements of El Cuartelejo were awaiting us. After we joined them with great pleasure to one another, we went on together the entire way. They came without arms, very happy and kindly disposed. They brought us much buffalo meat, roasting ears of Indian corn, tamales, plums, and other things to eat. In this way we continued together until we arrived on the last hill, where there was a most holy cross which the Apaches had set up.

A chief of the Apaches came to me and took me forward to where the most holy cross stood. After he had showed it to us, all the Spaniards and Christian Indians alighted, kissed, adored, and worshipped it. Then the Royal Ensign Don Francisco de Valdés took it up, and we carried it in the procession as far as the ranchería, which was very close, at the foot of the hill. From out of the huts or little houses[23] came Don Lorenzo and the rest of the Picuríes Indians, men and women who were with him. There we alighted a second time and embraced him and gave them to understand why we were coming,

68

having been sent by our governor and captain-general. After they understood everything, they cried for joy. We continued thus until we arrived at the plaza which the rancherías formed. The Reverend Father Fray Domínguez de Aranz took up in his hand the most holy cross and intoned the *Te Deum Laudemus* and the rest of the prayers and sang three times the hymn in praise of the sacrament. After these holy ceremonies were over, the royal Ensign Don Francisco de Valdés drew his sword, and I, after making a note of the events of the day and the hour on which we arrived, said in a clear, intelligible voice: "Knights, Companions and Friends: Let the broad new province of San Luís and the great settlement of Santa Domingo of El Cuartelejo be pacified by the arms of us who are the vassals of our monarch, king and natural lord, Don Philip V—may he live forever." The royal ensign said: "Is there anyone to contradict?" All responded, "No." Then he said, "Long live the king! Long live the king! Long live the king!" and cutting the air in all four directions with his sword the ensign signaled for the discharge of the guns. After throwing up our hats and making other signs of rejoicing, the ceremony came to an end.

We went down to the side of this stream and there set up camp. In it I received all the Apache chiefs and the rest of the people of the tribe to whom I showed the same equal good will. I made them gifts and good presents and assured them of our good intentions and certain friendship. I gave them to understand the purpose of our coming and how we had been sent there on behalf of Don Lorenzo, the Indian chief of the Picuríes, whom they had enslaved, having badly used the good faith which they [the Picuríes] had in them. For their own safety they had sent to us to ask for aid and protection which we as Christians could not deny them and that our captain had great forces and thus he had dispatched me. On account of this I advised them that they should not make the slightest objection in handing over the Picuríes, for otherwise they would experience the severity of our arms. To that they all answered they were ready to obey and carry out that which our captain had ordered. They said they would give up all the Picuríes, not only those who were there but also those who were scattered about in the rest of the rancherías and that in order that they would understand that our words were true and our friendship honest, while the Picuríes were being gathered, we were to go with them to attack their enemies, the Pawnee Indians, since it was only a seven days' journey across level land with sufficient water. To this I responded that another occasion would not be lacking in which to aid them; at that time I was determined only to bring back the Picuríes. Further, I might lose the largest part of my horses, as their feet had become very sore. Also, in order not to frighten and drive them away, I had not brought with me a bugle and a drum. Finally, it was very necessary for me to return shortly because of the winter which was coming; and that I would come another year in May or June and we would succeed in helping them against their enemies. They assented to this explanation and others that I gave them. [*Marginal note:* It is supposed that the Pawnees and French are united.] They told me that I could leave with them one of our useless guns, as the other Spaniards [i.e., French] who live further in also gave them to the Pawnees, their enemies, as I would see by the gun they had taken away from a "Spaniard" some six days ago whom they killed as well as his wife, who, because she was pregnant, had fallen behind the rest. These had come united with the Pawnees to attack them at the time when they were going out to hunt buffalo meat to entertain us, after they had received news that we were coming to their country. And having discovered one another, they had returned to assure the safety of their ranches and maize fields. The Pawnees and French, having learned this, retreated. The chief of this ranchería had sent some young men to reconnoiter the route taken by the French and Pawnees. This man and his wife, having become separated from the others, had fallen behind, and they had killed them in a little wood along a river, and taken away the gun. They sent for it and promised to show the rest of the spoils. Having brought the gun, it surprised us, particularly the Frenchman, Juan de Archévèque, whom we had with us. This man said he recognized the gun and that it belonged to his kinsmen.[24] Upon this news, the Apaches said that the man they killed was not a Spaniard but a Pawnee chief whom they knew well. They changed their story, perhaps through having noticed the too great care with which the gun was examined, and fearing apparently lest some injury on our part might be done them. Owing to this fear, they refused to show us the kettle, coat, and other spoils. We were unable to move them even to show them to us in the future. They excused themselves saying that the spoil was at the other rancherías.

Thursday, the fifth. Don Lorenzo came very early in the morning to our camp and told me that some Picuríes Indians of his tribe who were missing were scattered out in different rancherías. I, the sergeant-major, had to arrange for rounding them up since they had not been able to do it, as they had no horses and were completely destitute. For

70

this reason, it was not only necessary to lend him some horses to collect his people, but that it also should be ordered that some Spaniards go with the Indians whom he was sending so that by their visit and awe which they inspired there might not be any embarrassment. I comforted him a great deal, assuring him that I would bring them all back because it was in accordance with the order which I had from my governor and captain-general, Señor Don Francisco Cuerbó y Valdéz.

Thus I decided that they should set out in three groups: some to the ranchería of Nanahe, which I renamed the Ranchería de San Agustín; others to the ranchería of Adidasde, which I named the Ranchería of St. Joseph; and the last, under Captain Joseph Naranjo, to the Ranchería of Sanasesli, to which I gave the name of La Ranchería de Nuestra Señora de Guadalupe. The latter is forty leagues distant from the first two of Santo Domingo and Porsiuncula. It is a ranchería of very many people, very friendly and agreeable, subject to its captain-major, called Ysdelpain, who was very pleased when he had the news of the Spaniards coming to his ranchería. He, as well as his people, desired that we should come to his ranchería, and he was extremely sad on learning when Captain Naranjo arrived there that we were not coming. However, he entertained Captain Naranjo and his companions a great deal and gave them excellent quarters. They handed over to them without objection or argument, Juan Tupatú, an Indian chief, a very young man who was the son of Don Luis Tupatú, whom, since the year '80 of the general revolt of this kingdom, all tribes as well as the apostates and likewise heathen acknowledged as their king, as everyone knows. From this revolt it came about that Don Juan was held in estimation by all until, like the rest, they found themselves among the barbarous heathen, enslaved like all others. This man [Tupatú] came with eighteen persons, leaving four behind, two young men and two old women, because they were away from the rancherías hunting buffalo meat. Chief Ysdelpain assured them that he would bring them to their pueblo the next year at the time when they came in for the ransom. On this day I gave the chiefs and the rest of the Apaches many good gifts and presented them with knives, tobacco, biscuits, and pinole so that they were delighted.

Friday, the sixth. We improved our site by moving the camp to the first hill where the most holy cross was, thus leaving the knee of the Río de Peñas which is in a vale where the Ranchería de Santo Domingo is, and where we set up camp the first day. This change had been caused by the danger attending the great number of heathen who were

71

coming every hour from the different rancherías and who lodged themselves in this principal ranchería.

Saturday, the seventh, Sunday, the eighth, Monday, the ninth, Tuesday, the tenth, and Wednesday, the eleventh, we remained in this spot and camp to which I gave the name of San Lorenzo. On this day, Wednesday, Captain Joseph Naranjo came with Don Juan Tupatú and the rest of the Indians, men and women of his tribe, leaving behind the four persons mentioned above whom Captain Ysdelpain promised to bring to their Picuríes pueblo with two more women of the Tana or Tegua [Tigua] tribe whom they said were captives very far away. They belong to the people of the pueblo of Santa Clara who went in the company of Don Lorenzo, all of whom they killed, and the said two captive women they had certainly carried off.

During all these days I had long conversations with the Apaches. Out of these I noted some particular things which I shall set forth without making a great deal of details of little importance.

[*Marginal note:* Nature of the Apaches and their inclination toward Christianity.] The first thing is that they are a people more inclined toward our Catholic faith than any of all those that are thus reduced. Though heathens, the majority of the Apaches wear many crosses, medals, and rosaries around their necks. We knew they were very old because the crosses are covered with perspiration and the girdles or chamois bags in which they carry them are very grimy and have been repaired. We asked them the reason they had for wearing crosses, medallions, and rosaries without knowing what they wore. They replied that for many years they traded and had commerce with the Spaniards and they knew that because they wore crosses and rosaries and images of saints, that they are very valiant; that there is no nation that can conquer them, and that when the Apaches fight with their enemies, the Pawnees and the Jumanos, and become tired, they remember the great Captain of the Spaniards who is in the heavens and then their weariness leaves them and they feel refreshed. They knelt down every night that they saw us on our knees worshipping the rosary of Our Lady, the Virgin Mary, and other prayers, and although we spent an hour and a half which was the usual length of time, they remained on their knees. After this ceremony was finished, they did as the rest of the Spaniards and Indians, which was to kiss the sleeve of the holy garment of the padre and seek from me permission to go away.

[*Marginal note:* The fertility of the land and its good climate.] The second thing I noticed was the great fertility of the land and its good

72

climate, for at the end of July they had gathered crops of Indian corn, watermelons, pumpkins, and kidney beans. It was believed that crops of wheat [in case sowed] would be ready before the day of San Juan. So that, because of the fertility of the land, the docility of the people, and the abundance of herds of buffalo, and other game, the propagation of our holy Catholic faith could be advanced very much.

[The third point particularly was to give detailed information of many other tribes which live to the north, as well as to the east and south.] They are established on five large principal rivers. The first which has been spoken of, they call in their language the Napestle, to which I gave the name of the Great River of San Francisco; the second, Nisquisandi; the third, Sitascahe, and on this live the Pawnees in two large rancherías; the fourth, Daenasgaes; and the fifth, Nasatha. This latter the Apaches say is much larger than the first, the Napestle, or the Río Grande de San Francisco. All these [tribes], although enemies of one another, have trading relations with the other Spaniards who live farther toward the east. [*Marginal note:* Communication of some of these tribes with the whites; they do not know if they are English or French.] There are more people there than live in New Mexico although they cannot say clearly if they are English or French. From these they buy many iron things such as hatchets, swordblades, arquebuses, copper things. It appears from this information that a very great deal of land can be discovered.[25]

This day I told the Apaches I was not yet ready to go on account of not having the apostate Indians of the Picuríes together; they were to hand over to me the rest in their possession that were missing. I told them that although they had told me that they did not want to deliver them, that they would rather shoot them; I said to them also that there were men to defend them and that I did not believe what they said inasmuch as I had found them to be very good people and our friends. But that in case the devil had reaped them in, we would not fail to fulfill the order of our governor and captain-general which was that we should bring back the people. To this they responded that they had not said such a thing and that they would prove this by delivering at five in the afternoon all the people whom they had. They did but left five in the house of the chief, which information Don Lorenzo gave me afterwards. He showed a great deal of feeling and I consoled him, saying that I would call the chief again so that he could deliver them to me, which I did. The chief excused himself, saying that the five persons were Teguas [Tiguas], Tanas, and not Picuríes and that they

73

had bought them from a tribe which they called Andadores [Comanches?]. Notwithstanding, I told the chief that I was going to bring back those apostate souls without exception as to tribe, and that thus he should go and hand them over, since I was sending for them. This was done with considerable feeling. In remuneration for these I gave him a present of thirteen horses, from those which were brought by Captain Joseph Naranjo and the Indians who had been collecting the said Picuríes. These horses were considerably footsore and I could not bring them back. The chief prized this present highly and remained very satisfied. All the rest were in the same frame of mind.

Thursday, the twelfth. I formed a council of war to deliver the gun which I had sent for and offered it to the Apaches. We had agreed by common consent that it was better to hand it over to them so that in no way should they lack confidence in our word that it would be delivered. With cleverness I exchanged it with them for the large French gun which they handed over to me with much willingness. They have other firearms and among them three carbines which they said they had taken from the Pawnees in the spoils and seizures they had made at various times. They said further that the enemies, the Pawnee Indians, sell to the "Spaniards" the [Apache] women and children whom they take prisoners as they [the Apache] themselves sold to us those of the Pawnees they captured. So then it is inferred that they are very close to the French or Dutch, or whoever they are. After I had questioned them about the seas to the north and east, they said that they know about them only from other tribes that the seas were not very far, and before coming to that of the north, there are three days of long journeys beyond a tribe whom they call the Pelones. This road is without grass, for there are on the way only sand dunes of very fine sand. They did not know for certain the distance there is from their rancherías to the said seas. These were the most important details that they gave us.

Friday, the thirteenth. After I had left the Apaches very pleased and contented and subject to the obedience of his majesty, the king, I took my leave with considerable affection on both sides. [*Marginal note:* They bring back sixty-two Picuríes; Don Lorenzo and Don Juan Tupatú, his nephew, are the most important among them.] I brought back sixty-two persons, small and grown of the Picuríes who were living as apostate slaves, and as captives of the barbarity of the Apaches, among whom are two of the most noteworthy Indians of the entire kingdom and provinces; they are Don Lorenzo and Don Juan Tupatú, his nephew. I assisted them with particular care, both as to their sus-

74

tenance and as to lending them riding horses until they arrived at their pueblo. Having arranged to load some sacks of corn which the women and children were already bringing, we said goodbye and set out on our return, on this day, Friday, the thirteenth. I had previously given the staff of command of Captain-Major of all Apachería, because all regarded him as such, to a young Indian of fine body and countenance, called in their language Yndatiyuhe, a brother of six other chiefs of whom the two leading ones are called, one Yyastipaye, and the other Dabichildildixe. I commanded these expressly that they should venerate as much as possible the most holy cross; that they shall not take it from the spot where I have placed it, because the first thing we would look for on our return to the land would be its divine image. All together they agreed to this and were happy. I set it up in the middle of the square of the encampment and they promised me that it would be just as I was ordering them.

After we had passed the spring of Santa Rita, the ranchería of Our Lady of the Angels of Porsiuncula, we came to a stop on the waters of San Bartolomé.

Saturday, the fourteenth. We came to the stream of San Ygnacio, arriving upon it below the spot I named San Sebastián. This evening we had the greatest of storms, rain, wind, thunder, and lightning, that one can image. We put ourselves under the protection of the Queen of the Angels, the most holy Mary, because it was the eve of her Glorious Acceptation, who came to our rescue like a mother with serenity and peace.

Sunday, the fifteenth. We came to the Ojo de Nuestra Señora de Buen Suceso. On the road we found, without looking for them, six head of bison. By slaughtering them the whole camp was provisioned. In this spot we found the eighteen beasts which were left on the way. Because of the great deal of water there, we stopped over Monday, the sixteenth.

Tuesday, the seventeenth. We came to the San Buenaventura, and on Wednesday, the eighteenth, to the Río Grande de San Francisco; Thursday, the nineteenth, we reached the Río San Juan Baptista, having crossed the rivers of San Diego and San Antonio.

Friday, the twentieth. We passed Las Tetas de Domínguez and arrived on the San Valentino.

Saturday, the twenty-first. We crossed the rivers of Jesús María and San Panteleón, Las Piletas, and the spring of Jediondo, and reached the stream of Santa Rosa.

Sunday, the twenty-second. We descended the hill of Nombre de Dios and came to the Río de Santa Ana.

Monday, the twenty-third. We rested in this spot to give the horses a rest as they had become very footsore.

Tuesday, the twenty-fourth. We passed through the Canyon of Ulibarri and along the Río de Santiago and came to a stop on the Río de San Christobal.

Wednesday, the twenty-fifth. We crossed the ridge of La Jicarilla and the pass of Buena Vista, the ponds of San Pedro, and the stream of San Gil and halted on the spring of Naranjo.

Thursday, the twenty-sixth. We crossed the Río de Santa Catharina and arrived on the Río de San Blas, which we found very swollen and the bridge, recently built, gone.

Friday, the twenty-seventh. We were among the rancherías of El Coxo and the rest of the chiefs who were awaiting us, and who entertained us a great deal. They gave us the news that the Utes and Comanches had attacked two rancherías; one of the Carlana and Sierra Blanca tribe, the other of the Penxayes tribe. They delivered to us the beasts we left with them to look after. We crossed the Río de Santa Cruz, San Nicolás de Tolentino, and Santa María Magdalena, and came to a halt on the Río de San Francisco de Xavier. From there I dispatched Sergeant Bartholomé Sánches with two other companions to the villa of Santa Fé to give the news to the governor and captain-general, and advise him of the happy outcome of our expedition.[26]

Saturday, the twenty-eighth. I crossed the first part of the sierra and halted on the pond of Santa Tomá de Villanueva, having crossed the dry pond of Santa Cruz, Puerto Florido, and the valleys of Espiritú Santo and San Cayetano.

Sunday, the twenty-ninth. The camp halted in the middle of the hill and I went on to the pueblo of Taos.

Monday, the thirtieth. The company arrived at the pueblo of Taos.

Tuesday, the thirty-first. We all arrived at the pueblo and mission of San Lorenzo de Picuríes, where the very Reverend Father Prior Fray Francisco Ximénez, minister of the pueblo of Taos, received the apostate Picuríes and absolved them with all solemnity. It was a day of the greatest rejoicing which this kingdom has seen. The Reverend Father Minister as well as Captain Don Felix Martínez, alcalde mayor of the pueblo, gave authentic testimony of having received them.

Wednesday. September first. We arrived at the valley of La Cañada and on Thursday, the second, at this villa of Santa Fé, in the presence

76

of the governor and captain-general, Don Francisco Cuerbó y Valdéz, to whose Christian zeal, after that of the Divine Majesty, everything is owed, to the honor and glory of God, may he be rewarded in heaven.

JUAN DE ULIBARRI
[rubric]

A. Governor Cuerbó Reports the Return of the Picuries, 1706[27]

Most Excellent Lord,

With the second mail and latest dispatch (which in virtue of and in response to the command of your Excellency) I remitted to the court of your Excellency in compliance with my first obligation and office, I informed your Excellency of the campaign which I was making ready to send into the unknown lands and far flung provinces of the plains, inhabited by innumerable nations of the heathen Indians. There have been there, since the past year of 1696, of the third revolt of the pueblos of this kingdom, in captivity, the larger part of the Indians of the pueblos and mission of San Lorenzo de los Picuríes. Upon their petition, I dispatched armed forces to rescue them, as I set forth to your Excellency on that occasion. Considering the care which I have taken then and the Catholic zeal of your Excellency, I am now looking forward to giving the felicitous news of the achievement of my desires and the alleviation of those poor souls, who were living as apostates under the barbarous oppression of the Apache infidels, and in slavery to Satan.

There set out from this villa of Santa Fé, on July 13, a company of forty men of war, composed of twenty-eight presidial soldiers and twelve militiamen, settlers, and one hundred Indian allies from the Christians of the pueblos and missions, under the charge of General Juan de Ulibarri, sergeant-major of this kingdom. He passed through these provinces, among the broadest, most attractive and most fertile of that which has been conquered, before reaching the great settlement where the numerous rancherías of the Cuartelejos are, conciliating many tribes on his way. He explored many streams, among them the largest river that has been discovered. He took possession in the name of his majesty of all the territory which he discovered, calling it the province of San Luis and the great settlement of Santo Domingo of El Cuartelejo. With much affection, friendly feeling, and considerate treatment, relations have been established with the heathen nations.

He obtained from them sixty-four persons, adults and children of

77

the nation of Picuríes, which they meekly delivered to him. Among them were two chiefs of these pueblos, Indians of the greatest popularity, namely Don Lorenzo and Don Juan Tupatú. He attended to them with particular solicitude until restoring them to their original and ancient pueblo. There the sergeant-major delivered them to the Reverend Father Fray Francisco Ximénez, its minister, who absolved them with great solemnity, to the joy of all the inhabitants of this kingdom. Of this delivery, the father minister as well as the alcalde mayor of that jurisdiction, Captain Don Felix Martínez, gave testimony, which I remit to your Excellency, adjoining with the rest of the instruments and certifications and diary which the sergeant-major, Juan de Ulibarri, made on this campaign. To his excellent experience, military practice, and prudent resolution, I confided this undertaking, which with the favor of God and the intercession of His Most Holy Mother, he achieved with success and fortune, all at my cost and without expense to the royal treasury, as your Excellency will recognize according to the said instruments.

After reading them, you will decide upon that which you may find most convenient to the service of both majesties. Meantime, I am as required engaged in the consummation of the rest of the duties of which I will give an account to your Excellency, according to the cases and times, in order that in all those which might be of your most excellent pleasure, I may comply with satisfaction to the wishes of your Excellency. I offer just congratulations for the good outcome of this campaign, the reduction of the poor souls who were freed from the apostasy in which they were, and today are quiet and content in their pueblo.

Not having hope of giving other great news to your Excellency, may God guard your most excellent person and your most important life many happy years in His greater goodness for the greater increase of this new Christianity and glory of God, as can be, and as I supplicate it. Santa Fé, New Mexico, September 23, 1706. Most Excellent Lord. I kiss the feet of your Excellency, your best servant. Francisco Cuerbó y Valdes [*rubric*]. To the Most Excellent Lord, Viceroy, Duke of Albuquerque, my Lord.

México, October 10, 1706. To the Señor Fiscal with the antecedent, and with that which he may dispose to the General Council. [*Rubric* of Albuquerque.]

Most Excellent Lord: The fiscal of his majesty has seen this letter and the diary and the certifications of its proof, which the governor of New

Mexico remitted to your Excellency of the expedition entrusted to Sergeant-Major Juan de Ulibarri who undertook this campaign with twenty-eight presidials, twelve militiamen, and one hundred Indian allies, armed and provisioned at the cost of the governor. He entered the unknown land of different nations of Indians until he reached the new and widespread province of San Luis and the great settlement of Santo Domingo of El Cuartelejo, inhabited by Apaches. From their possession he took away sixty-four persons of the Picuríes nations whom he restored to their pueblo of San Lorenzo. Among them were two most important Indians, namely, Don Lorenzo and Don Juan Tupatú, who with the rest were made slaves and apostates in the power of the Apaches.

At the same time, he reports the docility and good humor of these and their inclination to the Catholic religion; the peace and good will with which they received Juan de Ulibarri and his people; the fertility, excellent climate; large flowing rivers, streams, fruits and other particulars, of those lands, and the different nations which inhabit them, and some others farther in who have friendship with other white people. They did not know if these be French or English, of whom there were few. The Apaches had killed a man and a pregnant woman who was accompanying him, from whom they had taken a cap, a kettle, a little powder, and a large fowling piece which they exchanged with Ulibarri for another which they asked of him. All this and the rest is particularly set forth in the diary and the certifications. Moreover, from this arise excellent hopes of extending into all those lands obedience to the dominion of his majesty and the Catholic religion, for the disposition of these nations seem to favor both.

It does not appear now that there is anything else to do but to give to his majesty account of all referred to so that with this information he may provide what may be his royal will. Your Excellency, being pleased, will command that thanks be given to both the governor and the sergeant-major for their service and that the aforementioned thanks may also be given in the name of his majesty and of your Excellency to the people with whom this undertaking was carried out, charging the chiefs and the rest of that kingdom to maintain the friendship and good relations with the nations, without attacking them nor making upon them any assault except in cases which necessary defense requires so that they may continue their present good disposition, in case his majesty disposes to introduce religion and government into those territories. Likewise they should be careful of the reëstablishment and conservation of the reduced Picuríes, for by means of them, they may be able so to expand as to attract others and to safeguard the few who have remained in the pueblo of San Lorenzo.

Above all your Excellency will provide that which you may hold the most advantageous which may be the best as always. México, December 22, 1706. Doctor Espinosa. [*rubric*] Most Excellent Lord, Viceroy, Duke of Albuquerque, my Lord.[28]

IV. COUNCIL OF WAR AND DIARY OF THE CAMPAIGN OF DON JUAN PÁEZ HURTADO AGAINST THE FARAON APACHES, 1715[29]

A. Council of War, Santa Fé, July 20, 1715

1. TESTIMONY OF DON GERÓNIMO, SANTA FÉ, JULY 20, 1715

[*Marginal note:* No. 384. Affidavits and council of war concerning the campaign of the Apaches, Chipaynes, and Faraones or Limitas and (torn out) which have been made: Diary and itinerary which General Juan Páez Hurtado made.] In the villa of Santa Fé of New Mexico on the twentieth day of the month of July, 1715, I, Don Juan Ignazio Flores Mogollón,[30] governor and captain-general of these provinces of New Mexico for his majesty, had appear before me Don Gerónimo, native son of the pueblo of Taos, and the lieutenant-governor of it. He gave me news through Captain Joseph Naranjo, an interpreter of his tongue, of how on the road to the plains there are some rancherías of Apaches whom they call Chipaynes or Limitas, who in their language are known as Sejines, and that these and the Faraon nation are one and the same. This nation in particular is the one which has always committed many robberies and murders in this jurisdiction. They are those who, when ransoming is begun in Pecos, mingle with the Indians of the plains who take them and go into the pueblo at peace with them. On leaving, they commit thefts of animals in this jurisdiction and in that of Cañada and among the Indians of Jicarilla who enter in peace in the pueblo of Taos and who have always kept it. He has known that these Indians have their habitation in the plains country where the grass that grows there is very dry, and for this reason their trail is very difficult to follow. They understood from Don Gerónimo that his people always desired arms to go and punish this nation. They offered to guide the Spaniards, since there is no road from La Jicarilla for more than five days with sufficient water for a large part of the horse-herd that might go. They know for certain that the little Spaniard whom they stole is the son of Jacinto Sánchez. They are the ones that

80

carried him away, as the Indians of Tesuque told Captain Naranjo, the interpreter. When they went out to follow the trail they recognized that the Faraons had come in by way of the Picuríes and that these two came to the ranch where they had kidnapped the boy and others. They had returned whence they had entered, carrying off the beasts which they needed from the canyon. The Jicarillas said that always when one goes to their land, there are many mules and horses in their possession which they have stolen from here. [He said] that in case a journey is ordered that no Indians of Pecos should go because they will inform this nation as the two are almost the same. For at the time of the conquest when the Pecos were reduced, the Faraons fled from them, these very same ones, and went to live on the plains. Likewise, the Queres Indians should not go on this journey either because they make a great noise when spies go out and thus advise the enemy to fly [so that] one may not take advantage of the opportunity of punishing them. Only the Tegua [Tigua], the Picuríes, and the Taos tribes go out together with all the Jicarillas who are many. These are sufficient. The Jicarillas offer both to attack their rancherías and to serve as spies.

The time they ought to arrive at their rancherías in order to take them together and to punish them is in the middle of August when the moon is almost full. At this time they are shaking out the grain from the ears of corn. Having finished doing this and having buried it beneath the soil, they all go on a hunt for buffalo where they maintain themselves until they return to sow which is at the end of April or the beginning of May. There they remain until they cut it. They will not find them in any other manner since they live where there is hunting and then invade this province for corn when they need it.

It appeared to Don Gerónimo wise to give me this news in order that according to it I could determine what may seem best to me. When I heard these details, I ordered them written so that I may use them as a measure for calling a council of commanders, active and retired, who, having understood its import, may give me their opinions concerning a campaign. So provided, ordered, and signed with my secretary of government and war. The said Gerónimo and interpreter did not sign it because they did not know how.

Don Juan Ygnacio Flores Mogollón

[*rubric*]

As ordered by the Señor Governor and Captain-General.

Roque de Pintto [*rubric*]

Secretary of Government and War.

2. TESTIMONY OF DON LORENZO, SANTA FÉ, JULY 22, 1715

In the villa of Santa Fé on the twenty-second of July, 1715, Don Lorenzo, chief of the pueblo of Picuríes and the lieutenant-governor of that pueblo appeared before me, Don Juan Ignacio Florez Mogollón, governor and captain-general of these provinces of New Mexico for his majesty. I asked them through the interpreter, called Luís, if they recognized the arrows which I showed them. These arrows had been left in the marsh of this villa by the Apaches who carried off as captive the son of Jacinto Sánchez. Don Lorenzo and the lieutenant-governor having identified them, said they belonged to the nation of the Trementinas[31] or Limitas and that, moreover, they always came to rob Taos, Picuríes, Río Arriba, and Chimayó. He knows this, for on the many occasions when the people of his pueblo had followed and overtaken them, they had left in flight some rope halters and hides of buffalo which Don Lorenzo had judged to belong to the Apaches Limitas.

Asked by me what the probable distance the said nation will be from their pueblo and if there will likely be sufficient water for a large cavalry, and what distance there is from one stream to another, he said that from the pueblo of the Picuríes to the first ranchería, composed of thirty houses of wood entirely smeared with clay outside, which is located on the banks of a river, there are ten days of marching with sufficient water every day because the springs are large.[32] Those who are accustomed to go beyond these a little find much sun and the water [torn out] The land is a plain going by way of Mora. The ranchería is also in good land, and without doubt more than [torn out] of the houses. He gave this same account to General Juan Páes Hurtado who signed it with me and my secretary of government and war. Neither Don Lorenzo nor the lieutenant nor the interpreter signed it because they did not know how. In order that it may appear, I ordered it placed for consideration with the preceding.

Don Juan Ignacio   Juan Páez Hurtado
Florez Mogollón [rubric]   [rubric]

As ordered by the Señor Governor and Captain-General

Roque de Pintto [rubric]
Secretary of Government and War.

3. ORDER OF MOGOLLÓN, SANTA FÉ, JULY 22, 1715

In the villa of Santa Fé of New Mexico on the twenty-second day of the month of July, 1715, I, Don Juan Ignacio Florez Mogollón, governor and captain-general of this kingdom and provinces of New Mexico for his majesty, said that I received a letter from the lieutenant alcalde mayor of the pueblo of Taos, in which he remitted me another which the father minister of Picuríes wrote him. In this he gives news that the Apaches had carried off the horseherd of this pueblo and that all their young men were setting out in pursuit for the purpose of following them to their lands. These papers I am ordering filed with this affidavit. I summoned the captain of the company so that he might prepare with dispatch as many soldiers as he could and set out for the pueblo of the Picuríes, following the trail of these natives in order to assist them. The captain, being present with General Juan Páez Hurtado, Sergeant-Major Don Alonzo Rael de Aguilar, and Lieutenant (retired) Francisco Montes Vijil, answered me that he found it impossible to set out himself because he had an infirmity in his leg. Although he could go about on foot, he knew he could not mount a horse. Having heard this, I ordered General Juan Páez to prepare himself to go as the superior chief and that he set out with the greatest promptness. Because the horseherd of the presidio was in the region of Chama and the soldiers could not find it today with fast animals, I ordered them to take their horses from the settlers in order that they could go to the horseherd and from there send back the [settlers'] animals with all care in order to deliver them to their owners. In that, the general, Juan Páez, will take all care. To him I gave the order in writing which must be executed. So provided and ordered and signed with my secretary of government and war.

<table>
<tr><td>DON JUAN IGNACIO
FLORES MOGOLLÓN
[rubric]</td><td>As ordered by the Señor
Governor and Captain-General.
ROQUE DE PINTTO   [rubric]
Secretary of Government and War.</td></tr>
</table>

4. ORDER FOR COUNCIL OF WAR, SANTA FÉ, JULY 22, 1715

In this villa of Santa Fé on the said day, month and year, I, the governor and captain-general, say that in compliance with the writ and order which I gave him for that, the general, Juan Páez Hurtado, set out from this villa with the military forces of this presidio to assist the Indians of the pueblo of Picuríes whose horseherd the Apaches had carried off and who went in pursuit. The general, having about arrived at the pueblo of Tesuque, met Diego Romero, an Indian of the pueblo of Taos, with a letter from the lieutenant alcalde mayor of the pueblo of Taos which gave him the news that the Picuríes had recovered their horseherd and are already in their pueblo. This paper I ordered placed among these affidavits with the others which the reverend father minister of the Picuríes wrote to the lieutenant alcalde mayor. Likewise, among these affidavits was placed the information which Gerónimo, the Indian son, the lieutenant-governor of the pueblo of Taos, Don Lorenzo, the chief of the pueblo of the Picuríes gave.

The active and retired chiefs of the company of this presidio were cited for tomorrow morning the twenty-third of the current month, in order that, informed of the said news and papers, they may give me their opinions to be able to coerce and punish this wicked tribe of Apaches for their haughtiness. So provided, ordered, and signed with my secretary of government and war.

DON JUAN IGNACIO FLORES MOGOLLÓN   Before me
        [rubric]   ROQUE DE PINTTO [rubric]
                                        Secretary of Government and War.

5. COUNCIL OF WAR, JULY 23, 1715

In the villa of Santa Fé of New Mexico on the twenty-third day of the month of July, 1715. All the chiefs, active and retired, of the company of this presidio came together in the courtroom of the governor. The news, affidavits, and the rest of the papers were read to them by the present secretary. When they understood the contents of all, they gave me their opinions in the following manner:

Retired Ensign Salvador de Santiestevan says it is necessary that war be made on this nation because of the many robberies they commit, as is known, on the pueblo of the Picuríes, having carried off their horseherd which the Indians of the said pueblo succeeded in getting back. He did not sign it as he did not know how.

The retired lieutenant Francisco Montes Vijil says he is of the opinion that, having understood the news given by the lieutenant of the alcalde mayor of Taos and the Indians, the robberies which the Apaches make require that war be made on them; that the month of September will be an opportune time for it; that there is much pasture and water for the horseherd; and that although the Indians say that in the middle of August the Apaches reap their maize, it appears to him that this is not possible, having sowed it at the end of April. But even reaping during August must require more than a month for drying it. He signed it.

Sergeant-Major Don Alonzo Rael de Aguilar says that he agrees in all with the opinion of Lieutenant Francisco Montes Vijil. He signs it.

The adjutant-general of the cavalry of the kingdom, Joseph Domín-guez, says he agrees with the opinion of the Lieutenant Francisco Montes Vijil, and that it is necessary notwithstanding that which the Indian Don Gerónimo said, that fifty Indians of the pueblo of Pecos go on the campaign. He signs it.

General Don Juan Páez Hurtado says that he agrees entirely with the opinion of Lieutenant Francisco Montes Vijil. He signs it.

Captain of the company of this presidio, Don Felix Martínez, says that he agrees entirely with the opinion of Lieutenant Montes Vijil. He adds that it is safer for the Indians of the pueblo of Pecos not to go on the campaign on the frontiers where the Faraon tribe is found. For it is a time when the Faraones can invade the pueblo, and that this presidio will be without men and unable to give it aid. He signs it.

I, the governor and captain-general, agree with the opinions given in the council that the month of September be decided upon for the departure of the forces; because a large part of the arms have to set out to escort the visitor-general of the kingdom who is to set out very soon to make his inspection.[33] On my return I will indicate the day on which the departure of the armed forces must be made and the spot that must be selected for the assembling of forces. It is to be understood that the Indians of the Queres nation are not to set out because the escort from Albuquerque must go on the campaign and the frontier must be guarded by the settlers and Indians. None of the Pueblo of Pecos must go because of the reason expressed by Captain Don Felix Martínez in his opinion. Only the Teguas [Tiguas], the Taos, and the Picuríes nations may go. At a convenient time I will give the order to the alcalde mayores in order that they may have the Indians ready. So provided, ordered and signed with all those of the council and my secretary of government and war.

MOGOLLÓN   FELIX MARTÍNEZ   JUAN PÁEZ HURTADO
   [rubric]   [rubric]   [rubric]

VIJIL   JOSEPH DOMÍNGUEZ
   [rubric]   [rubric]

ALONSO RAEL DE AGUILAR
     [rubric]

According to the order
of the Señor Governor
and Captain-General
ROQUE DE PINTTO
[rubric]
Secretary of Government and War.

85

B. Appointment of Hurtado, Santa Fé, August 20, 1715

In the villa of Santa Fé of New Mexico, on the twentieth day of the month of August, 1715, I, Don Juan Ygnazio Florez Mogollón, governor and captain-general of this kingdom and provinces of New Mexico for his majesty, say that in conformity with that decided upon in the council of war on the twenty-third of July, past, of this year, concerning making a campaign against the nation, Chipaines or Limitas, in which I determined that I would indicate the day as soon as I should return from making the inspection of the kingdom, that I appoint General Juan Páez Hurtado, who has come to this villa as superior head, to make this campaign because of the sickness of the present captain of the company. I ordered him to prepare with dispatch forty soldiers. They are to set out from this villa and jurisdiction of La Cañada, twenty settlers and one hundred fifty of the Taos, Pequríes, Teguas [Tiguas], and Pecos Indians. I designate the pueblo of Pequríes as the place the assembling of forces where they will be on the thirtieth day of this month; the armed forces of this villa to set out on the twenty-eighth. So provided, ordered and signed with my secretary of government and war.

Don Juan Ignacio Flores Mogollón   Roque de Pintto
[rubric]   [rubric]
                                      Secretary of Government and War.

C. Order to Hurtado, Santa Fé, August 26, 1715

[Marginal note: As much of the order as was given to General Don Juan Páez.] Don Juan Ignazio Flores Mogollón, governor and captain-general of this kingdom and provinces of New Mexico and warden of its forces and presidios for his majesty:

Wherefore, by means of a council and affidavits, I have determined that a campaign should be made against the Apache Indians, heathen of the nation Chipaines or Limitas, having named the pueblo of Pecuríes for the assembling of the armed forces on the thirtieth of the current month and appointed as principal head, General Don Juan Páez Hurtado, with forty men of arms from this presidio, a list of whom will be delivered to him; and twenty settlers and one hundred and fifty Indians. For this end I have commanded the alcalde mayores of the jurisdictions of this kingdom that on the above mentioned day they (the Indians) be in the said pueblo; I ordered and commanded General Don Juan Páez Hurtado to set out from this villa on the twenty-eighth of the current month, with the column of armed soldiers that I

86

have indicated, for the pueblo of Picuríes, where, having arrived, he will receive from the alcaldes mayores the number of Indians indicated. He will muster the soldiers, settlers, and Indians, a list of whom he will remit to me. When this is done, he will begin his march, making the journeys proportionately so that we may not lose the horseherd; he will take every precaution so that the heathen Indian allies who may be met on the route shall not be maltreated in any respect by the soldiers, the settlers, and the Indians of the pueblos,[34] since the purpose is only to punish the Apaches Chipaines or Limitas who are causing damages and robberies that have been experienced and as appear in the affidavits. On these war will be made, taking care that the women and children of the Chipaines are not killed by the natives and are apprehended and brought to my presence.

In everything, the general shall act according to his extensive experiences, love and zeal for the royal service, as he has for the present affair. He shall not allow the soldiers to gamble, nor barter arms or horses, with warning that I shall judge his tolerance.

It is dated in this villa of Santa Fé of New Mexico, on the twenty-sixth day of the month of August, 1715. I sign it with my secretary of government and war.

Don Juan Ignacio Florez Mogollón Roque de Pintto
        [rubric]   [rubric]
                                Secretary of Government and War.

I, General Don Juan Páez Hurtado, received the order set forth above drawn up by the Señor Governor and Captain-General Don Juan Ignazio Florez Mogollón and countersigned by the secretary of government and war. It is in my possession for its observance. In order that it may so appear, I sign it on the said day, month and year.

Juan Páez Hurtado
[rubric]

D. List of Soldiers with Hurtado, Santa Fé, August 28, 1715

List of the soldiers who are going on the campaign against the Apaches Limitas or Chipaines on which General Don Juan Páez Hurtado goes as principal head:

2. Adjutant Roque Madrid
3. Adjutant-General Joseph Domíng^z
4. Ensign (retired) Salvador de Santiestevan
5. Ensign Xptóval de Torres

87

6. Ensign Real Eusebio Rael
7. Captain of the Company Pedro Luján
8. Captain of the Company Al° Real
9. Captain Pedro de Chaves
10. Corporal Fran^co Thamaris
11. Corporal Lorenzo Rodríg^z
12. Corporal Antonio Tafora
13. Corporal Ber^do Casillas
14. Fran^co Javier Benavides
15. Ju^n de D^s Martínez
16. Joseph Montaño
17. Joseph de Salas
18. Manuel de Silva
19. Ju^n Phelipe de Rivera
20. Diego Velásq^z
21. Blas Lovato
22. Ju^n Rico de Rojas
23. Dom° Ram°
24. Ju^n Gallegas
25. Luis Ortiz
26. Ju^n Luján
27. Joseph Griego
28. Dimas Jurón
29. Joachin Sánchez
30. Ant° López
31. Alejo Gutiérrez
32. Ant° de Herrera
33. Pedro de Roxas
34. Miguel Durán
35. Simón de Córdova
36. Fran^co Trujillo
37. Dom° Trujillo
38. Ju^n Joseph Archuleta
39. Corporal Al° Garzía
40. Ant° de la Rea Clarinero

All of the above are at the orders of the General Don Juan Páez Hurtado, with warning that I shall punish the disobedient. Villa of Santa Fé, August 28, 1715, I place my rubric.

[*rubric* of Mogollón]

E. List of Settlers with Hurtado, Santa Fé, August 28, 1715
List of the twenty settlers who are going on the campaign of the Apaches Chipaines or Limitas, on which General Don Juan Páez Hurtado goes as commander:
1. Captain Luís Garzía, settler of Albuquerque
2. Ensign Miguel de S^n Ju^n, settler of Bernalillo
3. Captain Fran^co Lorenzo de Casados
4. Cap^n Ju^n de Archiuèque
5. Ensign Miguel de Coca
6. Adjutant Andres Montoya
7. Vizente de Armijo
8. Ju^n Ant° Rodríguez
9. Sergeant Diego Marq^z
10. Lorenzo Griego

11. Diego Martín	16. Luis López
12. Diego de Archuleta	17. Martín Fez [?] in the place of another
13. Ju^n Ant^o de Apodaca	18. Joseph Luján
14. Simon Baca	19. Marzial Martín
15. Fran^o Martín	20. Jazinto Martín

All these will be under the command of General Don Juan Páez Hurtado, with the warning that I shall judge any disobedience. I place my rubric upon it in this villa of Santa Fé on the twenty-eighth day of August, 1715.

[*rubric* of MOGOLLÓN]

F. List of Pueblo Indians with Hurtado, Santa Fé, August 28, 1715

List of the natives who are going on the campaign referred to, on which Don Juan Páez Hurtado goes as commander and who must be in the pueblo of the Picuríes on the thirtieth of this month.

Captain Joseph Naranjo	0.01
From the pueblo of Pecos, twenty-four	0.24
From San Juan, twenty	0.20
Nambé, ten with panchuelo	0.10
S^n Yldephonso, sixteen	0.16
Santa Clara, twelve	0.12
Pujuaque, eight	0.08
From Tesuque, twelve	0.12
Thaos, thirty-six	0.36
Picuríes, twelve	0.12
	0.151

That these natives will be at all the orders that General Don Juan Páez may give them, with warning that I shall punish the disobedient. Villa of Santa Fé, August 28, 1715. I place my rubric upon it.

[*rubric* of MOGOLLÓN]

G. Hurtado's Review of Forces and Equipment, Picuríes Pueblo

In this pueblo of San Lorenzo of Picuríes on the thirtieth day of the month of August of 1715, I, General Juan Páez Hurtado, principal commander of the campaign to the plains on which I am setting out today, this day, in compliance with that which was commanded by Señor Don Juan Ignacio Florez Mogollón, governor and captain-general of this kingdom of New Mexico: Wherefore, I have commanded to come together the body of the people of war, presidials, militiamen, and Indian people of the pueblos for muster in the following form and manner:[35]

In this pueblo of San Lorenzo of the Picuríes, August 30, 1715, I, General Juan Páez [H]urtado, commanding officer of the expedition to the plains, begin today fulfilling what was commanded by Señor Don Juan Florez Mogolló[n], governor and captain-general of this kingdom of New Mexico, for his majesty. Having commanded that the soldiers, presidials, militiamen, and Indians from the pueblos gather here, I reviewed them in the form and manner as follows:

1. Adjutant-general of the kingdom, Joseph Domínguez, fully armed and provisioned and .... 5 horses
2. Sublieutenant, detached, Salbador de Santiesteban, fully armed and provisioned and .... 6 "
3. Capitán de Campaña, Pedro Luján, fully armed and ... 4 "
4. Capitán de Campaña, Don Alonzo Real, fully armed and provisioned and .... 5 "
5. Royal ensign, Don Eusebio Real, fully armed and munitioned and one mule .... 3 "
mules 1
6. Captain Don Pedro de Chavez, fully armed and provisioned and .... 6 "
7. Corporal Francisco de Tamáriz, fully armed and provisioned and .... 5 "
8. Corporal Alonzo Garzía, fully armed and provisioned and .... 7 "
9. Joseph Montaño, fully armed and provisioned and ...... 4 "
10. Juan de Dios Martínez, fully armed and provisioned and 5 "
11. Juan Gallegos, fully armed and provisioned and .... 5 "
12. Joseph de Salas, fully armed and provisioned and .... 5 "
13. Juan Rico de Rojas, fully armed and provisioned and .. 5 "
14. Manuel de Silva, fully armed and provisioned and ...... 6 "
15. Nicolás Gallegos, fully armed and provisioned and one mule .... 5 "
mules 1

90

16. Francisco Gavriel Venavides, fully armed and provisioned and   5 horses
17. Corporal Lorenzo Rodríguez, fully armed and provisioned and   4 "
18. Corporal Bernardo Casillas, fully armed and provisioned and   3 "
19. Miguel Durán, fully armed and provisioned and   4 "
20. Antonio López, fully armed, provisioned and   4 "
21. Antonio de Errera, fully armed, provisioned and   3 "
22. Domingo Romero, fully armed and provisioned and   5 "
23. Bernabe Vaca, in the place of Juan Joseph de Archuleta, who was unprepared, fully armed and provisioned   5 "
24. Diego Velásquez, fully armed and provisioned and   5 "
25. Domingo Truxillo, fully armed, provisioned and   5 "
26. Pedro de Rroxas, fully armed, provisioned and   4 "
27. Joachín Sánchez, fully armed, provisioned and   4 "
28. Corporal Antonio Tafoya, fully armed, provisioned and   6 "
29. Blas Lobato, fully armed, provisioned and   4 "
30. Juan Luján, fully armed, lacking leather jacket, provisioned and   5 "
31. Joseph Griego, fully armed, provisioned and   4 "
32. Francisco Truzillo, fully armed, provisioned and   5 "
33. Dimas Jiron
34. Luys Ortís
35. Juan Phelipe de Ribera
36. Simón de Córdova, fully armed, provisioned   5 "

Settlers of Al Buquerque

1. Captain Luys Garzía, fully armed, lacking leather jacket, provisioned and one mule   10 "
mules
1
2. Sublieutenant Miguel de San Juan, fully armed, lacking leather jacket; four horses and one mule   4 "
1
3. Captain Antonio de Ulibarri, fully armed, lacking leather jacket, and provisioned   6 "
1

91

4. Captain Francisco Lorenzo Casados, fully armed, eight mules and six horses   6   horses

mules

8

5. Captain Juan de Archévèque, fully armed, provisioned and six horses and five mules; he takes an armed personal servant.   6   "

5

6. Adjutant Andrés Montoya, fully armed, provisioned, and seven horses and one mule   7   "

1

7. Bisente de Armigo, fully armed, provisioned   11   "

8. Juan Antonio Rodríguez, fully armed, lacking leather jacket, provisioned, and three horses and one mule   3   "

1

9. Captain Miguel de Sandoval, fully armed, lacking provisions, and three horses and two mules   3   "

2

10. Nicolás Griego, who volunteers, fully armed and provisioned, two horses and one mule   2   "

1

Settlers from La Cañada

11. Sergeant Diego Marqués, fully armed, one mare and two mules   1   "

2

12. Joseph Luján, fully armed, and lacking provisions; two horses and three mules   2   "

3

13. Luys López, fully armed, lacking leather jacket, two mares, and one horse, and one mule   3   "

1

Note. Lorenzo Griego, fully armed, lacking jacket, two horses. He remained because he was not ready.

14. Juan Antonio de Apodaca, fully armed, one horse and one mule   1   "

1

15. Diego de Archuleta, fully armed, lacking leather jacket, and four horses   4   "

92

16. Francisco Martín, fully armed, lacking leather jacket and sword, two horses ... 2 horses
17. Antonio Martín, for his father, Diego Martín, fully armed, provisioned, lacking leather jacket ... 3 "
18. Cristóbal Rodarte, lacking leather jacket, fully armed, and two horses, and two mules ... 2 "
2
19. Juan López, fully armed, lacking leather jacket, provisioned, and two horses and two mules ... 2 "
2
20. Simón Baca, fully armed, lacking leather jacket, provisioned, and one horse, and two mules ... 1 "
2
21. Juan de Candelaría, fully armed, lacking leather jacket, and four horses ... 4 "

Indian Warriors

From Pecos, thirty friends with Don Phelipe and Don Juan Tinde with guns ... 30
From Taos, thirty-six with Don Gerónimo with guns ... 36
From the pueblo of Nambé, ten, with blankets, leather jackets and guns, and those six from Pujuaque ... 16
From the pueblo of Tesuque eleven because one, being ill, remained behind ... 11
From the pueblo of San Juan seventeen, for three, having hidden, remained behind. The alcalde mayor will have to give account of them. ... 17
From Santa Clara, twelve, and these ... 12
From San Yldefonzo, sixteen, and these ... 16
From Picuríes, eleven, and these ... 11

All of those included in this muster roll are the ones that I am taking in my company on the expedition to the plains. I am starting from this place of mobilization today, August 30, having left behind Maestro de Campo Roque Madrid, and Marzial Martín, because they are ill of the flux.

In order that your Lordship may be informed of this leave-taking which is thus delayed, I inform you and sign it since it takes place the said day of August 30, 1715.

Juan Páez Hurtado
[rubric]

93

V. Diary of the Campaign of Juan Páez Hurtado Against the Faraon Apache, 1715

The diary of the campaign I made to the plains under orders from Señor Don Juan Ignacio Flores Mogollón, governor and captain-general of this kingdom of New Mexico is as follows:

Friday, August 30, 1715. I set out from the pueblo of Picuríes at about nine o'clock in the morning with thirty-seven soldiers, eighteen settlers, and one hundred and forty-six Indians. The chaplain of the army was the Very Reverend Father Predicator Fray Lucas Arebalo. We marched six leagues up the river to the east, for the heart of the sierra is very rough, mountainous land, and the river a narrow passage between the mountains.[36] We stopped at five o'clock in the evening in a sandy place, a cavern in a rock, where there was a good pasture. The river ran through the middle of it. [*Marginal note:* Six leagues.]

Saturday, the thirty-first, of the said month. We set out from this spot and marched along the edge of the river through rough land of steep slopes and precipitous descents. A league from the spot where we left the river of the Picuríes on our right hand we ascended a hillock on our left and marched down hill a short distance to another arroyo with very good water. This ran to the southwest among rough hillocks and canyons covered with many large oaks. I went down with the camp to the valley which is called Mora,[37] where there is an old house with adobe walls.[38] We continued to march four leagues and came to a halt where there was an abundance of pastures and meadows to refresh the horseherd. [*Marginal note:* Four leagues.]

Sunday, September 1. The first of September we set out from this above spot and marched for a league and a half along a good route among evergreen oakwood, poplar trees and pines. We halted in a valley three quarters of a league long. It has an arroyo running to the southwest filled with much good water and quantities of trout. I called it the Valley of Corncobs because of the great quantities there are in it; it is a land famous for grain and herds.[39]

Monday, the second. We set out from the above spot at seven in the morning, continuing in the same direction to the southwest along the stream for a league. There we left the stream on our left and marched off along a good road through a gently rolling plain until we arrived at an arroyo lined with many plum trees. We reached here about twelve o'clock. We named the stream Río de San Esteban of the Caves,[40] for there were some caves there which sheltered us from a short heavy shower. This day we had marched eight leagues. [*Marginal note:* Eight leagues.]

Tuesday, the third. We set out from the Río de San Esteban at six in the morning, and marched to the southeast,[41] quarter to the south over level country until we arrived at a stony canyon. Here were a few pine and piñon trees, many evergreen oaks, and many deep pools of water. For this reason I named the place the Canyon of Santa Elena of the Jagueyes. The march was some ten leagues. [*Marginal note:* Ten leagues.]

Wednesday, the fourth. I set out with the camp from this above spot at six in the morning and marched five leagues through a good country covered with hillocks. At the end of these appeared a small mountain of pines and piñons, and then a very long, rough descent; a little later another for about half a league. Afterwards, I marched through a broad glen, the two sides of high mesas, and along an arroyo which ran through the middle of many [groves of] poplars and white timber. I must have marched for some six leagues. At the outlet I found some watering holes of bad salty water. I named them the Salt Marshes of Santa Rosa del Viterbo, and the Water of the Shells, on account of some mussels found there. This day I traveled some eleven leagues to the east. [*Marginal note:* Eleven leagues.]

Thursday, the fifth. I set out from this above spot at sunrise and marched through a plain for some four leagues and stopped in a vale, where there were holes of salt water, to eat and to water the horses. At twelve we set out from the Río de San Raymundo, *nonnato,* so named because the river was discovered on his day. The march was to the southwest. The river runs through some mountainous mesas. The water is salty and the terrain red. For this reason the Indians call the river the Río Colorado.[42] On the way there were many mesquite bushes, and the heat was extreme. It rained during the whole march. [*Marginal note:* Nine leagues.]

Friday, the sixth. I marched with the command along the banks of the Río Colorado, leaving it occasionally. I stopped on a hillock on the bank. I remained here all day and night in order to pick it up on the seventh because it was distant and out of consideration for the horses. This march was three leagues to the east, which is the direction the Río Colorado takes. About this spot there are many deer and some prairie chickens. [*Marginal note:* Three leagues.]

Saturday, the seventh. The camp set out from this above spot at sunrise under the command of Francisco Tamariz with whom I had left it, for I had gone ahead the day before at three in the afternoon with a squad of nine soldiers and two settlers who volunteered to accompany me and nineteen Indians in search of a watering hole in order to continue the journey. At five leagues I found an arroyo of colored water in a salt marsh sufficient for the camp. From there two Indians were dispatched to order the command to come to the said arroyo and there await a new order. I set out to look for the Río Colorado which I had left on our left. After marching to the north a little more than a half a league, I was obliged to stop on account of a heavy shower of rain accompanied by such thunder and lightning that we waited on horseback. This lasted an hour. After that we continued our march until nine in the evening for the guide had lost the way. At the break of day we found ourselves upon a river with sufficient water from the rain. From here I dispatched some Indians ordering them to tell the commander to follow my trail as he did, arriving with all the camp at one in the afternoon at an arroyo of poplar trees which I called the Water of the Miracle of the Nativity of the Holy Mary because it was the eve of her day.

The camp stopped, for the river was some distance and we did not know if there was water. I sent Captain Naranjo with six Indians to examine it. He went down to the river three or four leagues and returned to advise me to continue the march to the ranchería. This march was eleven leagues to the east with a declination to the southeast. The land is [*Marginal note:* Eleven leagues.] a plain; on the sides of the mesas there are many mesquite bushes. The heat of the sun is intolerable. The land is not sandy.

Sunday, the eighth. I set out from The Miracle and marched to the north from seven in the morning (after having heard mass by the Reverend Father Preacher Fray Lucas Arevolo) to eleven o'clock, when we lost our way. I was obliged to return to the Río Colorado to follow its course in order to arrive at the ranchería of the Chipaynes. On this day Captain Naranjo discovered some tracks of Apache men and women and on the bank of the river he found three springs of good, cold, sweet-tasting water. I called them the Springs of San Joseph in compliment to Captain Naranjo. The river water is very brackish. The march today was six leagues to the north. [*Marginal note:* Six leagues.]

Monday, the ninth. I set out from this above spot at six in the morning and marched along the banks of the Río Colorado, crossing the stream many times, and at times ascending the low hills to avoid a

96

circuitous route. We marched east having sent ahead the captain with twelve Indians the day before to examine the river and the mesas. They did not find anything more than old tracks. The march was six leagues, the most of which was among sand dunes. I stopped with the camp in a beautiful pasture with much grass and cotton woods. There was a tiny spring of good water on the side of a hill where were also many grape vines. I named the spot San Juan Baptista in honor of my saint. In this spot there is a saline [deposit] with very white and colored grained salt, very heavy and good, and a spring of good water. [*Marginal note:* Six leagues.]

Tuesday, the tenth. I set out from the spot of San Juan at six in the morning, with the camp down the river. I marched east along the river crossing it many times. The land is miserable; on both sides are sand dunes. On this above spot was the horse of the soldier, Juan Gallegos, all saddled and bridled with an arquebus and saddle bags. Four soldiers went to look for him. The squad remained on the spot waiting for them. The tracks continued along the river, although somewhat more fresh. The march was six leagues. I called this spot San Nicholás de Tolentino where a glen running north terminated. [*Marginal note:* Six leagues.]

Wednesday, the eleventh. I set out from this above spot and marched along the banks of the river for three leagues. The river was dry in places because the water ran into the ground and came up again at intervals. Afterwards, I marched through its meadows some four leagues, having been on the march for seven leagues to the east. The land is very rough and partly covered with sand dunes; along the banks of the river are wild grape vines, white trees, some walnut trees, with small hard nuts. [*Marginal note:* Seven leagues.]

Thursday, the twelfth. I set out from the above spot along the bank of the river to the east, crossing it many times to save ourselves its many circuitous windings. The land is the same as on the preceding marches. I stopped on the banks of some marshes more salty than brackish, for the river had no water for a long distance, but only a pool for the command. Today about three in the afternoon I dispatched Captain Naranjo with twenty-seven Indians by another route to see if there was water at the foot of a mesa where the Picuríes said there was. I remained there. The sierra of sand divided us from where the rancheria was. I awaited his report in order to move camp. The march was seven leagues. [*Marginal note:* Seven leagues.]

Friday, the thirteenth. I set out from the above spot to a better location because Captain Naranjo advised me. He had found some marshes with much sweet water and good pasture and there awaited, as he did. The march was three leagues to the east along the banks of the river. I called these the Waterholes [*Marginal note:* Three leagues.] of the Exaltation of the Cross. This day I moved camp at ten. I marched five leagues to an arroyo of good water and pastures where Captain Naranjo was waiting, [*Marginal note:* Five leagues.] leaving the Río Colorado on our right because of some hills. At four in the afternoon we changed [course] again. I set out with forty-four soldiers and settlers and one hundred Indians to investigate a white sand hill which was near the spot and on which the guide said was the ranchería. Having marched some eight leagues, we came to an arroyo with much water and fine meadows of green pastures, but without a mark of ever having been a ranchería. On asking him for the site of the ranches and corn fields, he said that he did not know where they were, that he was already confused and that he did not know where he was nor where he ought to go. Seeing that we were approaching eighteen days marching with him as leader and that he was guilty of such negligence, I condemned him to be given fifty lashes with a whip. For this reason I called the place the Arroyo of the Whipping. From there I returned to join the camp. [*Marginal note:* Eight leagues.]

Saturday, the fourteenth. I dispatched Captain Naranjo with the Taos towards the north to reconnoiter some high mesas and come back to give me news of what he should discover. In compliance with this he marched six leagues, taking as a guide a Picuríes Indian. He reported a spring a league away sufficient for the horseherd. To this spot the Picuríes came when they left their pueblo. At this spring I found old tracks of many people and horseherds who had gone out for buffalo.[43] I presume that at the ransoming which they enter into at Pecos they had had news that the Spaniards were to set out in search of them. For this reason all absented themselves from the Río Colorado where they have their rancherías. With this information I decided to return to give an account to my governor and captain-general, and because I saw my supplies for the soldiers beginning to grow scarce. I did this along the same route I had come. In order that it may appear so, I signed it on the eighteenth day of September, 1715.

JUAN PÁEZ HURTADO
[*rubric*]

VI. COUNCIL OF WAR AND DIARY OF THE CAMPAIGN OF GOVERNOR VAL-VERDE AGAINST THE UTES AND COMANCHES, 1719[44]

A. Order for Council of War, Santa Fé, August 13, 1719

Year of 1719. No. 511. Proceedings and judicial formalities in which war was declared upon the Utes, barbarous Indian gentiles, because of the deaths and robberies which they have caused in this kingdom. For this purpose Señor Governor Don Antonio Balverde Cosio organized and held a council of war of the officials of this presidial fort together with the practiced and most experienced settlers, etc.

In the villa of Santa Fé on the thirteenth day of the month of August, 1719, I, the governor, Don Antonio Balverde Cosio, governor and captain-general of this kingdom and province of New Mexico for his majesty, say that I find myself with these letters:[45] The first from Captain Miguel Thenorio de Alva, alcalde mayor of the pueblo and valley of Taos and its jurisdictions, wherein he gives me news of how on the eighth day of the present month ten Indians, Utes, came upon Diego Romero, a Coyote,[46] and shot him with arrows in Arroyo Hondo near the pueblo of Taos. He escaped by fleeing. On that night in El Embudo[47] they ran off four animals and a boy belonging to Captain Xptoval de la Serna, who had come down from the pueblo of Taos. The second of the cited letters is that of Reverend Father Fray Manuel de la Peña, missionary minister in that of Cochití. He informs me that in the canyon of Los Dulraznos, near the pueblo some twenty Utes had murdered an Indian of the Queres nation of that pueblo. The alcalde mayor of that jurisdiction has set out, according to the news he gave me just now, with forty Indians in search of the enemy. They found the tracks of the Utes, some one hundred Indians more or less, and six tracks of women and of dogs which they were using. The third letter is from the Reverend Father Fray Juan de la Cruz, missionary minister of the pueblo of San Gerónimo de Taos, dated the twelfth of the current month. In it he informs me of the news reported by the alcalde mayor and adds that it is commonly reported that all that valley of Taos is harassed by a growing number of Utes. This is recognized by the many tracks which the captains of war have found. Accordingly, it is feared that they might attack the pueblo or do some injury. In pursuance thereof, I considered that this might occur, by virtue of their wickedness and the impudence which they have, since they are killing, and trying to do a thing which up to now we have not experienced from this nation. In order to repress them and punish their audacious-

99

ness, it has appeared convenient to me to take arms up against them. For this resolution, I command the military chiefs and the rest of the intelligent and experienced settlers, who, in a council of war, in view of these matters, to give me, each one, his opinion and belief over his signature.

Having named for this meeting the nineteenth of the current month, in view of the said opinions, I will make the decision which is convenient to the greater service of his majesty. In order that it may be evident, I command the council of war for the affair and that in it they attend to the things which may be proposed. So provided, ordered, and signed with my secretary of government and war.

Don Antonio Balverde Cosio
[*rubric*]

As commanded by the Señor Governor and Captain-General
Miguel Thenorio y Alva [*rubric*]
Secretary of Government and War.

[*Marginal note:* Order given and executed this day.] In the villa of Santa Fé on the fifteenth of the said month of August, 1719, I, the governor, Don Antonio Balverde Cosio, governor and captain-general of this kingdom, for the defense of the pueblo of San Gerónimo de Taos and its ministers, decree, in view of the council of war which I have ordered held in regard to the Ute nation, and order that in the interim Sergeant-Major Miguel Thenorio de Alva, alcalde mayor in the pueblo of Taos, who is in this villa, set out today from here with a squad of soldiers from this royal presidio. I order Corporal Joseph Griego, in the pueblo of Taos, to remain there with the above mentioned squad, if meanwhile I have not commanded something else. I order the alcalde mayor to give me news of what he may find, if it be worthy of report which will assist the council of war which I have commanded held. So provided, ordered, and signed with my secretary of government and war.

Señor Don Antonio Balverde Cosio [*rubric*]

B. Council of War, Santa Fé, August 19, 1719

[*Marginal note:* Council of War.] In the villa of Santa Fé on the nineteenth day of the month of August, 1719, I, Governor Don Antonio Balverde Cosio, governor and captain-general of this kingdom of New Mexico for his majesty, being in this palace of the villa, had appear in my presence for the council of war, commanded by me, the military heads and settlers of this kingdom, experienced in matters of war. Informed of the context of the cited letters which were read, they discussed this matter. Each one gave his opinion and belief as follows:

[*Marginal note:* Opinion of Captain Joseph Naranjo.] Captain Joseph Naranjo, captain-major of the war, his title which the most excellent lord and former viceroy, the Duke of Linares, bestowed, settler of the new villa of Santa Cruz, says that it is proper to make war on the Indians of the Ute nation, although this nation may always have maintained peace with the Spaniards. It is about a year since they have been carrying on robberies. Now, because it appears and has been experienced, that their intention is to murder, if they are not punished this insolence will fall upon the settlements and the people will not be secure in their own homes. To avoid this situation, the armed forces should set out in search of this nation, who since it appears so close may attack the people. For on the other hand, an unfortunate result is to be feared. He gives this as his belief and opinion, according to the God and the experience which assists him. He did not sign because he did not know how. I, the governor, signed it with my secretary of government and war.

[*Marginal note:* Opinion of Nicolas Ortiz.] Captain Nicolas Ortiz, who has been with the militia of the villa of Santa Fé and a settler of it, says that it appears to him to be convenient that war be declared on the Indians of the Ute nation, since it has been recognized that their friendship has been only a cloak and under it they have been stealing continuously horseherds from different places, more than at present. They are now proposing to commit murder. If this wickedness is not punished, they will leave safe neither our few possessions nor our lives. This is his opinion and he signs it.

[*Marginal note:* Opinion of Diego Manquez.] Diego Manquez, a settler of the new villa of Santa Cruz, said that his opinion is that war should be made upon the Indians of the Ute nation since these for a long time have under the voice of peace entered to commit robberies among horseherds and steal cattle. He does not exculpate them by saying that they are Comanches because he has suffered from both who live and coöperate in attacking these vicinities. He gave this as his belief and opinion. He does not sign it because he does not know how.

[*Marginal note:* Opinion of Juan de Mittas.] Juan de Mittas, a settler of this pueblo of Pujuaque, said that he is not of the opinion and belief that war be made on the Indians of the Ute nation, notwithstanding the reasons which they may have given, since for many years it is known that this nation always maintained peace and that they do so now. These actions are for vengeance because of those whom the Pueblos have killed of their nation in defense. This is permitted. It may be that these are allied with the Apaches and with the domestics of the Pueblos. In this eventuality, seeing the armed forces going out, they can bring about a revolt in the center of the kingdom. This is his feeling and belief which he signs.

[*Marginal note:* Opinion of Captain Joseph Truxillas.] Captain Joseph Truxillo, settler of the jurisdiction of the new villa of Santa Cruz, says the he holds it very advisable that war be made on the Ute Indians in order to restrain them. For, on the other hand, considering the manner they are carrying on, committing robberies of horseherds every day, they will cripple the neighborhood in such a manner that the settlers will not be able to march out in defense, the more so when their audacity extends to murder, a thing which up to now they have not committed. This is his opinion and belief which he signs with me and my secretary of government and war.

[*Marginal note:* Opinion of Alejo Martin.] Alejo Martin, settler of Río Arriba, jurisdiction of the new villa of Santa Cruz, said that he is of the feeling that the armed forces should be directed against the Indians of the Ute nation, since, although up to the present they have shown themselves friends of the Spaniards, yet under this friendship they have carried off some animals. They have been tolerated in order to conserve friendly relations. But now they have dishonored themselves and have begun to commit murder. He maintains that it is proper that they should defend themselves and go out to punish this nation. This is his opinion. He does not sign it because he does not know how. I, the governor, signed it with my secretary of government and war.

[*Marginal note:* Opinion of Sergeant Juan de Pineda.] Sergeant Juan de la Mora Pineda, who is drill sergeant of the company of this presidial fort, said that he is of the feeling and belief that war should be made upon the Indians of the Ute nation and that the armed forces be directed against them in order that they may experience their rigor. For, in scorn of them, their insolence is such, that in their sight they not only come to steal animals but attempt murder, as they did among the Queres of the pueblo of Cochití and the wounded ones of the pueblo of Taos. According to what the reverend father missionary of the pueblo points out, they intend to destroy his mission and attack it as they did the pueblo of Picuríes, so that if this is allowed and no defense made, as is proper, they may go on to more excesses. Conspiracy with the Pueblos is not to be suspected when they are attempting the murders which they commit on these natives. The departure to punish the enemy should be made with the greatest promptness possible. This is his feeling and opinion. He signed it with me and my secretary of government and war.

[*Marginal note:* Opinion of Ensign Xptoval Tafoya.] Ensign Xptoval Tafoya, who has served his majesty in this kingdom for twenty-two years, a settler of the jurisdiction of the new villa of Santa Cruz, said that he is of the opinion and that it comports with the service of his majesty [and the] peace and quiet of this kingdom, that the armed forces set out to punish the excesses committed by the Indians of the Ute nation. Moreover, now and for a long time, this nation has been committing under the guise of peace, robberies of beasts, shooting the larger herds and whatever they find. The departure for defense and punishment should be with all promptness. This is his belief and opinion. He does not sign. I, the governor, sign it with my secretary of government and war.

[*Marginal note:* Opinion of the Captain of the Company Pedro Lujan.] Captain of the Company Pedro Lujan, who is captain with office in this presidial fort and who has served his majesty in this kingdom for forty years, said that, having informed himself of the letters which were read to him, it was manifest therein that the Ute nation is declaring war. This fact is verified by the things done, their committing of murders besides the robberies which they make of horseherds. He is of the opinion that the armed forces should go out to punish them and repress their insolence. This appears to him to be convenient. He did not sign; he does not know how. I signed it with my secretary of government and war.

[*Marginal note:* Opinion of Captain Sebastian Martin.] Captain Sebastian Martin, settler of Río Arriba, who has served his majesty in this kingdom in its pacification and conquest for thirty-four years, says that he is of the feeling, notwithstanding the letters of the reverend father missionary ministers and those of the alcalde mayores which were read to him, that squads of armed men and Indians of the pueblos should be placed where the Ute nation commonly enters in order to ascertain whether those who come in to commit hostilities are Utes or Comanches. Then the Utes, it is his feeling, whom the Spaniards by recognizing and inquiring can identify, may be many times

103

Comanches. Thus, by this means, the one committing these robberies having been determined, may be punished and the innocent not injured. This is his opinion and he signs it with me and my secretary of government and war.

[*Marginal note:* Opinion of Ensign Xptobal de Torres.] The Ensign Xptobal de Torres, who has been a presidial of the fort and at present is alcalde mayor and captain of the new villa of Santa Cruz and its jurisdiction of this kingdom, and who has served in it his majesty for forty years, says that it is his belief that war should be made upon the Indians of the Ute and Comanche nations since these always go about allied. Although it is true that they may have kept the peace, under the cloak of it they have been committing robberies among the horseherds for many days. Today, proceeding to commit murders, they have declared themselves enemies as is known. Because of what has happened, they have at present no reason on our part for this hostility. This is his opinion and he signs it with me and my secretary of government and war.

[*Marginal note:* Opinion of Balthasar Trujillo.] Captain Balthasar Trujillo of the militia of the jurisdiction of the new villa of Santa Cruz and Cañada, settler of the pueblo of Pujuaque, said that he is of the feeling, having seen the letters of the father missionary ministers and those of the alcalde mayores wherein they set forth what was done by the Indians of the Ute nation, that war be made upon them. They have declared themselves enemies because of the murders and robberies they are committing. Now and up to the present, they have been tolerated under the pretext of peace, which, as he sees it, they will never maintain since under it they have attacked like the rest of the enemies. This is his opinion. He does not sign because he does not know how. I, the governor, sign it with my secretary of government and war.

[*Marginal note:* Opinion of Ensign Bernardo Casillas.] Ensign Bernardo Casillas, who is a former settler of this presidial fort and who has served his majesty in this kingdom for eighteen years, said that he is of the belief that war should be made upon the Ute nation and Comanche nations, who, always united, have been committing robberies of horseherds in the name of peace. In the shade of it they have come in and have been admitted into the kingdom. They have done much more at present in the jurisdiction of Cochití and Taos, as appears from the letters of the reverend father missionaries of the said districts, that of the alcalde mayor of Taos and from the verbal account

104

of the alcalde mayor of Cochití. This is his opinion, which he signs with me and my secretary of government and war.

[*Marginal note:* Opinion of Captain Miguel de Coca.] Captain Miguel de la Vega y Coca, who has been a militiaman of this villa and has served his majesty for twenty-five years in this kingdom, said that he is of the belief and opinion that war should be made on the Indians of the Ute nation. For besides the robberies which under the name of peace they have committed, in this kingdom, they have now declared themselves as enemies as appears from the letters of the reverend father minister missionaries. This nation and that of the Comanche commonly go about together for the purpose of interfering with the little barter which this kingdom has with the nations which come in to ransom. They prevent their entrance and communication with us. This is his opinion, which he signs with me and my secretary of government and war.

[*Marginal note:* Opinion of Captain Miguel Thenorio.] Captain Miguel Thenorio de Alva, alcalde mayor and war captain of the pueblo of Thaos and its jurisdiction and secretary of government and war who served his majesty for twenty-five years, said that it is very convenient that the armed forces go out against the said Ute and Comanche Indians, for, besides having previously committed robberies, today they are becoming more wicked in committing murders. Those who have done these things have declared themselves enemies. For this reason, the armed forces should restrain them. Although in his letter, he has said that they are Utes who killed Diego Romero, a settler of Taos, they are Comanches as is also declared in the letter. The Indians who carried off the beasts of Captain Serna were also Comanches. These followed the same trails as the Utes. This is his opinion which he signed with me, the said governor.

[*Marginal note:* Opinion of Xptoval de la Serna.] Captain Xptoval de la Serna, who has been captain of this presidial fort and has served his majesty in this kingdom for twenty-five years, says that his feeling and belief is, because of the experience he has, that the armed forces be sent above to punish the Ute and Comanche nation. For since the time when the Marqués de la Peñuela governed this kingdom, these two nations have entered it to beg peace.[48] This was given them.[49] The effect was that on their departure for their boundaries they stole beasts which they found. They have continued from then until now under the shade and cloak of peace on whatever occasion that offered itself to do this stealing and have succeeded greatly. Now that they have declared themselves enemies, let war be made. This is his opinion. He signs it with me and my secretary of government and war.

[*Marginal note:* Opinion of Captain Don Francisco Bueno y Bohorques.] Captain Don Francisco Bueno y Boharques, alcalde mayor and war captain of this villa, said that, having heard and understood the context of the letters of the reverend father missionaries and the alcalde mayor of Taos, and in view of what was ordered in the decree of the señor governor and captain-general, he is of the opinion that it will be very much to the service of both majesties to send out the armed forces against the two nations of Utes and Comanches who have declared themselves enemies, not only by the extensive hostilities of robberies and deaths which they have made as is verified by the letters and by the opinions above. To this end, because, according to the common opinion of the Indians of the rest of the frontiers, they have appeared in greater numbers than that in which they are accustomed to go about, he recognizes that they are coming determined to declare war. This is a matter worthy of great punishment as a warning for the rest of the nations. He signed it with me, the governor, and my secretary of government and war.

[*Marginal note:* Opinion of Ensign Ygnacio de Ruybal.] Ensign Ygnacio de Ruybal, who is ensign of this presidial fort, having served his majesty for twenty-six years, said that he agrees with the preceding opinion given by Don Francisco Bueno that the armed forces must go out against the Ute and Comanche enemy. For being in sight of the two nations, they may be reprimanded peacefully, or in case they take up arms, war may be made. This was his opinion. He signs it with me and my secretary of government and war.

[*Marginal note:* Opinion of Ayudante Salvador de Santistevan.] Ayudante Salvador de Santistevan, who is adjutant in service, said, having informed himself of the context of the letters of the reverend father missionaries and that of the alcalde mayor of the valley of Taos and of the news provided by that of the jurisdiction of Cochití, he is of the opinion that war be declared on the two nations, Utes and Comanches. For they are of great prejudice to this kingdom with their hostilities which they have committed while at peace. It can be expected that they will continue if they are not controlled. He did not sign because he did not know how. I, the governor, signed it with my secretary of government and war.

[*Marginal note:* Opinion of Juan de Archibeque.] Juan de Archibèque, settler of this said villa who has served his majesty for twenty-

106

five years, says that it is very just that war be made against the Ute and Comanche because it is evident that for more than seven or eight years they have come to steal horses and rob herds and run away with the goods in the trade which this kingdom has with the Apaches of El Cuartelejo. Since they have committed three murders, the present is very opportune to make war upon them; the least that can be done. This is his opinion which he signs with me and my secretary.

[*Marginal note:* Opinion of Captain Thomas Olguin.] Captain Thomas Olguin, who has been captain of this presidial fort and has served his majesty in this kingdom for thirty years, says that having understood the above mentioned letters of the reverend fathers ministers and of the alcalde mayor of the pueblo of Taos and the account given by the alcalde mayor of Cochití, it seems expedient that the armed forces go out to repress the boldness and wickedness of the two nations, Ute and Comanche. These are to be understood as one with respect to their speaking a language and going about together, and to be punished as one nation. For if they are not punished and the forces do not go out for defense, very promptly, it is feared that they may do some considerable injury, since the number of Indians which appears to have come to Cochití intimates that they may be coming to an engagement of importance and not simply to cause the deaths which they have caused. These two nations are those which under the name of peace have been plundering this kingdom. This is his opinion. He signs it with me and my secretary.

[*Marginal note:* Opinion of Captain Francisco Casados.] Captain Francisco Casados, a settler of this villa, having served his majesty in this kingdom for twenty-five years, said that, having seen and understood the letters of the reverend father minister missionaries, Fray Juan de la Cruz and Fray Manuel de Sopesta, that of the alcalde mayor of Taos, the report which the alcalde mayor of the jurisdiction of Cochití made verbally, the one substantiating the other with regard to what was done by the Indians of the Ute nation. Therefrom it ought to be assumed that it is coöperating with that of the Comanche, because they are allied with one another. He is of the opinion that the armed forces should be sent against them, particularly when they have declared themselves as enemies and have made known the false peace which they have held, committing under it robberies which have been made known. Now, their insolence is such that they have reached as far as the center of this custody in increased numbers to commit injuries. It is not fit that they be remonstrated with in a matter so well verified,

107

but that war be made upon them and they should be made to experience the rigor of the armed forces. This will be the only means of restraining the others and the rest who are near. This is his opinion which he signs.

[*Marginal note:* Opinion of Adjutant-General Joseph Dominguez.] Adjutant-general of the kingdom, Joseph Domínguez, who has served his majesty in this kingdom for thirty-seven years, said that his opinion is that war should be made upon the two nations, Ute and Comanche, because they have declared themselves enemies on this occasion as their act manifests. War should be declared without waiting for them to commit any attack. Since their people are coming in numbers to the old pueblo of Cochití, the trail of whom he saw and recognized, it is apparent that they are having a great meeting and are undertaking to commit some injury. The armed forces should be hidden and spies dispatched to see whether an attack could be made upon them, as a result of which they would be punished for this insolence. This is his opinion and he signs it with me and my secretary of government and war.

[*Marginal note:* Opinion of Captain Diego de Arias.] Captain Diego de Arias de Quiros, a settler of this villa, who has served his majesty in this kingdom for thirty-four years, said that he is of the opinion that if the armed forces should set out at once, the Ute and Comanche nations could be punished, since they deserve it so much for what they have done in the way of atrocities they have committed. This he gives as his opinion and belief which he signs with me and my secretary of government and war.

[*Marginal note:* Opinion of Lieutenant of the Company, Franco Montes Vijil.] The lieutenant of this presidial company, Francisco Montes Vijil, who has served his majesty for twenty-five years, said that, having understood the context of the letters which were read to him, and in virtue of the order of the señor governor and captain-general, he agrees entirely with the opinion which the sergeant of the company, Juan de la Mora Pineda, gave in this council. This is his opinion and he signs it with my secretary of government and war.

[*Marginal note:* Opinion of the Sergeant-Major of the Kingdom.] The sergeant-major of the kingdom, Don Alphonsso Rael de Aguilar, who has served his majesty for thirty-seven years, said that he has been informed of the letters of the reverend father minister missionaries, the alcalde mayor of the pueblo of Taos, and the report which that of the jurisdiction of Cochití made, together with the decree which

108

in virtue of them, the governor and captain-general of this kingdom provided. With his great zeal for the service of his majesty, holding the war justified for the motives and reasons which these letters set forth, he commanded this council of war held for the great success of the undertaking. He is of the feeling that war should be declared on the said enemies, the barbarous Comanches and Utes, because of the grave injuries, murders, and robberies which they have committed without making any remonstrance with them. This is his opinion and he signs it with me and my secretary of government and war.

[*Marginal note:* Opinion of the Captain of the Presidial Company.] Captain Don Joseph de Tagle Villegas, who is captain in active service with the company of this presidial fort, said that he agrees with the opinion given by Captain Francisco Casados. In it he finds stipulated all the necessary requisites so that war may be made on the enemies justly. He gave this as his opinion and belief. He signs it with me and my secretary of government and war.

[*Marginal note:* Opinion of the Lieutenant-General of the Kingdom, Don Pedro Villasur.] The lieutenant-general of the kingdom, Don Pedro de Villasur, said that, having informed himself of the context of the letters of the reverend father missionaries, it appears from them that those of the Ute nation have declared themselves as enemies without reason, for which they may now be held. Besides, they have committed robberies under the artful peace they have maintained. He is of the feeling that war should be declared and that the armed forces should set out to punish their insolence. In no way is this opposed to that which his majesty (may God guard him) has provided for in repeated orders and in this council of war. This is his opinion which he signs with me and my secretary of government and war.

The señor governor and captain-general of this said kingdom, Don Antonio Balverde Cosio, has seen the opinions of this council. The enemies' murderous attacks and robberies on the frontiers of this kingdom are well known and their wickedness proved with which they are acting. It appears to all, since their own lands are more than two hundred leagues away from this kingdom, that according to the reports they are coming to attack us on sight. It is evident that they have the deliberate intent of causing what damage they may be able and of provoking these arms. To tolerate them longer would aid them in the future on the rest of the frontiers. On this account, I concur with the opinions that war should be made upon them, to take place when convenient, that they may be driven to their lands, and these frontiers

109

freed. This was the opinion of his lordship. He signs it before me, Captain Miguel Thenorio de Alva, with the rest of those mentioned in this council.

Nicolas Ortiz; Sebastian Martin; Miguel Joseph de la Bega y Coca; Xptobal Torres; Ygnacio de Roibal; Thomas Olguin; Juan de Mittas; Joseph Truxillo; Bernardo Casillas; Xptobal Serna; Don Franco Joseph Bueno de Bohorques y Corauesa; Juan de Archivèque; Franco Lorenzo de Casados; Diego Arias de Equiros; Alphonsso Rael de Aguilar; Joseph Domínguez; Franco Montes Vijil; Joseph de Tagle Villegas; D. Pedro de Villasur; D. Antto Balverde Cossio [all with rubrics].

Before me

Miguel Thenorio de Alba [rubric]

Secretary of Government and War.

VII. Diary of the Campaign of Governor Antonio de Valverde Against the Ute and Comanche Indians, 1719[50]

No. 510.

The diary and itinerary which General Don Antonio Valverde Cosio, governor and captain-general of this kingdom and provinces of New Mexico,[51] made on the campaign which he carried out against the Ute and Comanche nations because of the hostilities, murders, and robberies they have made upon this realm. For the solution of this, a council of war was held of the military heads of the royal presidio and the experienced settlers of the villa of Santa Fé.[52] The decision was that the military forces should set out to curb the boldness of the enemy. This the governor did execute. [Marginal note: General Valverde, September 15, 1719.]

On the fifteenth of September, 1719, he set out from this villa of Santa Fé for the valley and pueblo of Taos, twenty leagues distant, which he designated as the mustering point. Having arrived at Taos with the Reverend Father Fray Juan del Pino, devout friar of our Father San Francisco and missionary minister in the pueblo of Pecos, who was going on the campaign as chaplain. The governor on the nineteenth of the month, after hearing mass, checked the roll of the military forces, horses and munitions, and the troops who were ready for this campaign in the [torn out] and following manner: sixty presidial soldiers of the villa of Santa Fé answered the roll call with their arms, horses, and munitions; and afterwards, before the governor,

110

forty-five settlers and volunteers, who offered voluntarily to serve his majesty on this campaign, answered the roll.[53] To these, on account of the impoverished condition of some, it was necessary to supply powder and balls and distribute among them ten leather jackets, which his lordship had brought and had made. He ordered divided among them a quantity of pinole, and likewise seventy-five horses and mules, all his own. After this had been done, he had the settlers assembled and addressed them, graciously thanking them in the name of his majesty for having volunteered like loyal vassals. This made them all happy and pleased, for they were wishing that an occasion would offer itself in which they could manifest their good will. They applauded the governor for his solicitude and the kind thoughtfulness with which he looked after them. He assured them that they would suffer no need, as he would supply them with the provisions and the other essential things which he was carrying, as soon as he noticed they were wanting. Likewise there answered the roll because [torn out] and thirty natives of [torn out] prepared for war with their arms. They numbered some six hundred with as many horses. Of these the camp was composed, together with the soldiers and settlers, the larger number being presidials, as the Indians were numbered apart.[54]

On the twentieth of the said month of September, after hearing mass, the governor and command set out from the valley of Taos in prosecution of his journey. They arrived at the spot which they call La Ciéneguilla,[55] distant eight leagues through painful mountain trails, forest, and underbrush. The march was attended with much suffering, which obliged the soldiers to divide the horseherd into groups in order to drive it. In this place captain-major of the war, Joseph Naranjo, who has his rank from the superior government, was waiting in accordance with the order that had been given him. He had gone on with some natives with whom he joined the command.

Today, the twenty-first of the month, after mass was heard in this place of La Ciéneguilla, because it was the day of the Apostle St. Matthew, the command set out for the region of the stream of San Joseph, the name which his lordship gave it. It is distant some seven leagues of very difficult travel through heavy timber. After the descent of an extensive slope which appears to be some two and a half leagues long, there are found at intervals many stone landmarks placed by the heathen Indians of the Apache tribe so that they may not lose themselves. Before reaching this place, there is a small lake with water, and opposite at a distance of a league, there are some red hills with

111

many outcroppings of ore, apparently mineralized. The river at this spot of San Joseph is very pleasant and wooded.[56]

At about one-half league away, Ensign Bernardo Casillas, a member of the expedition who had been sent off by order of the governor, found a small adobe house where there were some pagan Apaches, who had sown and reaped their maize-fields.[57] As soon as these Apaches learned of the coming of the Spaniards, they came to see the governor, who received them very kindly and gave them tobacco and something to eat. The pagans, after giving many signs of pleasure, said that their enemies, the Comanches, were persecuting and killing their kinsmen and others of their nation. They declared this through the interpreters, captain of war, Joseph Naranjo, and Don Gerónimo, an Indian of the Taos tribe, both of whom were well versed in the Apache tongue. The señor governor, having heard their story through the two interpreters, told them that his journey [torn out] and that he had set out personally to punish these nations for their infidelity and wickedness, for, under the guise of peace they had made attacks, committed murders and robberies. Whereupon the entire camp which was listening became excited. All the Apaches were very happy and appreciative of the benefit they were accorded of being safe in their lands. Thus they returned home with their wives.

This same day about four o'clock in the afternoon a troop of heathen Apaches arrived from the ranchería of La Jicarilla. An old Indian woman on horseback said that their kinsmen had given them word that the governor had come and that they were coming to put themselves at his service. Having come into his presence, they dismounted at a distance of some fifteen steps. Their chief carried as a standard a most holy cross, at the foot of which was an engraved parchment, whereon there was an image of Mary, our most holy Lady, in adoration of the rosary. The chief, bearing in his hand so sovereign a standard without any injury whatsoever, gave it to the governor and the reverend father chaplain to kiss, who did this with all veneration, and to the soldiers and settlers who had gathered about at the news. After this incident had passed, touching as it was, because they all adored on their knees this most holy wooden symbol of our redemption, the governor welcomed the chief and all the rest. Having seated themselves, the Indians said through the interpreters, already mentioned, that they were very sad and discouraged because of the repeated attacks which their enemies, the Utes and Comanches, make upon them. These had killed many of their nation and carried off their

112

women and children captives until they now no longer knew where to go to live in safety. Their greatest sorrow was that, since they had carefully wrapped up and guarded this image of the most holy Mary, they had found on opening it three drops of blood. For this reason they feared something was going to happen to them. Upon hearing this with all attention and kindness, his lordship told them they should not be disconsolate, and that they should keep this lady in their hearts, being certain that if they truly called upon her and reduced themselves to the fold of the Church [torn out] they might attain victory. From [torn out] and that the señor governor was setting out in person on a campaign to look for the Comanche enemy to punish and make war upon them. The blood, he explained, which they said the most holy Lady had, signified that they should abandon their heathen and barbarous life in which they lived and make Christians of themselves. If they should decide upon doing this, she would aid and assist them in everything for their welfare and being. He set before them, with Catholic and Christian zeal, other effective arguments so that by this means their reduction could be achieved. The Apache chief with all the rest who accompanied him said that the governor was their father whom they loved a great deal since he spoke courteously to them, and was going to defend them. If his lordship should wish it, he continued, they would receive the water of holy baptism, upon which Valverde rejoiced greatly. The governor had chocolate given to them all and to the settlers who were there, and tobacco distributed among the heathens. He commanded that if they had need of anything, they should let it be known so that they could be helped immediately. They answered that they needed nothing. After which the heathen went away quite satisfied, offering to accompany the governor on the campaign.

On the twenty-second of the present month of September the señor governor set out with all his followers from the region and river of San Joseph. After marching a distance of three leagues over level ground, they arrived on the river the Apaches call La Flecha;[58] the governor called it Nuestra Señora del Rosario.[59] On it they found some fields of maize, frijoles, and squashes which the Apaches had planted. Moreover, as soon as the fields were noticed, the governor gave the order that under no circumstances should anything be seized, so that the military chiefs proceeded with great care.

Above on the river at the distance of an arquebus shot, a house of adobe was found where some Apaches were living with their women

113

and children. On the flat roof of the house there was erected a most holy cross, about a yard in height. Farther up the river eight other houses were found where some families of the Apaches dwelt.[60]

While the governor was eating with the reverend father chaplain and other military chiefs of the presidio of the villa of Santa Fé, an Apache chief called Carlana [torn out] the Sierra Blanca[61] arrived and in his company three others. As soon as they were before his lordship, Chief Carlana said in a clear voice, *"Ave Maria,"* and his lordship and the above mentioned ones responded, *"Sin Pecado Concevida."* The governor ordered him to dismount, and he and the rest having done so, his lordship gave him the plate of boiled meat and vegetables from which he was eating. After Carlana had taken it he ate the mutton and left the chicken, which surprised all. After he had eaten, the governor asked him through the interpreters what he was doing and why he had come. To this he answered that he had come fleeing from his country, the Sierra Blanca,[62] with half of his people to get the help of the Apaches of La Jicarilla. The rest of his people, he said, had gone for protection farther into a land of Apaches whom Chief Flaco[63] governed, because of the continual war that the Ute and Comanche enemy made upon them. Although, he continued, he had news that the governor was coming with the Spaniards, he had not believed it entirely because no governor had ever entered the land nor had sent any of his captains to his country.[64] In order to verify it he had ascended a high hill, looked towards the open country and made out the dust. This was the reason of his coming, and he was greatly delighted because he had seen the governor.

After the governor had pleased and gratified him with a present, he told him also that the Ute and Comanche enemies had done great damage among the settlements of this kingdom, causing deaths and robberies. This had moved him to go out on a campaign and hunt the enemy to punish their wickedness and let them experience the rigor of the arms of our king and lord, Philip V (may God protect him). After the Apache chief, Carlana, had been informed of this, he said that he was very pleased that the said señor was going to make war upon them and that all his people would go with them and serve as guides for the camp, showing them the best spots and springs so that they could reach the unknown land of the Ute and Comanche enemy. These would be recognized because [torn out] nation. The señor governor [torn out] and entertained them all that he could. Then, having said good-bye, they went away greatly contented.

114

On the twenty-third of the month the governor with his camp set out from the river called Nuestra Señora del Rosario in prosecution of his journey and camped at a distance of two leagues on a small river where the Apache ranchers of La Jicarilla were living. Their chief is the one whom they call El Coxo [who] on this occasion was absent because he had gone to the Navajo province.[65] This news his two sons gave, who, as soon as they had tidings of the arrival of the governor, came out with the rest of their people to see him. He received them with his accustomed kindness, entertained, fed them and gave them tobacco. These said that on the very site and spot where the camp was placed, the Comanche and Ute enemies had attacked a ranchería of their nation, causing sixty deaths, carrying off sixty-four women and children, burning and destroying a little house in the shape of a tower which was there, and even the heaps of maize. There were none of their possessions that were not destroyed. For this reason, they had deserted that locality a year ago and had gone up the river to live. Since that had happened they were sad and filled with misgivings and fear that the enemy might return and finish them entirely. Upon hearing this, the governor consoled them with explanations and kind words, telling them that he had already set out on a campaign to punish this nation which had caused such great damage to all of them. They received this news with much exulting.

On this day, about three in the afternoon, the señor governor mounted his horse in company with the reverend father chaplain, the captain of the presidio, Don Joseph de Tagle Villegas, his lieutenant, Francisco Montes Vijil, and some soldiers and, marching up the river a distance of a league and a half, found seven terraced houses where some Apaches lodged. They welcomed the señor governor with great rejoicing. At the same time it was observed that many women and children, a mob of heathens who heard the bustle and confusion at the arrival of the governor, fled to the hills. It was seen that they had already gathered their crops of corn because they had placed it in the shape of a wall about a half a yard high. Many rows of the same [torn out] abundance, from which it was evident that the land is very fertile. On it they have many ditches and canals in order to irrigate their fields. Some had not finished harvesting and there was much corn in heaps not yet husked.[66] In this spot and region where the chief, Carlana, was domiciled there were counted twenty-seven tipis. The Indians showed great hospitality because they gave the soldiers many ears of green corn. On this occasion, Chief Carlana

115

himself offered to go with all his people on the campaign, repeating the proposal which he had made previously; the Apaches of La Jicarilla did the same. For this the governor showed his gratitude and returned to his camp.

On the twenty-fourth of the month the señor governor set out, continuing his journey, and having marched eight leagues arrived at an arroyo which the Apaches called the Río Colorado.[67] His lordship gave it the name of Nuestra Señora de la Soledad. It has very little water but is lined with considerable timber. A little while after he had arrived there, twenty Apaches of those that live on the river which they call La Flecha appeared and joined the expedition for the campaign. They said that the Comanche enemies had attacked two houses which were over there and had burned the people who were living in them.

On the twenty-fifth of the month the said señor governor with all his camp left the spot and river of La Soledad and marched about nine leagues. He crossed a mountain ridge with so many forests, ravines, canyons, and narrow places that it was necessary that day to divide the cavalry into ten groups to get it over such a difficult trail. In this the soldiers worked considerably in order not to lose many beasts. With which care and divine favor intervening, they succeeded in bringing the horseherd safely as far as the Río de las Animas, a name his lordship gave it, where the camp was placed thankfully, because the spot was pleasing.[68] The river was lined with luxuriant foliage and had considerable good water. The many poplars and elders found furnished a supply of wood with which they could warm themselves because they suffered this day from great cold, for the north wind blew with such biting sharpness all had arrived on the spot numb.

The morning of the twenty-sixth of the said month dawned overcast in all directions. So much snow had fallen that the said governor had to order [illegible] them not to leave the spot.

The twenty-seventh of the month dawned as the preceding day; with much more snow and rain. The señor governor, with the wisdom of experience, commanded that the horseherd should not be collected until the weather cleared up. He distributed this day [torn out] pinole and mutton, giving it to the ones who were sick from an attack of an herb called ivy, caused strangely by lying down upon it or being near it. Those affected swelled up. He ordered Antonio Durán Armijo, a barber by trade who had some knowledge of blood letting, to attend and assist them and that whatever might be necessary

116

should be asked for, and his lordship with his charitable zeal would order it be done.

On this day about ten o'clock in the morning Chief Carlana, the Apache chief of the Sierra Blanca, arrived in camp with sixty-nine Apaches of his ranchería and tribe. They circled the camp on their horses, jubilantly singing and shouting. In the evening these same messengers danced according to their custom, some covered with red and others with white paint. They came to the tent of the said governor, who received them with great kindness. After they had danced for a good part of the night, he ordered them entertained and feasted.

On the twenty-eighth of the month, the weather having cleared, the camp set out from the above mentioned spot and river. After marching some six leagues, they arrived on an arroyo with little water but much timber, where the camp was supplied with wood. On this journey they caught many deer so that the Indians were sufficiently provisioned with good fat meat. While the command was camped in this spot, Chief Carlana of the Apache nation came to the tent of the governor about four o'clock in the afternoon with seven young braves of his ranchería, all armed with arrows, machetes, and oval leather shields. By means of the interpreters, he told the governor that now was the time to send out spies to reconnoiter the regions in which their enemies, the Utes and Comanches, were. To this the governor responded that it seemed very wise, and after ordering them to be given chocolate and tobacco, he sent them off, impressing upon them the care and vigilance they ought to exercise in this affair in order to bring about the success and happy outcome of this campaign. The governor blessed the spot.

According to the order he gave to Ensign Torres and Captain Luís Garzía, in whose care the Indian pueblo people had come, the horse-herd that the natives were bringing was counted. When done, six hundred and eighty beasts were found. These horses were never mixed in the number or body of the horseherd of the presidio and settlers.

The twenty-ninth day of the month, on which is celebrated the festivity of the glorious archangel San Miguel. After mass was said, to which the whole camp listened, they set out from this locality. Having crossed the river, they arrived at another more pleasant, with a grove of plum trees, many willows and many wild grapes, from which vinegar was made. In the woods some deer were caught by the Indians who, surrounding them, drove them into the camp, at which there was great glee and shouting. The journey this day had been five

117

leagues up to their arrival on the river, which the señor governor named the San Miguel. It has plenty of good water and runs through a very broad and pleasing valley. A number of deer were caught, for many abound in this valley, thus verifying what the Apaches had said on many occasions, namely, that there was good hunting here. But from fear of the Utes, they are fleeing from their hunting grounds, which those of their nation have, where they were maintaining themselves and securing many pelts.

On the thirtieth of this month of September, the governor in prosecution of their journey moved the camp from this spot on the San Miguel River a distance of two leagues. They always followed the route to the north, leaving a high sierra on the west, with much level ground stretching towards the east,[69] On the road they hunted many deer, with which the camp was supplied. A halt was made on the river, where they arrived at ten o'clock under the guidance of the Apache chief, Carlana. In this region, for greater protection, the said señor governor ordered four squads of settlers formed as a guard, in whose custody the camp would be during the night. For this purpose, he named four leaders under the orders of Sergeant-Major Don Alonso Real de Aguilar of this kingdom. In the camp there were seven soldiers and some settlers considerably ill from the evil effects of the ivy mentioned above, for stepping on it or passing near it causes such great discomfort that their bodies swell, they appear hydropical, and the skin peels off. The most harm is done to the genital organs. From this sickness they suffered for some time when relief was found by chewing chocolate and then applying and rubbing the saliva on the parts. This remedy, accidentally discovered by Francisco Casadas whose face had swollen, relieved him to a great degree. The rest of the sick followed his example.

Today the señor governor ordered Salvador de Anaya, the head of the squad, to count the horses which the Apache Indians, who had volunteered as guides on the journey, were bringing. One hundred and three were found. The night before, the Apache chief, Carlana, sent out four spies of his nation to examine the country and to find out if there were any tracks of the Comanche enemies. When the governor, coming in the vanguard with the presidial soldiers, arrived at the aforementioned spot, the same four spies were seen coming towards us with their eyes on the ground as if they were trailing. Realizing this, the governor commanded a halt, ordering that no one should move on because the trail ought not to be effaced. Captain

118

Joseph Naranjo, Don Gerónimo, the Taos Indian, and Chief Carlana went to where the spies were. The latter said that they were following five trails of the enemy who had come to the site of the apachería of chief Carlana, who had fled with his people so that they might not be killed.[70] Not having found where they fled, the said five enemies had returned from whence they had come, having lost hope of finding Chief Carlana's apachería. This was verified by the information given through the interpreters to the governor. He ordered the command to camp in this place.

While here, about four o'clock in the afternoon, a shout was heard at which the whole force became excited. Three Apaches were seen coming towards the camp. The Corporal Antonio Tafoya, with the soldiers of his squad, went out to meet them and recognized them to be the spies who had gone out on the twenty-eighth of the present month. They were received by those of their tribe with great rejoicing. They came in surrounded by the squad; as soon as they arrived the Indians closed in about them. The Christian Indians tried to go where the latter were, but the governor would not allow it, but kept them alone.

In order to deliver the report which they were bringing, Chief Carlana shortly came together with the interpreters, the three spies and others of his tribe to the tent of his lordship, who was awaiting them. Received with great affection, they said that after they had set out as they were ordered, to spy on their enemies, they found very fresh tracks of three of these. They followed this trail, always hiding themselves in the thickets, until they made them out very close, but they had not followed further to overtake them in order not to be perceived. They had returned to give this news, for it was a sign of being very near the enemies' rancherías.[71] It would now be necessary for the camp to draw near the mountains and march by night to hide until the attack at daybreak. At this news all the settlers gathered around the tent of the governor. He ordered them seated and chocolate brought to them. Considerable tobacco was given to the Apaches and the interpreters, for this is the best gift that can be made to them. After manifesting his great generosity, together with that of his ardent devotion to the most holy Mary of the Rosary to whom he is devoted, for it was the eve of her day, he mortified himself considerably by omitting the salute to prevent the noise of the arquebuses and military instruments. At their report and the echo the enemy would fly, as possibly some were close to the camp, since they were already in the enemy's

119

country and hunting grounds. In order to avoid difficulties and be able to travel at night, the governor ordered the sheep that were being driven killed and dressed, to be carried upon the pack animals.

On the first day of October of this year, after hearing mass, the señor governor, with all of the camp and the Reverend Father Chaplain Fray Juan del Pino, prayed with great zeal to the Holy Mary of the Rosary. This was the day on which by her intercession her most holy Son granted that celebrated victory which to all Christendom has been, is, and will be one of great rejoicing. After the governor and the reverend father chaplain had breakfasted with some persons and settlers whom he wished to entertain to express the joy he had on that day, they were served some very good glasses of wine that he brought prepared beforehand for whatever should occur. All joyfully toasted his health.

The command set out on the road and, having marched on this day four leagues over level ground, keeping the route to the north, arrived at a river which the governor called Santo Domingo; a very rocky stream between the mountains. In order to avoid difficulty for the next day, he ordered the camp to cross to the other side; this was done with great inconvenience. In order that the mules which were carrying the provisions should not fall, the governor ordered that they be taken across on the right; this movement succeeded well, as the stream was crossed without damage and the camp set up on that side.

After drinking some chocolate, the governor mounted his horse and with Lieutenant-Captain Francisco Montes Vijil again crossed the stream, as all the horseherd had not yet crossed and had not drunk, because of the formation of both banks of the river as already mentioned. In order that the horseherd might drink, the governor ordered it divided into many little groups. In this manner, breaking up the formation it had, the horseherd was able to drink, though with great difficulty. The governor assisted personally with this, as otherwise a great number of beasts would have been endangered on the precipices and rocks.

Today the señor governor had news that one of the settlers in camp, Christóbal Rodarte, was dangerously ill, so that it was necessary to administer the sacrament of penitence to him. The governor ordered that they should bring him to his tent for the best attention and care. This was done. Had not the governor exercised this mercy toward this poor man, giving him medicines that appeared proper for his case (these medicines and others he carried as a precaution) which were

120

administered to him, there is no doubt but that he would have died. Our Lord will reward him for this as for all the rest of the things that he was doing on such an extensive journey through unknown regions. Likewise, the governor ordered the sergeant-major, Don Alejandro Rael de Aguilar, to bring together all the settlers in order to provision them. This was done. After being supplied as ordered, the settlers said that God, our Lord, would reward the governor, for they were already in considerable need, having sustained themselves the day before with nothing but meat from the deer which they had caught, and that no other governor of the past had done as much. They then went away exceedingly pleased by his fine manner and his mode of treating them, saying God grant that he be perpetuated in the governorship. They were grateful for so many favors that they went to give him their thanks.

On the second of October, the governor with all his camp set out from this river of Santo Domingo. Having marched some four leagues all over level ground, the route always to the north, and the river on the left hand, they came to where another, which comes down from the north with more copious clear water, joins it. At the union of both streams they put up the camp at about the middle of the day. The señor governor called this river the San Lorenzo. It has many plums, which though wild are of fine flavor and taste. With these and many very delicious wild grapes the people satisfied themselves. It was leafy here and the command took a nap, enjoying the coolness and shade of the many poplars and deep woods. While they were in this happy state, a bear came out of the thicket and threw the entire camp into an uproar. The people took great delight in teasing it for some time until they killed it.

On this day the señor governor took advantage of his many experiences in military affairs in this country, as he had been reared from a tender age in its service, and ordered the army to set out at sunset from this spot, and march during the night in order to avoid the great deal of dust that was made, as this could be a means by which the enemy might learn that they were being followed. After setting out they marched about two leagues to a river they call Chiopo, to which the governor gave the name of San Antonio. It is an admirable stream much resembling the Del Norte because of its large volume of water and broad, spacious meadows, filled with poplars.[72] On its banks camp was set up at about ten o'clock at night. At about three or four o'clock in the morning three Apaches of the spies who set out

121

from the spot of the sacrament, arrived with the news that on the road, of the many which go to and fro from Santa Fé and its settlements, which goes to the Teguas [Tiguas] they found that three Comanche and Ute enemies had with them twenty beasts and a colt, whose trail led straight to their land and ranchería.[73] They themselves returned in order to communicate the news they had. At this very hour Chief Carlana sent out other spies whom he ordered to report immediately and without delay what they discovered.

On the third of October, the governor set out with the camp from this river San Antonio and after marching over level ground some four leagues, arrived at a very pleasant river with many large poplars and other graceful trees. To this river his lordship gave the name of San Francisco. Here they hunted and caught many deer and a lot of good fat prairie hens with which they made very delicious tamales. After recognizing that the river did not have good watering places for the horses to drink, the governor mounted his horse and with some of his military chiefs went out to find where they could do this more favorably. This having succeeded, the horseherd was divided into groups and drank until satisfied. Afterwards, the governor returned to his tent, where the Reverend Father Fray Juan del Pino was.

He wished to entertain him, as he did. They celebrated together with the military chiefs the eve of the glorious patriarch San Francisco, having ordered out a small keg of rich spirituous brandy made at the Pass of the Río del Norte of the governor's own vintage. It was of such good flavor, taste and quality and though vinted without the carefulness with which other wines are made, that that of Castile does not surpass it. The health of the reverend father chaplain was toasted in celebration of his patriarch. This they did, both the governor and the others who were present, wishing each other fortune with pleasure and concord.

The señor governor, having received news that the Apaches had found a horse which was believed to belong to their enemies, had called the Apache and Chief Carlana to learn and investigate the truth, so that through the interpreters the latter should tell what it meant. Having demanded of him why he had not given an explanation of the horse that had been found, he answered that when the enemies were attacking the Apaches of La Jicarilla, they had left there that horse which they had taken from them. Then the governor ordered the horse returned [to the Jicarilla] and gave them pinole and tobacco.

122

On the fourth of the month of October, the señor governor set out with all his camp from this spot and river of San Francisco. After mass was heard and after the governor and the father chaplain and officers of war had breakfasted, his lordship ordered a cask of wine which had been made at the pass to be brought out. With it they all drank to the health of the governor and of the chaplain, and celebrated the saint's day of San Francisco. To this the chaplain, who had behaved on this campaign like a real true son of such a good father, responded with propriety and urbanity. The governor himself so declared in toasting his saint's day, with appropriate actions both as to what has been referred to, as well as in the great pleasure he had in regaling them under the circumstances with the best rich bread and melon preserves he carried for such an occasion to entertain the reverend father chaplain and himself.

The expedition having set out as said above, from this locality, crossed the river, the route to the north, and went along its meadows for four leagues over level ground. While so marching they recognized two tracks of some of their enemies, which were followed a considerable distance. For this reason his lordship ordered the camp to stop on the same Río San Francisco, giving to the place the name of San Francisco. It is a very cheerful spot, with a beautiful view and excellent springs and many thick poplar groves. On the left hand, about three leagues away, there is a range of mountains and on the right, a very extensive plain in the distance.

On this road today many deer and prairie chickens which moved about in flocks were caught to such an extent that nowhere else were more caught because of their abundance in this region. The governor hunted deer and chicken. Having been given news that one of the settlers was very sick with a pain in his stomach, the governor ordered him called to his tent and a cup of tea given him to strengthen him. This made him better, and he sent him something to eat every day, for which he was very thankful. On this day a mountain lion and a wildcat were killed. At about sunset some Indians came in, running from a bear which plunged into the middle of the camp, throwing the people into confusion. With great shouting and uproar, they killed him with many spear thrusts and arrows. His strength and size were so formidable that the governor was impelled to go with the chaplain to view it.

On the fifth of the present month, the señor governor and his command left this site of San Onofre and River of San Francisco, keeping

123

it always on the left hand and the mountain ridge also.[74] Having traveled two short leagues, the governor commanded the expedition to stop because Chief Carlana said that in the region where they were to spend the night there was but little water. The governor, accordingly, guided by experience, ordered a halt so that the horseherd might drink. The place where we rested is very pleasing, with large groves of plum trees and cherries, so that the soldiers gathered considerable. After the siesta was over and the horseherd brought in, the governor ordered the march to proceed, still keeping the range of mountains on his left hand. Having traveled some four leagues, keeping the route always to the north and following a dry creek on his left hand, a short distance opposite the brook, they made camp, on a spring which the governor called Nuestra Señora de Dolores. It was mountainous all around. Plum trees, roses of Alexandria, and a great deal of rockrose were found. There was sufficient water for the people, and they dexterously gave the horses, that came saddled, water they poured out in containers.

On the sixth of the present month of October, the señor governor and all his camp left this spring of Nuestra Señora de Dolores and marched over level land and through many good pastures because it was grassy. On the road to the left was a summit sloping to the east heavily wooded with pines.[75] Having traveled some six leagues, they arrived at a spring which had considerable water. There the camp was put up and the governor called it Nuestra Señora del Carmen. On this day before the halt a bear was met. It was larger than the preceding ones, for its size and height were probably greater than that of a donkey. One of the soldiers went out and put a spear into him up to the middle of the shaft. The brute, turning around, seized the lance and grasped the horse by the hocks. At the same time another soldier went to the rescue and gave the bear another spear thrust. The bear, seizing the horse by the tail, held him down and clawing viciously, tore a piece of flesh off the rump. Having tied the bear up finally, they finished killing him. The soldiers who were bringing up the rear guard of the cavalry met a female and two cubs, which they also killed.

On the seventh of this month of October, the señor governor with the command set out from the spring named Señora del Carmen and, having journeyed some seven good leagues bearing toward the east, they arrived at a canyon in which there were many sandy creeks.[76] The señor governor called it Santa Rosa. It has many good pastures.

The weather this day was very distressing. From the spot called Señora del Carmen, two leagues were marched over a flat land among many pine trees. They went down to the canyon and creeks and upon entering therein they met some herds of buffalo, so that the whole camp was provided with meat. His lordship went hunting and on this occasion more than twelve head were killed. Farther down a spring was found from which a little pond was formed. The chaplain called it San Ignacio, and as soon as the camp was made on this spot and creeks, Chief Carlana went to examine some tracks he had seen. He found that their enemies, the Utes and Comanches, had ranched on that spot. He recognized that they had set up more than sixty tents, and following the trail along the road by which they set out, he found at a little distance the track of the tent poles which they were dragging along. He reported this information to the governor, who appreciated it greatly and rewarded him with meat and flour. This made him very happy. Along the shoulder of a hill close by, there was found a herd of bison which, according to appearances, must have numbered more than two hundred head. The governor ordered that it should not be hunted, since the enemy might hear it if it were frightened. Because there was no wood in this spot, a cook fire was made with buffalo chips, of which there was an abundance. On this day a soldier ran down a buffalo, but when he was about to spear it, the animal turned around with such speed that he drove the lance through the flank.

On the eighth of this aforesaid month, after hearing mass, the governor with his command left this spot and marched five leagues. The day was unpleasant, being cold. Their route was to the south. They set up camp in an arroyo with many poplar trees. Since it was in a sandy place, the water that was found did not run and the arroyo was dry. In this spot the trail was found where the enemy had camped; some eighty ranchos with their tents were counted. The trail was observed to be fresh, as the enemy had gone away but a few days previously leaving many heaps of wood. To this spot and dry creek, the governor gave the name of Santa Efijenia. On this day, the sky began to cloud and sleet began to fall.

On the ninth of the month, the morning dawned with the same storm. For this reason the camp remained in the same place.

On the tenth the weather cleared, and although the north wind was very cold, they raised camp from this spot and marched some six leagues, wholly along the river; the banks of which were covered with many poplars. The route was northward. On the road some signs were found where the Ute and Comanche enemies had camped. The camp was placed on a creek which had a great deal of marsh grass. The señor governor called the marsh San Phelipe de Jesús. Along it a short distance away they found many herds of buffalo, of which the Christian Indians and the heathen Apaches killed about fifteen head. This same day about four in the afternoon, the governor ordered Captain Alonso Rael and Ensign Christóbal Tafoya to go out separately with six soldiers and drive a herd of buffalo toward the camp. The señor governor went out to watch the affair. In this way they succeeded in provisioning the camp with meat. At sunset the señor governor ordered the Apache chief Carlana called and, when he was in his presence, told him through the medium of the interpreters, with his accustomed kindness, that it seemed to him a wise thing to send out some spies to the east and south in order to ascertain the whereabouts of the enemy so that they might not be left in the rear. For, he said, he had a great desire to punish their insolence so that they might experience the rigor of the arms of the Spaniards, whose kindness and good nature they had abused up to this time. Chief Carlana agreed to this. It was decided that in order better to bolster up the fidelity of the Apaches two of his nation should go with four outside Indians, two of the pueblo of Taos and two of those from the Picuríes. All these were quite experienced because of the long time that they wandered among the heathens, for as apostates they fled during the rebellion which they had. He made them a long speech, saying that they should not omit any circumstances looking towards the attainment of the good object for which they were dispatched. The señor governor noticed that Chief Carlana had not gone out to get meat on account of the great irritation he felt in not having found the enemy whom he desired punished if a good opportunity should present itself. He wanted the enemy restrained from the attacks they were making each day on his rancherías, killing many and capturing their women and children. The señor governor consoled him with gentle words designed for that purpose and presented him with a quantity of meat, tobacco, and pinole, with which he went off very pleased.

On the eleventh of the month of October the camp set out from this spot, following its route, and marched about a league, always down the river, where camp was made because the night before he had told the spies they would wait for them there.[77] He named the place Santa María Magdalena. At about five o'clock in the afternoon the señor

126

governor again dispatched other spies by different routes to see if the enemy could be found. They were unsuccessful.

On the twelfth of October, the governor with his command set out and continued down the river, following the route to the east. After traveling some four leagues, they halted on the banks of the said river. The name of San Nicolás Obispo was given to the spot. That night about eleven o'clock, while the governor was talking around the fire with the sergeant-major and the lieutenant of the company, and Captain Miguel Thenorio de Alva, such a furious hurricane came up that it obliged them to withdraw to their tents, which it seemed would be uprooted. The hurricane lasted all night.

On the thirteenth of the month the governor with his camp set out and marched down the river, keeping the route to the east. After we had marched some six leagues, camp was set up on the banks of the river; the spot was called Nuestra Señora del Pilar de Zaragosa. Along the way on the journey, they noticed where their enemy had stopped. According to the ranchos and the fires they made, they must have exceeded two hundred. From this it ought to be understood that there were no less than five persons, and in some cases more, about each fire. There were also many buffalo herds, walking about feeding and wandering in all directions on those plains which are so extensive that nothing is seen to obstruct the view.

On the fourteenth of the aforesaid month, the governor with all his camp set out downstream, always keeping his route to the east. After they marched some two leagues, the track of the enemy was recognized, which left a clear trail wherever it went, both on account of the great number of people and the multitude of horses, as well as the tent poles they carried dragging along behind. Their road went northeast. Marching on, the governor ordered a halt. He told the Chief Carlana through the interpreters that he was going immediately to where it appeared to him that the enemy was, according to what he judged from the trail. He was minded to follow it until they should all be punished. To this reasoning the Chief Carlana responded that it would not be possible to follow them because they had changed direction and had taken another route along which there were very few springs, and those too scanty to support the main body of the horseherd and command.

After listening to these reasons which Carlana had given, the governor called a council of all the soldiers and settlers. Assembled, he told them that they should give their opinions as to what ought to be done in the light of what Chief Carlana had proposed.

His lordship told them that he had still sufficient vigor and strength for greater campaigns and journeys, and that he was entirely unaffected by the severity of the weather and the few conveniences which these journeys hold out. But as they were aware, he knew how to perform and bear the hardships that had presented themselves on other occasions, so that they should set forth, without respect to him, according to their experiences that which appears to them ought to be done. All having understood this, and in compliance with what was ordered, answered unanimously that they were of the opinion that the señor governor and all the camp should return, for by continuing to follow the enemy there was a manifest risk that thereby all the cavalry, which was the principal means by which the kingdom was sustained, might be lost. This his lordship well knew, for he was familiar with the rigor of the snow and cold weather, which in these lands is so extreme that it benumbs and annihilates. Such had happened in the year '96 under the governorship of the Marqués de la Nava de Brazinas, when his lordship was captain of the presidio. At that time the Picuríes Indians had abandoned their pueblo and, uniting with the Apaches, become apostates from our holy Catholic faith. He set out to punish them. In his pursuit at this very time of the year he lost the major part of his horseherd. Valverde was a good witness of this event, as he was commanding the armed forces. These latter remained helpless for a long time until delivered by Providence.

To fulfill his obligation in the royal service—since no other person would have penetrated through so many and such unknown lands, never before seen or discovered by the Spaniards, as those his lordship has explored in the present campaign—he has demonstrated his great zeal in the service of his majesty. For these reasons, it appeared that his lordship should suspend following the enemy and retire with his army to the presidio in the center of the kingdom.

Having heard these reasons mentioned above, the señor governor agreed with their judgment and gave the order to camp on the river in the place most suitable both for pastures and for wood, and that the settlers and two squads of soldiers should go out, together with the Indian people, to kill some buffalo for meat because they no longer had any other provisions. This was done about ten o'clock and the camp put up on that spot, which was named La Exaltazión de la Santa Cruz. Some four leagues were marched that day.[78] Joseph

128

Naranjo, captain of war, having gone out with some Christian Indians to examine some tracks which the Apaches had seen, arrived at this place about four o'clock in the afternoon and told the señor governor of having seen the trails left by four horses, some of a previous day and others of that same day. He followed this trail which led toward the Río Napestle. In this direction the expedition itself was already moving.

At about eleven o'clock on the night of this day ten Apaches arrived at the camp from the region of El Cuartelejo.[79] Being in the presence of the señor governor, they told him that they were sent from their chiefs who were on the Río Napestle with all their people. In all they amounted to more than two hundred tents, and they had moved from their land in search of his lordship because the news had been brought to them that he was on a campaign with soldiers to punish the Comanche enemy. The señor governor entertained them all that he could and had them retire until the next day.

On the fifteenth of the above mentioned month, the governor with all his camp, after having heard mass, because it was the day of Santa Theresa, set out. After some four leagues were marched, they found a little bad water. In order that all the troop could drink, the governor ordered four wells made in a creek which was already dry. The horses drank from a small pond where a dead wolf was found. He called this spot after the saint of the day. Having seen a great herd of buffalo, the señor governor mounted his horse and with his adjutant and other soldiers went among them. He isolated a cow and ran it a good distance until he killed it with a spear. He told the soldiers to avail themselves of the meat, and to bring him the tongue only. On this day all the command killed many buffalo.

On the sixteenth of the above mentioned month, the governor, wishing to visit the numerous ranchería which was coming from El Cuartelejo in search of him, set out from this spot of Santa Theresa with his entire command. Having marched some ten leagues, they arrived at the Río Napestle, which is a very copious and pleasant river, with many poplars and extensive flatlands.[80] On these latter there were great herds of bison so that in the distance they looked like rolling hills. From what the plainsmen said, more than eight thousand head could be seen. Here much meat was secured by killing them. The governor named this spot San Pablo.

On the seventeenth of the above mentioned month, the governor ordered a sojourn in the spot, so that they could dry the meat and rest the horseherd from the strenuous journey of the preceding day, because of the little water and poor pastures they had had.

On the eighteenth of the month of October, the governor ordered that they should continue in camp as on the preceding day so that the horses might recover their strength. On this day he sent out two Indians of the Taos nation, to the spot where the Apaches of El Cuartelejo were camped, with a message to give the chiefs, saying that he was waiting to talk with them and assuring them of his good faith and friendship. Having done this, the envoys returned with the reply. They said that as soon as the Apaches were informed, they set their ranchería in motion to come to see the señor governor. They were bringing in their company another nation or ranchería of the same Apaches whom they called the Calchufines. They likewise gave an explanation for the tracks which Captain Naranjo went to observe on the fourteenth of the present month. The governor, realizing that the Apaches were already late in arriving, again dispatched War Captain Joseph Naranjo, to tell them that he could not delay much longer because other matters of the royal service which had to be taken care of were pressing him.

On the nineteenth of October, the governor remained in camp for news of the Apaches, to whom Captain Naranjo had gone. He came at the time of the evening prayer and said that the Apaches would come on the following day.

On the twentieth of the month the governor, finding the camp so increased in size because the return was accidentally postponed longer than he expected, and the supply of provisions already used up, determined with his good sense to send Captain Miguel Thenorio y Alva, alcalde mayor of the pueblo of Taos, with two companions to Taos, as it was the closest settlement, with a letter to its minister, the very Reverend Father Fray Juan de la Cruz, in order that he might aid him with provisions and come to meet him on the road. He informed him in the letter of his great want, which made it necessary for them to eat buffalo meat and gruel made from corn meal, and for some this was scarce. Likewise he wrote to his lieutenant-governor, Don Pedro de Villasur, giving him notice that the governor with his camp was already marching on his return to Santa Fé, as he realized that the lieutenant-governor would be anxious on account of the great period of time that had elapsed on such a journey.

A short time after these affairs were attended to, a chief of the Apaches of those of the ranchería of El Cuartelejo came. Being in the

130

presence of the governor, who received him with great expressions of pleasure, the chief said through the interpreters that he [Valverde] should delay, for all his people who were coming, even the women and children, wished to know him because of his great fame. After understanding this, the governor responded that it gave him pleasure to await until the ranchería would arrive to see and become acquainted with them. He assured them of the spirit of good friendship that he wished to establish with them.

He made a memorandum that the French were settled in the region, of their distance, and of the arrangement of their settlements, to be able with great detail to inform his excellency, the viceroy, of this New Spain. His lordship was pleased to command Valverde to solicit by all means possible the reciprocal friendship of the Apaches of El Cuartelejo, both for the good purpose and Catholic zeal of his excellency to convert them to our faith, and to be able, by means of them, to attain a knowledge of the location, designs, and movements of the French.[81]

On the twenty-first of the said month, the rancherías of the Apache of El Cuartelejo reached this Río Napestle and camped on the other side of the river. They numbered more than two hundred tents, and more than three hundred Indians under arms. Together with the crowd of women and children there were probably more than one thousand persons. As soon as they arrived and were encamped in the form according to their custom and military arrangement, they came to see the governor, who received them with his accustomed kindness and entertained them as best he could. They gave many demonstrations of being pleased and happy. Through the interpreters they said that they had the news, as did the other rancherías of their nation, that the señor governor was on a campaign through these remote countries and that this news had given them great delight because they had never seen any other governor in that country. This was the motive of their setting out to meet and see and know him. Other tribes were coming, clamoring for the same purpose. Having heard them, the governor gave them many thanks, esteeming the good faith which they were manifesting in their friendship. His lordship mounted his horse, and with the reverend father chaplain, Captain Don Joseph de Villegas, Lieutenant Francisco Montes Vijil, the Royal Ensign Don Joseph de la Fuente, and other active and retired officers went with the Apache chiefs to see the rancherías on the other side of the river. There they saw the dogs, on which were loaded the poles for tents and other utensils they used. They were considerably surprised to behold that

131

aggregate of heathenism and to see so many souls apart from our holy mother Church. In order that he might more quietly and peacefully enjoy rest from his weariness, the governor returned to his camp, and the Indians continued making up their own.

On the twenty-second of the aforesaid month the governor had information that one of the Apache chiefs of that ranchería had a wound which appeared to be from a gun shot. To inform himself of this, he ordered Lieutenant Frances Montes Vigil to bring him into his presence. This was done. When the Apache had come with many other Indians of his tribe, the governor examined the wound, asked him who had given it to him and with what had he been wounded. He answered that while he and his people were in his land, which is farther in from El Cuartelejo, on the most remote borderlands of the Apaches,[82] the French, united with the Pawnees and the Jumanos,[83] attacked them from ambush while they were planting corn. Placed on the defensive, they fought, and it was then that they gave him that oblique wound in the abdomen which was still healing. The Apache also said that had not the night settled on them, so that they could escape from their ranchería, none would have remained. They have seized their [Paloma] lands, and taken possession of them and held them from that time on.[84]

The French have built two large pueblos, each of which is as large as that of Taos. In them they live together with the said Pawnees and Jumanos Indians, to whom they have given long guns which they have taught them to shoot. With one of these they had wounded him. They also carry some small guns suspended from their belts. At the time of the fight the Apaches had told them that they would advise their friends, the Spaniards, in order that they might defend them. To this the French responded that they were greatly pleased to have them notify them and bring them there, for they are women *criconas* (these are words, however rude, that the Indians are accustomed to use to incite ire). All the enemy were dressed in [torn out] that they have done them much damage in taking away their lands and that each day they are coming closer. This is the reason that moved the Apaches to come, establishing themselves on this lower part of the river[85] to be able to live in safety from their enemies. Likewise, they added that the French have three other settlements on the other side of the large river, and that from these they bring arms and the rest of the things they bring to those which they have recently constructed.[86] They know this because they were told by some women of their tribe who were

132

made captives among the French on the occasions when they had war, but who had fled and returned with their kinsmen.

The governor gave all his attention to the above because it was of great import to the royal service. He determined that as soon as he arrived at a suitable place he would send the news to the viceroy of New Spain in obedience to his superior command. He told the Apache chief and all the rest who were there that they were admitted to the protection of our king and lord, in the name of his majesty. As his minister and servant he offered them his aid, against the French and the nations with which they were confederated, in order that they could live securely on their land. He would expel the French from it as the lands belong only to the majesty of our king and lord, Don Philip V (may God guard him many years). The others, he said, were thieves and intruders on that which did not belong to them, and that this was the land of the king, and his vassals, ourselves, and the Apaches also. They would see that the Spaniards were coming with their power and strength to attack and drive the French out of the land and destroy their pueblos and villages.

With this discourse the Apaches were consoled and pleased. They told the governor that he should wait a little while until the rest of their ranchería, which was coming, had arrived for they had great desires and yearnings to know him. Whereupon the governor assured them that he could not comply with what they asked for two reasons: the first was that he had suffered great anxiety notwithstanding the precaution he had taken, for he had no news of the kingdom in his charge; and secondly, that the supply of provisions had failed. Thus having taken leave of the Apaches, the governor set out with his command from the spot, the march all being made along the Río Napestle, on which they had been going.[87] [torn out] .....

VIII. A PORTION OF THE DIARY OF THE RECONNAISSANCE EXPEDITION OF COLONEL DON PEDRO DE VILLASUR[88] ALONG THE PLATTE RIVER, 1720[89]

The tracks which we found led us to a place where we believed there was information of a band, which, according to all signs, was not very far from some village. We decided to camp in order to see what had to be done. The lieutenant-general had assembled all the officers, active and retired, and the settlers. To them he said that a savage had reported to him that he had found some leaves of fresh sand cherries which seemed to be the remains of a meal of some troop which had passed there lately. He next set forth for consideration the

133

length of the journey we had made, which in his belief was about three hundred leagues.[90] Then he proposed for consideration whether we ought to await the orders of the viceroy of our New Spain, who had sent this detachment to try to discover by means of the infidel nations if there were any French established in these regions, or whether, since we had not up to the present found any indication which would convince us of such, we should continue our search among the Pawnee nation, the only one which may be able to give us some light, through which we could be able to communicate with them.

The council was composed of Captain Thomas Aulguin, Aide-de-Camp Joseph Domínguez, Ensign Bernard Cazille, Captains Manuel Thenorio de Albas, Alonzo Raeld, and Pierre Lucan, Corporal Joseph Gregoire, Manuel Thenorio de Alba, Laurent Rodríguez, Captain Christophe de la Serne, Captain Jean Archive; the two last named are settlers.[91] All were of the opinion that it was necessary to look for the Pawnees to learn the truth from them, or to learn whether the Apaches had deceived us; that to this end the detachment should cross to the other side of the river and that then all convenient measures be taken to reach the end that had been proposed.

Upon this resolution, the lieutenant-general ordered some savages to look for the ford across the river so that the command might gain the other side. After dinner, they began to take over the baggage on rafts and on the backs of the savages. It was not possible to get them over otherwise. The large number of islands which are in this river makes navigation with pirogues absolutely impracticable. As the day did not suffice to take over all, our camp was divided the following night by the river; moreover, we did not wish to expose our Indians to crossing at night because it was so cold.

Wednesday, the seventh of the month of August. At daybreak, the rest of the baggage and our people were brought over from the other side of the river Jesús María. This was not without a great deal of trouble, but we finally found ourselves together at midday.

Thursday, the eighth. We left the river Jesús María following the trail of the Pawnees. The savage of Captain Serne boasted of his good understanding. He lost his way, however, and returned to camp. He was sent out again and Captain Joseph Narvarnno,[92] four corporals, and two soldiers dispatched to accompany him. A servant of Captain Serne, Pawnee by nation, said he remembered although he had been taken away quite young, that the village of his kinsmen was situated

134

on the bank of a river, facing north. Our soldiers were charged with determining the truth of this assertion. They were commanded at the same time when they should be near the settlement, to let the savage talk alone to those of his nation to tell them not to have fear, that we were Spaniards, their friends. In case they should not find anyone in the village, they were to cross to the other side up to a point from which they could return to camp on the same day or in the following night.

After we had left the river of Jesús María, we gave our attention to following the tracks which we had found before us and which we believed to be made by the Pawnees. We found, at a league from that river, a large creek which it was necessary to cross. We thought from the water, which was very warm, that it was a branch of the river which had its current from west to east.[93] We marched then into a plain, following always the tracks of those who had gone before us. We discovered a quantity of trees at a league from us, and we found one of our savages who was from the detachment of Captain Narrans and who had an order to await us to tell us to follow the stream and that he was following the tracks of those who were going before him, not having found anyone in the villages. The command arrived on the bank of the stream, and as it was impossible to cross it with arms, we were obliged to continue along the side of the stream and follow the same route as that which Captain Narrans took. We had already made three leagues to reach this stream; we marched another three to reach a plain. There we halted so that those who had to come after us might not lose the way. There arrived at the same time two savages of Captain Narrans to tell the lieutenant-general that he should not be disturbed if he should not come to camp the next night; that he was following the tracks of the Pawnees who, according to all appearances, were not far away and that the main body of the command should march, because he planned on rejoining it soon.

Friday, the ninth. When the camp was ready to move, we saw at more than a league someone coming at a gallop. We went on and found that he was from our people who had gone ahead. He told us that at eight leagues from us, on the other side of the stream which we were following, they had found the Pawnees in a bottom, singing and dancing according to the custom of savages. There had appeared to be a large number of them. It was not judged fit to approach them nearer for fear of frightening them in the night.

135

Upon this news, the command was at once given orders to cross to the other side of the stream. This was done with such good fortune that everything went over without anything getting wet, although the horses were in water up to their girths. We traveled three leagues along the stream and found it convenient to halt at a distance of five leagues from that band, following the advice of those who had given us the news. As soon as we were encamped, the lieutenant-general sent the savage of Captain Serne to see and talk to those of his nation, reassuring them of our friendship and good will, and that we were taking these measures to advise them, for their observation, of our good faith. Although the lieutenant-general wished to dispatch two soldiers with this savage to prevent him from being attacked by his nation, the savage said to him that there was nothing to fear for him and that it would be better for him to go alone. If the soldiers accompanied him, they could believe that there might be some deceit and bad faith in that which he was to propose to them. This was approved and the savage left at eleven o'clock in the morning to go and see that nation. May God and the Holy Virgin his Mother wish that he have success! The general called the stream the Saint-Laurent; the river Jesús María unites with this stream at the point where we are, so that if we had not crossed, it would be impossible to do it.[94]

At six in the evening, we saw coming at a gallop François Sistaca, which is the name of the savage of Don Christophe de la Serne, who related to the lieutenant-general and to all the others that he had been looking for this band which he had seen the preceding night. Not having found it, he had continued along the stream, and he had seen them crossing from the other side, where there was a village and some people. Having halted on the bank of the said stream, after dismounting, he called to the people who were crossing the river, making signs of friendship and of peace, which are the usual ones, to the savages. As soon as they had seen him, many savages came towards him and among others, four, who walked before the band, with hatchets in their hands, without bows or arrows, uttering cries. Seeing them approach within a stone's throw, he became frightened. This obliged him to make signs with his hat as if he were calling people behind him. Having mounted his horse, he fled as far as the camp, the whole of the eight leagues, without stopping.

Saturday, the tenth of this month, the feast day of the Glorious Martin, Saint Laurent, Spaniard. The camp marched along the river following this band, and having discovered on the other side of the

136

stream a village with a number of houses and some people who were crossing by a ford from one side to the other and calling out to us, which could be understood, the stream only being between us.[95] We made signs, which we mentioned before, of peace and friendship. Twenty-five or thirty savages came to the bank of the water on the other side of the stream to talk with our people. All that they were saying was easily understood. The savage of Don Christophe Le Serne, who recognized the language of his nation, said to the lieutenant-general that they were asking peace and that he was to come among them.

They made signs, looking towards the sun, which meant that the Spaniards and they could not confer together that same day. On the spot, the savage of Don Christophe la Serne decided to cross to the other side, notwithstanding the fear he had had the day before. The camp halted opposite the village and the savage undressed to swim across with the consent of his master. The lieutenant-general instructed him to tell his nation that he was coming to see them and without any intention of causing them the least injury, as they could well understand since he had just discovered them without using strategy, as he could have, when he was apprised that they were dancing and singing, being then distant from them only two leagues. Accordingly, they could treat with us in all security concerning the peace and good relationship which was and ought to be between us and them, as brothers and subjects of the same king. The lieutenant-general gave some tobacco to the savage to take to them, which is the reasoning ordinarily used at these conversations.....[96]

IX. Proceedings Concerning Designs of the French on the Northern Frontier, 1719-1727

A. Plans for the Occupation of El Cuartelejo, 1719-1727

1475

Taken from a cuaderno which has the title: Document XX.

New Mexico, Year of 1719, Superior Government. Xicarilla Apaches.
Proceedings Concerning What Was Advised by the Governors of
Parral and New Mexico Regarding the Designs of the French
to Penetrate into These Regions,[97] *1719-1727*

1. CRUZ TO VALERO [TAOS, 1719]

1. *Most Excellent Lord:* For some time I have found myself in the quiet and peaceful possession of my mission, the sole and only end of

137

my journey from our beloved Spain to these countries. This consideration, Sir, for which I have voluntarily exiled myself, for the greater
glory of God, does not excuse my concern and obligation to the person
of your Excellency from writing these words. It will please me if they
find your Excellency in perfect health. Considering then the holy
desire of your Excellency to improve souls, especially in these parts
where heathenism is so widely spread, I must look to your Excellency
without doubt, whatever the undertaking will be, to bring with great
joy the light of the faith and disperse the shades of idolatry.

I am, Sir, in a mission called San Gerónimo de los Taos, so close to
heathenism, that, as is commonly said, we are shoulder to shoulder. A
tribe of heathen Apache, a nation widely scattered in these parts, of
whom it may be said as is mentioned by the Venerable Madre Sor.
María de Jesús of Agreda as a matter of great good for the future[98]
have come to ask for holy baptism. Having examined their intents and
persuasions, I found them to be truly religious. In this affair I am
now engaged, so that, it having been decided what ought to be done
in a case of this kind, the immediate undertaking will continue. The
governor, Don Antonio Valverde, Sir, a nobleman of much fear of
God and zeal for His greater honor and glory, assists greatly. Availing
himself of his experiences in the country, prudence, zeal, and charity
in his government, he not only allays whatever troubles that may be
encountered, but likewise encourages and aids us in carrying on the
cause of God and our king (whom God may guard). Truly I say that
I have labored and thus I say, Sir, that in this kingdom, judge thou
how I have worked to carry on the cause of God, who may guard your
Excellency for me many years in His love and grace. Your humble and
loyal chaplain who kisses your hand. Fray Juan de la Cruz. Most
Excellent Lord, Marqués de Valero, Viceroy of Mexico.

2. ORDER OF VALERO, MÉXICO, AUGUST 1, 1719

2. Mexico, August 1, 1719. With reference to what this father of the
Apache Indians writes, let a dispatch be prepared for the governor
ordering him to employ with the greatest efficiency all his care to
allure and entertain them extensively, as all that is spent in this will
be compensated as soon as he advises its import.[99] Warn him that it
is necessary to hold this nation because of the hostilities which the
French have launched among the Tejas, because the Duke of Orleans
has threatened to declare war on our crown, in which France is not
participating.[100] As the Apache nation aided by ourselves could inflict

138

considerable damage on the French and block their evil designs, the governor must assist with all the people that he can and on such occasions which offer themselves as await his zeal. Having recommended this to the governor, this father will be advised that the governor himself concurs in subjugating and entertaining the Apache Indians, taking advantage of the occasions which they have given, concerning which he wrote. Endorsed by his excellency. These dispatches dated this day.

3. VALERO TO CRUZ, MÉXICO, SEPTEMBER 3, 1719

3. In the same memoranda the following documents were found. In the understanding of your Grace's letter of the third of August, last, together with the testimonies which accompanied it about the imprisoning and seizure of the goods of the French, which your Grace has done, of those who have been found in the district of your government, in accordance with the notification which I received under date of July 3, last, about this matter, I remit to your Grace the adjoined dispatch so that in accordance with its contents and the royal purpose of his majesty, observance may be arranged concerning the treatment of this nation. That is, in the case of those who are established in these countries with royal permission and have given no suspicious indications, no indignities may be done them. With regard to the English, your Grace will be on the alert for whatever may occur in your district, to defend it from the hostilities which they might attempt. May God guard your Grace many years. Mexico, September 3, 1719. The Marqués de Valero. To Señor Don Manuel San Juan de Santa Cruz.

4. DURÁN TO VALERO, MADRID, JANUARY 30, 1719

4. *Don Baltasar de Zuñiga, Gúzman, Sotomayor y Mendoza, Marqués de Valero, of Ayamonte and Alenquez, Gentleman of the Bedchamber of his Majesty, of his Council Chamber, Chamber and Council of War of the Indies, Viceroy, Governor and Captain-General of this New Spain, and President of its Royal Court:* Whereas, the Lord Secretary Don Miguel Fernández Durán has written me this letter: The king finding himself with certain information that the duke regent of France, taking advantage of the occasion of the minority of her most Christian majesty, has made an alliance with the archduke, the duke of Saboya, and the king of England, and declared war against Spain, altering the reciprocal union, friendship, and good relations which the two crowns have maintained so long, and has already had

French troops march to the frontiers of this kingdom to enter it, his majesty has commanded me to advise your Excellency of this. In your understanding you may fulfill the duties of your office with all care in safeguarding and defending the plazas and presidios of this kingdom, advising the governors not to admit to their ports, on any pretext or motive whatever it may be, any French ship arriving at them and that in case any enter, their people be seized and kept secure, and their effects put in safe-keeping and kept in close custody until a new order comes from his majesty. But that concerning those French who are established in these parts with the permission of his majesty, no violence may be permitted because of the affection and reverence which all this nation has for his majesty, lamenting the irregular procedure of the duke regent who governs it.

In England an armament of ten warships and other vessels has been brought together for the purpose of crossing to this America, likewise two frigates, one of forty-six cannon and two hundred and seventy men, and the other thirty-six, and one hundred and sixty men, all English. These, for some days, have been only awaiting favorable winds to put out from the Downs and voyage to the South Sea with authority, and as nominal captains of the archduke, hoping to be able to plunder the ports of the coast of Chile and Peru, to capture the vessels which they meet on that sea, and sailing on to do likewise to the galleon of the Philippines on its arrival and departure from Acapulco, also attacking the coast of that kingdom. I am informing your Excellency of the order of his majesty so that you may communicate this news immediately to the presidents of the audiencias of Guatemala, Manila, and Guadalajara and to the governors of the coast of the North and South Seas of this kingdom so that each one, at the point which concerns him, may exercise care and corresponding alertness to avert the attacks and hostilities which the English intend, your Excellency providing everything that you can, or may be necessary to obstruct it. I desire that God may guard your Excellency many years. Madrid, January 30, 1719. Don Miguel Fernández Durán. To Señor Marqués de Valero.

5. ORDER OF VALERO, MÉXICO, JULY 13, 1719

In view of this and that it may be carried out according to the command of his majesty, as he advised me in the inserted letter, I order that circular letters be dispatched immediately so that the end may be achieved; that the governor of Parral have this intelligence and take the precautions which he might deem the most efficacious with all vigilance and care so that on those coasts and in those ports the designs which are expressed may not be attained. In case of vessels arriving at any of the ports which are referred to, let what is ordered be carried out, its people seized and safeguarded, and the effects of these put in safe-keeping until a new order comes from his majesty. But that concerning the French who are already established in those parts with the royal permission, let them suffer no extortion because of the affection and reverence which all that nation has for his majesty. I order the present writing be expedited with all exaction to avoid the attacks and hostilities which the English are intending to make, and avow that on my part everything will be provided him which may be necessary to hinder it. Mexico, July 13, 1719. The Marqués of Valero. As ordered by his excellency. Antonio de Aviles.

6. VALVERDE TO VALERO, SANTA FÉ, NOVEMBER 30, 1719

5. *Most Excellent Lord:* I have given an account to your Excellency in the previous mail of his majesty of the campaign I was preparing to make on the Ute and Comanche nation, known because of some attacks and robberies on the dominions of this kingdom. After a council of war was held concerning them, I determined to set out to punish them in person. I did this.[101] Now it is necessary to advise your Excellency. Having set out on the fifteenth of the month of September last from this villa for the said campaign, I took with me sixty soldiers from this royal presidio and forty settlers who volunteered to do this service for his majesty (to some of these because of their poverty I furnished arms and horses) and two hundred allies of these pueblos. This preparation was necessary because of the great number composing the Ute and Comanche nation. After we had arrived at the pueblo of Taos, the frontier whence we were to take the trail, I set out for La Jicarilla, the ranchería of Apaches, of whom I have already informed your Excellency.[102] These had the news that I was going to make a campaign against the Utes, who are their enemies on account of the serious losses they have suffered from them, because of murders and thefts which they have perpetrated on their families, women and children whom they take to sell in this kingdom when they are at peace, and came out to meet me with great rejoicing, one of them carrying a holy cross and an image of the most holy Mary, Our Lady. Twelve offered to accompany me on my journey, which they did. In this ranchería, although at some distance from one another, they have

flat-roofed houses, and, in many of them worship with great veneration the most holy cross. Thus I found these people very close to
embracing our holy faith. As I have informed your Excellency on
another occasion, they lack only missionaries who may instruct and
convert them. They work hard, gather much Indian corn, squashes,
and kidney beans, lay out ditches to irrigate their crops, and have
always maintained and at present maintain friendship with us.

6. From here I continued my march to the ranchería of the one
whom they call Chief Coxo of the same tribe. These friendly and
kindly disposed Indians came out to meet me because of the reasons
which I have given above. There I also found houses and sown land.
I greeted one and all with signs of friendship and good faith. While I
was in this ranchería, the Apache chief of the Carlanas, who have
their location in the Sierra Blanca, came to see me. He told me through
an interpreter that he was very glad that I had come to his lands, and
that he was withdrawing with his people in fear of the Utes and
Comanches who had caused them so much damage, and who have
destroyed their tribe. This is true because I passed through many
depopulated rancherías where ruins only were to be seen. He promised
to accompany me with those of his ranchería until he placed me in the
land of the Utes and Comanches, and that he would aid me in their
punishment. This I accepted because they are acquainted with the
country. Chief Carlana did this with great willingness, omitting no
diligence on his part, and sending spies out in all directions. After we
had marched and examined all the water holes and places where this
nation is ordinarily accustomed to be, they could not be found, because
they are a vagrant people, without permanent location anywhere. They
are brought into these lands by the interest they have in robbing the
enclosures that exist in the rancherías of the Apaches. The latter live
in constant alarm and at night they leave their houses and retire to
the hills to insure their lives.

[*Marginal note:* The Carlanas are located in the Sierra Blanca.]
I arrived on the Río Napeste, a very pleasant and full flowing river,
competing in its beauty with that of the Del Norte.[103] [*Marginal note:*
Río Napeste which the French call Acansas.] I crossed many arroyos
with very delightful valleys in which there were pasturing numerous
droves of buffalo, which from the distance appear like mountains.
There are, too, prairie chickens, deer, and antelope.

7. I penetrated from there much more country toward the north[104]
and found myself at a distance from El Cuartelejo, which was accord-

142

ing to some experienced men who were going with me, some four or five days' travel. Not having discovered the Utes and finding at the same time that the provisions were growing scarce for the number of people who were with me, and not wishing my journey to be extended too long, I determined to hold a council, as I did, of the experienced military leaders and settlers who were with me. Therein, it was resolved not to continue farther, because it was already the end of October and storms were expected which would make the way out impossible, and the horseherd might be lost in the many snowstorms which fall in the winter. I returned by a different route from that I had been following and again came upon the Río Napeste lower down. There an Apache Indian overtook me and, being in my presence, asked through an interpreter that I stop and wait for the ranchería of the Palomas and various others, all of the Apache nation, that would come. [*Marginal note:* No Spaniard had reached the Palomas Indians.] [He also stated] they had the news given them by some Indians of El Cuartelejo of their tribe who had come to trade in the pueblo of Taos where I was then. They had told him that I was going on a campaign. For the purpose of becoming acquainted with me, the old people, women, and children had left their rancherías to see the great captain. This was their way of explaining themselves because they had not seen any other Spaniard come this far to see and talk with them. I awaited them six days, at the end of which time the tribe began to arrive with their chiefs, whom I received with much affection and entertainment such as the situation demanded. They were happy and placed their camp where I showed them. I went to visit them and found there were set up more than two hundred war tents. These they carry on dogs. After I had returned to my tent, I learned that one of the Apaches had a wound in his belly. I ordered him sent for, and when he was present, I examined the oblique wound. I asked who had given it to him, and he answered that, while he and others of his tribe were fighting with that of the Cancer[105] nation, they gave him a bullet, as he expressed it. [*Marginal note:* Cancer Indians fight with Palomas.] He said that with the nation of Cancer are united some white men who in our understanding are French; [*Marginal note:* French united with the Cancers in 1719.] that these have friendly relations with the Cancers, Texas, and Pawnees; that their [French] first settlement was among the Cadodachos; [*Marginal note:* Cadodachos settled among by the French before the Cancers.] carry some long muskets and go about on foot, dressed in red clothes with their hunting caps of the same color; [*Marginal note:* The Cadodachos carry large flintlocks and go dressed in red.] that in the fight which they had they were able to escape only because night came; that the French have their settlement on a very large river which here is known as the Jesús María, the name which Captain Naranjo gave it on a journey which he made there, as I have already notified your Excellency.[106] The Apache also added that the French had lately established two other settlements up the river on the north bank; that they were confederated with the Pawnees and Jumanos to whom they have given firearms, which as he showed, they fire on forked sticks. Many other questions were asked him by me, and without repeating what is mentioned above, he added that many Indians of his tribe, who were captives among the French and had fled, say that from those old settlements they are reënforcing those they have recently built with arms and everything that was necessary; that among the French there are beautiful white women. He made motions to show that they wear their hair tied together on the crown of the head. These Indians told me that those of their tribe who were settling in El Cuartelejo had deserted the spot and were dispersed among the other rancherías of their tribe because they were molested and persecuted by the Utes. Thus, most excellent Lord, having solicited this news of the French by all means from these Indians, I found it to agree with that understood by Captain Naranjo, with whom I counciled and with those whom I marched on this journey. Having informed myself of the country, I conclude that this villa is distant two hundred leagues more or less from the settlement of the French. The purposes of the enemy appear accordingly to be to penetrate little by little inland. This country is very suitable for doing this because of its abundant meat, game, streams, and plains.

8. I treated the Indians with much love and kindness. I gave them to understand the power of our king and his people, who desired only the salvation of their souls, peace, and comfort in temporal things; that they should be confident that he would protect and defend them from their enemies; and I told them that those white men who were subjects of another king sought nothing else than to tyrannize over them as they were already experiencing. This they acknowledged and went away contented and happy.

I returned to this villa, having marched two months. The journey coming and going consumed some three hundred leagues. This news

144

being of such service to his majesty that it may be of moment to the high measures your Excellency is now considering for protection from these enemies, in order that they may not gather on the boundaries of this kingdom, which though far removed is the bulwark of New Spain, obliges me to dispatch the present mail so that with the knowledge of this report, your Excellency may order that which I ought to do. I am prepared for the time being, as I mentioned in my former letter, to attend to the matter personally, or my lieutenant-general will do it until the enemy is seen, so that I can report to your Excellency in regard to everything with more certain knowledge, if in the interim I have no new superior order.

For your high consideration, I must put before you, for whatever importance it may have, the very small amount or entire lack of munitions of war in this kingdom. It is likewise without sufficient force for any emergency that may occur. Although there are some stone mortars belonging to the royal exchequer in this capital, they do not have gun carriages nor are they in a condition to be used. There is no one who knows how to manage them. There is also wanting in this country persons to whom one can entrust a military operation, though the people of the land are very suitable for being commanded under arms, as on all emergencies that have presented themselves they have shown their aptitude. Concerning this I have had sufficient proof since I came to this kingdom.

9. In the dispatch your Excellency was pleased to send more than two years ago according to which I should report on the French who are in this kingdom and the rest of the things expressed therein, I have given notice that there is one, Juan de Archévèque, and according to the order, the manner and means of his coming here. He is today married, with some means of supporting himself honestly, and a very good servant of his majesty. He accompanied me on this journey as a settler and as an interpreter of the tongue of his nation; he is ready for all that one may command of him in the royal service.[107] I am giving this information for whatever value it may have, to your Excellency, who, in view of everything, will take the measures you may consider proper. I beg our Lord in His infinite goodness to guard your most excellent person many happy years. Villa of Santa Fé, November 30, 1719.[108]. Most Excellent Lord. At the feet of your Excellency, Antonio de Valverde Cosio. To the most excellent lord, Viceroy Marqués de Valero.

145

10. *Most Excellent Lord:* In a letter of November 20, past, I have reported to your Excellency the receipt of the dispatch of July 20 of this year with the insertion of the letter of January 30 of the señor secretary, Don Miguel Fernando Durán; the measures taken in virtue of it for the security and safeguarding of these provinces and what has been done for that of the galleon of China;[109] and how I have conducted myself concerning the release and discharge of the persons and goods of the French who were imprisoned and seized at the order of your Excellency because it did not appear that they had license from his majesty to have entered these provinces. Concerning all this, on the same date and separately, I prayed your Excellency be pleased to tell me what I should do. I also supplicated your Excellency that, with regard to men, arms, and munitions necessary to attend engagements which demand them, your Excellency, as a precaution, may be pleased to command that five hundred long-range guns be sent me, the equal of those which the enemy uses. In order to present opposition to the enemy, the soldiers and settlers should use them, prohibiting them firelocks of three-quarter caliber[110] as no better than arrows because of their short range; fifty quintals of good powder; twenty-five quintals of ball; and various persons who have served up to the grade of sergeants, ensigns and captains,[111] in order that the sergeants, ensigns and lieutenants may be used in the paid companies and the alcaldes mayores, lieutenants and adjutants in the jurisdictions to train and discipline therein the soldiers and settlers in military service.

[*Marginal note:* The soldiers of New Mexico serve only to fight with the Indians; not with the Europeans.] In consideration of the training and instruction with which up to now they have had, they are only sufficiently trained for the Indians and not for other enemies who may not be of this kind, such as may be considered the English, French, or any other foreigners. Likewise, may your Excellency be pleased to provide powder for military drill for both, and that the soldiers be paid monthly in reales in cash so that thus these provinces may experience the effects of your good precaution with regard to the continual menace of Indian enemies and what might occur in the future, as will more extensively appear to your Excellency from the letter referred to and from the testimony of the affidavits which accompany it.[112]

11. News has since come unexpectedly from a soldier passing through from New Mexico sent to your Excellency by its governor.[113]

The information, as the captains of Conchos, Campana, and the alcalde mayor of the valley of San Bartolomé gave it to me, is that at seventy leagues from the villa of Santa Fé there are six thousand French. They obliged the Indians of the Apache nation, some of whom were wounded with balls, notwithstanding that that nation is their enemy, to take refuge in the pueblos of the frontiers of that province. They had four hand axes and two guns which they took away from the French. Thus it is evident that they or other enemies are in the above mentioned region. Now as for the rest spoken of, the governor of that province will give your Excellency an account, although he has not advised me.

To guide me in the safeguarding of these provinces and the consequent advantages, I convoked a council. To it was submitted the news which I had of the enemies and the measures I had asked of your Excellency, in the letter referred to, considered necessary, according to the circumstances up to that time. Added to this information was the report from New Mexico. It was decided by common consent among those present that I should compose and dispatch a letter, as I did, to the governor of New Mexico. Since I lack official confirmation of this matter may your Excellency inform me concerning it. Further, I pray your Excellency may be pleased to provide this government, including that asked for in the letter referred to with one thousand large guns, a thousand bayonets, a thousand sheaths, five hundred pairs of pistols, five hundred lances, one hundred quintals of powder, and one hundred quintals of balls which may be made here by sending the moulds to utilize the lead at convenience, and charge the cost to his majesty, in order that all this may be available for exigencies which demand it; and with different persons who may have served up to the grades referred to, for use, as I said in the above mentioned letter, in the paid companies and jurisdictions to drill the soldiers and settlers. For this purpose powder should be provided for both and that which they may have need be given them without the increase of four reales, which is the price according to the monopoly in this town, since it [powder] sells here at twelve reales. Generally, both the soldiers and settlers use large guns corresponding to those which the French and English carry. The firelocks of three-quarter caliber should be prohibited because they are of no use, as I said in the aforementioned letter, being no better than the arrows of the Indians because of their small caliber and range. With respect to the aforementioned number of six thousand French, there are in the companies and squads of this government only three hundred and eighty-three enrolled soldiers including their

147

officers. They make up its dotation and may be used at such places and in regions so urgent that those which they vacate demand immediate attention. The distance of the French is considered to be two hundred leagues from the boundaries of this government. They are drawing nearer, chiefly across open land, without forces or trained men able to resist them. Accordingly, they will come closer swiftly and easily.

May your Excellency be pleased to command that people be recruited in the boundaries of this government whom your Excellency may consider proper and sufficient to resist and restrain them; that as to these people as well as to those of the companies referred to and the squads mentioned, be paid monthly in reales in cash in order that they may be prompt and prepared for everything. This cannot be achieved by paying them annually. For when it comes to paying them yearly, some owe already six months of it and others more or less. Because of this fact they do not get out of debt to their creditors from whom, with prompt salaries, they will free themselves. Thus these measures and forces may produce the good effects which such precautions promise.

To the end that your Excellency may be pleased to provide all effectively, I am dispatching mail to your Excellency, as I am doing with testimony of everything in order that in view of it and the report above mentioned which the governor of New Mexico is making clear, your Excellency may be pleased to supply provisions as promised me, chiefly, when your Excellency so offered in the cited dispatch and the señor secretary so wrote me in the letter charging me with the safety of these provinces, and whose written evidence tells me to turn to your Excellency for whatever I may need and which I might not have.

May God guard the most excellent person of your Excellency many years in His greatest goodness. Parral, December 11, 1719. Most Excellent Lord: at the feet of your Excellency, your best servitor, Manuel San Juan de Santa Cruz. To the most excellent lord, Viceroy Marqués de Valero.

12. Mexico, December 28, 1719. To the lord auditor-general of war with the letter written by Don Antonio Valverde, which is in the possession of the fiscal attorney, in order that in view of both, and recalling the opinion of the latter, and the difference between the account of Valverde and that of San Juan, the señor auditor may give his opinion.

8. REVOLLEDO TO VALERO, MÉXICO, DECEMBER 29, 1719

Most Excellent Lord: In view of this letter of the governor of Parral which is accompanied by an affidavit of the testimonies made concerning the orders he has given both to the governors, as well as to the alcaldes of the pueblos and coasts of his territory for their protection, in compliance with the superior order of your Excellency and that of his majesty; also, in regard to the news secured from a soldier of New Mexico, which his captains communicated to him, that at seventy leagues from Santa Fé there were six thousand Frenchmen, and the measures he asks for defense; also, in regard to the point concerning the embargo and seizure of the goods and persons of the French who are in this country without royal license; in view, likewise, of what the governor of New Mexico wrote to your Excellency on the thirtieth of November of this year which (not conforming with the information given out by the governor of Parral) refers to his having set out on a campaign with sixty soldiers, forty settlers, and two hundred Indians, and arrived near El Cuartelejo, a spot which belongs to the heathen Apaches; to the friendship with which they received him in their country; to their being industrious and very much disposed to receive the Gospel; to their having crosses; that one of these who set out to greet him had an image of the most holy Mary; their lamenting that the Utes and Comanches attack them; and also to the Cancers, who are confederated with the French established at a distance of two hundred leagues from that villa, according to the news which a wounded Indian gave him; and that in the year coming, he will try to penetrate as far as these settlements; also in view of the reply of the fiscal, who says that your Excellency, being pleased, can command the letter be acknowledged to the governor of Parral with thanks for the measures he has taken, and the care he has had for the security of the kingdom, and that to this end your Excellency will do everything necessary for its protection, but that for the time being he should detain in prison the French and keep their possessions until a new order arrives; with regard to the rest of the points he expressed and soldiers which he asks for the military instruction of his presidials and militia, your Excellency may take this proposal before a council of war as the fiscal petitions.

[*Marginal note:* The lord auditor gives his opinion here that the French are continuing to fortify themselves in the neighborhood of New Mexico.] With regard to those precautions which must be taken to impede the French in their ingress towards New Mexico by means of the confederations with the Canceres, and other nations and the settlements they have made and which it is said they are fortifying by means of others which it is said they had previously, and which appears

149

to be either the ones they possess on the Río Missouri, or on that of the Cadodachos,[114] which this letter mentions, both of which enter the great river of the Mississippi, thus the greatest care is necessary to insure more defense.

13. [*Marginal note:* The señor auditor wishes that in El Cuartelejo a presidio be placed with a mission of friars.] That which has suggested itself to the auditor general is that in El Cuartelejo, to the vicinity of which the governor of New Mexico penetrated, and where he intends to go in the coming year, a presidio be placed with twenty or twenty-five soldiers and two or three missionary fathers who should instruct the Apaches and establish a perpetual alliance with those who are in their nation very numerous. By this means and that of military forces, the boundaries of the kingdom may be safeguarded, and the ingress of the French impeded. In order that the military discipline which is practiced be taught them, some trained officials should go there from this kingdom. To this end, on the journey which the governor of New Mexico is contemplating this year in that country, he should take them with him and establish them in El Cuartelejo where there is known to have been a presidio or settlement of Spaniards in former times, or in lieu of that, whatever is most suitable both for defense as well as for the welfare of the inhabitants. For this same purpose some settlers of that villa should go. He should persuade the Apaches that for their safety they congregate about the presidio, and at the same time take advantage of their alliance and work in the fields, for sowing and other necessary things. The light of the Gospel and the royal protection will be given them. It should also follow that, being so scattered they extend to the Tejas and the Mississippi River, we shall use them as an auxiliary in those parts for defense. The expense of the presidio, which the royal treasury will necessarily have to bear, the council could avoid if your Excellency would decide to detach these soldiers from the hundred which the villa of Santa Fé and its government have. Then no expenditure would be necessary because no new drain would be made on the treasury. Whatever your Excellency is pleased to decide in reply to Governor Valverde, may your Excellency command. It can also be written to the Marqués of San Miguel that the Apaches have accepted our attachment throughout the country touching New Mexico and that he solicit the same from those of Texas, telling them of this in order that we may have them united in all parts and our allies.[115] Your Excellency with regard to everything

will decide as always for the best. México, December 29, 1719. Doctor
Juan de Olivan Revolledo.

14. Letter written to the most excellent lord, Marqués de Valero
by the governor of Parral, D. Manuel de San Juan Santa Cruz.

Most Excellent Lord: In the dispatch of July 13 of this year, which
I received on the thirteenth of the present, with the letter of the third
of September inserted in it, that of Señor Secretary Don Miguel Fernández Durán, your Excellency was pleased to command me to take
the most efficient measures which I might so that the designs of plundering the ports and coasts of this government by the English enemies
might not be achieved nor of capturing the Philippine galleon, and
that which I ought to do with the French ships which arrive, their
people and effects. Your Excellency commanded me in the letter referred to, to carry out the tenor of the dispatch concerning those who
found themselves imprisoned by order of your Excellency and who
had license from his majesty. At the same time, I received a letter from
the lord president of Guadalajara in which he tells me of two ships
having been descried on those coasts and that it is possible that they
may be the same ones which were advised to be about to sail from the
Downs. The French being near the Texas and New Philippines with
the intention of marching towards the new dominions, as is clear to
your Excellency, has necessitated taking manifest measures to restrain
them. Because this government is so close to that of the new kingdom
of León and Coahuila (the former bounds on that of the villa of
Saltillo of this government at a distance of about sixteen leagues from
the city of Monterrey; and the second along a canal of the same villa)
and because the coasts are menaced by these enemies, the said lord
secretary, having warned me of the order of his majesty of the care I
ought to have for its safety and defense, asked me for a list of the
men paid and the militiamen in order to arrive at an understanding of
the state of these provinces and the resources which they have. I have
ordered the militia enrolled and the mulattos of Mazatlan to continue
their vigils on the coast, having so commanded them previously in
order to have possible warning of what might occur.

15. As soon as I received the dispatch your Excellency referred to
and the letter of the lord president of Guadalajara, I sent orders to the
jurisdictions of Sonora, Cinaloa, Vayoreca, Rosario, Chametla, Mazatlan, and Californias, which include the coasts of the sea, advising them

of all referred to in the command, so that the civil officials and military chiefs, in whose charge they are, could fulfil them with care, so that the English nor any other foreign enemy who might arrive there could neither disembark nor commit any hostilities, nor even replenish supplies, nor do anything else to facilitate their remaining. I ordered them to put out competent watchers in appropriate spots, taking in their herds and whatever other supplies they had so that they [the enemy] might not benefit by them; that the paid military men be prepared to reconnoiter the coasts and ambushes, as weather and occasion best permit, to resist any disembarkation which may have covenant with others. The word is to be passed from one place to another so that the best advantage for defense and their punishment may be had. They are to report to me that which might be needed for this so that I may provide it as far as I am able, but if not to appeal to your Excellency.

16. With regard to the Philippine galleon, notwithstanding the lack of ships which there is on the said coasts and ports, lest some might possibly see it, the officials may attempt to give notice by fires either on tops of mountains or as best they can so that it may be known that there are enemy ships on the coast. The Captain of Sinaloa with all promptness is undertaking to inform the captain of the ship by placing someone on the cape of San Lucas. He is to go regularly between there and the Island of Guadalupe,[116] for it may happen that the galleon may pass beyond the island mentioned, and it must be warned and reënforced with men. He may have whatever may conduce to that end and whatever his favor and zeal in the royal service may dictate as the most suitable to prevent the enemy from learning the measures which may be taken inasmuch as they may be in these very spots awaiting the galleon.

17. With regard to the French who have royal license, let that which your Excellency is commanded by his majesty be done. As to the rest who do not have the license referred to, they are to be imprisoned and seized. Your Excellency is consulted (as I do in this letter) concerning what ought to be done because it appears that they have entered without the license of his majesty, evident from the adjoined affidavits, as the unprotected state of these coasts will also permit in the immediate future. With respect to what has been referred to, i.e., these provinces so menaced by enemies, it ought to be considered how much I leave to the sovereign consideration of your Excellency. But that there may yet be an assured time in which the use of arms for their defense may not be mandatory and punishment necessary. Because of the continu-

ous assault which the province suffers from the Indians, invaders, barbarous gentiles, apostates, and rebels, I cannot but repeat to your Excellency the representation that the companies and presidios of this government and its militia are scarcely sufficient to repulse these Indians both on account of the manner in which they are paid, which I have reported to your Excellency, especially in the letter of July 22, of the past year, with the testimony of the affidavits of the inspection which I made of the greater part of the companies and presidios, as well as because the discipline of both is not sufficient to resist trained troops such as will be those of the above mentioned enemies. This government is without the proportion of arms, powder, and ball which generally must be provided to those who need them, as appears from the testimony of the certification adjoined given by the royal officials. Those which are found in the military stores of this government are one hundred sixty-eight cartridge belts, which are neither sufficient nor of use because they are not up-to-date. Because up to now these companies may have been considered sufficient for the Indians, their discipline and arms makes them incapable of resisting trained troops because the firelocks which they commonly use are about five spans long and of such small caliber that they serve only for defense against arrows and not for firelocks and other guns of range, which must be considered with regard to any enemies other than Indians. Because of this, I cannot avoid fulfilling my obligation and setting forth to your Excellency my limited means to guard against whatever eventuality that may occur, both as to the regions referred to and the coast of the sea with respect to these nations or others of the enemy who intend to force their entrance and commit hostilities.

18. The first being (as I have before represented to your Excellency) that the soldiers be white men of pride and honor, and that those not of this kind, which by necessity were tolerated up to this time, be excluded; that their salaries be paid monthly in cash to them personally so that they may be provided with everything necessary; that both these soldiers and the settlers have large efficient guns which ought to be considered with regard to these enemies; that your Excellency be pleased to furnish various soldiers who may be conducted to this kingdom, having served up to the grades of sergeants, ensigns, and captains and that of these, three be lodged in each company and presidio: one a lieutenant, another an ensign, and the other a sergeant; in each of the jurisdictions three others be placed: one an alcalde mayor and captain of war, the other a lieutenant, and the other an

153

adjutant, so that with their skill and practice they may drill the soldiers and settlers of the said companies, presidios, and jurisdictions with the constancy that is required, in order that they may be skilled in the use and management of arms. No doubt that in this way, with the care which this government will take, they will be expert whenever an occasion arises, for the native Spaniards in the country, even though they should not flock from other places as they would with good, prompt pay, are quick and naturally very apt, so that thus properly trained they will make a favorable showing whatever the undertaking. In addition, the lack of active firing exercises, which are obtained on occasions of combat, must be considered. But this can be supplied in part by continuous reviews and drills which ought to be made. Your Excellency being pleased to provide the powder necessary for it, plus fifty quintals more of powder, twenty-five quintals of balls, and five hundred guns, with an armorer to look after them and have them clean and in respectable condition to await occasions which present themselves. This is what I consider necessary to conserve these provinces in case that they are not to be overrun. Your Excellency, offering to provide me with all that were or may be necessary, I supplicate that your Excellency will be pleased to furnish me the above with the exactness which I beg because it conduces to the service of both majesties. May God guard the most excellent person of your Excellency many years in His great goodness. Parral, November 20, 1719. Most Excellent Lord: at the feet of your Excellency: your best servitor. Manuel San Juan de Santa Cruz. To the Most Excellent Lord, Marqués de Valero.

10. ORDER FOR COUNCIL OF WAR, MÉXICO, JANUARY 10, 1720

19. The following documents were also found in this same file. Year of 1720. The councils which General Don Antonio Valverde Cosio, governor and captain-general of the kingdom and provinces of New Mexico, ordered convened in virtue of the dispatch from his most excellent lordship, the Marqués de Valero, viceroy, governor and captain-general of this New Spain. He was pleased to send this on the tenth of January of the present year of 1720 in accordance with the decisions of the lords of the council of the treasury with regard to placing twenty-five men in El Cuartelejo, and the rest of the points which are set forth in the superior dispatch.

11. VALVERDE TO VALERO, SANTA FÉ, MAY 27, 1720

20. I, General Don Antonio Valverde Cosio, governor and captain-general of this kingdom and provinces of New Mexico for his majesty,

154

reached this royal presidio of the Paso del Río del Norte, to which I came down because it was necessary to take some precautions. Three days after my arrival, which made it the fourth of March, past, of this present year of 1720, the messenger of his majesty delivered to me the dispatch above, which consists of the five preceding pages. It appears that his most excellent lordship, the Marqués of Valero, viceroy of this New Spain, had ordered a council of the treasury held, which was done by the lords. In it there was set forth, in virtue of the reports made by Don Manuel de San Juan, who was governor of New Vizcaya, and one of mine of November thirtieth, past, in which I gave an account to his Excellency of the expedition I had just carried out to punish the Utes and Comanches and in which I mention the rancherías of the Indians and the rest which appeared pertinent so that his Excellency was well pleased. He deigned to approve that which was determined upon by the lords in the council, one of the points being that I or my lieutenant-general should set out at an opportune time to reconnoiter the settlements which it is said the French nation has. This journey I am now preparing for and it will be carried out with the greatest dispatch by my lieutenant-general, as I was commanded. His excellency approves the detaching of twenty-five soldiers and commands that they be taken from this royal presidio of the villa of Santa Fé and stationed in the region of El Cuartelejo, which is some one hundred and thirty leagues distant from this villa. [*Marginal note:* The one hundred thirty leagues from El Cuartelejo to Santa Fé, plus the seventy from El Cuartelejo to the Pawnees, compose the stated two hundred leagues from Santa Fé to the French possessions.] This distance more or less conforms to the opinion of some in this kingdom who went to bring back from that spot to the pueblo of the Picuríes fugitives who were there. The rancherías of the Jicarilla and Sierra Blancas are in the territory between them. Of these and others I have given an account in the former report. They are the ones who received me with the image of Our Lady the Sainted Mary, and they are a little more than forty leagues distant from the villa. Thus, in what was determined upon by the lords of the council and ordered carried out by his excellency, there appears, and I find an error: namely, that it was commanded me to establish twenty-five men in the spot of El Cuartelejo, which is at so great a distance, in the center of Apachería, that they could not be assisted with military forces. I find this location in its present state useless. I feel doubtful whether that which was decided upon ought not to be understood to be the spot of La

Jicarilla. There, according to the above mentioned dispatch, it is conceded three religious could be assigned to administer, instruct, and guide those heathen in the mysteries of our holy faith. In order better to present to his excellency this point which I set forth, I am ordering a council held of the most experienced heads of this royal presidio of the villa of Santa Fé, and other settlers who have information and who went out when the pueblo of the said Picuríes was restored. These will set forth in their own words what they have seen and understood of that place and ranchería. To these the dispatch was made known so that, having been informed of it, each could state his opinion so that I could give an account to your Excellency, who, in view of this will decide what he considers best and give me the orders I am to execute. So provided, ordered, and arranged for by my secretary of government and war. In this villa of Santa Fé, May 27, 1720. Antonio de Valverde Cosio. As ordered by the señor governor and captain-general. Miguel Enríquez de Cabrera, secretary of government and war.

12. COUNCIL OF WAR, SANTA FÉ, JUNE 2, 1720

21. In the villa of Santa Fé, the capital of the kingdom of New Mexico, on the second day of the month of June, 1720, in virtue of that which was provided for in the above writ by me, General Don Antonio Valverde Cosio, governor and captain-general of this kingdom and its provinces, [assembled] the heads of the royal presidio and the settlers who seemed fit because of their experience and knowledge in the material which would be considered in this council, which was held at my order. Having been informed of the text of the superior dispatch, they gave their opinions in the following form and manner:[117]

22. Opinion of Captain-Major of War José Naranjo. Captain José Naranjo, who is war major of the inhabitants of this kingdom with his title from the superior government, deposed that: having been informed of the dispatch above from his excellency and of the writ drawn up by me, the governor and captain-general, in view of the experiences which guide him and four expeditions that he has made to the country of El Cuartelejo and some distance beyond,[118] as far as the great river which he called Jesús María, which river is about seventy leagues more or less from the region of the people (of El Cuartelejo), that the vicinity of El Cuartelejo is not appropriate nor has it the conveniences which are necessary to establish either a presidio or a settlement. [*Marginal note:* This Río Jesús María appears to be that of the Pawnees, spoken of in Alcedo's *Dictionary*,[119] word *Panis*.]

These accommodations are only seasonal because there is little water and no wood so that after harvesting their crops, the Indians leave the spot.[120] It is at such a great distance, and the great number of Indians of different nations, all numerous, who surround the place naturally make it an unadvantageous site in which to place a presidio of twenty-five men. In fact a force of fifty men would not be sufficient, for they could not live safely, according to what he supposes from the expeditions which he has made under orders for various reasons, in the time of different governors who have been in this kingdom. If it is the intention to seek the conversion of these Indians of the Apache nation, because of the disposition that is found in them, he was of the opinion that, notwithstanding the spot promises great resources since its valley have a great abundance of water and timber, twenty-five men were not even sufficient for the post of La Jicarilla, because it is forty leagues distant from this villa, is very rough, and the number of Apaches is great and that these have great readiness in assembling. It has not come to his notice that there had been a settlement of Spaniards at any time in the region of El Cuartelejo nor has he heard it reported, but he certainly considers that in this spot a presidio should not be placed or established.[121] This is his opinion. He did not sign because he did not know how to sign it. I, the governor, signed it with my secretary of government and war.

23. Captain Miguel Tenorio, a soldier of this royal presidio and the alcalde mayor of the valley of Taos and Picuríes, having been informed of the above dispatch in the preceding pages and the writ of my said governor, declared that he is of the same persuasion and approves likewise what Captain José Naranjo has said; that it is not convenient that the presidio of twenty-five men, which is intended, be placed in the neighborhood of El Cuartelejo. Besides the few or utter lack of necessities which the site presents, a great number of savages surround it. This he saw on the journey which he made to El Cuartelejo when he went to bring back the people of the Picuríes, when Don Francisco Cuervó governed this kingdom.[122] At that time, the Apaches who were ranching there told them that as soon as they harvest their crops (which, as was apparent, are of a seasonal nature) they retire to other parts where they can resist the rigor of the winter, because there is a scarcity of wood in that spot. Because of the wish of his excellency that a presidio be established to avoid the ravages which the Utes and Comanches make on the rancherías of the Apaches, their conversion begun, he is of the opinion that the presidio should be placed in the

157

valley called La Jicarilla, as it is close and armed assistance can be rendered. He is also of the same opinion that twenty-five men are too few for the great number of the heathen, for he has seen the valley of La Jicarilla many times and it is very abundant in water and forests, which promise many conveniences. He is informed that between the valley of Taos and that of La Jicarilla, there are veins of minerals in the range which divides the two valleys, so that this valley developed and settled, some wealth could be hoped for, and it is the key of the frontier of the northeast. Concerning the settlement in the region of El Cuartelejo, which some Spaniards are said to have had in former times, this was inauspicious news for when he was there he found nothing more than some ruins, which according to the reports, were made a long time ago by the Taos tribe which fled as fugitives to this spot.[123] This is his testimony. I, the governor, sign it with my secretary of government and war.

24. Deposition of Captain Juan de Archévèque. Captain Juan de Archévèque, a settler of this villa, having been informed of the dispatch of the most excellent lord, the viceroy of New Spain, and the writ provided by me, submitted that at the time when they went to bring back the pueblo of Picuríes fugitives who had fled and established themselves in the spot of El Cuartelejo, he was one of those who took part in this affair. He inspected closely the region so that, with reference to the presidio which his excellency, in accord with the council, was pleased to decide be established there, he agrees entirely with the testimony Captain José Naranjo has given, on finding it to be according to what he had learned. That if his most excellent lord is deciding to undertake the conversion of the Indians of the Apache nation who are closest in the region of La Jicarilla, he is of the opinion that this may be found very suitable to the service of both majesties; that the presidio of twenty-five men, which number may be found for the present sufficient, could be situated in this valley in the part that would be most convenient. It will thus adequately serve the kingdom in acquiring news with the greatest facility, regarding the nation of his kinsmen, the French, and be in the vicinity of these armed forces. This is his opinion, and I, the governor, sign it with my present secretary.

25. The remainder who comprised the council mentioned differed in nothing, entirely agreeing with these testimonies. They were Captain José Domínguez, Captain Tomas Olguín, Sergeant-Major Don Alonso Real de Aguilar, and Lieutenant-Captain Francisco Montes Vigil.

26. I, General Don Antonio Valverde Cosio, governor and captain-general of this kingdom, having seen the opinions above, given by the military men and intelligent and experienced settlers, by virtue of the council which I convened, on account of the dispatch the most excellent lord, the Marqués de Valero, viceroy, governor and captain-general of this New Spain, was pleased to send on the tenth of January of this present year, 1720, encompassing what was decided upon in the council of the exchequer, which had been assembled for this purpose. Informed of its context, I wished to reply according to the dictates of experience. I am instructed concerning the situation of the presidio which his excellency is ordering established in the region of El Cuartelejo from what I learned on the journey I made during the past year in search of the Ute and Comanche nation. I agree with the opinion of Captain José Naranjo, and the rest of those who confirm him. With respect to my journey, I always marched at eight or ten leagues from the sierra which was on my left hand towards the west. The route was north,[124] [as] far as the boundaries of the Texas and Pawnee nation.[125] [*Marginal note:* The nation of the Texas is contiguous with that of the Pawnee.] Their plain is so extensive that all agree it embraces not less than one hundred and fifty leagues more or less, and there is not on the whole of it anything more than some briar bushes and a few poplars along the rivers and small streams which cross and water it. It is peopled with different tribes which are in the vicinity of the site of El Cuartelejo. If it is the wish of his majesty (may God guard him) and of the most excellent lord, the viceroy of this New Spain in his royal name, to invite and convert this Apache nation to their obedience and to the fold of our sainted Mother Church, it seems to me that it will be very practicable to do this in the valley of La Jicarilla in the part which may be found most convenient to establish the presidio. However, I find, according to my experiences, the number of men, twenty-five, too small. The reason is that, although these Apaches acknowledge their submission, since they have offered themselves for catechizing, they have for enemies the Ute and Comanche tribes in the northeast, and to the east the Faraon, which, although an Apache tribe, is ordinarily hostile.[126] [*Marginal note:* Utes and Comanches to northeast of the valley of La Jicarilla.] This being the situation, it is necessary for arms to defend and protect them from their enemies. It is certain that such a small number of men cannot make sallies and reconnaissances, making safe the kingdom and the settlement, which we must consider should be done. If the presidio

referred to is placed in the manner that may seem fit, the evangelical ministers whom the lords of the council propose to his excellency can take possession without fear. From it I promise much gain that must be of great service to both majesties; a protection to the realm, and a means of bringing the numerous nation of the Apachería to our devotion.[127] So, then, my feeling is that, his excellency electing to place the said presidio in the spot and valley of La Jicarilla, I believe the number necessary for such a situation is fifty men. In everything, I subject myself to your superior inclination, which will always be for the best and the most prudent. This is my testimony and I sign it with my secretary of government and war on the said day, month, and year as above. Antonio Valverde Cosio. Before me, Miguel Enrique de Cabrera, secretary of government and war.

27. In the villa of Santa Fé, on the third of June, 1720. I, General Don Antonio de Valverde Cosio, governor and captain-general of this kingdom and provinces of New Mexico, having examined the preceding opinions of the chiefs of this royal presidio and the experienced settlers whom I convened for this purpose, and it having appeared from them the small benefit that can follow from the situation of the presidio of twenty-five men in the region of El Cuartelejo, both from the small number of people as from the absolute lack of conveniences which the vicinity has, for it is at such a great distance, it has seemed proper for me to represent this situation to his most excellent lordship, the Marqués of Valero, viceroy of this New Spain, deferring to his superior order so that he may command me that which I ought to do. I remit these proceedings by his majesty's mail as it appears to me to belong to the royal service. So provided, and signed with my secretary of government and war. Antonio de Valverde Cosio. As ordered by señor governor and captain-general. Miguel Enríquez de Cabrera, secretary of government and war.

13. VALVERDE TO VALERO, SANTA FÉ, JUNE 15, 1720

28. *Most Excellent Lord:* During the past month of February, I was obliged to go down to the jurisdiction of El Paso del Norte both to take measures there looking towards the preservation of the peace which the Indians of the nearby nation of Apaches maintain with those of the Zuma tribe and to supply that presidio with the best equipment of arms. A few days after my arrival there the messenger of his majesty arrived and delivered to me the above dispatch from your Excellency. In this your Excellency was pleased to command that

160

as soon as the time is opportune either I, personally, or my lieutenant-general should make the journey I had promised to reconnoiter the French in the region where they are situated; and that by virtue of a council of the exchequer which your Excellency deigned to convene, which, moreover, accorded with opinions given in it by the ministers, who all concurred, I be ordered to establish some twenty-five men in the vicinity of El Cuartelejo, taking the men for the present from this royal presidio. On account of the reasons and purposes which were set forth in the above council, it appeared to me that there was a misunderstanding, since it did not provide if the site of the presidio should be placed in the spot of El Cuartelejo—whose distance is more than one hundred and twenty leagues from this villa; [*Marginal note:* One hundred and twenty; in No. 20 he said one hundred and thirty.] and wherein few or no conveniences are accessible for the purpose of establishing a presidio; where small returns can be expected since the Indians, who ranch there seasonally, gather the scanty harvests which the place provides, and retire to other spots to pass the winters which are rigorous, and where there is no supply of wood for many leagues or whether it is to be understood that the presidio be placed in the valley of La Jicarilla. Finding myself in these doubts, and to be better able to inform your Excellency, I determined to convene a council of the principal heads of this royal presidio and experienced settlers in the country, who would be able with the greatest intelligence to give light and express their opinion.

These had made an expedition when it was decided to bring back the people of the pueblo of Picuríes, who were fugitives during the rebellion they had in the year [16]96 and had fled for refuge among the Apaches. From the said council there issued the opinions embraced in the proceedings which I am sending the highness of your Excellency. It being my feeling, because of the experiences I have gained from serving his majesty for twenty-seven years [128] in this kingdom in military affairs, that the opinions are wholly in agreement with the common belief of all who have traveled back and forth between these spots. Thus, if the intervention of your Excellency is to begin in the region of La Jicarilla, where the natives have given hope of submitting themselves to the fold of our Holy Mother Church and to the obedience of his majesty, as they have so shown and manifested their good will towards us up to the present, they are very close to that desired end which may be attained.

Since this place is such as appears from the opinions expressed in the

161

council and in which I concur, it appears to me that the presidio which your Excellency ordered me in the above dispatch to establish in the region of El Cuartelejo should be placed in that of La Jicarilla, which is at the short distance of forty leagues from this villa on the frontiers of the valley and pueblo of Taos, the most remote settled jurisdiction of this kingdom. Then for the attainment of the desired object, which the catholic zeal of your Excellency has, you had best assign three religious for this region, and site, and heathen. These with more security can fulfill their ministry, and the natives will be protected by our arms against their enemies who disturb them so much. Excepting the better opinion of your Excellency, who has such great zeal for the royal service, I hope to decide what is best and the most judicious.

I cannot omit giving notice that on the seventeenth of the present month, in compliance with the superior order of your Excellency, my lieutenant-general will set out from this villa with forty soldiers from this royal presidio and seventy Indian allies of this jurisdiction to make a reconnaissance of the settlements which they say those of the French nation have established. As to what will result I shall inform you, as my obligation bids me.[129] In compliance with that I am sending this present mail with that of his majesty's in order that according to it, your Excellency will properly decide to command what I ought to do concerning the placing of the twenty-five men, whether it would be better in this site or in that of El Cuartelejo. I am of the feeling as expressed above, in which everyone here generally agrees. I cannot neglect to place again before the high understanding of your Excellency the great need there is in this kingdom of an armorer, a smith, and two carpenters, so that in whatever may arise in the service of his majesty (may God guard him) the end can be attained with the perfection required. In everything I am awaiting your Excellency to command that which might best be done, which will always be the most prudent. I pray our Lord will guard your most excellent person many years in his greatest nobleness. The villa of Santa Fé, June 15, 1720. Most Excellent Lord at the feet of your Excellency. Antonio de Valverde Cosio. Most Excellent Lord, Marqués de Valero. [*Marginal note:* The resolution was that the presidio be placed in the valley of La Jicarilla.]

14. VALVERDE TO VALERO, SANTA FÉ, OCTOBER 8, 1720

29. *Most Excellent Lord.*[130] Sir, the mail I sent to your Excellency the twelfth of June (this is a mistake; it did not go then, but on the

fifteenth of the said month[131]) of this present year in which I recounted to your Excellency that my lieutenant-general, who was Don Pedro de Villasur (may he rest in peace), had resolved to leave this villa of Santa Fé promptly on the sixteenth of the month referred to, to make reconnaissance of the French as your Excellency ordered me. He actually began his journey the intended day, acting with such precision in the discharge of his obligation that he preferred rather to lose his life than to return to the royal presidio without bringing back particular information of the region where the French were, because if he did not bring this information, he would endanger his reputation in not satisfying the great desire of your Excellency, who must be advised with exactness in this matter. (In the third part, which concerns the compliance of the royal order of May 20, 1805, we have copied the documents by which this note or reference is proved; although with these same judicial proceedings and with documents of other proceedings we show that the erection of this presidio was never effected.[132])

The most necessary and proper orders having been given to the said Don Pedro both by word of mouth and in writing, he set out with forty soldiers, some settlers, and Indian allies. Having marched with good fortune, he arrived on the banks of a large river (*Note:* it appears this is the river of the Pawnees) which divides the tribe of the Cuartelejo Apaches, who are our allies, from the Pawnees, who are those of the French. He ordered the camp set up, whence at a distance a settlement of Pawnees could be seen. Having foresightedly brought along in his command an Indian of their tribe as an interpreter, the servant of Captain Christóval de la Serna, a settler, who voluntarily offered himself for this campaign, he managed to inform himself through some of the Pawnees of the region where the French were said to be. They came to inspect our [forces] and said there was a Spaniard among them. For this reason, he ordered Captain Juan de Archévèque of the French nation, also a settler in this villa, to write a letter in his language. The Indian interpreter, having taken it, went away at once and brought back a reply on old paper which our Frenchman did not understand in the least. At the same time, an Indian of theirs came with a linen flag.[133] To him he gave another letter. Because of a lack of white paper, perhaps, the writing was in such form that it could not be deciphered. In order that they might communicate, another letter was written in the Spanish language with paper, ink, and quills, so that they could have something that they might comprehend. They waited two days and, when they did not answer, fear arose that they were planning some trickery, and such was the case, as may be inferred from what later occurred.

30. Seeing the delay of the messenger and the reply, the general determined to improve his position to assure the safety of his person and that of his men. He retired up the river some eight or ten leagues. When it appeared that he was in less danger, he set up camp and charged his subalterns to be vigilant. In this way they were well prepared for the entire night. But as one cannot easily be forewarned nor advised of all accidents, such as treacherous perfidy, where they thought they were secure occurred the most outstanding misfortune that has come to pass in this country.

31. Here most excellent Lord, a digression is necessary because my heart is broken with the unhappy thought of having to relate this sad tragedy. When I contemplate those fields with the spilt blood of those who were the most excellent soldiers in all this realm, and who sacrificed their lives in the service of God and the king, my master, at the hands of the impious barbarousness of the enemies of our holy Catholic faith, I am persuaded that some were heretical Huguenots whose insolent audacity did not even spare the innocence of the priest who went as chaplain. I would well wish that my perfect loyalty to the royal service would excuse me from giving an account of such lamentable news as that which today floods this miserable realm, which, although so poor, is the bulwark of all New Spain. But my obligation does not excuse me from giving an account to your Excellency, accordingly as I have learned it from the few who escaped from the encounter. From these I tried to secure the truth, and I have formed an honest narrative; thus I return to the relation of the event.

32. I said that the general had withdrawn up the above mentioned river, because the enemies had captured one of the Indians of our auxiliaries, who with too much confidence had gone to bathe with one or two others. The latter, by dint of assiduity, saved themselves. On the following day at daybreak, he commanded that the horseherd be brought to the camp and that the horses which they had saddled to catch the others be untied, unseasonably and contrary to the usual procedure of this country (since the custom of launching an ambush is just before daybreak); these scoundrels, in order to take advantage of their dastardly purpose, remained in hiding until after the sun had come up, giving time to our people to lessen their precaution, some being engaged in catching horses, others gathering the utensils, and all busy. It is thought that the advice of this situation may have come

164

from the Pawnee Indian who, disloyal, had remained in the enemy camp. Only with that warning could they have attacked at such a time and caught them on foot; otherwise our men could have retired in the face of the great number who attacked them. These in the opinion of all were more than two hundred soldiers using arquebuses, with an endless number of Pawnee Indians as their allies. The discharge of the musketry, the confusion, the yelling of the Indians, threw our cavalry into a stampede so that it was necessary for those who had charge of them to restore order, which they did, taking them a short distance from the camp where, because of the smoke and dust which was raised, they could hardly see one another. But distinguishing the voices of the few who were spiritedly defending themselves against such a multitude of enemies, the intrepid corporal of the cavalry threw himself into the battle with three others, who followed him. They opened the ring which the enemy had made, killing many of the Pawnee Indians. Taking advantage of this, seven of our men came out, although two were very badly wounded with shot and arrows, having left the said corporal and a companion dead in the attack.

33. Thus, most excellent Lord, those who perished in this attack were my lieutenant, Don Pedro de Villasur, the Reverend Father Chaplain Fray Juan Mínguez of the Seraphic Order, five retired squad corporals, nineteen soldiers, the Frenchman Juan de Archévèque, [Note: Juan de Archévèque killed at the hands of the French] Captain Christóval de la Sierra [Serna], four of my servants, and the eleven Indian allies, with the captain-major of war, José Naranjo. In all the number amounts to forty-five persons. Those who escaped with life were a retired officer, a corporal of the squad, eleven soldiers, and a settler, all very badly wounded.[134] Although the enemy had the victory and all the supplies and provisions of war, they did not come out very cheaply because, according to what I am told, some of them died with their chief, so the escaped ones affirm. These on their return had the good fortune of finding refuge among the Indians of the Apache tribe who came out to meet them with great tenderness, giving signs of much sympathy on account of the misfortune of those who were left dead. It must be wondered at that they, being heathen and seeing our men so weakened in health and strength, did not attempt to take away the horses they had with them; otherwise more than those who perished in the encounter would have been lost. They not only did not do this, but kept them in their company with much

kindness for two days, supporting and succoring them with their poor provisions. Their excellent conduct did not stop here, but they all offered to take revenge, manifesting a great desire that the Spaniards return to those frontiers in order that, allied together, they could make war effectively on the French and Pawnees.

They said the manner of living of the French was in strong round houses, which hold four persons. On the roofs were large arquebuses, which in my understanding are stone mortars or field pieces. They have seen four settlements which are the closest ones to the region which our men reached, being but three or four leagues away. Two Indian women, of their Apache nation whom the French had as captives and who had escaped, saw these individually.[135]

[Marginal note: The French have made strong houses which they have designed.] Since your Excellency may perhaps wish to be more extensively informed of the event, I am sending this mail by one of those who was in the fray who, as an eyewitness, will give a complete account of what happened.[136]

34. I am now going to place before the sovereign consideration of your Excellency the condition in which I may find myself in this realm, which is by nature poor, without any resources. What grieves me most is the need of thirty men, the best trained and most experienced in the engagements of this warfare which is constantly active in this kingdom. The great number of heathen, the Utes, Comanches, and Apache tribes of Faraons, invade the kingdom with death and robbery. They have their habitation within the territory around this villa as far as the jurisdiction of the Paso del Río del Norte and the Junta de los Ríos. To the defense [of this kingdom] I was ready to march out personally as soon as my lieutenant-general and his companions had come to headquarters. I have been forced to alter my purpose because of the fatal occurrence, though I am determined that the campaign will be made to restrain their boldness with the soldiers of that presidio, twenty of whom I shall detach from this [presidio] under the charge of the Lieutenant-Captain Don Juan Domingo de Bustamante, because of the great confidence which I have that he will know how to discharge his obligation to the royal service.

35. Because, in the previous report I have given an account to your Excellency of the lack of supplies for war which there is in this kingdom, I am mentioning it again in compliance with my duty, because of what the moment may bring forth. At present, it is presumable that the French may wish to take advantage of the opportunity with

166

the guidance of the Pawnee Indian who remained among them and the other they captured, to which could be added the diary and itinerary which my lieutenant-general was making at my order for the purpose of putting it in the hands of your Excellency as soon as he should return. Now most excellent Lord, having made known the shortage in the kingdom caused by the loss of the men who died on this campaign, it is very opportune and necessary to put before the high comprehension of your Excellency the usefulness of recruiting thirty or forty men to fill the vacancy. It should be said that it is very important that they be Spaniards, advanced in years in order that they may become proficient (those who may be inclined) in military matters, so that the governors who may come to administer this kingdom will have them at hand for the many occasions which would offer renown. However, I grant that in order to fill the quota of one hundred soldiers which his majesty (may God guard him) has assigned to this kingdom, there are enough of them to be just soldiers, but not with that aptitude which responsibility may bring out of them; and they should not have a too limited intelligence.[137]

All of which I place in all humbleness before the sovereign greatness of your Excellency in order that you may determine that which you may find to be most proper and to whose opinion I subject mine with all humility. I pray his Divine Majesty to guard the important life of your Excellency in His greatest nobleness. Villa of Santa Fé, October 8, 1720. Most Excellent Lord. At the feet of your Excellency. Antonio de Valverde Cosio. Most Excellent Lord, the Marqués de Valero.

15. VALERO TO SAINZ, MÉXICO, NOVEMBER 3, 1720

35. Mexico, November 3, 1720. To the fiscal attorney, who will see immediately what this means. Rubric of the Lord Marqués, Viceroy of Valero.

16. SAINZ TO VALERO, MÉXICO, NOVEMBER 4, 1720

Most Excellent Lord: The fiscal attorney has reviewed this report and says that although it did not come according to established rules, as it should have with testimonies which may confirm the narrative of its context, he defers, as should be done, to the great veracity and well known fidelity of the governor of New Mexico. What he sets forth is a notorious contravention of the truces which in other councils of war and exchequer have been considered at length, to the testimonies of which your Excellency may be pleased to order that this

167

report be added. Therein, the repeated royal orders appear to the effect that the French shall not penetrate into the territories of this royal domain, for which purpose, concerning the province of Texas, various precautions have been taken and very large amounts have been expended, consigned to the disposition of the Marqués of San Miguel de Aguayo.[138]

36. In the last council which was held concerning this, various measures were taken according to the state of the news of the truces. It was inferred at that time that the preceding provisions were not necessary because it was not to be supposed that on our part the pact would be violated. Notwithstanding that, the fiscal attorney was always mistrustful that the other side might be lacking in the required fidelity, in which it would appear that the determinations of the first councils which were held, without news of the treaties, should continue to exist in their strength and vigor. The most unfortunate case which this report refers to has made certain and patent the misgivings which the fiscal attorney always had. The contract of truces has failed. By no means should the other side maintain them. It will be agreed, as the fiscal attorney says, that the first decisions of the councils concerning the expedition for Texas be given an absolute and legal effect.

In this report the governor of New Mexico has not indicated which is the river along which the French advanced to make their perfidious attacks. According to the previous councils, the information which they had concerned only the Río Missipipi (Mississipi, it should have been written) and that of the Palizada (that is the same as the Mississipi, not different).[139] The fiscal attorney, having desired to acquaint himself with this, inquired concerning it of the soldier who came with the mail. He was informed that it was another very different river by which the French are directing their travels further toward New Mexico, though according to this report an opposite meaning can be understood. They could come by the Río del Norte to El Paso, from whence they could with ease penetrate even to Parral and the rest of the presidios to the destruction of the royal dominion, because further to the north of New Mexico there are deserted lands and a very long road to the boundary of Holland, from whose remote regions some Indians have come to New Mexico. They give an account of the distance which they explain in their manner. The distance is eleven moons journeying over broken ground. For this reason, the fiscal attorney is persuaded that this is not their [the French] route, but that they follow the Río del Norte as far as the Paso del Norte which they call the Río del Norte. [*Marginal note: Note:* The lord fiscal attorney knows little of the geography of these countries, since he errs in these few writings.] There, the same General Don Antonio Valverde for many years was captain. At this pass the rigor of the winters freezes this river so that with sand the carts which go from New Mexico can cross.

In this matter the fiscal attorney holds very justly and properly for the royal service that measures be taken for which the governor of New Mexico prays, supplying him with as large a number of militiamen as may be possible because of the need which he mentions exists. For the most prompt assistance the militia could be taken from the closest places. At the same time a dispatch should be issued with this news for the Marqués of San Miguel de Aguayo, so that as to Texas, he should proceed to a defensive and offensive war. (*Note:* The lord fiscal attorney asks the Marqués de San Miguel de Aguayo to make an offensive and defensive war in Texas) in conformity with what was decided upon in the first councils. The presidios should be established that were resolved upon in the last, and should be placed in the region which appears to be the most convenient, so that the French may not invade New Mexico by the Mississippi River and the Palisada, for the fiscal attorney is persuaded that the other river of which the soldier informed him may possibly be a branch of the Mississippi or of the Palizada.

Concerning everything, may your Excellency be pleased to command, after referring it to the lord auditor-general of war so that he may answer, that it be taken to a council of war. Above all your Excellency will decide as ever for the best. México, November 4, 1720. Master Sáinz.

Mexico, November 6, 1720, to the lord auditor of war, who will at once see that he agrees so that the council may be called soon. Rubric of his excellency, the Lord Marqués de Valero.

17. REVOLLEDO TO VALERO, MÉXICO, NOVEMBER 12, 1710

37. *Most Excellent Lord:* The narrative of this letter is short. It will be advisable for the messenger who brought it to be examined concerning the event and its circumstances; the distance from the region where the battle was fought to the site of the villa of Santa Fé, the capital of that kingdom; and the terrain in which are established the four settlements or fortifications of the French; their number, and that of the Pawnee Indians, Yutes, Comanches, and Canceres, who are

their allies; the countries in which these have their abodes, or rancherías; the distance it is to the Sierra Blanca [*Marginal note:* Sierra Blanca. The Carlana Apaches who are our allies live in it.] where the Carlana Apaches, our allies, have theirs; if it is the Río Napeste or the Río Jesús María, on which the battle was fought; where the French have constructed their strong forts; the route of the journey which they made; the days they delayed; the halts they had; the dwellings they found, and the kind of streams, mountains, or countries over which they crossed to reach the spot of the battle; the leagues from there to the junction of Los Ríos, Culebras de Conchos, and New Mexico, where the Indians of the Six Missions have rebelled, of which an account has been given by the governor of Parral. Thus your Excellency will order that this messenger and Captain Martínez[140] go to the residence of the auditor-general of war to be interrogated on these points and others which might occur to him. He can with those which he will bring out and with the information they have of that country set forth more perfectly his opinion, or whatever may be the pleasure of your Excellency. México November 8, 1720. Let Captain Martínez and the testimonies on this point be sent. So be it: Don Juan de Olivan Revolledo, Mexico, November 12, 1720.

18. ORDER OF VALERO [MÉXICO, NOVEMBER 12, 1720]

As the lord auditor says, let the testimonies and Martínez be sent immediately. Rubric of his excellency, the Lord Marqués de Valero.

19. DECLARATION OF MARTÍNEZ, MÉXICO, NOVEMBER 13, 1720

38. In the city of Mexico, the thirteenth day of the month of November, 1720, Lord Doctor Don Juan de Olivan Revolledo of the Council of his Majesty, his Judge in this Royal Audiencia, and Auditor-General of War of this New Spain, in compliance with what was ordered by his excellency in his decree which precedes, Captain Don Felix Martínez, a life-tenure captain in New Mexico, being present in order that he depose before me, the scrivener of war, received the oath which he took before God, our Lord, and the image of the Holy Cross, according to law and promised to tell the truth. Questioned about the tenor of the contents in the reply of his grace above, he said he thought from the capital of Santa Fé to the site on which the battle occurred there are some two hundred leagues, because he, the witness, had traveled from the capital to the pueblo of Taos, which is thirty leagues to the north, from there northeast to the pueblo of La Jicarilla, fifteen

leagues, where is a nation of the Apache, and from this sixty leagues to the same northeast to the Río Napestle, which he reached when he was captain of the presidio of New Mexico; [*Marginal note:* Distance from Santa Fé to the Río Napestle, to El Cuartelejo] that from this river to the same northeast there are about fifty leagues to the pueblo of El Cuartelejo, a nation of the Apache, and from this there are about another fifty to the Río Jesús María, on whose banks, he had heard from the messenger who came with the news of the rout of our people, was the spot on which this took place;[141] that he has information that along the margins of this river, Jesús María, those of the Pawnee nation have their rancherías; they are white Indians with pierced ears; the witness affirms that these Pawnees are those who attacked our men, because on this river they have four or five settlements, according to what he had heard said to these same Pawnees who were captives in New Mexico;[142] that the Sierra Blanca, where the Apaches Carlanas, our allies, are ranching or settled, is between the Río Napestle and La Jicarilla, twelve leagues to the north and runs east and west, and that on the eastern extremity is where the Canceres are, allied with the French;[143] according to what is said, the Utes and Comanches are to the north of Santa Fé about one hundred leagues distant more or less, and that they are like republics or itinerant nations who today dwell in one place and tomorrow in another, and carry with them tents of bison hides to camp when it occurs to them. [*Marginal note:* If he does not believe they were French, he ought to credit that they were French, because they have a fort on the spot from which they go out to oppose the Spaniards, as appears in 38 and 39, the Indians aiding them with guns which they give them.]

Those who surprised our men on the above mentioned spot are the same Pawnee Indians who are white, wear clothes, and use firearms like the French, from whom they secure or acquire them in order to roam about over their confines. Because if they had been French, they would not have killed so many, but would have managed to make them prisoners and taken the horses which they lacked. [*Marginal note:* Bad inference: The French would not only have made them prisoners if they could have, but they would have killed them as surely as they were killed, so that the Spaniards could not seize and dislodge them from that spot, since they came furtively, hiding themselves as much as they could from the Spaniards;] because in the security of the eight leagues which the Spaniards made from the river to the site of the combat, being French infantry they could not have made such a long march in one night, and not having cavalry to hasten the journey, since the declarant knew absolutely that they did not have horses in those countries; that from this site to the capital of Santa Fé, as he has said,[144] there are some two hundred leagues, that from the capital to the junction of the Ríos Conchos and del Norte by the usual road, there are two hundred and forty leagues. Consequently, these distances being so great it does not appear possible that the Pawnees and French can aid the Julimes Indians, who are those of the rebelled missions and who reside near the junction of the two rivers mentioned above.[145]

From the capital of Santa Fé to the Río Jesús María there is no range of mountains to cross,[146] but all is plain-like, and these two rivers, the Napestle and Jesús María, that may be forded without danger; as there are no land obstacles, one may arrive in a very short time by cavalry marches from Santa Fé as far as the settlements of the Pawnee, which he believes are very distant from those of the French. This is what he knows and has heard as one experienced; he has lived twenty-eight years in the capital of New Mexico, and it is the truth as required by the oath he has taken. He declared his age as more than twenty-five years. He signed it and his grace placed his rubric on it. Felix Martínez. Rubric of Señor Olivan. Before me, Juan de Valbuena, royal scrivener of war.

[*Marginal note: Note:* This Martínez did not know nor suggest the site on which the battle had occurred, but that, as it appeared to him, it was between the Río de Acansas, or Napeste, and Missouri on the river which they call the Panis. See the *Geographical Dictionary of America* of Alcedo, word "Panis."][147]

20. DECLARATION OF GARDUÑO, MÉXICO, NOVEMBER 15, 1720

39. In the city of Mexico fifteenth day of the month of November, 1720, the lord auditor general of war, in compliance with what was ordered by his excellency to have Bartolomé Garduño declare, I had him appear before me. He said he called himself as mentioned above; that he is an ensign-corporal of the presidio of Santa Fé, New Mexico, where he has served his majesty as a soldier for twenty-seven years, and that for the space of four years he has been in this city in a lawsuit with the soldiers of the said presidio. Before the scrivener of war he received the oath which he took before God, our Lord, and the image of the Holy Cross, according to law, and promised to tell the truth. Asked the tenor of the opinion of the said lord, which is in the two pages before this, the declarant said that according to the news which

he had from some letters that had come from New Mexico, as well as what the messenger who had brought them had told him, that the site where the battle was fought was distant from New Mexico two hundred and twenty-five leagues; that the declarant had twelve years ago[148] set out from the capital of Santa Fé as sergeant with thirty soldiers and two hundred Indians, to rescue twenty families who were captives of the pueblo of San Gerónimo, serving some Indians close to El Cuartelejo; and then he saw and knew that it was two hundred leagues from the capital of Santa Fé to El Cuartelejo; and that one sets out from the said capital of Santa Fé and goes to Taos, which is thirty leagues; that from this spot to La Jicarilla there are about ten leagues; that from here to the Río Napestle there are forty leagues, and that the Carlana Apaches have their dwelling place on its borders; that from this site to that which they call the Spring of Our Lady there are twenty leagues; that from here to what is called La Persingula (that is, La Porciuncula) fifty leagues; and from this to El Cuartelejo there are another fifty leagues, which are the two hundred leagues there are from the villa of Santa Fé to El Cuartelejo; that on the occasion that he traveled there, the Indians reckoned it was twenty-five leagues to where the Pawnee Indians have their dwelling place on the other side of the river which they call Jesús María; that the Pawnees were the enemies of those of El Cuartelejo, and that in the forays which they have made on them, they have taken from these Pawnees some fowling pieces, clothes, small short swords, and French iron axes which the declarant saw, and a foot of a gilded silver chalice, which they sold to the declarant for two yards of sackcloth, and two French guns for two horses. Likewise, the witness saw that the captain of the Indians of the said El Cuartelejo wore on the neck of his horse a little silver bell with lettering which read: *Jesús María.*[149]

Many of these Indians of El Cuartelejo told him how the Pawnees are living with Spaniards who are well clothed, and with white women, and go about on the sea in their houses of wood, giving him to understand they are small craft, and that in that region the sea is close; that the above mentioned distance of two hundred leagues is across passable land, a hard plain, with very much grass or hay and considerable streams; that the Sierra Blanca, in the understanding of the declarant, was seventy leagues distant from the villa of Santa Fé [*Marginal note: The distance of Sierra Blanca is seventy leagues from Santa Fé.*] and from there to El Cuartelejo one hundred and thirty; that the two junctions of the rivers of New Mexico and Conchos, which flows

173

towards the presidio of El Paso, are distant from the villa of Santa Fé two hundred leagues, and from El Cuartelejo another two hundred leagues, so that there are more than four hundred leagues from the said junction to the Río Jesús María; that the Canceres were living at the eastern point of the Sierra Blanca which extends from east to west; that on its shoulders which face south the Sierra Blancas have their rancherías and range and that to the north are the Utes and Comanches; [*Marginal note:* Utes and Comanches are to the north of the Sierra Blanca.][150] that the battle was fought at the rising of the sun on the day of San Hipolito, thirteenth of August of this year; that the French and Pawnee attacked unexpectedly all men who were dismounted, [*Marginal note:* Here it appears that the French with Pawnee Indians killed the Spaniards.] except ten who were mounted on the horses which were within the camp where the horseherd had just come in for mounting again; but the enemies did not give them the opportunity for that, because they had been spying on them all night; that the witness knew all this mentioned above from letters and what the messenger who came said; that although they had spies and these were warned by the barking of a dog and by having heard a rustling, it was not considered; that on the dismounting of the last of our men, the French attacked them, and that this above mentioned is what happened and the truth as charged in the oath which he had taken. He affirmed and ratified it, after it had been read to him. He declared his age to be more than twenty-five years. He signed it, and his grace attached his rubric. Rubric of the lord auditor of war. Bartolomé Garduño. Before me, Juan de Balbueba, royal scrivener and that of war.

21. DECLARATION OF TAMARIZ, MÉXICO, NOVEMBER 15, 1720

40. In continuance, the said lord auditor had appear before him a man who said he called himself Felipe de Tamariz, who had come with the mail from New Mexico dispatched by Don Antonio Valverde Cosio, its governor, to his excellency. In order that he declare before me, scrivener of war, he was given the oath which he took before God, our Lord, and the image of the Holy Cross according to law, and promised to tell the truth. Asked the purpose of the said opinion, he submitted that he was a sergeant who went on the reconnaissance of the French settlements. He had made a diary which was lost the day the combat occurred, which was the thirteenth of August of this year; [*Marginal note:* It is most unfortunate that the diary of this

messenger may have been lost.] that the declarant composed another one of everything which happened to them on the trip going and coming from the villa of Santa Fé to the Río de Jesús María; the marches they made; the leagues they traveled from the sixteenth of June of the said year, when he set out with the command from the villa referred to, up to the sixth day of September, when he arrived in the villa with the news of the event. There he did this, so that the circumstances of this accident might not be forgotten. Having arrived at this court, the declarant himself put the diary in the hands of his excellency.[151] He refers to it under the oath he has taken because all that it contains is the truth; and on this occasion, it is affirmed anew because it is correct and the truth, as charged by his oath. He declared his age to be thirty-one years. He signed it, and his lordship placed his rubric on it. Rubric of Lord Olivan. Felipe Tamariz. Before me, Juan de Valvuena, royal scrivener and of war.

22. REVOLLEDO TO VALERO, MÉXICO, DECEMBER 9, 1720

41. *Most Excellent Lord:* In view of the letter of the governor of New Mexico, the reply of the fiscal, and the information received, it is understood that the site on which the Pawnees and French attacked our men is on the Río Jesús María which is to the northeast distant two hundred leagues from Santa Fé, the capital of New Mexico;[152] that the way is flat, without obstruction such as mountains or rivers; that we lost forty-five of the best trained soldiers in the attack; that because of this event and the alliance which the French have with the Pawnee heathen, with the Canceres, with the Utes, and with the Comanches, and with the Pawnee Indian, who was taken by our men to guide them, and who betook himself to his own people, they can without impediment penetrate into that realm if our allies, the Carlana Apaches, do not block their passage; that for its defense, it is necessary that the number of soldiers who were killed be replaced; that they may be selected in this capital from among those who have served his majesty in Europe, for which purpose your Excellency may order that they present themselves, those who have this qualification, in your royal captaincy-general. For this end a proclamation may be published in order that at the cost of their salary they may be conducted, equipped and armed, not only that that governor may find himself with soldiers instructed in European military discipline, but also that they may teach the rest of the presidials and settlers of that capital to defend themselves against the French, preserve the conduct of military

175

matters as it is practiced and established in Europe; and await the attack the messenger predicts, for they are not only settled, but fortified and supplied with ammunition in the manner referred to in the letter and in the investigation.

42. That the event reveals a flagrant act of breaking the truce of which your Excellency will be pleased to give an account to his majesty with the testimony of these proceedings; that there may be erected the presidio deliberated upon in the councils, and decided upon by your Excellency to be in the region of La Jicarilla, forty-five or fifty leagues distant to the northeast of the capital of Santa Fé, to aid the assembled Apaches in this very area of La Jicarilla, and to serve as a bulwark for that realm because it is on the road which goes directly to the settlements of the Pawnees and French; that the twenty-five men which were ordered to occupy this presidio may also be from those who have served in Europe; and that arms and supplies be sent that might be necessary for their establishment.[153] The French and Pawnees are unable to have contact with the Julimes of the rebellious six nations, situated near the junction of the Río del Norte and Sacramento, both, because of the great distance, more than four hundred leagues, which there is from San Juan to the Jesús María, on which are situated the Pawnees and French, as because in the intermediate distance, and in the surrounding territory in the center, there are different tribes, some antagonistic like the Apaches, and others with neither dependence upon nor alliance with them, like the Conchos and Zumas,[154] and others, so that we do not have to fear either that the French and Pawnees may abet the Julimes, or that the latter may aid the others.

43. These French, who are on the Río Jesús María according to the history of this affair, appear to be at thirty-eight or thirty-nine degrees of latitude. They make a triangle with respect to the capital of Santa Fé, and the capital of Texas, the latter in thirty-three degrees of latitude, and the former in thirty-six. The distances between these because of the variance of the degrees of longitude in which they are, constitute the three points in the situation. It appears that the French came to that river of the Pawnees by the Missouri River, and that this flows into the Mississippi and crosses the plains two hundred or three hundred leagues north of Texas. It will be well to inform the Marqués of San Miguel de Aguayo of the news of this event, in order that he may take the necessary precautions concerning the things that have been written him always to suspect the French, and if any Pawnees arrive there or others who have been in their settlements, to inform himself

of the distance there is from them to those of Texas, and to have the same mistrust of the Pawnees which he has of the French, their confederates, of the Canceres, the Utes, and the Comanches, their allies, because it may be that the said French may avail themselves of either under the specious name of peace, or of piety, and go to decoy them from our Catholic and holy religion, or having subverted their zeal in a catholic manner, the French may invade them with these same enemies whom they may receive as friends. Inform them how affectionate are the Apaches of La Jicarilla, in El Cuartelejo and in the Sierra Blanca towards our people, in order that those of this neighboring tribe, the Texas, may know of their good relations and assure them ours, and that they will be defended and protected by our arms from their enemies and the French allies of these same enemies. Your Excellency, remembering what has been referred to and the diary which the messenger says he put in your hands, will determine whatever may be useful in the council which the fiscal attorney proposes. There the auditor-general of war will express what more suggests itself to him. Mexico. December 9, 1720. Dr. Juan de Olivan Revolledo.

23. MARTÍNEZ TO VALERO [MÉXICO, 1720]

44. *Most Excellent Lord:* Captain Don Felix Martínez has placed himself at the feet of your Excellency for the most favorable appeal, without prejudicing anyone who may assist me, all having given a solemn declaration previously so that I might use them where, how, and when it may be convenient to me. I say that, commanded by your Excellency, I made a deposition before the lord auditor-general of war in regard to a report made by Don Antonio Valverde concerning the command of the soldiers of the presidio of New Mexico which the Pawnee Indians sent to their deaths the thirteenth of August past of this year. Being competent to make this representation, and in order that the entire event may not be so misrepresented to your Excellency as to conceal the grave crime which Valverde has committed, so that I may not be held responsible at any time, it is necessary to place before your Excellency the following consideration:

45. That while in the office of governor of New Mexico[155] I maintained all that kingdom in entire peace and tranquillity; the Indian allies remained in subjection with great satisfaction. The enemies were restrained with great fear by the campaigns which I had made and the happy successes which through the mercy of God were given me over them. Your Excellency was under the influence of the sinister repre-

sentations of Don Juan Flores,[156] former governor of that kingdom, and Don Antonio Valverde, captain of the Pass of Río del Norte. Both were joined in a great friendship and allied against me by the great hate which they bore me: Don Juan Flores, because I had taken from him the provisioning which he wished to supply to the presidio at excessive prices, and Don Antonio Valverde, because he had also both supplied provisions to the soldiers of his presidio from the time that he entered into the office of captain and had had the collection of their salaries to augment the great fortune which he has. He feared with this example the soldiers of El Paso also might try to take away the provisioning from him. Thus both with different proposals obliged with persuasion and violence the soldiers of New Mexico to make declarations and papers which they forced them to execute and give up their provisioning. Having given me charge of campaigns which I carried out, they influenced the thought of your Excellency against me in such manner that in view of all, the greatness of your Excellency was pleased to send a dispatch so that Don Antonio should take certain testimonies and that I deliver the government to him and come to this city. This, as is publicly known, was put into effect on the ninth of December of the past year of 1715 by the same Don Antonio Valverde.[157]

To him I responded that with regard to my coming to this city as your Excellency ordered I was promptly executing that which my obligation required. But that with regard to delivering the public employment to him, speaking with veneration and reverence due, I was not consenting for the reasons which I would set forth to your Excellency by word of mouth. To possess it [the office of governor] I had taken an oath, had contracted and had sworn homage for it. For this reason, I was ready to leave a person to my satisfaction in its government, until your Excellency informed of the truth in view of my report, would decide that which was most expedient, as all appears in the principal affidavits which were made concerning this matter. But in spite of an action so well taken, a resolution so fitting, and a reply so much to the service of the king, your Excellency had me charged with disobedience.

46. In fulfillment and obedience to the mandate of your Excellency, I came to this city, where as soon as I arrived I put myself at your feet and informed your Excellency of the state in which I had found the kingdom and the state in which I had left it. I reported that I did not deliver the government to Don Antonio Valverde, although your

178

Excellency so ordered me, because you did not know him and were guided solely by the reports which Don Domingo de la Canal, Cavallero of the Order of Calatrava, correspondent, sponsor, and patron of Don Antonio Valverde and of Don Juan Flores, had made to you. This man, devoted to them and corrupted with hate against me, directed them solely to the end to which he was inducing your Excellency, that of removing me from the government and giving it to Don Antonio, to whom I had not dared to deliver it because of the knowledge which I had of his person and the fear that he would ruin it. Further, because of the great detestation with which the soldiers of New Mexico regarded him, because they had been made to lose more than forty thousand pesos in the litigation with Don Francisco Cuervó,[158] as they have represented it, though even after his influence had been counteracted, they pretended to have received it and been satisfied.

What principally moved me was the knowledge and experience which I had. Since Valverde had come in as captain of the presidio of El Paso, I had never seen him execute with his soldiers any operation in which he might discharge his obligation. It was necessary to utilize for the undertaking, whatever it was, the soldiers of New Mexico. Such happened in the year 1711 when the Indians of the Manza[159] nation and those of the Suma rose up and, leaving their pueblos, went to the sierra because of bad treatment given them and because the Zumas' land had been taken away for cultivation. This is patent even today, since he maintains possession of them, having profited from that said year until the present from the very extensive crops of wine, wheat, maize, beans, and other grains. The poor Indians, because they have no lands nor pueblo where they can sow, go about perishing, acquiring bad habits, and are obliged to rob to maintain themselves.

Thus, if it were not for the soldiers of the villa of Santa Fé, they would not have been reduced even yet because his own soldiers are and have been kept so badly disciplined that they do not even merit the name of soldiers. Because he does not look after anything else than the provisioning of the soldiers, the interests which he was advancing in the increased prices he was charging for them, the collection of their salaries, the ranches which he had acquired and the herds of cattle which he had formed, the soldiers do not have any other occupation than that of muleteers, herders, teamsters, and other employments of husbandry and service directed to his affairs and profits. This work is paid for with the wages of the king.

179

47. This truth, most excellent Lord, which is widely known in all that kingdom, and the knowledge and experience which I have of it from the time I entered at its conquest was that which obliged me to respect some really great soldiers, experienced, disciplined veterans like those they had in the presidio of New Mexico. This is really the principal, only, and entire defense of the kingdom. They have been corrupted at every point: they do not have to make henceforth any proper [military] operation, and they have even the reputation of losing whatever undertaking they attempt. As this was to the detriment of all the kingdom, in disservice to his majesty and contrary to the zeal of your Excellency, it appeared to me that the greatest favor I could do for your Excellency and the greatest fidelity to his majesty was to suspend the delivery of the government to Don Antonio Valverde until giving your Excellency an account. Having taken, as I had, the employment under oath, and had contracted to do homage in it, I was not complying with my obligation by delivering it to one to whom I was commanded without a knowledge of the person and of the unhappy consequences which could follow. For if an unfortunate event should occur, not only his majesty and the most excellent lord viceroy, but your Excellency could hold me liable for not having suspended the delivery, while I was informing you of the truth and the very great inconvenience which could follow the delivery of the government to Don Antonio Valverde.

48. All this, most excellent Lord, I informed your Excellency of when I came, though it seemed the effect of my desire was to maintain myself in the government, which I never had, because the position had not served to advance me an ounce of convenience, nor have I taken from it the best interest as the same affidavits show nor anything more than many difculties and controversies in which Don Juan Flores and Don Antonio Valverde have thwarted me, taking away even my honor, or exculpate myself from the disobedience which was imputed to me. They accused me of calumny; even the detestable crime of infidelity was not ignored. Your Excellency, having ordered me imprisoned in the body of the guard and inferred as fit that General Juan Paez Hurtado, to whom I had left the government as my lieutenant because of his great courage, his many experiences, his prudence, and good will among the soldiers, should deliver the government to Don Antonio Valverde as he did.

As soon as Don Antonio received it, without cause nor any motive for it, he put in prison all the regidors of this city because he considered that they were complaisant in the resistance to delivering the government, attributing this to my influence and not to the knowledge of the truth which we all had that he must ruin the kingdom. This was the only thing which obliged us to resist his entrance for the service of both majesties, for at the same time that surrender in the human is hazarded, faith in the Divine is necessary. Thus your Excellency, to my great grief, experience, turning to God and defending my veracity, has so proved my contention. For the Ute Indians having committed so many robberies and attacks, their audacity becoming so great that they came in near the pueblo of Taos where they killed an Indian and ran off some horses, that Don Antonio Valverde was forced to declare war upon them. To this end he set out in the month of September of the past year of 1716 [sic] with more than one hundred soldiers and settlers and three hundred Indian allies. It was necessary to follow their trail to punish them. In order not to overtake them and see himself obliged to enter battle or retire ignominiously, he took another route. With this news of his cowardice, the Indians came so close to him that there was no more than a hill between them, as an Indian woman declared who fled from them and came to our camp. [Marginal note: See Document 25, number sixteen, where Valverde is cleared of these accusations and the true account of these matters is given.] Yet, having such a good opportunity to punish them, if it were no more than to restrain their insolence, he made his men march in another direction, leaving them more boastful with his flight than they might have been with their own victory.

49. Having marched four days he met by chance some Indians of the Apache nation of El Cuartelejo, among whom there were two other wounded ones. Asked who had wounded them, they replied the French had fallen on their ranchería two days before [Marginal note: The French attack the Indians as they also do the Spaniards; this is contrary to what is said in his declaration No. 38.] and had killed some Indians and wounded others. If he wished he could still overtake them, they said, for they were no more than two days' march from there and they could kill all with great ease because they were few, on foot, and careless. They also proposed to aid, adding themselves to our men for a greater body of troops. With an occasion like this, Don Antonio found himself with more than one hundred Spanish soldiers, three hundred Indian friends, with whom he could with such great facility undertake so glorious an enterprise of so much service to his majesty, and of such great utility to the entire kingdom. Even if they

181

were not French, but Indians with the former's dress and arms, who because of their friendship and alliance have such things, the deception might have been unmasked. If they were French, he might have advanced the security not only of that province, but of all the kingdom with their conquest and capture. Yet against the opinion of his chiefs, he did not wish to continue their pursuit, but judged it better to return to inform your Excellency what he had done, dispatching a messenger with this news. Thus, while he was considering again whether they were Indians or French, they retired further within their land without being punished, and the kingdom (still held the Ute) enemy as powerful as though they were victorious. Even the Indian allies with this example were encouraged with the knowledge of his cowardice for any altercation whatever.

But his [mis]management did not end here. He, having requested of your Excellency to be given an order that he ought either execute in person or dispatch another to his entire satisfaction and confidence, the affair was remitted by your Excellency to the council. Therein it was resolved that a person go with that number of people who appeared fit to him for such an undertaking, and of that which might result he should give an account to your Excellency in order that commands be sent him. That which he did in view of this was to organize a camp of forty-two soldiers, three settlers and sixty Indian allies and name as head Don Pedro Villasur, giving the pretext that he was ill to excuse himself from going personally on this affair.[160]

50. Here, most excellent Lord, the first thing which comes to your eyes is that your Excellency and the council resolved that he should go personally on this affair, without giving him the alternative of delegating another, for no other reason than that they decided because of his courage, knowledge, and the military experiences which he ought to have, he could conduct the campaign with such ability that the glorious end which was desired would be attained; secondly, the unfriendly intent with which, from its inception, Don Antonio resolved to block the affair, as he did in the fatal outcome which he brought about. It was impossible, morally speaking, that it should be successful because, if with more than one hundred Spaniards and three hundred Indian friends, Don Antonio had not dared to continue the advance and confront those said to be French, for fear that they could defeat him, it was not possible that the same Don Antonio could think that only forty-two soldiers and three settlers with sixty Indian allies could conquer them. Thus, the disposition erred at once, either because of malice,

182

which is not too much in one who held so detestable the sergeants and soldiers of New Mexico as to deliver them over to the very knife of a powerful and resourceful enemy, or because of ignorance which is not excusable in a captain, who by his profession is obliged to know the means which he ought to take for the success of his operations, with such reasonable judgments that although, by misfortune or by accident, as many times happens, his successes may not correspond to them, less blame can be imputed to him. Thirdly and finally, failing in the order because he did not wish to expose his person to danger, he adopted the pretext of sickness. This was so false that at the time that he sent off the command and while this was occupied in its expedition, Don Antonio himself went out on an inspection. He went out on this and on it received the news of his ill fortune.

He had in that presidio many chiefs, so valiant, so experienced, and with such great knowledge of the country, though of none he made use, but sent to New Vizcaya for Don Pedro de Villasur. This man in all the days of his life that he had served the king not only had not the least knowledge of the land, nor was practiced nor experienced in war, nor understood that which he was to fight, much less govern and direct. Thus, he admitted not only a serious risk in the unwise selection of the chief, but also in the low spirits of the soldiers and chiefs of New Mexico, because of the lack of confidence for their persons; veterans and experienced men subjected to a visionary man, who did not understand in all the days of his life more than on paper in what manner he had won the pleasure of Don Antonio de Valverde. In order to disengage himself of all its affairs, for it appeared to Valverde that it is the same to dispute with the pen as with arms, he gave over so daring an undertaking which required captains and soldiers to go discontented for fear of its evil end.

51. Would to God the experience had not proved thus. But, having set out from the villa of Santa Fé the sixteenth of June last of this year, they marched fifty days, having camped twelve others. They arrived on the banks of a very full coursing river which has an island in the middle of it where there is a very large settlement of Indians of the Pawnee nation. They are very friendly with the French and have important relations and trade with them; they buy arms of them and learn from them their use and many of them wear the same garb. [*Marginal note:* The Pawnee Indians wear the costume of the French.] Our men, observing that they could not cross, sent an Indian of the same nation, who was a servant of Captain Christóbal de la Zerna, to

183

reconnoiter the settlement and its attitude, and bring news from them. This he did not do, but remained in it, and the Indian with a white flag on a stick came, whose language no one could understand, nor what he was saying. Having taken the flag from him, Juan de Arché-vèque, a Frenchman who was accompanying our command, gave him another of white cloth, and a paper written in the French language, in order that it might be given to the chief of that people. With this the Indian left and on another day, another Indian returned with an old ragged linen cloth as a flag, asking that they take it and return the one the first Indian had brought over, and also an old paper written in a language that the Frenchman did not understand. All this showed not only the bad intentions and contempt with which they regarded us, but that all was a piece of cunning to take the measure of the command and to attack it when they could not resist them.

All this obliged the head chief to be watchful and have care. This he did by moving the camp and, having marched some distance, halted. The master of the camp, Tomas Olguín, recommended that since the retreat had begun, he should continue it, because the enemy was near and the spot in which he had ordered camp made was not fit to resist the enemy. Villasur replied to him that was fear and that there they were going to stop. He answered that he had never known fear and spoke only what appeared wise to him.[161] Notwithstanding, the chief maintained his opinion, encamping in very thick grass higher than the stature of a man. From there he sent the horses to pasture, leaving the men on foot and without the least kind of sentinel for the enemy, who went to bed to sleep with as much insouciance as if they were in their homes.

52. And thus, at the break of day of the thirteenth of August, the enemy fell upon them, and without losing a man, our men neither firing a gun nor being scarcely able to draw a knife, they killed all who were found in camp. Only those escaped who were guarding the horses who, seeing all their companions slain, fled for the villa of Santa Fé, where they arrived on the sixth day of September. Not finding Don Antonio in it, because he was out on an inspection, they went to give the news to him in the pueblo of Santo Domingo, where he was. This, most excellent lord, is the real and true account of what happened on this campaign. However much it may wish to be misrepresented and painted to your Excellency, it is the saddest, the most lamentable, and the most fatal event that has happened in New Mexico since the time of its conquest. Outside of Father Friar Juan

184

Mínguez, a Franciscan religious who went as chaplain, and the commander, Don Pedro de Villasur, they killed thirty-three of the best officers and soldiers that that presidio had, as appears in the list in the margin,[162] and eleven of our Indian friends. Thus in the villa of Santa Fé, thirty-two widows and many orphan children, whose tears reach the sky, mourn the poor ability of the governor, pray God for his punishment, and await the remedy of your justice.[163]

This is not the worst of the damage which has happened or which may happen since the least is that the neighboring Indian enemies, viewing this defeat, have assumed greater insolence. The greatest is that even the allies are so overbearing that little lacks for them to declare themselves enemies, because the valor and experience which those dead had was the bridle which restrained them. These being absent, they consider themselves superior to all who have remained in defense of the villa. The evident proof is the very example that they have given of their boldness, since the same messenger who brought this fatal news, with a ten soldier escort, makes known that the Indians in the intervening distance between Santa Fé and the Presidio del Norte attacked them and killed a soldier, wounded three and carried off almost all the horses. What is more, they had the daring to attack an entire pueblo of Indian allies, that of San Felipe, killed three Indians, and ran off a portion of their horses.

This is certain: That when cancer moves about in the body, there is no security for the heart; when there is a raging fever in its parts, it is very close to reaching the head. We are able and must fear with great reason and prudent conjecture that even the Indian allies in the vicinity of the villa of Santa Fé are as warlike. This was shown and experience shows, in the past revolt, in which they killed twenty-two religious, more than one hundred and sixty persons, and even obliterated the name of Spaniards, throwing off totally the yoke of vassalage and obliging his majesty to conquer them anew at the very greatest expense. This the Marqués de las Navas Brazinas did, with whom I entered to serve, engaging in the most important encounters, and in the siege of the very villa of Santa Fé until achieving its surrender. There is no certain instant in which that kingdom may not be lost.[164]

53. All this, most excellent Lord, is said to your Excellency with truth, candor, fidelity, and loyalty that I profess to his majesty, in whose service I have been, nevertheless, despoiled of the office of governor. Though, because of the experiences I had had for more than thirty-eight years, since from a soldier I have risen and attained by my own

185

hands promotion, I was worthy, and the most excellent lord, the Duke of Linares honored me with the governorship,[165] it would appear to me a species of treason not to disabuse your Excellency in order that in view of this representation you could approve or disprove, praise or blame, or decide upon that which is the most acceptable for the service of his majesty. Neither for that nor for the declaration that your Excellency ordered, should I have had, nor have I had, any other purpose than to give assistance to that realm, the protection of those dominions, and the conservation of the Faith, without passion, hate, or ill intentions toward Don Antonio Valverde, notwithstanding that by him and Don Juan Flores I was dispossessed of the governorship, flung into prison, and foresee myself in this city perishing, having fought up to the moment against the ill-intention of their reports which have injured me. However, through the mercy of God they have been vanquished by the same testimonies.

Because fealty is my defense, which I swore to in the office and oath I took to maintain it, I resisted delivering the post before informing your Excellency of the truth so that in its light you might command me to do that which I ought. Thus at no time can I be charged with this affair, nor of any of the most pernicious consequences which can flow from it.

54. To your Excellency: I beg and supplicate with the profound humiliation which corresponds to my veneration that you may be pleased to command that I be given an affidavit of the dispatch in which I was commanded to deliver the government to him; of the reply which I gave, word for word; and with regard to how by this I was accused in the common trial which was drawn up against me; of this representation and decree which might be issued for it (i.e., the representation); both word for word, for my safety. Thus I may be provided with a defense for whatever charge that may be imputed to me. This is the justice which I hope for from the greatness of your Excellency. Felix Martínez.

55. List of soldiers killed on the thirteenth day of August of this year of 1720. The chaplain, Fray Juan Mínguez; the principal commander, D. Pedro de Villasur; Adjutant General José Domínguez; master of the camp, Tomás Olguín; Captain Christóbal de la Zerna; Captain Miguel Tenorio; Captain Pedro Luxán; lieutenant of the presidio, Bernardo Casillas; Corporal José Griego; Corporal Lorenzo Rodríguez; Manuel de Silva; Pedro Segura; Lorenzo Segura; Juan de Archévèque, interpreter of the French language; Diego Velásquez;

Ignacio de Aviles; José Fernandez; Simón de Córdova; Francisco Gonzales; Francisco de Tapia; Francisco Perea; Bernardo Madrid; Pedro de Agüero; Nicolas Girón; Domingo Romero; Luis Ortiz; Juan Gallegas; Ramón de Medina; Antonio de Herrera; Domingo Trujillo; Juan Río de Rojas; Pedro Lugo; José Naranjo; Juan de Lira; Pedro de Mendizábal; and eleven Indian allies.[166]

24. MARTÍNEZ TO VALERO, MÉXICO, 1723

56. *Most Excellent Lord:* (I supplicate the greatness of your Excellency that these writings be read to the letter and that the assessor of your Excellency be not present because he is a lawyer for the other side.) I, Don Felix Martínez, governor of the kingdom of New Mexico in the judicial proceedings which were conducted upon the inspection of the presidios of the land within which Captain Don Antonio Cobián Bustos went to execute, and especially of that of the presidio of the villa of Santa Fé of New Mexico and the rest of the matters which may have a more important place in law, appear before the greatness of your Excellency. I say that on the occasion that Don Antonio Cobián, having remitted the testimony to your Excellency in five parcels of paper bound together, which your lordship had forwarded to the lord auditor, in the reply which he gave he was of the opinion that the judicial proceedings be returned to Don Antonio Cobián and, among other things, that he inquire into and establish the real motive which Governor Don Antonio Valverde had in not going personally as he was ordered by the most excellent lord, Marqués de Valero, on the reconnaissance of the Río Jesús María, on whose banks were established the settlements of the Pawnee Indians allied with the French, [*Marginal note:* Here it is seen most clearly that the River of the Pawnee is the Río Jesús María.] with whom they dwell and with whom they attacked and surprised those whom the same Valverde sent under the command of his lieutenant, inexperienced in military affairs and the management of arms. Because of his carelessness in this attack before they were arranged in battle order, forty-five veteran soldiers of those who had reconquered that kingdom of New Mexico were killed in camp, as is more extensively contained in his said reply.

Because your Excellency was pleased to concur, as up to the present the dispatch does not appear to have been sent, nor the return made, because the attorney, Francisco Antonio Rosales, took these judicial proceedings which he held in his possession from the twenty-eighth day of June of the present year, having delivered them, as he delivered

187

them, to Captain Don Domingo de la Canal. The latter, having been presented with a memorial by my attorney, had to return them and they were delivered to him. All this, most excellent lord, because I do not consider so much the inspection which Don Antonio made because it concerns me, as the reply of the lord auditor, since Don Domingo de la Canal protects Don Antonio Valverde. The opposing attorney, with the pretext that he is defending the presidial troops, did this thing.

57. I am presenting the following memorial in order that your Excellency with your great sense of justice, prudence, and wisdom, so experienced and practiced in matters of war, may be informed of the things which have occurred in that kingdom in the time when the said Don Antonio Valverde governed, the crime so grave and other things which he committed and whom it has been attempted to exculpate and protect, and has been protected, to my great discredit, taking away my life and honor by having issued affidavits, wherein I have a deposition made, before the lord auditor, Don Juan de Olivan. Likewise, may you be informed of the judicial processes which were prosecuted in New Mexico and were prosecuted by Don Juan Flores Mogollón against me, and in which Don Antonio issued an accusation against me. This was prosecuted, charging me with not delivering the government to Don Antonio Valverde. The aforesaid maintained himself against all reason in his glory; all his forces and artillery have been directed against me because of the influential persuasions and agencies of Don Domingo de la Canal.

I am submitting, with the solemn and necessary oath, a copy of a memorial from two which I presented of the same tenor to the most excellent lord, Marqués de Valero, the predecessor of your Excellency. On one of them, because of the interposition of the lieutenant of the scrivener of government, Don Antonio de Aviles, no measure was taken. The other I delivered into the very hand of the said most excellent lord. I was frustrated everywhere. The scrivener neither wished to take my deposition nor return the writing to me. Thus justice up to the present has been denied me. The great goodness of God has caused the lord auditor to see the clear injustice which has been worked against me and in favor of Don Antonio Valverde by the visitor of the said presidios, as the above may have showed. According to his words, may the greatness of your Excellency be pleased to favor my just claim that Don Antonio may not remain without condign punishment, having been the formal cause of the death of forty-five veteran soldiers, naming for them an inexperienced commander as the affidavits

188

which I have cited reveal. May the lord auditor have them search for the official letter and deliver it to me; likewise, let the scrivener, Don Antonio Aviles, certify that, as mentioned above, I had presented the memorial to the Lord Marqués de Valero and that no measure was taken. This reservation being made, I may allege whatever befits me. In the meantime, nothing should be done to my prejudice.

To your Excellency I pray and supplicate that you may be pleased, having been presented with the said memorial, to command and have determined everything as I refer to it with justice and costs. I swear to God and on the cross to be certain in my soul of what is herein contained. Felix Martínez. Licenciado Christóval Moreno Avalos.

57. México, September 15, 1723. To the lord auditor, with a rubric of his excellency.

25. REVOLLEDO TO CASA FUERTE, MÉXICO, SEPTEMBER 22, 1723

Most Excellent Lord: It is well known that the supplicant went in the company of the Marqués de Barzinas, Don Diego de Bargas Zapata y Luxán to the kingdom of New Mexico. This fact weighs much. He reconquered and reduced it to obedience and vassalage of the king. For this and other merits, the supplicant was made a captain in that presidio, which office he exercised. Afterwards he governed that kingdom because of the resignation which Don Juan Flores submitted over various lawsuits sued between him, the supplicant, and the soldiers in that presidio. All or the largest part of the litigation was about the great interests which Don Juan Flores pretended to have: about the supplies and provisions made to his soldiers both by his predecessor, the Marqués de la Peñuela, as well as by the provisioner, Don Pedro de Otero, by the authority the Duke of Linares[167] gave the latter for this purpose; and about the supplicant, forbidding Don Juan Flores to sell to the soldiers the goods which belonged to them, bought and paid for with their salaries, and remitted on the account of these same soldiers from this Mexico to that New Mexico, and that he held them illegally making extravagant profits by their sale at the high prices of New Mexico, to these same soldiers who were the rightful owners of those same goods of which he was not the owner, neither could he have been.

The same Don Juan was and is engaged in an important legal battle, and even today is in jail in the captaincy-general of your Excellency.[168] He is represented in a great file of papers which the auditor saw, having been named by the most excellent lord, [the] Marqués de Valero, as judge together with the Marqués de Villa Hermosa and Lord Don Antonio Terreros, because three other lord ministers had been challenged, as afterwards the auditor and the two above mentioned judges were. After having seen this great collection of papers and having been given an opinion, he concluded that if there had not been the salaries of the soldiers, there would have been neither litigation nor challenges, nor would those interested have been swindled so much.

58. Don Domingo de la Canal as a friend of Don Juan Flores ought to believe in him and support him. That his faith would be in what was right, is presumable, to fulfil the duties which are delegated by his friend, in the opinion that he was furthering justice. The same as regards Don Antonio Valverde, governor of this same New Mexico, who is a man of merit and honor and in common belief would not do a thing which he might consider intrinsically sinful. Although according to his best intentions, as is presumable, he did injustices, even though they were accidental, if they were born of sincere intention, he is absolved with regard to this point, according to the feeling of the jurists and moralists and in the sense in which they discuss and decide these matters.

With regard to the second point, it is certain that a file was made up according to the report and affidavits which the same Don Antonio Valverde remitted concerning the fatal happening, namely, that the French, allied with the Pawnees, killed forty-five men, the most veteran ones of that presidio, at a distance of two hundred leagues from the capital of New Mexico. A file was formed in which it is understood by the auditor who dispatched it, that the defendant, at the order of the most excellent lord, Marqués de Valero, should set forth his plea.

Let the rights of the supplicant, to the extent that he has rights, be protected. This is well assured in the known equity which your Excellency administers; he should await the justice that you may have for him. Your Excellency, willing it, can order that Don Antonio de Aviles certify as he prays; that this file of papers be looked for and the other which he cites, and that they return them to the auditor, both executed, if it pleases your Excellency or that which your Excellency may consider more just. México, September 22, 1723. Doctor Juan de Olivan Revolledo.

59. México, September 23, 1723. As it appears to the lord auditor, with a rubric of his excellency.

190

In compliance with that which was commanded by the most excellent lord, Marqués de Casa-Fuerte, viceroy, governor and captain-general of this New Spain and president of the royal audiencia of it, in his above decree which goes before, and in view of the point concerning me contained in the writing of the pages before this, that which I can certify is that I do not recall, because I do not remember whether or not I gave the memorial which Don Felix Martínez specifies, through my interposition to the most excellent lord, Marqués de Valero, the predecessor of your Excellency, nor whether his excellency took any action touching the above mentioned because one was of the various and repetitious writings, reports, papers, and the rest of the matters which were being repeatedly presented to the affair of the trial and placed in the affidavits of the material for the parties; the other, the passage of time, variety and confusion of affairs which have been dispatched. They are in the office of the government under my charge. Of these an understanding is not easy in the regular course of human affairs because they are innumerable, as is well known. México, September 25, 1723. Antonio de Aviles.

27. REVOLLEDO TO CASA FUERTE, MÉXICO, JULY 11, 1724

60. *Most Excellent Lord:* In view of the preceding certificate, your Excellency being pleased may command that I give to Don Felix Martínez the testimony of the two writings which precede, together with the opinion of the auditor and decrees of your Excellency. Likewise that I give testimony of the writing presented by Francisco Antonio Rosales in the name of the presidials of New Mexico, the opinion of the auditor, decrees of your Excellency and also the declarations which he made at page sixty-six (in this, our copy, it is *ante* at number thirty-eight.) of these affidavits in order that he may make use of the testimony, among that which he is submitting with these same presidials and their governor, before your Excellency, which is the place where he ought to continue his suit, and seek that which touches his interests.

However, because he has been made a captain by the king of the presidio of New Mexico, to whose reconquest he went with the Marqués de Brasina, Don Diego de Vargas Luján, wherein he has served many years with skill and valor, it was more worthy of him to engage his person in the service and employment in which the king placed

191

him by royal cedula, wherein his rank was conferred upon him, than uselessly to lose his time in litigation which an attorney, well instructed as to his rights, could do. Your Excellency will determine that which may be most just. México, July 11, 1724. Doctor Juan de Olivan Revolledo.

61. México, July 19, 1724. Let the testimonies be given him for which he prays for the purpose which he represents with citation of the lord fiscal, and on behalf of the presidials. Rubric of his most excellent lord.

28. ROSALES TO CASA FUERTE, MÉXICO, SEPTEMBER 25, 1723

Most Excellent Lord: (I,) Francisco Antonio Rosales, in the name of the presidials of New Mexico, in the affidavits together with D. Felix Martínez concerning accounts and the rest, say that on the opposing side an extensive writing was presented which the auditor had brought to him, since concerning my data he had to be satisfied.

To your Excellency I supplicate that you be pleased to command that the affidavits be transferred and for that purpose be delivered to me. I pray justice, costs, etc. Francisco Antonio Rosales. México, September 25, 1723.

To the lord auditor, with a rubric of his excellency.

29. REVOLLEDO TO CASA FUERTE, MÉXICO, OCTOBER 11, 1723

Most Excellent Lord: Your Excellency has a file of papers pending in your captaincy-general at the instance of Don Felix Martínez, former governor of New Mexico and captain of those presidials, in which the lord auditor gave an opinion to your Excellency so that this file might be put with other files concerning the same thing, in order to submit an opinion to your Excellency in their light. From them, it will be seen whether or not the copying requested by the attorney of these presidials has been done, as he maintains should be in his above opinion. Your Excellency will command that which you estimate most just. México, October 11, 1723. Dr. Juan de Oliván Revolledo.

62. México, October 13, 1723. As it appears to the lord auditor, with a rubric of his excellency.

30. REVOLLEDO TO CASA FUERTE, MÉXICO, APRIL 10, 1724

Most Excellent Lord: These affidavits, which were taken to the auditor to give an opinion concerning whether or not they have been delivered to the attorney, who says he is the attorney of the presidials of New Mexico, with regard to what was prayed for by their captain,

192

Don Felix Martínez, were returned to the office of the government to be put with those of the account of Señor Marqués de San Miguel de Aguayo, as governor of Texas. It is said that these belong there under the name of the Fourth File so that they might go to the royal *tribunal of accounts* for review of the account given by the marqués.

With regard to this matter, these affidavits are brought together concerning the matter of the presidio of New Mexico, which is totally different and distinct from that of Texas, and they have no relation with those of Texas nor with the account of the Marqués of San Miguel. Your Excellency will command that this file of papers must be separated from those of Texas and that the testimony be taken out which concerns only Texas. This is the information which was ordered given to the Marqués de San Miguel de Aguayo in the council at pages thirty-nine and over, [*Marginal note:* This council which is mentioned here is not copied because it is copied in document twenty-five of this, number 228.] of the Apaches having come to our alliance throughout New Mexico and that he solicit the same of those throughout the country of Texas. This testimony was put in the affidavits of the Marqués de San Miguel in order that it appear that there was nothing else in them and they be not esteemed lessened in value for whatever determination that may be taken concerning them.

With regard to those of New Mexico, your Excellency will command that they be given for review to the lord fiscal and returned to the auditor with that which the former might say. México, April 10, 1724. Dr. Juan de Oliván Revolledo.

31. ORDER FOR COUNCIL OF WAR, SANTA FÉ, 1723

63. In the same file the memorandum that follows was found.[169] New Mexico. Xicarilla Apaches. Year 1723. Judicial proceedings and measures taken concerning the Apaches of La Xicarilla and the rest of the heathen of those countries who have begged for the water of holy baptism and to be brought into the fold of our Catholic religion, offering vassalage to his majesty. For this purpose, they have prayed to be subjected and congregated in a pueblo, before General Don Juan Domingo de Bustamante, governor and captain-general of this kingdom and provinces of New Mexico and warden of its forces and presidios for his majesty, etc.

32. DECREE FOR COUNCIL OF WAR, SANTA FÉ, NOVEMBER 8, 1723

Decree. In the villa of Santa Fé, New Mexico, on the eighth day of the month of November, 1723, I, General Don Juan Domingo de

193

Bustamante, governor and captain-general of this kingdom and provinces of New Mexico for his majesty, said that on the instance of this date Captain Carlana, with other captains of the heathen Apache nation, having appeared and represented to me that the heathens of the Comanche nation, their enemies, had attacked them with a large number in their rancherías in such a manner that they could not make use of weapons for their defense. They launched themselves with such daring and resolution that they killed many men, carrying off their women and children as captives. Because they recognized that they are not safe from their enemies any place, they are asking me to protect and shield them with the arms of his majesty. Concerning this, they have conferred and communicated with the rest of the captains and people of the rancherías of their nation, because they have the same fears. In order to get away from them, they are seeking more pleasant living in entire peace and tranquillity under the security of the arms of his majesty, giving him henceforth the required obedience. For this reason, they are praying that I administer to them the sacrament of holy baptism, and their entire nation, having received it with all their heart, will settle in their pueblos in the same form and economy with which the Christian Indians of this kingdom live; that priests be assigned them to teach and instruct them in the mysteries of our holy faith, and that an alcalde mayor govern them. They will submit themselves to everything with punctual obedience commanded them, since they realize that the ruin they have suffered and which their enemies have inflicted on their rancherías has been because they have been remiss in coming to the fold of our Catholic and true religion. For the success of their good desires they have asked me, the governor, to go to the valley of La Jicarilla to survey the place and situation which offers the most advantages for the foundation and establishments of the said pueblos with their lands so that they may reap their crops. At this moment, I am prepared to make a campaign with the arms of this royal presidio against the barbarous and heathen tribe of Faraone Apaches, who attack the frontiers and pueblos of this kingdom. This being an occasion so opportune for the greater good in the royal service of his majesty, as are my greatest desires, it appeared to me just to call a council of war of the military of this royal presidio and the most practiced and experienced settlers so that, in view of this decree, each one may state his judgment and opinion as to whether the campaign should be superseded or we undertake that which these Apache captains solicited and have represented to me. For this reason, the present

194

secretary of government and war has made known to them this, my determination, and is summoning the persons according to the list I have given him, to assemble tomorrow morning, the ninth of the present month, in this palace presidial fort, the date which I indicate for the affair. So provided, ordered and signed with my secretary of government and war. Juan Domingo de Bustamante. Before me, Miguel Enríques, secretary of government and war.

33. COUNCIL OF WAR, SANTA FÉ, NOVEMBER 9, 1723

65. Council. In the villa of Santa Fé of New Mexico, on the ninth day of the month of November, 1723, I, General Don Juan Domingo de Bustamante, governor and captain-general of this kingdom and provinces of New Mexico and warden of its forces and presidios for his majesty, decree that, in conformity with that ordered by the writ which was provided by me, who is in command of these, the present council be formed and in it opinions stated to reach the best result to be inferred from the above mentioned writ. To carry out this there were present in the room of the palace of my dwelling: Captains Alonso Musguia, Alonso Real de Aguilar; Ayudante Salvador de Santistevan; Captain of the Company Antonio Tafoya; Captains Juan de la Mora, Pineda and Francisco Lorenzo de Casados; sergeant of this presidio, Juan Vijil; Ayudante Don Francisco Guerrero; Ensign Don José de la Plaza; lieutenant-captain of this presidio, Antonio de Ulibarri; D. Francisco Bueno de Bohorques, alcalde mayor and captain of war of this villa; Captain D. Antonio Pérez Velarde; Sergeant-Major D. Alfonso Real de Aguilar; Lieutenant-General D. Juan Paez Hurtado; the Reverend Father Preachers Fray Antonio de Savaldon, Fray Juan del Pino, Fray Francisco de Irazaval, Fray Domingo de Arans, Fray Antonio Camargo, procurer of this holy custody; Fray José Antonio Guerrero, guardian of the convent of our Father San Francisco of this villa; and the very Reverend Father Preacher Fray Francisco de Lepiane, custodian and ecclesiastical judge in ordinary of this holy custody.

Having understood the context of the above mentioned writ, for which purpose it was read, all, each one for himself unanimously and in agreement, after they had conferred at length on this affair, said that the conversion of the souls which are outside of our true and Catholic religion, and who have come with the desires they are manifesting to receive the water of holy baptism, of congregating and reducing themselves to live in their pueblos, rendering vassalage and obedience to his majesty, is of such service to God, our Lord, and to

195

the pleasure of his majesty (God preserve him) that favorable results are promised. Their example may cause all the rest of their tribe to do likewise, which is so dispersed and large that they live on the spaciousness of the plains as far away as the boundaries of its nations, the Pawnees, the Cagodachos (Cadodachos, it should have been written), the Canzeres, and other tribes who are their opponents. Consequently, the settlements will serve as a bulwark for this kingdom, for its greater security from French arms and settlements which are on the Mississippi River, as the valley of La Jicarilla is where they can come through. For these reasons the campaign ought to be suspended [*Marginal note:* The French are established on the Mississippi River.] which, I, the governor, had determined beforehand to carry out against the enemy Faraones to end for a time their plundering and the rest of their attacks, and offer these (the Jicarillas) the royal protection of his majesty, under the arms of whom they could live safely and be defended against their enemies. Accordingly, they are of the opinion that I, the said governor, should go with fifty soldiers from this presidial fort to the above mentioned valley of La Xicarilla, call together the captains and the rest of the heathens who are there, and set forth the motives and consideration that, I, the governor, have had in going to their rancherías. If their accounts are in accord with the ones which these captains have represented, he could at once assign them their site and precinct where they can construct and assemble their pueblos. Of these measures, let an account be given to his most excellent lordship, Viceroy Marqués de Casa Fuerte, in order that in view of them, his highness, with his just zeal, in the greatest service of both majesties, may command measures be taken for the greatest success of this undertaking, which the most excellent señores viceroys have solicited with such ardor, the request for which they have given by their superior order to preceding governors.

Likewise, the measures were explained to those Apache captains, who were present, by means of Gerónimo Ylo, Indian chief of the pueblo of Taos, and Juan Luján, a soldier of this royal presidio, who served as interpreters, the reason for having held this council, and that in it had been determined that I, the governor, should set out on the day mentioned for the valley of La Jicarilla to effect that which they have prayed for, and that when I arrive they should have gathered together all the captains, and the rest of the people. Over this they were pleased, manifesting their satisfaction and saying that they wished to go to carry out that which was ordered of them. All that which has been

196

referred to is what has happened and been decided upon in the council, nothing else being offered to them for the present.

After I, the governor and captain-general, had seen all that had been determined and conferred upon in the council, I agreed with it to accomplish all in the greatest service of the divine and human majesty. In order that I fulfil the prospected arrangement, I ordered the lieutenant of Captain Antonio de Ulibarri immediately to prepare fifty soldiers of the company of this presidial fort for the seventeenth day of the current month of November, which is that which I marked for my departure and march to the before cited valley of La Jicarilla. In order that it may so appear, I signed it in the council with the persons who attended and with my secretary of government and war, Alonzo Mizguia. The signature of all the ones mentioned above composing the council follows.

34. DIARY OF GOVERNOR BUSTAMANTE, NOVEMBER 17-27, 1724

66. The governor sets out from the villa of Santa Fé for the valley of La Jicarilla. In the villa of Santa Fé on the seventeenth of the month of November, 1723, I, the governor and captain-general, depose that in conformity with what was confirmed in the antecedent council and for the execution of that which was resolved therein, I am setting out today, this date, for the valley of La Jicarilla with fifty soldiers of this presidial fort, and in my company [is] the very reverend father preacher, Fray Antonio Camargo, proctor of this holy custody. So that it appear so, I sign it with my secretary of government and war. Juan Domingo Bustamante. Before me, Miguel Enríques, secretary of government and war.

67. The governor arrives at the valley of La Jicarilla and on the chief river, called Guadalupe. [*Marginal note:* Río de Guadalupe is the principal stream of the valley of La Jicarilla.] On the twenty-fifth day of the month of November, 1723, I, General Don Juan Domingo de Bustamante, governor and captain-general of this kingdom of New Mexico and warden of its forces and presidios for his majesty, state that after having arrived today, this recorded day, on this spot and Río de Guadalupe, where the valley of La Jicarilla begins, Captain Carlana with six other captains and (fifty young men), who arrived in a body, one of whom was carrying a holy cross, came out to receive me. With joyful demonstrations, they manifested the happiness which they had because I, the governor, had come to their land. What they desired was to receive the water of holy baptism and to render obedi-

ence to his majesty which they did, thus ratifying and corroborating the same which they had previously represented to me in the villa of Santa Fé. After I had heard them affectionately, by means of the above mentioned interpreters, Gerónimo Ylo and Juan Luján, I reiterated to them the same thing which I proposed to them in the villa of Santa Fé: namely, to protect and defend them from their enemies with the arms of his majesty, in whose royal name I would receive them immediately as his vassals, and have them showed the site and location where they would have to construct and establish their pueblos and live like Christians, devoting themselves to the land for its crops. After they had been informed concerning the above mentioned, they said that they would go further in where other captains were with their rancherías and determine that which they ought to do concerning this matter. In order that this may appear so, I, the governor and captain-general, sign it with my secretary of government and war, Juan Domingo Bustamante. Before me, Miguel Enríques, scrivener of government and war.

68. The governor reaches the ranchería of Captain Churlique. On the twenty-sixth of the said month and year of this date, I, the governor, having set out from the above mentioned spot and Río de Guadalupe, arrived, at a distance of five leagues, at the ranchería of Captain Churlique with Captain Carlana and the rest of the captains mentioned. When I was near Captain Churlique came out to receive me with an engraving of Our Lady the Virgin Mary, which he had wrapped in a buckskin. I took this holy image in my hands and with devoted reverence kissed it, and held it above my head and with this opportunity, I gave them a long discourse on the mysteries of our holy faith, saying that up to the present time they had lived blindly and were slaves of the Devil, that they should give thanks to our Lord, the Creator of the heavens and the earth, who had enlightened their understanding so that they should come into a knowledge of his holy law (which is the true law), in order that their souls might be saved, and that this was the greatest desire of the king, our lord (may God guard him). For this end he had placed me in the position of governor and captain-general and was paying the soldiers who were under my command. In the same way I was assisting the priests with alms so that they could administer the holy sacraments to the Indians of the realm, who were living quietly and peacefully, because they were always protected from the enemies who were attacking them. In the same manner I would do so for them, having been influenced to come to this land

because those captains who were present in Santa Fé had sworn obedience to his majesty and intended to receive the water of holy baptism. To this he (Churlique) responded, with much rejoicing, that they would be baptized (being ignorant of undertaking the first perquisite of the mysteries of our faith). Moreover, he continued, saying that I should join their people who were in other rancherías distant from his to make a campaign against their enemies, the Comanche nation, because they found themselves suffering from the havoc they had wrought on one of their rancherías, as he went on to explain. To these propositions, I, the governor, responded that there was a time for everything, that I supposed that their pretension was to reduce themselves to our Catholic religion as they said, that they should discuss the situations where they had to build their pueblos in order to divide up the lands among them which they needed so that they could be assigned and adjudicated for them in the name of the king, our lord, and that missionaries for whom they ask be sent them for their teaching and instructing in the mysteries of our holy faith, as well as an alcalde mayor to govern them. This having been carried out, it was my obligation to defend them from their enemies, making war on them as they would discover upon occasions which presented themselves. Concerning this, he was pleased, convinced entirely of what I had proposed. For the final decision, he begged me to go on the following day to another ranchería which was close to his, and there everything which had been expressed could be deliberated upon with the captain of that ranchería, and whatever else that might conduce for the best. In order that it appear so, I, the governor and captain-general, sign it with my secretary of government and war. Don Juan Domingo de Bustamante. Before me, Miguel Enríquez, secretary of government and war.

69. [*Marginal note:* The governor approaches the ranchería of Captain Cojo.] On the twenty-seventh day of the month of November and year of the date, I, the said governor, having set out with the soldiery and with the said reverend father procurator, Fray Antonio de Camargo, from the cited ranchería of Captain Churlique, and having marched about four leagues through the said valley, arrived at the ranchería of Captain Cojo, who with all his people was waiting for me. He welcomed me with many demonstrations of gratitude for having come to his land because he desired this very much. For this show of friendship I embraced him affectionately, indicating to him by means of the said interpreters the reason for having come to his land, giving them the explanation as I had to the previously mentioned

199

captains, and adding with pleasure that their people were swearing, as they had, obedience to his majesty and would receive the water of holy baptism. Captain Coxo begged that they, who had on another occasion repudiated the water, should be baptized immediately. Through the interpreters, I gave him to understand that it was necessary to absolve him of the apostasy which he had committed. Because he was a Christian, they could receive the water but once. In this way they would return to the fold of our Catholic religion. With regard to this, he was satisfied with these explanations and many others which the father proctor, Fray Antonio Camargo, made clear to him, leaving to my care the defense and protection that they would have to have from the arms of his majesty from their enemies. The king, our lord (may God guard him), would look after them and give them tools to cultivate their lands and carry on their labors. Because of this they exhibited much pleasure. All the rest of the people, who were dispersed among the other rancherías and were of the same mind as they, would unite with them and in the spring of the coming year they would advise me for the purpose of bringing them the missionaries and the alcalde mayor. Better to attract them to our devotion, I presented to each one of the captains a horse and to all generally a certain amount of flour that I had provided for this purpose, this being the means of encouraging their stability and permanence.

70. I, the governor, recognized and replied to the discourse which the three captains made before me in the villa of Santa Fé, together with those and all the demonstrations which they had manifested. There are a great number of people of both sexes, who by giving themselves to God our Lord, and to the king our lord (may God guard him), add many souls to his vassals and extend his dominions in these regions. The valley is particularly abundant in springs and rivers embracing luxuriant woodlands; and because of the fertility of its soil, plentiful crops will be secured by its cultivation. For this extension, I ordered the royal ensign, Don Miguel Enríquez de Cabrera, my secretary of government and war, to wave the royal standard of his majesty over its broad surface. This was done with a three-gun salute. I commanded the military to discharge their weapons, declaring in a loud voice that I was taking and took royal possession in the name of his majesty the king, our lord, Señor Don Philip V [*Marginal note:* Royal possession which I, the governor, took in the name of their majesty.] whom God guard many years. I received and admitted under the royal protection all those vassals who were present and all the rest

200

who were absent and were natives of those rancherías. To these words all said: "Long live the king many years." All of this was explained to the captains and the rest of the heathens, who received it appreciatively. I took my leave of them to return to the villa of Santa Fé.[170] In order that it may appear so, I sign it with my secretary of government and war. Don Juan Domingo de Bustamante. Before me, Miguel Enríques, secretary of government and war.

35. BUSTAMANTE TO CASA FUERTE, SANTA FÉ, JANUARY 10, 1724

71. *Most Excellent Lord:* In compliance with my obligation I am giving your Excellency an account of how on the eighth of November of the present year, three captains of the Apache nation appeared before me, representing to me that those of the Comanche nation, their enemies, attacked them. They assaulted with a vast number one of their rancherías in such a manner that they could not defend themselves. They attacked with such determination that they killed many young men and carried off their women and children captives. They had the misgiving and fear that the said enemy would return to harass them. To escape them, they petitioned me to protect and defend them with the arms of his majesty (may God guard him). They promised to give him at once the required obedience, pleading that the sacrament of holy baptism be administered to them together with all those of their rancherías, and to come together to live in their pueblos in the same form in which the Christian Indians of this kingdom dwell. For this end they begged that missionaries be given them and an alcalde mayor to govern them, and that they would subject themselves to me in everything that will be commanded of them, with entire docility. They had a clear understanding that the calamity they had experienced was due to the omission and unwillingness they had in coming into the fold of our Catholic religion. They supplicated me insistently to go to their land, the valley of La Jicarilla, where they have their dwelling, to make a reconnaissance of the site and spots that would be the most profitable to establish their pueblos. Because I was about to make a campaign with the arms of this royal presidio against the nation of the Faraon Apaches who assail the frontiers of this kingdom continually, it appeared proper to me to order a council convened of the military men of this presidio and the experienced and practiced settlers, the reverend father custodian, Fray Francisco de Lepiane, and the rest of the religious who were in this villa, so that with mature resolution they could offer judgment as to whether the campaign referred to ought to

201

be suspended, or do that which the captains solicited. This was held, and they were of the opinion that the campaign referred to should be suspended; that with the time in which it could be made, I could protect these heathen under the arms of his majesty and go to the valley of La Jicarilla on a reconnaissance of it and of the rest of the heathen if the latter agreed with the things which the three captains have fittingly set forth. Accordingly I conformed with what was set out in the council, recognizing the conversion of souls to be a great service to God our Lord, and the greatest pleasure of his majesty.

72. Having set out from this villa on the seventeenth of the month referred to, November, with fifty soldiers of this presidio and with the reverend father preacher, Fray Antonio de Camargo, procurer of his holy custody, for La Jicarilla, I arrived at it, on the twenty-fifth of the said month. Bearing a holy cross, the aforesaid captains, together with fifty young men and others, advanced to receive me. These were the captains who had come to this villa. They manifested with repeated demonstrations the pleasure they felt for our having visited their land. Having surveyed the rest of the rancherías, they received me in the same manner as the others, one chief bringing out an engraving of Our Lady, whom he had wrapped in a buckskin. This holy image I took in my hands, kissed, and exalted it above my head, giving all the heathen to understand the purpose I had in coming to their land. With great rejoicing they answered that they wished to become Christians and vassals of our king, that in the springtime they would notify me so that I could show them the spot and site where they would have to establish their pueblos, and that I should bring them religious to teach and instruct them in the mysteries of our holy faith, together with an alcalde mayor. Having recognized that it accorded with their wishes, I offered to protect and defend them in the name of his majesty with his royal arms from all their enemies. As its consequence, I accepted and admitted them as his subjects and took royal possession of all that valley, hoisting the royal standard with the rest of the ceremonies which are observed in like cases. I bid them farewell most affectionately, making them presents of what I was carrying along for this exigency, as more extensively appears in the adjoined affidavits which I am remitting with all humility to your Excellency, before whose high comprehension I put information of such great and appreciable import so that his majesty may enjoy the firmness and permanence that is required.[171]

Indispensable is the presidio of fifty soldiers, most excellent Lord, which was ordered by command of the former lord viceroy, Marqués de Valero, with the resolution of the royal junta of lord ministers, to be situated in the valley of La Jicarilla.[172] Under the shelters of this they will live secure from their enemies, and in subjection so that the religious who administer to them may fulfill their obligation in the holy calling and as a consequence will serve to impede their giving away to French arms. These are trying to penetrate into this realm, according to the notices which the Jicarilla gave to my predecessor, General Don Antonio de Valverde, and because of which the most excellent lord, viceroy, Marqués de Valero ordered him to take the necessary precautions more particularly in that quarter because of the great number of enemies who surround it and commit hostilities there. For equipment and fortification there is necessary dwelling places for the fifty soldiers with their fortified towers, commanded by a gate, competent religious ministers, ornaments, and the rest of the jewels of the divine ritual and the provision for them for the period of one year until they harvest their crops, sets of tools, large hoes, plough shares for the cultivation of the land, and axes to cut wood to build their houses.

All that I have referred to as has appeared to me should be placed before the sovereign attention of your Excellency, promising on my part to assent to everything that may be for the greater service of his majesty with the careful attention and vigilance I owe and have executed. In everything your Excellency will determine that which may be best, and whose commands will find in me the most exact observance. In the interim I take advantage of this happy occasion and pray our Lord to guard the important life of your Excellency in his greatest goodness the many years of my wish. Villa of Santa Fé, January 10, 1724. Most Excellent Lord, at the feet of your Excellency, Don Juan Domingo de Bustamante. Most Excellent Lord, Viceroy Marqués de Casafuerte.

73. México, February 18, 1724. To the lord fiscal with the reports of the missionaries which accompany this, and affidavits which the government may have, with a rubric of his excellency.

36. REPLY OF THE FISCAL, MÉXICO, APRIL 2, 1724

Most Excellent Lord: The fiscal has seen the affidavits and measures taken by the governor of New Mexico concerning the Apache Indians of La Jicarilla and the rest of the heathens of those countries having petitioned the water of baptism, offering themselves to the fold of our holy mother church and to the vassalage and obedience to his majesty, praying that they be gathered together and reduced to their pueblos, which is set forth by the religious of that custodia, and by the said governor.

The fiscal deposes that both because of the many convenient and favorable consequences and estimable virtues that are represented in the confirmatory reports and which are obvious from the affidavits themselves, as well as the precise obligation which the laws require for the very special care and vigilance in the conversion and voluntary submission of the Apaches and the rest of the heathen and because of such great service and glory to both majesties, the greatest attention and application are necessary to take the requisite measures for the increase of our holy faith in those parts, and extending, guaranteeing, and conserving the dominions of his majesty. Accordingly, your Excellency will be pleased, with your well-known zeal, to command that a dispatch be issued, entrusted to the said governor, as one who understands the necessary measures so that the holy faith and Catholic religion be planted in those places; that those Indians be instructed with the doctrine and Christian documents, in conformance with the Law of Title V, Book I, of the *Recopilación de Indias*. This petition and undertaking should be made known to the superior prelate of that custodia so that on his part he may have ready the religious that are judged necessary to form missions adequate for those countries, in the manner traditional and provided for by the royal regulations, which may be assisted by all necessary, in accordance with what has been the custom which has always been observed in the rest of the missions of that kingdom. Likewise let contributions be made to it, as provided in the laws 5, 6, and 7, Title 2 of the cited Book I for the adornment and divine worship of the images which are made in the said missions. The governor also should take suitable measures to the end that the Indians be reduced to settlements and be taught and instructed in political and rational life in conformance with that established in the laws of Title 4, Book 4 of Title 3, Book 6 of the same *Recopilación,* assisting each pueblo with the tools that are necessary for the cultivation of the land, according to and in the form and amount that has always been usual and which the royal regulations command.

74. With regard to the formation of the presidio which is represented to be necessary for the security of the missionaries, fortification of the settlements, defense of their Indians, protection of the dominions, and preservation from invasions of Indian enemies and penetration of the

French, being so useful and indispensable as is expressed, to achieve these purposes, your Excellency may be pleased to order that the governor go, with the least cost to the royal treasury, establish the presidio, with entire care, consideration, and economy, in the spot that may be considered most opportune and appropriate, putting in it the soldiers who may be required. These may be collected and detached from the other presidios in which they are not necessary in order to encompass the proposed purposes with the least expenditure of the royal treasury, putting in charge one of the principal military heads in whom he might have the greatest confidence and in whom the qualities and requisites of the laws coincide, in order that the administration of justice and ordinary jurisdiction of the pueblos or reductions may be under his control, proceeding in everything which he proposes in his report according to the royal laws and with the prudence, zeal, and practical wisdom which such an important affair requires. Of all this he will report with affidavits to your Excellency in your superior government of the measures he might take as proper, which likewise he must do in justice and conformably with the royal laws, the fulfillment of which in everything the fiscal prays. México, April 2, 1724. Licenciado Palacios.

75. México, April 24, 1724. To the lord auditor, with a rubric of his most excellent lord.

37. REVOLLEDO TO CASA FUERTE, MÉXICO, JULY 12, 1724

According to three councils of war and exchequer celebrated since January 2 of the year [17]20 it was ordered that a presidio of soldiers be established in the region of La Jicarilla. The number of these, twenty-five, was first estimated sufficient; afterwards fifty were thought necessary with the circumstances which were set forth, and two or three missionaries for the administration of the sacraments to the Apache Indians of the valley of the same Jicarilla, who, with those of El Cuartelejo, and Sierra Blanca of the same nation of Apaches, esteem the Spaniards of New Mexico either because of the preference they have for our people or because of the hatred they have for that of the Comanche, who attack them together with those of the Canzeres and Pawnees with whom the French are allied.... [*Marginal note:* French confederated with the Pawnee and Canzeres who live with them at a distance of two hundred leagues from Santa Fé] and who dwell among them in their own pueblos at a distance of two hundred leagues from the villa of Santa Fé, capital of New Mexico, as all appears from

205

the first file of papers of this affair. According to the report which the new governor of that kingdom made who examined three captains of these very Apaches, they solicited baptism, extended obedience, and offered to reduce themselves to the dominion, vassalage of his majesty. Also the governor himself, having gone to their country, fifty leagues distant from Santa Fé, that nation had received him with the greatest good will. Accordingly, the most suitable situation appears to erect effectively a presidio with the missionaries and circumstances provided for in the cited council [among them] because of spiritual and temporal interests which make them both Catholics and vassals. They are entitled to be protected and defended from their enemies, the Comanches, who are allied to the nations referred to and who abide in alliance and devotion to the French. It being thus, your Excellency will be pleased to command it done.

Since in the same councils it was provided that the soldiers be married and skilled, those who would seem to be most fit are those of New Mexico, experienced in the same country where they must be established and who, without much cost to the royal treasury, could carry out the foundation of the presidio in the region of La Jicarilla, or in the most suitable place in its valley, which is rich in products, with abundant water, and woods in the mountains which it has near. For this end fifty of that presidio could be detached for this new one and be replaced shortly from the presidio of Conchos, and that of Casas Grandes,[173] taking from each one of these twenty-five men and leaving in each twenty-five of the fifty of its complement. Truly with twenty-five, every one of these remains sufficiently garrisoned. The case is clear because that of Los Conchos and that of Casas Grandes are already centrally situated since they have pueblos and haciendas in their vicinity, and since the purpose of the civil and royal laws of Spain in looking to the construction of presidios within its boundaries, was to hold adjacent enemies within their confines and to drive them back from the portals or limits of the empire, because within the kingdom justice defends it from lawless subjects. The building of towns about presidios in itself makes them inland and without border significance. But it will be wise to continue the conquest until all the enemy be exterminated.

These presidios of Conchos and Casas Grandes are situated in La Vizcaya, distant from Santa Fé, the capital of New Mexico, some one hundred and fifty leagues. From the latter city to the settlements on its boundaries there are probably thirty-five leagues; possibly less than this between both presidios. The fifty soldiers which may be detached for that of La Jicarilla can be replaced from other older and less useful presidios. The auditor, having decided which they are, will either inform your Excellency or set forth by other means at what extra cost to the royal treasury the presidio of La Jicarilla may be founded and maintained.

76. The Apaches who dwell in this valley plant corn and other seed. At twenty leagues from these is the pueblo of Taos, which is composed of Catholic Indians subject to New Mexico, who also plant so that the soldiers will have at once the corn which they need to support themselves in La Jicarilla. By having allotted to them small strips of cultivated land and ploughshares for tilling, axes and tools to cut wood from the neighboring mountain range, they could easily do their sowing, cut wood, and carry meat from New Mexico at little cost, because it is twenty leagues from their pueblos. It will be possible to apportion their land and water, with which that region is well provided. License could be given them to establish in it settlers of New Mexico who might wish to go there, dividing among them also the lands and waters for houses and haciendas like the soldiers. To the two or three missionaries there should be assigned the salary which is provided for the rest of New Mexico. In order that these, both fit and necessary, be assured to them, the reverend father commissary-general of the order of Our Father San Francisco, should be prevailed upon and charged to this effect, giving salary to these fathers for chalices, bells, and the rest. With respect to this point, Don Felix Martínez, captain of the presidio of New Mexico who resides at this court, will be able to give information, as one expert and practiced in that country concerning the prices and value which the needed articles may have there, in order that they could equitably obtain them. The help that can be given to the soldiers for their transportation should be allowed with the least expense to the royal treasury. This work which is so important for the salvation of those heathen who so much desire and long for baptism to submit themselves to attain it, your Excellency above all will decide concerning the noble purposes of religion and the extension of the Catholic dominion, that which you estimate is the most essential for its end. México, July 12, 1724.

It appears proper to the auditor, although it is the point of another inspection, to set forth to the piety of your Excellency that since in New Mexico, which exists today garrisoned with many pueblos and settlers, an auxiliary bishop should be established with six thousand pesos income which could be charged to some of the episcopal accounts of this kingdom. It will be greatly to the advantage of the dominion if with the advice of his majesty it should be decided that way. Don Juan de Oliván Revolledo. [*Marginal note:* The auditor advances that a bishop be placed in New Mexico. An idea held before; see Cedula of nineteenth of May [16]31 of our document thirty-nine, number four and that of June 23, 1635, number sixteen.][174]

38. BUSTAMANTE TO CASA FUERTE, SANTA FÉ, MAY 30, 1724

77. *Most Excellent Lord:* Sir, I received that of your Excellency, its date March 8 of this present year, in which you are pleased to desire me to take all care that the Indians of La Jicarilla be conserved in peace and quiet and that their conversion may be augmented. In the interim the necessary measures are being taken. In order that your Excellency may know of the manner in which I have acted to achieve what your Excellency commands, I report: having announced a campaign against a nation whom they call the Faraons, who harry with their plunderings the frontier of the villa of Albuquerque, the Jicarillas came to represent to me that the nations Ute and Comanche had attacked them for a second time and abducted their women and children, and that since they had sworn obedience to our king, whom God guard, and I on my part had offered to aid them in the name of his majesty, [they required] that I do so. In order to decide, I called a council of war with the settlers and soldiers most experienced in this kingdom; and they were of the opinion that I should aid them first rather than to carry out the campaign referred to against the above mentioned Faraons. I respected the opinions given me and conformed to them, because it appeared to me to be more a service to both majesties. Having set out to execute it, I had the fortune to restore sixty-four persons. They were gratified, without having committed any infraction of peace. We both remain in friendship, I having protected them in every way that my weak forces permitted, as is known. Notwithstanding all this, they have returned to cause another vexation. They have decided, since their persons are not being protected, to go to the province of the Navajos.[175] If they do that it will be difficult to secure their reduction. All that I have set forth, I find essential to place before the high comprehension of your Excellency to determine the most expedient thing. In the interim, I am hoping that your Excellency may command of me that which is your pleasure.

I pray God to guard your important person many years. Villa of

Santa Fé, May 30, 1724. Sir, at the feet of your Excellency, Don Juan Domínguez de Bustamante. Most Excellent Lord, Marqués de Casa Fuerte.

78. Mexico, October 5, 1724. To the lord fiscal, with a rubric of his excellency.

39. REPLY OF THE FISCAL, MÉXICO, OCTOBER 20, 1724

Most Excellent Lord: The fiscal does not find himself possessed of entire information concerning the affidavits of this affair and can only offer to pray that your Excellency provide that which may be the most efficacious and proper, to the end that the Indians of La Jicarilla be reduced and not escape to the region of the Navajo, and that they be conserved in peace and quietude. For this success it would be worth while to place them in a spot ample and close to the reduced pueblos where they might live,[176] and what is necessary the first and second year may be assigned from the means of the royal treasury for their maintenance in the form provided for by the laws concerning which your Excellency will take measures with regard to what you may judge most appropriate. México, October 20, 1724. Licenciado Palacios.

40. ORDER OF CASA FUERTE, MÉXICO, OCTOBER 21, 1724

79. México October 21, 1724. Let these be delivered to the Brigadier Don Pedro de Rivera[177] so that in view of this representation asked for by the lord fiscal, and the affidavits which he might take in the matter, he may inform me that which I might do advantageously.

41. RIVERA TO CASA FUERTE, PRESIDIO DEL PASO DEL RÍO DEL NORTE, SEPTEMBER 26, 1727

Most Excellent Lord: By decree of October 21 of 1724, issued by your Excellency in view of the affidavits made by the governor of New Mexico concerning the reduction of the Apache Indians of the valley of La Jicarilla to our holy faith and the opinions given to your Excellency by the same lords, the fiscal of his majesty and the auditor-general of war, with regard to their inclination and concentration in pueblos and their defense with arms in protection from the nation of the Comanche, who attack them, to the erection of a new presidio and its form in the said valley, to the assistance of parish priests, to the provision for supplies for the material foundation of the presidio, and materials and tools for its crops, and ornaments for the new churches, your Excellency was pleased to command that the affidavits of this matter be delivered to me so that in view of them, and of that prayed

209

for by the said lords, I might inform your Excellency that which you ought conveniently to do.

According to the affidavits and representations made by the governor, by the councils of war formed by the superior government of your Excellency, and by the above mentioned opinions, I recognize everything recapitulates itself thus: That the Indian Apaches of the Jicarilla nation are soliciting to be reduced to the yoke of our holy law and obedience to his majesty, offering to receive the water of holy baptism, asking for parish priests, and to be defended with arms in protection from their enemies, those of the Comanche nation. Thus persuaded, the lords, fiscal and auditor, like those who composed the councils, of the legitimate proposals and conversion of these natives, pray that they be admitted and reduced; that to achieve this end they point out that it is recommended by laws which they cite; that they be assigned lands and waters, furnishing them with tools and supplies for their crops on the account of his majesty, and parish priest ministrants necessary to their new establishments of the same, with their usual alms, vessels and sacred objects and works of churches; and besides, in order that they be protected and defended with arms, a new presidio be founded in that spot, entrusting to the governor the building and equipping with the greatest saving to the royal treasury.[178] In order that it may be garrisoned with soldiers without new expenses levied on it, fifty be detached from that of New Mexico and settled in that valley, giving them lands and waters for their aid because of the fertility of the country; that it be restocked, twenty-five soldiers are to be detached from the presidios of Conchos and Casas Grandes, considering for these presidios, already midland and without need of much garrison, the rest of its complement would be adequate. For the understanding of this, the lord auditor disclosed the distances from the presidios of New Mexico, and other circumstances which appeared conformable to his zeal, making the reservation to replace these soldiers from those of other older presidios, which because they are inland will not need so large a number of them, as he sets forth more extensively in his opinion.

80. The lord fiscal in his latest opinion concludes, setting forth that it would be well considered to give to these heathen a suitable spot close to the reduced pueblos where they might live, supplying them the first year with what was necessary for their crops. Since I had been given supervision of everything, on the occasion of having been in the capital of that kingdom, in charge of the inspection of that presidio,

and the rest of the affairs of my office, I undertook to investigate carefully all matters concerning it, for the purpose of attaining full knowledge both of the pueblos reduced, their tribes, locations, and distances, as well as of the valley of La Jicarilla, and the rest of the savage nations, and to acquire exact information of everything in order to make to your Excellency the report which you commanded of me with the candor which I profess and desire so that there may be neither mismanagement of the funds of the royal treasury nor the established practice amongst all the presidios reversed, considering the inconveniences that could follow from its procedure, and the attainment of the good result which is desired and sought.

Because my vigilance has increased in the time that I remained in that capital and the experience which the present affair develops in me, I must inform your Excellency, first, that I know that the nation of Apache Jicarillas, who live in the region and valley of this name, is sixty leagues from the capital of that kingdom. This nation is commonly harried by the nation of the Comanches, which although it is the most barbarous which is known in the north, conserves such solidarity that both on the marches which they continually make, wandering like the Israelites, as well as in the camps which they establish where they settle, they are formidable in their defense. Although it is not understood for a certainty the country from which they are originally, there is an ancient tradition from a variety of reasonings which recognizes it to be that of Teguayo, [*Marginal note:* Teguayo has its sovereign crowned, according to Señor Rivera; but travelers have not found this kingdom. See the dissertation on La Quivira.] and distant more than three hundred leagues to the northwest of that capital and its sovereign is crowned. As it is argued, there are a great number of aborigines who inhabit that country and they travel in the manner stated, from the northwest, whence they appear near the east between the rivers of Missouri, close to the settlement of the Pawnees, Case, and Napeste. (It ought to read Kanses, as the French call it or Canseres, like the Spaniards name it.) They dominate with the power of arms all the nations who live in that region, because they terrorize them with the ferocious war which they make.[179] All close to New Mexico will wish the arms of the king to protect them as appears, since the Cuartelejo Apaches are also asking primarily not to be converted to our holy faith, but in the shade of it to be protected and to have satisfaction for the hostilities which they suffer from the said Comanches. This is the motive which the Apaches Jicarillas have had in ask-

211

ing for holy baptism, as may be recognized from the affidavits; their petition for arms for defense is so evident as to be the principal affair. Though the valley of La Jicarilla is distant twenty leagues from that of Taos, a pueblo of those under the jurisdiction of that kingdom, the Jicarilla have frequented it. There is not a case of baptism, which substantiates what all feel, because it is so obvious, that they have no other aim than the purpose of their safety—to be secure from the enemies who attack them.

81. In order that one may come to a full understanding of this truth [let it be recalled that] the larger part of this nation fled to the said pueblo of Taos in order that it might serve them as a refuge, because of news which they had that the Comanches were coming. I, having had word that they were in the said pueblo, requested the reverend father missionary of the cited pueblo to advise, induce, and persuade them to remain in the vicinity of that pueblo, as the lord fiscal suggested in his last cited opinion of October 20, 1722. [*Marginal note:* It was a mistake of the señor brigadier, as may be seen in number 78; it is of 1724.][180] On no other occasion and in no better place could the settlement of the said nation be confirmed, even though it were larger because in the neighborhood of the said pueblo of Taos, the best of that kingdom, there are valleys as rich and abounding with water as there are in that of La Jicarilla. With the cost alone of what the tools and the corn which they could consume in a year would amount to, they could be settled in the cited spot at the greatest security for them and without the increased expenditure which would ensue with the erection of a presidio. For in crossing from the pueblo of Taos to that of La Jicarilla a ridge of mountains intervening makes traveling less easy in case of the necessity of succoring them. Accordingly, I consider that the neighborhood of Taos would be most appropriate in which the Jicarilla Indians may be established. Thus, if this report should appear well conceived to your Excellency, your greatness may be pleased to command the governor of that kingdom to confer with them concerning the affair and draw up treaties which prudence might dictate to attain this end.

Because I, having reflected on the matter, do not find advisable the establishment of a presidio in that spot, since if the end is to reduce and take these Indians in custody, that may be achieved with the measure which is proposed. But if it is to extend the dominions, there is nothing easier, Sir, than to extend them for the king in that direction. For if one wishes to control El Cuartelejo, which is less than two hundred leagues distant to the northeast from that capital and is a country, according as all say, very abundant, the effect can be achieved by establishing a presidio; if it is desired, among the Moquis, who are one hundred leagues distant to the southwest of this capital, and who before the rebellion of the year 1680 were a colony of that realm, that, also, may be achieved with another presidio; [the same may be attained] if it is wished to possess all the province of Natagées, which is in the neighborhood of this presidio of El Paso and that of New Mexico on the part to the south of the Sierras de los Organos, and region of the Siete Ríos.[181] It is a country very abundant with streams and everything else for cultivation. If it is wished to place another on the south of the Sierra of Sandia where still remain the pueblos preserved which existed before the uprising, that could be done. It is a plenteous country, since at the end of so many years, the fruit trees which it had then still remain. With the introduction of arms one could do likewise in an infinity of places, as could be done at the pueblo of Socorro which is in the neighborhood of the road of this presidio to the presidio of Santa Fé, where I have gone, and is a country which delights one to see, because it derives everything from the banks of the Río del Norte. But as I consider that one ought better to conserve that which is acquired, to enjoy the fruit which has been cut, than to augment the dominions without any hope, I conjecture for these reasons that the presidio in La Jicarilla would be unproductive, when there are so many spots, discovered and known, that could be populated. But if, as is adverted to in the said opinions, one could populate the valley of La Jicarilla with the settlers of New Mexico, it would be well if the neighborhood be fertile. But there is so much land that can be occupied which is subjugated in that kingdom, and even if there were people to enter, there is land more than enough for all. For from the villa of Santa Fé to the pueblo of Zuñi, distant seventy leagues to the west, there are very few spots populated; in the neighborhood of the pueblo of Taos, as I have already stated, there is abundant land. Because there is much of this and few settlers, if these were detached for the valley of La Jicarilla, being now competent to withstand any onslaught which might occur in that kingdom, the province would be left too feeble to withstand those who might attempt to attack.

82. From this presidio of El Paso to the villa of San Felipe del Real de Chihuahua there are ninety-four leagues, and within this distance few settlements, not exceeding two ranches which are Carrizal and

213

Ojo Caliente,[182] within the jurisdiction of this presidio, and two other haciendas near Chihuahua. Thus in this distance and its surroundings there are more than three hundred leagues with very few inhabitants (though there are spots very appropriate) and because of lack of arms to take care of them against the Indians that are not subdued. They are closer than La Jicarilla, El Cuartelejo, and the rest, since from Chihuahua to this presidio one cannot come without an escort, and to go to New Mexico, the same is true, between the two of which are another two hundred and twenty-five leagues. It appears incompatible that we leave unprotected such a great amount of land and so useful to what we have already acquired, to populate that which imports so little. I speak about temporal matters since what is relative to the spiritual is looked after by reducing the Jicarillas, in the manner I have suggested, to the pueblo of Taos. For if their conversion is genuine, by making some offers which will attract them, I consider practicable the attainment of what is desired. Throughout all the parts I passed, on whatever occasion the reduction of Indians was spoken of, no person of any rank had any other remedy than that of founding presidios, saying that the king has his royal desire always disposed for the excessive expenses which are needed for such cases without taking any account of the considerable expenses which the increase of presidios promote and are without any use (save that of augmenting religion) which the king perceives. Accordingly, I suggest to your Excellency that if every proposal for the foundation of presidios for reduction were acceded to, the treasury of Midas would not suffice. Because, as I have said, in whatever spot from Durango to New Mexico, and from here turning towards the Californias, and from there to Los Adaes,[183] one would wish to place presidios (that is, speaking against the Indians) no one will be astonished if I consider this expense would be useless because arms alone would serve for which the barbarian nations have respect and perhaps the reduction of not one to the holy Catholic faith would be achieved.

It appears to me for colonial purposes the Faith is sufficiently spread out, and that one ought to try in these regions in which some of them are reduced to solicit the adherence of those nearby, as well as the cultivation and settlement of that vicinity. This will happen in the present case with the foundation of the presidio in La Junta de los Ríos. Not only will those be maintained who are already in peace and are being instructed, but that in view of this force the nearby tribes who attack all the neighborhood will be pacified. The effects of this

214

truth we have already experienced practically, by having reduced to a settlement the nation of the Zumas, who were those who assisted in attacking the nations of the Junta de los Ríos.[184] For even at the time when I arrived here to go to New Mexico, they came to me offering peace, praying for a site to be established. I showed to them that where they are today. My activity might not have been sufficient (although I attempted by all means that I could to reduce them) to have mollified them with such facility, (since for forty years, according to what everybody says, this reduction to a pueblo was solicited and could not be achieved) if it had not been for the inclination the presidio that was erected at the Junta de los Ríos had produced in them. Considering those nations and these arms, which will unite without leaving them any recourse in this situation, I believe that the said Zumas have been converted by seeing themselves constrained by the armed forces. For this same reason, another ranchería of this nation which is in the Sierra de la Candelería to the south of this presidio, twenty-five leagues distant, is about to be subdued, too. These results imply favorable consequences for the possibility of colonizing the banks of this river and the territory between it and the villa of Chihuahua. This land, being colonized, will be more easily defended from any nation whatsoever, though it be European, which might attempt to attack it.

83. For this reason I consider the valley of La Jicarilla will not be suitable because the same defense which can be given from the above mentioned valley can be carried out by the arms of the presidio of that kingdom, since from the most distant end of settlement in that direction, which is the pueblo of Taos, there are only twenty leagues to La Jicarilla. I infer that establishing a seat there as a barrier would be suitable for defense of that kingdom. The reason is, although those who made up the council for the admission of the Jicarillas set forth as a fixed principle that those reduced would serve to withstand the French from the Mississippi, the same end can be realized from the above mentioned pueblo of Taos. Because, although the French of Canada are closer than those of the Mississippi, and are little different from one another, the same opposition can be made to them from the valley of La Jicarilla that can be made from the said pueblo of Taos, distant twenty leagues, which is in the direction of Santa Fé, one of our towns.

With regard to what the lord auditor prepared in his opinion concerning the detachment of twenty-five men from the presidials of Conchos and Casas Grandes because these are midland, I must say

215

that although that of Conchos is surrounded on the south, the west and the north, though at a distance from any settlements, it has none on the east. Moreover, the existence of Conchos is not considered necessary, yet nine leagues away is the sierra of Terrazas, where enemies dwell. With respect to that which was disposed for the erection of the presidio, in order that the soldiers who were commanded be detached from La Junta de los Ríos, I protest, for the reason that the auditor proposes concerning this presidio. With regard to Casas Grandes (alias Janos) I ought to say that although I have not seen it, I know it, and it appears to me that, being where it is, it needs more garrison than the twenty-five men whom the lord auditor proposed, because the Indians whom it holds back are the nation of the Apache Xilas [Gilas], and others, who being all formidable require these forces to restrain them. Accordingly, I am of the opinion that the five men who are being taken out for the said Junta de los Ríos are, it seems to me, all those who for the present can be detached from the said presidio. The former is some two hundred leagues from Santa Fé, and that of Conchos some two hundred and seventy. In these distances there are no more people than the villa of Chihuahua, and some haciendas and ranches. The villa of Chihuahua and the presidio of Janos make a triangle with this [El Paso]. The circuit which is contained between these and La Junta de los Ríos is the same which I conjectured appropriate to colonize with the protection of the arms which is established in the Junta de los Ríos.

Because I am of the opinion that the foundation of the presidio in the valley of La Jicarilla is not convenient for the reasons I have expressed, I think the reduction of those Indians to our holy faith can be done by moving them to the valley of the pueblo of Taos, where all those of that nation are now, fleeing from the Comanches, and where they can live protected with arms, without the cost which the royal treasury would have in the support and erection of a new presidio. This is as much as my poor ability has been able to deduce concerning the affair with the little knowledge of that locality which I have acquired. It may be that another with greater intelligence may reason better concerning the matter and what is needed. I must assure your Excellency that all my mind I have applied for the best understanding and that, with this report going to the hands of your Excellency, you can with your high and sovereign comprehension resolve that which is convenient to the service of both majesties. May God guard the most excellent person of your Excellency many years as I

216

wish and have need. Presidio of Paso del Río del Norte, September 26, 1726. Pedro de Rivera.[185]

84. México, November 14, 1726. To the lord fiscal, with a rubric of his excellency.

42. REPLY OF THE FISCAL, MÉXICO, DECEMBER 14, 1726

Most Excellent Lord: The fiscal of his majesty, in view of these affidavits made concerning the conversion and reduction of the Apache Indians of La Jicarilla, the erection and foundation of a presidio for the custody and defense, and of the report of Brigadier Don Pedro de Rivera, visitor of the royal presidios, made in virtue of the order of your Excellency, says that because of its location it is manifest that the site of La Jicarilla which was selected for the foundation of the said presidio is neither suitable nor appropriate for them with respect to the distance of the villa of Santa Fé, capital of New Mexico, and the rest of the reasons which he proposes; that the purpose of this presidio is to serve as a defense and custody of that kingdom and as a fortress to prevent entrance to the rest of the nations and the French, and the hostilities which they can carry out, that same thing can be achieved by establishing them in the site called Taos, which because of the proximity and nearness to the said capital offers great possibilities and service to that kingdom, and to the very same Indian Apaches because of its fertility, and abundance of lands and waters; that reduced to this country they can take advantage of the garrison and protection from the attacks of their enemies and live in security; that the governor of that kingdom negotiate and confer with them and facilitate the movement with treaties, considerate and prudent, which he may make with them. Likewise he sets forth that it is not convenient that soldiers, necessary for the conversion and defense of the said presidio, be detached from that of Casas Grandes. These have already been taken from the latter for the newly founded presidio on the Río de las Juntas; nor from that of Janos, because the maintenance of those which it has is necessary to withstand the nation of the Xila Apaches and other formidable ones which attack it. In this matter various councils of war have resolved that the foundation of the projected presidio in the site of La Jicarilla be made, influenced by the judgment and opinion of various soldiers skilled and experienced of the distances, situations, and locations of that kingdom, who estimate it useful and fit for the business of the settlement of the aforesaid nation of the Jicarilla Indians and of aid and protection to impede the influx and progress of the French.

217

Your Excellency may be pleased to command that this file of papers be taken to a council of war in order that, in the understanding of what the said brigadier sets forth, and the inconveniences which touch the said foundation and the utilities and interests which can result from it, according as the governor and the rest of the persons of that kingdom propose; of that which was done in previous councils, what ought to be done may be resolved and determined, in case it is deemed useful and necessary, the form, order and manner of garrisoning the said presidio in its erection with the least cost to the royal treasury and without prejudice to the rest of the presidios in the detachment which might be made from them of soldiers for conversion to the former; and that both be fortified and prepared for defense against the invasion of the enemy nations who attack these countries, concerning which the justness of your Excellency will determine that which may be regarded according to justice, the fulfillment of which the fiscal prays. Mexico, December 14, 1726. Licenciado Palacios.

85. México December 17, 1726. To the lord auditor-general of war, with a rubric of his excellency.

43. REVOLLEDO TO CASA FUERTE, MÉXICO, MARCH 31, 1727

Most Excellent Lord: As prudence furnishes the means for the end which it attempts, so the excellent understanding of your Excellency will be pleased, for now the brigadier proposes the means to win over the Apaches of La Jicarilla who, harried by their enemies, wish to be reduced to the faith and law of God and of the king, and settled in the neighborhood of the pueblo of Taos, distant twenty leagues from the capital of Santa Fé of New Mexico;[186] that to this end the governor show them the sites most fit, useful, and well supplied with water, from which they themselves may choose in order that they may be catechized, baptized, and indoctrinated by the father missionary of the pueblo of Taos, and that for this a dispatch be issued; that he report the cost which the corn and the rest of the seeds for their sowing may be for the first year; and the oxen, hoes, and tools which may be given them for their cultivation in order that the expenditures may be passed upon by your Excellency; and the end which is desired of reducing to the Gospel be achieved, particularly today, of those Apaches, fugitives from the depredations of their enemies, whom the brigadier affirms are in that pueblo, suspending for the present the execution of that which was provided in the opinion of the three general councils.[187]

Let there be presented to the council this file for this resolution, as the lord fiscal prays, since it conforms to the results provided for by the laws, which when there is no order of the king to incur expenses for the royal treasury, his majesty desires they be made with the consent of the council. Though it having been decided by three councils that the presidio be placed in La Jicarilla at the charge of the royal treasury, the council has not yet been required to disburse moneys in establishing it. Your Excellency now having ordered that it be not founded, there is no expense which can be incurred. This can be deliberated upon in the council, for the trifles involved in the cost of the corn, grains, tools, and implements have already been decided upon in the three antecedent ones. In conformity with which, your Excellency being pleased may order that it be so carried out and command a dispatch be issued with the insertion of chapters six, seven, and eight of this letter-report of the brigadier so that the government of New Mexico may undertake its execution, giving an account with the greatest promptness of its outcome in order that in view of it, your Excellency may decide that which you may esteem most fit. México, March 31, 1727. D. Juan de Oliván Revolledo.

44. ORDER OF CASA FUERTE, MÉXICO, APRIL 1, 1727

México, April 1, 1727. As it appears to the lord auditor of war, with a rubric of his excellency. Date of the dispatch for the governor of New Mexico, as prepared on April 5. Here ends the said file of papers.

NOTE:The words of the lord brigadier to which the lord auditor refers are from the clause: "And because my vigilance has increased," as far as he says, "the treaties which prudence may dictate."

NOTE: This file continues in document twenty-five.

X. PROCEEDINGS OF THE TRIAL OF GOVERNOR DON ANTONIO DE VALVERDE, 1726-1727[188]

Number 21 of the papers of
the Superior Government   370   Number 1
Superior Government   1726

Affidavits taken by Brigadier Don Pedro de Rivera in the matter of the complaint against Don Antonio de Valverde, former governor of New Mexico, for having entrusted the reconnaissance of the Río Jesús María and the settlements of the Pawnee Indians, allied with the

French; and for not having gone himself, as he was ordered by the Lord Marqués de Casafuerte:[189]

S^{RIO} Gorraez

Expediente No. 1. Pages, 78. Interior Provinces of the West

A. Writ of Rivera, El Paso, May 13, 1726

In the royal presidio of Nuestra Señora del Pilar and the glorious Señor San José del Paso of the Río del Norte on the thirteenth day of May, 1726, Señor Don Pedro de Rivera, brigadier of the royal armies and visitor-general of the interior presidios of these kingdoms, deposed that the most excellent lord, Marqués de Casafuerte, viceroy, governor and captain-general of these kingdoms, in virtue of a royal order from his majesty (may God guard him), dated in Madrid, the nineteenth of February of the past year, 1724, and countersigned by Lord Don Antonio de Sopena, was pleased to bestow upon his lordship the office of visitor-general of the presidios referred to, giving him secret instructions found in the principal dispatch of his commission, forwarded to his excellency, with the knowledge of the lords, the fiscal of his majesty and the auditor-general of war, on the sixteenth of October of the same year, 1724. In accordance with this, after having inspected some of the presidios of the kingdom of New Vizcaya, he was to go to the province of New Mexico to review those established there. On the occasion of the above mentioned inspection-general, by order of his excellency and prayer of the said lords, the fiscal and auditor-general of war, several memoranda of testimonies were delivered to his lordship, drawn up by Don Antonio Cobián Busto on the inspections which he began in these and other presidios of the said kingdom of La Vizcaya in conformity with the commission of the most excellent lord, Marqués de Valero, former viceroy and governor and captain-general of these kingdoms, so that his lordship (Rivera) might continue and substantiate them in the matter which they concern, with respect to which the said Don Antonio Cobián had remitted in summary. One of the memoranda referred to above which he drew up was for the inspection of this presidio, its proprietary captain being General Don Antonio Balberde Cossio, begun on the twenty-second of October, 1722. The other he put with it proceeded against the same Don Antonio Balberde, then governor and captain-general of this kingdom of New Mexico. In view of these, according to the disposition set forth by the lords, the fiscal of his majesty, and the auditor-general of war, under dates of March 10 and May 19, 1723, his excellency was petitioned to

220

command that he proceed both to the substantiation of the aforementioned attestations and to the investigation of other particulars which the auditor-general set forth. In consequence of which and in accordance with his instructions, they were delivered to his lordship.

As it was convenient to transact the business before the inspection of this presidio, the particular officials were taken to the villa of Santa Fé, the leading city of this kingdom, in which were to be verified the proceedings prepared by the lord auditor-general, these being the citation and trial of General Don Antonio de Balberde, who is present in this presidio. His lordship had to prescribe and command that he be notified that within the end of one month, he be present in person (in the villa of Santa Fé) for the purpose of hearing and answering the testimonies and proceedings that might be required. For those which concern this presidio, because of the lack of other facilities, this tribunal of inspection is declared adequate. Therein will be held the judicial proceedings which may be proposed. They will have as much force and effect as if they were carried out on his person present. There will be continued the record of these dispositions and judicial proceedings, which by command of his lordship have been prepared, because what was necessary was not in New Vizcaya nor in this kingdom.

By this writ it is so provided, ordered, and signed in triplicate. Don Antonio Balverde. It is well.

PEDRO DE RIVERA
[rubric]

Before me
FRAN^CO SAN^S DE S^TA ANA
[rubric]
Royal Scrivener

B. Notification to Valverde, El Paso, May 13, 1726
Notification:

In the royal presidio of El Paso del Río del Norte on the said day of May 13, 1726, I, the scrivener, read to and notified General Don Antonio Balberde Cosio in person of the antecedent writ so that he would appear in the villa of Santa Fé for the purpose which was expressed and set forth, namely, the prosecution of the proceedings and the substantiation of the affidavits which the foregoing contains. He understood all and said that he attended it and that he would present himself both as cited for the proceedings which might be proposed in the villa of Santa Fé, as well as for those which may be carried out in

221

this presidio and that which concerns the petition by which he is
arraigned, he is ready to do; and that he will set out from this villa
for Santa Fé at the same time as the señor visitor-general does, in order
to take advantage of a convoy and safe escort, because of the danger
from enemies presented by the distance of the said villa, and because it
was not opportune to detach other soldiers from this presidio for his
guard. This he submitted as his reply and he has signed it.

ANTT^O DE BALVERDE COSSIO
[rubric]

FRAN^{CO} SAN^S DE S^{TA} ANNA
[rubric]

C. Valverde to Rivera [Santa Fé, 1726]

Señor Brigadier and Visitor Don Pedro de Ribera: When trouble
arising out of malice has sprung up, if no adequate means for its remedy could be found, hope would surrender to iniquity and the mind
would devote itself to grief. My purpose is nothing else, Señor, in this
communication, but to throw myself on the protection of the impar-
tiality, uprightness, and rectitude of a minister so conformable to
justice as you are, to clear my injured reputation attacked by the de-
praved purpose of false impostors who taunt me with epithets. Since
their malice is restricted by perfect knowledge of how to group factions
and unite them for their purposes, they do not allow me the justification of carrying out with exactness the inviolable command of the
Señor Marqués de Balero, viceroy of these kingdoms, who confided in
me in his dispatch free action so that either I, personally, should make
or that I should order my lieutenant-general [to make] a reconnaissance
of the location of the French and their fortifications, and of forwarding
the expressed reconnaissance with everything that conduced to that end.

Because I found myself on that occasion with duplicate orders and
unavoidable obligations to the lord viceroy from which I could not
excuse myself because they subjected me to command, I turned this
over to the person of my lieutenant-general, Don Pedro de Villasur,
a native of the kingdoms of Castile. This circumstance is that with
which my enemies and adversaries confute me and concerning which
they write, and against whom I protest as false accusers so that I may
take advantage of all my prerogatives and rights. These accuse me of
the loss of the said Villasur and of complete defeat, styling him as
inept. From this proceeds the citation that was commanded of you that

I be made to appear in the villa of Santa Fé at the trial of this particular by virtue of the authority of his excellency. Censorious words are being repeated and spread about among their followers, to stir their peaceful minds with hateful chimeras, out of which disturbing and inimical consequences are being prepared.

In order that you may be impressed with my rights and those of him who was Don Pedro de Villasur, and in order to destroy and unveil malice and by its consequence you may approve my lawful choice and reflect entire approbation, esteem, and fame on this deserving person, I say that the following offices converged in this individual: Ensign of the royal presidio of El Paso, as appears from his titles of: captain of the said Paso; alcalde mayor and captain of war, formerly of the province of Santa Bárbara in the kingdom of La Biscaya; visitor of El Rossario and its jurisdiction for Don Joseph de Neyra y Quiroga; alcalde mayor and captain of war of the fort and mines of Cosaguriache; alcalde mayor and captain of war of the villa of Chiguagua, whose inhabitants asked his reëlection. To this man I entrusted this affair. Worthy because of his merits and great importance, because of his prudence, valor, and immediate dispatch which his resolution had made effective and because of other qualifications which assured a successful outcome of the undertaking, he would have achieved his object on this occasion if it had not been thwarted by the carelessness of the subaltern, maestro de campo, Thomás Holguín, who, in the opinion of all in the kingdom, was reputed to be its best soldier.

Don Pedro de Villasur, having arrived with his detachment on the banks of this part of the river and having inferred that on the other bank was the location of the French and the Pawnees, his experience and practice in military affairs pointed out the danger he was incurring in remaining on the said bank. He determined in consultation to retreat. He did this, accelerating the march over the same road he had come as much as he had traveled before in two days. Having quartered on the shores of the other river [Río de San Lorenzo], placed sentinels, and given orders for the best security of the camp, he retired to his tent and ordered that he should be given an account of everything. A report was made to the subaltern by a corporal of a squad of the approach of an enemy, of whom he had not previously been aware. He considered it fictitious and as evidence of the lack of courage of the head of the squad, for he did not confer with the chief, Don Pedro de Villasur, who without doubt would have repaired the blunder of the subaltern which cost so much.

223

That is, in summary, the most substantial part of the event which I set forth and offer (with other things concurring when the trial arrives) to represent and submit before you with the four or more eyewitnesses who escaped from the attack and who are in the villa of Santa Fé, and others who are well known, whom I supplicate you will examine according to the interrogatory[190] arranged at this, my trial, bidding fair that you may accept the course I took as justified (without exception), and approved in all touching this matter by the Señor Marqués de Balero, assured prudence being natural in that lord with the same degree as it is in your lordship. I have the fixed belief that Divine Providence will free my reputation from blemish (because justice is on my side). Let what may fall into your hands, where wisdom and piety are sons of the great ability of your lordship. There I place my recourse with the certainty that my reputation will come out unsoiled and that my opinion and fortune will run a different course.

I also hope that your great ability, understanding, and good zeal may be means of conserving peace in this kingdom; and, understanding the goodness of your lordship, I believe you will find the means for its total relief. May God guard you many years in the means and manners which are meet.

ANTT^O DE BALBERDE COSSIO
[rubric]

D. Writ of Rivera, Santa Fé, June 7, 1726

Decree. Villa of Sta Fé. June 7, 1726

Let this writing be placed with the writ of notification to this report in the presidio of El Paso del Norte so that it may appear in this villa in pursuance of the subject matter which it contains. Señor brigadier and visitor-general so decrees and signs it.

PEDRO DE RIVERA	Before me
[rubric]	FRAN^{CO} SAN^S DE S^{TA} ANNA
	[rubric]

Stamped for the year of 1726. [rubric]

Writ:

In the villa of Santa Fé, on the twenty-eighth of June, 1726, Señor Don Pedro de Rivera, brigadier of the royal armies and visitor-general of the interior presidios of these kingdoms for his majesty, witnesses:

Whereas, one of the particulars the señor auditor-general of war set forth, among others which he selected in view of the different memoranda of testimonies which Don Antonio Cobián Busto began in the kingdom of New Mexico for the inspections of the administrations of the former governors and the one who was [governor] of the kingdom up to the past year of 1722, is that which he chose concerning the case from those of the inspection at the time when Don Antonio Valverde supervised this kingdom.[191] In this he petitions his excellency that the real motive be investigated and established which the governor, Don Antonio Valverde, had in not going personally as he was commanded by his excellency, Señor Marqués de Balero, on the reconnaissance of the Río Jesús María, on whose banks were situated the settlements of the Pawnees, allies of the French, with whom they live and with whom they attacked and surprised those whom the Don Antonio sent under the command of a lieutenant, inexpert in military affairs and in the management of arms, and because of whose carelessness the enemy killed in the camp before they could arrange themselves in battle order, forty-five soldiers, veterans of those who had reconquered this kingdom and sustained it with credit. There ought to have been reviewed in the inspection which Antonio Cobián made, the reason that he [Balverde] had for not having obeyed the order of his excellency and for not having gone personally on that campaign, as Don Antonio had himself offered to do. With this opinion, his excellency agreed and to this end the affidavits referred to were delivered to his lordship.

In order that it be conducted in the best possible manner and that the directed investigation be prepared, citation was served on Don Antonio Balverde and his appearance demanded in this villa for the substantiation of the charge in accordance with what was set forth. His lordship ordered that secret information be received as coming within the nature of the *juicio de visita* from persons who may have knowledge of the case. These were sworn according to form and asked questions according to the tenor of the above mentioned particular, independent of that which Don Antonio sets forth in the writing he submitted so that in view of it there may appear what is suitable.

PEDRO DE RIVERA
[*rubric*]

Before me
FRAN^{CO} SAN^S DE S^{TA} ANNA
[*rubric*]
Royal Scrivener of the Assessor

225

E. *Testimony of Aguilar, Santa Fé, July 1, 1726*

Stamped for this year of 1726

[*Marginal note:* Volume I. Yldefonso Rael de Aguilar. Ratified.]
In the villa of Santa Fé on the first day of the month of July, 1726,
señor brigadier and visitor-general, in conformity with his antecedent
writ, had appear before him Yldefonso Rael de Aguilar, a Spanish
settler of this villa and one who had been a soldier of its presidio. Upon
being present before me, the scrivener, he received the oath which he
took before God and the image of the holy cross. So charged, he
promised to tell the truth concerning that which he knew and what he
might be asked. Being informed as to the material which the said writ
contained, he testified: Although the witness was one of those who
went on the expedition which the writ mentions,[192] he never knew nor
had he heard stated the motive that Don Antonio Balverde had in not
going personally on the said expedition, nor whether he refrained from
doing this with just cause or without it; that from hearsay he supposed
he was ordered to go by his most excellent lordship, the Marqués de
Balero, the former viceroy and governor and captain-general of these
kingdoms; that he knew the reason he had for having ordered Don
Antonio to go on the above mentioned expedition was that while Don
Antonio was on a campaign along the Río Napeste, an Indian of the
Apache nation informed him that the French were close neighbors of
the Pawnees, who had wounded him with gunshot and killed many
others of his companions. This news he [Valverde] communicated to
his excellency and from this originated the order mentioned.

In accordance with it he detached from this presidio some fifty men,
according to his memory, placed under the command of Don Pedro
de Villasur, lieutenant-general of Don Antonio Balverde. They set out
from this villa on the fourteenth day of June of the past year 1720, as
he recalls, the witness being one of the fifty soldiers, as he has declared.
For this reason he knows that they consumed, on arriving at the Río
Jesús María and the lands of the Pawnees, sixty-three days from the
day which they set out from this villa; that they marched always
between the north and east; and that having come to a halt on the
banks of the river, and in view of a village of the Pawnee nation which
was on the other bank, the commander, Don Pedro de Villasur, sent
across an Indian of the same nation who had been raised among the
Spaniards and whom they had brought along to serve as an interpreter.
To him, he [Villasur] gave some knives and some bundles of tobacco

226

to distribute among the chiefs to please them. This Indian remained there, and one of those of that village came, but they were unable to understand anything he said; on the following day there appeared on the other bank of the river among the Indians of that village the one mentioned before as having been sent as interpreter. They asked him why he did not return and if there were Spaniards [there]; and what conditions existed among that tribe. He answered that they were well disposed and that he did not know if there were any Spaniards (that is the name which they give to all those who are white), and that they were not allowing him to return.

This having been noted, the commander, as mentioned, convened a council of war of the most experienced men who were there. Although the commander wished to cross to the other bank of the river to satisfy himself with evidence which he could not secure by sending the interpreter, those of the council dissuaded him, pointing out the peril they were in and the danger to which they would be exposed if they should go over to the other bank; moreover, because of the large volume of water which the river carried they would be in danger in fording it. What they decided was to retreat, to give up the enterprise, because it seemed that little could be gained and because the Pawnees, by having detained the Indian interpreter, indicated their malice.

The commander, convinced by these opposing arguments, retreated to the Río de San Lorenzo, the same from which he had set out two days before. Having made camp for that night, the witness says that a little after nightfall many of his companions heard the barking of a dog and the noise of people who were crossing the river. This news was made known to the commander, who ordered that the ones in charge of the horseherd be careful, and sent some of the Indians (whom he brought with him from this kingdom) to discover what was occurring along the river. Those (judging by what happened) did not investigate, since they advised that there was nothing. With this assurance the horseherd was brought together at daybreak to continue the journey. They unsaddled, all at the time, to exchange horses. At this very moment a horde of men who were in ambush near them attacked both with guns and arrows and wrought the havoc that is known. Although our men defended themselves, considering that they were few with regard to that multitude, it was impossible to hold out. While those who were mounted were sufficient to make that host retreat, the rest were unable to aid, as they were already dead. Those who remained fled, rescuing only the witness, who had nine wounds

227

of great severity. The Indians also cut off a braid of his hair. Besides this the witness might have noticed on that occasion another thing which occurred. He knew that the twelve fleeing ones, who were able to escape from the encounter, retreated with the bulk of the horseherd, having left in the camp all their equipage and provisions; and that of the sixty Indian allies who accompanied them, twelve or thirteen died in this attack; and that the soldiers who escaped with the witness were Manuel Thenorio, Phelipe Tamariz, Matheas Madrid, Joseph Mares, Juachín Sánches, Jacintto Perea, Juan Antonio Barrios, Antonio de Armenta, Joseph de San Tiestevan,[193] Melchior Rodrígues, and Diego Tafoya. He did not remember if there were any more than these mentioned. What he had said and declared is that which he saw and what occurred as he knew it and the truth as charged in the oath which he has taken. After being read to him, it was affirmed and ratified. He declared he was competent to testify and that he is thirty-six years old. He signed it with his lordship, to which I testify.

PEDRO DE RIVERA
[rubric]

ALONSO RAEL DE AGUILAR
[rubric]
Before me
FRAN^{CO} SAN^S DE S^{TA} ANNA
[rubric]
Royal Scrivener of the Assessor.

F. Testimony of Tamariz, Santa Fé, July 2, 1726

[Marginal note: Volume II. Phe. Tamaris. Ratified.] In the villa of Santa Fé on the second day of the month of July, 1726, señor brigadier and visitor-general in the prosecution of these proceedings had Philipe Tamaris, the head of a squad of the company of this presidio and one of those mentioned by the previous witness, appear before him. Upon being present before me, the scrivener, he received the oath which he took before God our Lord, and the image of the holy cross. So charged, he promised to tell the truth concerning that which he knew and might be asked. Being informed of the purpose of what the auditor-general of war demanded in the antecedent writ, he said that it is true that he had been one of the soldiers who were detached for the reconnaissance of the river called Jesús María in the month of June of the past year, 1720; that he had not known and had not heard the reason which Don Antonio Valverde Cosio, who on that occasion was the governor of this kingdom, had for not going personally on the said reconnaissance

228

nor whether he was ordered precisely by the most excellent lord, who was viceroy of these kingdoms at that time. That which the witness did know was that Governor Don Antonio Balverde had set out in the preceding year on a campaign and, having arrived on a river (which they call the Napeste) in the lands of the tribe of Cuartelejo Apaches, he met a group of Paloma Indians who had coming fleeing, routed by the nation of the Pawnee Indians and French. Among these were some wounded by gunshots whom the governor, Don Antonio Balverde, examined. He learned that the French were establishing themselves in the region of Río Jesús María, on whose banks were settled the Pawnees. He gave an account of this investigation to his excellency from which he, the witness, understood had resulted the reconnaissance expedition. In the execution of this they marched some two months until the tenth day of August. They arrived opposite the rancherías of the said Pawnee Indians. To these the commander, Don Pedro de Villasur, sent one of the Indian allies whom he was bringing along because he was of the same nation and would serve as interpreter. He was to tell them that he was coming in peace and only to make a note of the peoples who might have introduced themselves into their lands. The commander sent them, as evidence of his friendship, bundles of tobacco and other things with which he tried to win their favor. The interpreter did not return and although on the same day some came from that nation, they never secured from them any reason for the reserve which they maintained. From this it could be seen that they were filled with distrust. The commander, having held a council of war with Thomas Olguín, his subaltern, and other officials, made known his desire to cross the river. They had already found a ford on the said river to do so. As preparations were being made, the Pawnees surprised some of our Indian allies who had crossed to bathe and carried off one of them. This occurrence gave indication of the dangerous intentions which the Indians had. Because of this, they again held a council and decided to retreat. This they put into execution on the following day and marched until crossing the Río San Lorenzo and about four in the afternoon halted on its banks. That night, said the witness, who was with the horseherd, a corporal on behalf of the subaltern warned them that they should be very careful because they said a noise had been heard on the river as though people were crossing it. The horseherd had been gathered at daybreak; and, at the time when all the soldiers were exchanging horses, an ambush of some five hundred enemies fell upon them with firearms, lances, and arrows. The nearby discharge of the fusillade threw the horseherd into a stampede. As the witness was on guard over it, he aided the rest of his squad in overtaking it; and, having stopped it for a moment, they found themselves immediately attacked by a great number of enemies, whom they repulsed three times. The number quickly grew so great that they could not resist longer than to free three of their companions who, badly wounded, had escaped from those in the camp. With the Indian friends who freed themselves, they retreated with the horseherd. Besides that, the witness thought of no other thing, except that the individuals who could give more of an account of what happened were Melchior Rodríguez and the three who escaped. That which he has said and declared is that which he knows to be the truth, as charged according to the oath which he took. After it was read to him, it was affirmed and ratified. He declared he was competent to testify and forty years of age. He signed it with his lordship, of which I testify. Corrected. Valid.

PEDRO DE RIVERA   PHILIPE TAMÁRIZ
        [rubric]   [rubric]
Before me
        FRAN^{CO} SANC^S DE S^{TA} ANA
Royal Scrivener and of the Assessor

G. Confession of Valverde, Santa Fé, July 5, 1726
Confession:[194]

In the villa of Santa Fé, the fifth day of the month of July of 1726, Señor Don Pedro de Rivera, brigadier of the royal armies and visitor-general of the interior presidios of these kingdoms on behalf of his majesty, in conformity with his antecedent writ, had appear before him the man prosecuted in these proceedings for the purpose of taking his confession. Upon being present before me, the scrivener, he received the oath which he took before God and the image of the holy cross. So charged, he promised to tell the truth concerning that which he knew and in whatever he might be asked. Being informed of the purpose of these writs and of the opinion set forth by the auditor-general of war at page 89,[195] and following, of the file of testimonies which contains an account of the various inspections which Don Antonio Cobián Busto had made in this kingdom, the following questions were asked him:

1. He was asked his name, where he came from, his quality, state,

230

profession, present location, and age. He testified that his name was Don Antonio Balverde Cosio; that he was a native of the region of Villa Presente in the mountains of Burgos, kingdoms of Castile; that he is Spanish, a bachelor; and that his profession has been that of a soldier, having obtained the offices in this kingdom of captain of its presidios and governor and captain-general of it; and that at the present his residence is at the presidio of El Paso del Río del Norte; and that he is fifty-five years of age; so he answers.....

2. Asked in virtue of what title and how many years he had held the employment as governor of this kingdom and who was administering these kingdoms, he replied that during the year of 1716 the most excellent lord, Marqués de Balero, being governor and captain of these kingdoms, remitted to him the commission according to certain files of papers which his excellency placed in his care in that villa, and which he offers to produce, and conferred upon him at the same time the office of governor *ad interim* of this kingdom; that being in actual possession, his excellency conferred upon him by royal title the government in his own right during the year of 1718 and that he exercised it up to the succession of him who is the present governor.[196] So he answers.....

3. He was asked with what motive or cause was the expedition carried out, for which he detached a number of soldiers from the company of this presidio and others who were Indian allies, for the purpose of reconnoitering the Río Jesús María, and to state and declare the order he had for that; with what he prepared this undertaking; and in what time, and the real purpose to which it was directed. He said that the origin of the said expedition was that the most excellent lord, the viceroy, upon finding himself with a report from Captain Diego Ramón, formerly of one of the presidios of the province of Texas, wherein he informed his excellency that a number of the French nation were marching for the mines of the villa of Santa Fé, ordered the defendant to send a squad of soldiers to reconnoiter where they were, what manner of living they pursued, how many there were, and other particulars, and that when done he inform his excellency so that he might take precautions. As he received the order delayed, he represented to his excellency that he felt to season to be passed in which he could execute it with safety, proposing that in the following springtime, it being his pleasure, he would execute it in person or through that of his lieutenant-general.[197]

In the meanwhile, it happened that the nation of the Comanche

231

attacked this kingdom so that it was necessary for the confessant, in order to ward off the destruction which they threatened, to hold a council of war to determine the remedy required. From this it resulted that it was expedient to send out with arms to restrain them. For this purpose, the confessant took the armed forces of this presidio and went in search of the Comanches, penetrating some two hundred leagues to the northeast.[198] There were congregated in the spot known as La Jicarilla, Indian Apaches to the number of one hundred who offered themselves as auxiliaries to the confessant to lead him to the spot where he could find the Comanches. Having arrived on the river called Casse[199] where the Comanches ordinarily live, two hundred leagues distant from this villa, and not having found them, these Jicarilla Apaches advised him that they ought to retreat as they thought that the Comanches, not having been found there, had hidden themselves. To this he agreed because the provisions were beginning to shrink and winter was approaching. Both reasons predicted clearly an untimely end for the expedition. In order to retire, he held a council of war of the most experienced men he was leading and they agreed to retreat because, if they did not do it then, the horseherd would be exposed to total loss since the snows were beginning to fall there. He directed his march by a different route as far as a large river called Napeste near El Cuartelejo, an Apache settlement of this name. There two Indians from the settlement overtook him asking him to delay two days so that their ranchería could arrive as the women wished to see him. He did this notwithstanding the scarcity of provisions which he had.

The ranchería having arrived, there was among the chiefs who came to talk with him, one wounded with a gunshot who informed him that he received the injury in an encounter which his nation had had for the space of a day with that of the Pawnees and their allies, the French. They had escaped together, protected by a walled ditch. From this they got out during the night of the day of the encounter. On this occasion the governor was informed of the region where the French were, their fortifications and circumstances. From this [it appeared] that the French were established within the Pawnee nation, that they had strong houses with a single door and large arquebuses on the roofs, that they wore red clothes, and had white women. Having asked the Apaches if they had seen them, they said that they had not, but that their women who had been captives and had escaped, maintained it to be so. Having continued his march and having arrived at

232

this villa, it appeared to him who was confessing, that the information being that which his excellency desired, he sent a courier informing him of the aforesaid, stating he would suspend the execution of the order which his excellency had given him, the confessant. All of the above, he said, will appear in his reports to the superior government of his excellency.

Notwithstanding, his excellency ordered him by special dispatch to carry out what he had commanded of him personally or by means of his lieutenant-general, setting forth the rest of the measures which he had ordained as appears from the above mentioned dispatch. In complying he sent forty soldiers and sixty[200] Indian allies under the command of Don Pedro de Villasur, his lieutenant-general and his subaltern, Thomás Olguín, official of this presidio, equipping them with all that was necessary and with effects to entertain the Indians in conformance with the particular order of his excellency. So he answers.....

4. Asked why, since the aforesaid was an expedition of the importance he set forth, to which he ought to have devoted his attention for its success, he confided it to his lieutenant-general and did not carry it out in person as he had proposed to his excellency, who had placed it in his care, he said that the first reason he had in not going personally on the said expedition was that he remained to carry out other orders of his excellency regarding different affairs which he had placed in the care of the confessant; and the second was that he had confidence in the experience and good management of his lieutenant-general, acquired in these kingdoms in various offices in Vizcaya where he had discharged his obligation. So he answered.....

5. He was asked why he says he did not go in person when, besides having offered to his excellency to go on the expedition and having been ordered to do so, he failed in this order, conferring it on his lieutenant-general, a man inexpert in military affairs and the handling of arms, and because of whose negligence many of the soldiers and Indian allies whom he was taking along were killed without being put in order for battle. He said that the most excellent lord, the viceroy, had not ordered the confessant expressly to go on this expedition, but that he left it to his choice. He ordered him to go or to send his lieutenant-general, in accord with the precautions which the dispatch contained, and he offered to prove that this lieutenant was a man trained in the war of these kingdoms, of tried valor and skill, both of which are verified by the offices which he had held and as appears from the instruments which he offers to present. So he answers.....

233

6. Asked: How can he assert the good management, experience, and practice of the commander since both the opinion of the lord auditor-general and the fact of the defeat show he was inexperienced, and since it is to be seen from the testimonies and investigations made in this affair that Don Pedro de Villasur was a man of little experience, as he had placed the camp in an exposed position and did not take the precautions which he should have, he said that concerning the inexperience of Don Pedro he repeated what he had deposed touching the lack of foresight of which he was accused, and he will prove that the commander had not been the cause which brought on this defeat, but that he had complied with what he ought to do, as everything serves to prove. So he answers.....

He was asked other questions and cross-examined touching the case, and to all he responded and answered that all that he had deposed and confessed is what happened without proposing anything else than declaring under the promise which he has made to justify it, and that which he had said and confessed is that which he knows and the truth as charged in the oath which he has taken. After this was read to him, it was affirmed, ratified and signed by his lordship, to which I testify. Attested to by one being present. Valid.

PEDRO DE RIVERA   ANTONIO DE BALVERDE COSIO
[rubric]   [rubric]
Before me
FRAN^{CO} SAN^S DE S^{TA} ANA
Royal Scrivener and of the Assessor.

H. Council of War Ordering Presidio at La Jicarilla[201]

Don Balthasar de Zuñiga y Guzmán Sotomayor y Mendoza, Marqués de Valero, Ayamonte and Alenquer, gentleman of the chamber of his majesty, of his council chamber and council of war of the Indias, viceroy, governor and captain-general of this New Spain and president of the royal audiencia of it, etc.

Whereas, I have ordered the following council formed: In the council of the exchequer and war which I, most excellent Sir, Marqués of Valero, viceroy, governor and captain-general of New Spain, and president of the royal audiencia of it, have ordered called today the seventeenth of September, 1720, with the lords: Don Joseph Juachín de Uribo Casttejón y Medrano, Cabellero of the Order of Santiago; Don Gerónimo de Soria, Marqués de Villahermosa; Don Juan de Olivan

Rebolledo, as auditor-general of war, all of the council of his majesty; and judges of this royal audiencia; Don Sevastián Rodríguez de la Madrid of the order referred to, Marqués de Villamediana Regente; Don Gabriel Guerro Ardila, chief clerk of both the royal audiencia and audiencia of accounts of New Spain; Don Simón de Carragal and Don Pedro de Larburo, official judges of the royal exchequer and office of this court; also present, Master Don Joseph Sáenz de Escobar as fiscal attorney of his majesty. There not being present: Colonels Don Julio Eusebio Gallo, warden of the royal forces of the fort of Acapulco; Don Francisco Aguinaga Comendio, and the master of the field of credit and commerce; Don Pedro Sánches de Tagle, Marqués of Altamira, the first two of the Order of Santiago and the said Marqués of Calatrava who expressed themselves as indisposed.

The statement of the context of the council of the exchequer held on the second of January past of this current year was read, in which were the testimonies taken concerning the report by the governors of Parral and New Mexico with regard to the designs of the French to penetrate into those countries, and likewise a report sent to his excellency by Don Antonio de Valverde Cosio, who is governor of New Mexico. This was dated in the villa of Santa Fé on the fifteenth of July of the same year.

He reported to his excellency that he had to go down during the month of February to the territory of Paso del Río del Norte, both to take some measures there to keep the Indians of the nation of Zuma at peace and to inspect that presidio for the better organization of its defenses. A few days after his arrival there, the mail of his majesty had delivered to him a dispatch from his excellency in which he was pleased to order him that, as soon as the time was opportune, he should depart and execute the journey which he had promised to do to spy out the French in the place where they were situated, either in person or in the person of his lieutenant-general, as was clear from the dispatch. Therein, he was required to place in the region of El Cuartelejo a presidio of twenty-five men to be withdrawn at that time from the villa of Santa Fé for reasons and purposes which were set forth.

But it seemed to him that there had been an error, since it did not provide whether the placing of the presidio must be understood to be in El Cuartelejo, whose distance was more than one hundred and twenty leagues from that villa and which had in it few or no conveniences that could be used in the said spot to effect the establishment of a presidio and from which little return could be assured, since the

235

Indians, who farm there for only a certain space of time, harvest the small crops which the region offers and retire to other parts to pass the winters, which were rigorous, and [since it is] without a supply of wood except within many leagues, or whether it ought to be understood to be in the region and valley of La Jicarilla. The governor, finding himself in these doubts, in order to be better able to inform his excellency, determined to hold a council of the principal leaders of the presidio of Santa Fé, who with more understanding would be able to enlighten him and give their opinion, and of some experienced settlers who were in that country and who had entered when it was determined to bring back the people of the pueblo of Picuríes who were fugitives in the revolt of the year of [16]96 and had fled for refuge among the Apaches. From this council issued the decision that appeared in the proceeding which he remitted to his excellency.

The governor is of the belief, because of his experience which has assisted him for twenty-seven years, the time he had served his majesty in that kingdom in the exercise of military affairs, that the opinions were entirely in accord with the common feeling of all those who had traveled to and fro between those spots; thus if it were the intention of his excellency to establish a post in La Jicarilla, whose inhabitants had given hope of reducing themselves to the fold of our sainted mother Church and obedience to his majesty, as they have so demonstrated and have manifested their good relations up to the present, they were very close to that end, so much desired, it might be achieved. This post, with the circumstances which appealed to the council and which were apparent to the governor from his visit, is at the short distance of forty leagues from the villa on the frontiers of the valley and pueblo of Taos the extreme end of that kingdom in which there was a population. From this it seemed wise that this presidio which his excellency ordered in his dispatch above placed in the spot of El Cuartelejo, be placed and organized in that of La Jicarilla. Therefore, for the attainment of this desirable end which the Catholic zeal of his excellency had, he should assign for the post and gentility three religious who with more certainty could secure fulfillment of their ministry, and the natives would be protected by our arms from the enemies who harassed them so much.

He gave notice also at the same time that on the day, the seventeenth, of the above mentioned month of June, his lieutenant-genral would set out from the above mentioned villa of Santa Fé to carry out, with forty soldiers of the presidio of the villa of Santa Fé and sixty Indian allies of its custody, the reconnaissance of the settlements which they say those of the French nation have established, and the result of which he would give an account. He also set forth that there was need in that kingdom of an armorer and two carpenters.

An account was also given of the proceedings of the council of leaders which the governor Antonio Valverde Cosio held in the villa the second day of the above mentioned month of June, before Miguel Henríques de Cabrera and what the fiscal attorney of his majesty stated in his reply of the twenty-ninth of August past of this current year with the rest which was seemly.

It was unanimously resolved, in accordance with the above mentioned council of the exchequer of January 2, that the greatest care and observation was necessary to block the French in their penetration towards New Mexico, [being carried forward by] means of confederations they have established with the Canceres and other nations, and by the establishments which they have made; and are said to be fortifying; and by others which they are reported to have had previously which appear to sustain them on the Missouri River and that of the Cadodachos, both of which empty into the great river of the Mississippi. [It was also resolved] that the strictest orders should be given by his excellency to the above mentioned governor of New Mexico so that when it was time, as he said, he should make a second entrada to reconnoiter the enemy; that a detachment be made up of twenty-five married soldiers with families, from the most experienced whom they had in that villa, to be transported to the site of El Cuartelejo, of which there was a report that a presidio or settlement of the Spaniards was there in ancient times, or in the spot which the said governor should find most fit for the defense as well as the convenience of the inhabitants whose territories he entered where they were to settle. After the lands were divided for them to erect houses upon, the fields should be cultivated and sown and whatever is necessary for that purpose they should have. To each one of the twenty-five soldiers everything else should be assigned that has been referred to: the annual salary they earn as presidials in Santa Fé, arms, powder, and horses which they need. For the deficiency created by the withdrawal of these from the villa, as many others should be put there in the place of those so that the number of its complement should be maintained. The governor, Don Antonio Valverde, was to carry out what was determined in the region and valley of La Jicarilla. Because he did not suggest to his

237

excellency, the captain, whom they were to have as he advised, he was to nominate three subjects so that his excellency could elect the one from these who appeared to him the most fit and assign his salary. In the meanwhile, the governor should place a subject in charge to command the soldiers.

Likewise, it was resolved by the said council that the liaison, union, peace, and confederation which the Apache Indians, whose nation is most numerous and widespread, have solicited from us, is very important both for the said location as well as for the service of God, our King. The measures to be taken by his excellency were that two or three missionary fathers should be present there to instruct the Apaches in the light of the Gospel and arrange with these a perpetual alliance. By these means and that of our arms, the confines of that government would be protected. Having attained this, the Apaches, being so scattered that they extend as far as Texas and the Mississippi River, we could avail ourselves of their aid throughout these parts for defense, and the French in their penetration would be impeded. The corresponding salary was to be assigned to the fathers, and his excellency was to supply all things needed from the royal exchequer for the divine cult of these missionaries in winning the Indians.

Moreover, because of the lack which there was stated to be in that villa of supplies, munitions of war, and people who would know how to manage artillery and stone mortars, he should take all those measures which with his mature wisdom and love of the royal service he thought might be useful. His excellency, with the authority which his majesty gave him, should send some expert officers from this kingdom for the purpose of giving military training, so that the governor might utilize this discipline. Nothing else in particular was set before the lords of this council, only that his excellency may be pleased likewise to provide, outside of the above, an armorer, a smith, and two carpenters whom the governor stated in the above mentioned report he needed. In order that this judgment be precise, proper dispatches were sent; so it was decreed. They placed their rubrics upon it. Sealed with eight rubrics.

In order that the above mentioned governor, Don Antonio de Valverde Cosio, may have knowledge of this resolution to observe, respect, fulfill and execute in full everything according to and in the manner which is required in it, I state and declare and command that the present writing be forwarded, of the receipt of which and of that which

238

he does in virtue of it, the said governor will give me information. México, September 26, 1720.

M^S DE BALERO
[rubric]
By Command of his Excellency
Affirmed   ANTT^O DE AVILES
[rubric]   [rubric]

In order that Don Antonio Valberde Cosio, having conformed to what was determined upon in the council above, attached, he may proceed to the formation of a presidio in the region of La Jicarilla at the setting out of his lieutenant-general to reconnoiter the settlements which the French have among the Tejas, and the rest which was provided for in the council according to the reasons which were set forth in it.

1. Council of War: The Punishment of Valverde [México], 1727[202]

1727   No. 590

Don Juan de Acuña, Marqués de Casafuerte, Cavallero of the Order of Santiago, commander of Adelfa in that of Alcantara, of the council of his majesty, in the supreme one of war; captain-general of the royal armies, viceroy, governor and captain-general of this New Spain and president of the royal audiencia of it, etc.

Wherefore: Brigadier Don Pedro de Rivera, visitor of the interior presidios of the land within, by virtue of my orders being engaged in his inspection brought together a collection of testimonies in the villa of Santa Fé, capital of New Mexico, continuing those which Don Antonio Cobián Busto had left in summary when he was engaged in an inspection of that kingdom. This collection was delivered to the brigadier to conclude various matters. Having gone to the villa of Santa Fé before beginning his inspection, he attempted to inquire into the motive which General Don Antonio Valverde Cosio, then governor of that kingdom, had in not going in person with the necessary detachment to reconnoiter on the Río Jesús María a settlement of the Indians of the Pawnee nation allied with the French, as he had promised the most excellent lord, Marqués de Balero. For this undertaking the viceroy sent a dispatch on the twenty-sixth of September of the past year 1720, with the insertion of the proceedings of the council of war held for the purpose in which suitable orders were advised for its success. Because he had confided this expedition to Don Pedro de Villasur, his lieutenant-general, a man little trained in military affairs,

239

followed the deaths of several veteran soldiers of that presidio who were detached for that affair. In order to investigate the truth and establish the guilt for this negligence, the above mentioned brigadier had appear before him Don Antonio Balverde and, having received information from various witnesses, took his declaration.

In this he stated the reasons which prevented his going, the confidence which he had in Don Pedro de Villasur, his lieutenant, answering in detail each one of the questions and cross-questions, and concluded according to affidavit on July 5, 1726. The case having been concluded within the fixed time, was received here for disposition.

The two charges were deduced against the said Don Antonio: the one, for not having gone on the said expedition personally, as he proposed and was ordered; the other, for having confided it to his lieutenant-general, inexpert in military actions and the management of arms, as was manifest in the lamentable event of many deaths which would not have occurred if they had proceeded in military fashion. Proof was given by Don Antonio, with nine witnesses who deposed before the brigadier to the tenor of the interrogatory arranged. He alleged that he was within his rights. In view of everything the affidavit was provided by the brigadier on the tenth of July of the cited year of 1726, in which he declared the case concluded and awaiting sentence. In this manner he forwarded it to my superior government with his report of the twenty-fourth of the same year. Having referred it to the señor fiscal of his majesty for review, he gave me this reply.

J. Reply of the Fiscal, México, November 23, 1726

[*Marginal note:* Reply of the fiscal.] *Most Excellent Lord:* The fiscal of his majesty, in view of these affidavits made by Brigadier Don Pedro de Rivera, visitor of the royal presidios of the kingdom, concerning the investigation of the motive which Don Antonio Valverde had in confiding the expedition and reconnaissance of the Río Jesús María and the settlement of the Pawnee Indians allied with the French to his lieutenant-general and in not having gone on it personally as he was ordered by the most excellent lord, Marqués de Balero, because of which the deaths of many soldiers occurred: states that from the verbal process issued by the above mentioned brigadier it appears that on the fourteenth of June, 1720, he detached a body of fifty soldiers from the presidio of Santa Fé, which was under the command of Don Pedro de Villasur, for the purpose of carrying out the inspection referred to above. And, having arrived there after sixty-three days, they

240

were attacked by Indians at an early hour when they are usually accustomed to make their attacks.

It is to be noted, then, that during this time the dispatch of the excellent lord had not been sent, because of the date of it, which is in these affidavits of September 20 of the same year, when the attack itself was already very near, this having been sixty-three days after the departure from the said villa. Accordingly, it could not have reached the hands of Don Antonio at an opportune time. Since it had happened thus, he could not be advised that he personally should make the reconnaissance. On the other hand, the freedom from restraint is found in his account which explains his selecting for it his lieutenant-governor. Perceiving, likewise, the sequence of the trial, he could not have been charged with fault or mismanagement of the latter for the above mentioned negligence, since, through the fault of the subaltern, the fear which was felt by the sentinel was not communicated to him; nor for ignorance in the management of arms, because he (Villasur) had been acquiring skill for a long time in many diverse employments.

The fiscal does not find any merit upon which he can establish an accusation against Don Antonio. In consideration of this may your Excellency be pleased to acquit him of the charges which were made against him by the above mentioned brigadier. Concerning that your Excellency will determine that which you believe more conforms to justice, the fulfillment of which the fiscal prays. México, November 23, 1726. Licenciado Palacios.

[*Marginal note:* It continues.] By decree of the twenty-sixth of the same, I commanded that the testimonies be taken to the lord auditor-general of war, whom I beg that in order to resolve with the fullest knowledge of the material the preceding affidavits be delivered to him. When delivered, I beg afterwards that in this matter a copy of the letter be placed with them of the penultimate chapter of his opinion of May 19, 1723, which is that in which he advised that Brigadier Don Pedro de Rivera investigate the motive which Don Antonio Balverde had had for not going personally to the Río Jesús María and the rest which is mentioned in it. The testimony of the said paragraph put in and the affidavits turned over to the lord auditor, who in its light set forth the opinion of the following tenor:

K. Revolledo to Casa Fuerte, México, May 29, 1727

[*Marginal note:* Opinion of the señor auditor.] *Most Excellent Lord:* Don Antonio Balverde Cosio, governor of New Mexico, gave an ac-

241

count that on the campaign which he made, having found an Indian wounded by a musket shot, which he said he had received from the Pawnees or French, he suggested that in the following year he would go himself or his lieutenant-general to reconnoiter the site of the Pawnee or French. In view of this, with the concurrence of a council of war and the fear that the French had declared war, it was decided as the governor proposed. A dispatch was sent in the belief that his lieutenant would be so expert that he could substitute his powers and discharge his obligation. The governor could not go and sent his lieutenant with soldiers from that presidio and Indian allies.

When he had arrived to make the reconnaissance of the settlement of the Pawnees, in which the French were living, he sent a Catholic Pawnee so that he could express to his kinsmen that they were coming peacefully.[203] He remained among his people, and these sent some Indians with a reply which was not understood, but their reserve and hypocrisy was perceived. The lieutenant determined to cross the river which separated his camp from the settlement. While looking for a ford, he learned that the Pawnees had taken prisoner one or two of our allies who were in the river. Because of this, a council of war was held in which retreat to the other river was decided upon, distant from this one a day's travel. This stream, reached and forded, camp was set up and the watch of the river entrusted to the Indian allies. Night having come, a noise of swimmers in the river was heard. Because of this, warning was given to the squad which was guarding the horse-herd so that they would be careful. Afterwards, the barking of a dog was heard, but not regarded. At daybreak the soldiers of the squad herded the horses into camp and, while all were moving about at the same time, the Pawnees and French attacked. They had hidden themselves and were awaiting to take advantage of the discharge with the least risk. They attacked with guns, lances, and arrows. At the noise of the shots, the horseherd stampeded. The squad which was watching it recovered the animals, and was able on the three occasions on which this squad charged the enemy to rescue three who were wounded from among the dead of our camp, who were more than forty. With these and the Indian allies, they fled and saved themselves, according to the declarations of six witnesses. Of these three soldiers, as eyewitnesses of this sad tragedy, deposed in verbal process.

It is certain that although Don Antonio himself might have had the just cause he alleged for not going on this expedition, as he offered, he ought not to have confided it to this man, his lieutenant, so little expert, as the sequence of these established facts shows:

If he had been experienced, he would not have wished, as he did, to cross the river close to the Pawnees to enter their settlement with his people. For without having cordial relations previously established and certain of them, to enter without this security was to sacrifice it; the more so when the suspicious attitude of the Pawnees was known, both by their having detained the messenger of the Spaniards and by having sent to the Spanish camp Indians whose reserve and apprehensiveness was recognized. Secondly, his inexperience is perceived in his having sent the Pawnees to ask what people were living among them, without having previously made sure of their good disposition. Having French among them when the latter nation was at war with ours, it was necessary that they should answer the question only with arms. Thirdly, having declared their meaning the more by having taken prisoner our allies in the river, because of which retreat from that to the other river was decided upon in the council of war, he ought, because of this to have posted the most careful sentinels of our Spaniards and not have confided in the Indians who were worn out with the march of the day and naturally careless. It was very likely and necessary that they should give themselves up to sleep, as happened. Fourthly, since he was in enemy country, he ought to have posted Spanish pickets to observe the movements of the enemy, already declared by their actions. Fifthly, since a noise was heard, in the silence of the night, of swimmers in the river, believed made by the enemy, he ought to have increased his care and posted sentinels over the camp itself for its guard. Sixthly, since the dog with his barking gave them warning of his owners, the Indians, he ought to have awakened them from the carelessness in which they were sleeping, and kept the squad united which was in charge of the horseherd, close to them, and not have ordered it to withdraw as was done.[204] Seventhly, that if this squad alone was sufficient to drive back the enemy three times, as appears from the soldiers' testimony, witnesses of this action, then forcibly united to all the camp, they would have put them to flight. Yet, because of the carelessness of this lieutenant, arising from his inadequate military knowledge and discipline, the soldiers of his command and many of the Indian allies, surprised at the discharge of the guns, arrows, and lances, were killed disgracefully with him. Under other circumstances, they would have sold their lives at a cost of their opponents', without leaving to the

243

enemy so cheap a victory, more a triumph of their treachery than that of their arms.[205]

This event establishes the defect of experience in the lieutenant because of its circumstances, and overcomes the presumptions on paper, which are the testimony of the employments which he had, but not of his acts. It is a testimony of honors, which are accustomed to be given *ad honorem,* but not of military activity which supplies experiences. Then his titles, which are presented in order to accredit him with them, do not prove nor relieve the responsibility which falls upon him who selected him so that the former should pay for all the damages and injuries which his lieutenant caused by his unfortunate conduct. For it is according to law that he must select one as fit, as vigorous, as prudent and as expert as the governor himself. Because of his defect, he is subjected to this satisfaction, conformable to the laws practiced wisely in the chancery of Valledolid, which pronounced a judgment on the secular revenues against the vicar-deputy of its bishopric for not having carried out an order by force. Because the vicar-deputy himself had no property, the bishop was fined for the election which he made. The chancery of Granada assessed the señor duke of Vejar because of the selection which he made of an ecclesiastical judge who did not carry out another order also by force, as Señor Amaya certified at sight. Although Señor Amaya considered these laws a long time, and Señor Solorsano accused as seriously the general of a flota which the Dutch seized because of another's carelessness similar to this, the lord fiscal does not indict this governor because of the selection which he made of his lieutenant for this expedition, because he did not consider sufficient the proofs referred to of his carelessness to sustain charge and merit the share of the damages caused.

Your Excellency will be pleased to free Governor Don Antonio Balverde from the prosecution of this judgment and condemn him to pay fifty pesos alms for masses for the souls of the soldiers who died on this campaign, and one hundred and fifty pesos for aid in the purchase of chalices and ornaments for the missions of La Junta de los Ríos, letting this be given as a fund for charity to the missionary fathers, and applied also for the souls of these deceased. He will deliver this to the Reverend Father Varo, its president, for which he will also send a receipt. The necessary dispatch may be sent for this or that which your Excellency may deem the best. México, May 29, 1727. Don Juan de Rebolledo.

[*Marginal note:* It continues:] With this opinion, I concur in my

244

decree of the eighteenth of the current month. In conformity, and remembering the principles deduced by the lords fiscal and auditor-general: For the present I absolve the above mentioned Governor Don Antonio Balverde Cosio of the prosecution of this judgment. I condemn him to the payment of two hundred pesos, fifty of which are to go to charity masses which must be used for the souls of the soldiers who died in the above mentioned action; and the one hundred and fifty remaining for aid in purchasing chalices and ornaments for the missions of the Junta de los Ríos.

XI. Investigation of Illegal Trading between French Louisiana and New Mexico, 1723[206]

A. Order for Council of War, Santa Fé, April 19, 1724

Edict. Villa of Santa Fé, the nineteenth of April, 1724. General Don Juan Domingo de Bustamante,[207] governor and captain-general of this kingdom and the provinces of New Mexico for his majesty, having received on the tenth of the said month a letter from his excellency, the Marqués de Casa Fuerte,[208] viceroy, governor and captain-general of New Spain, dated the twenty-third of October of last year, inserted it in this decree, as follows:

Letter. By a royal dispatch of the tenth of May of this year his majesty is pleased to inform me of the fact that the Spaniards of this region have been buying from the French in the colony of Louisiana merchandise to the amount of twelve thousand pesos, and on this information his majesty orders me to proceed to punish most severely those who may be found guilty of this illicit commerce. In consequence of this intelligence, I notify you to make an investigation of those persons who may have done this in contravention of royal orders. Put them on trial and secure them (if you prove the fact), exerting the greatest energy and vigilance in preventing by every possible means and effort any illegal trading with the French that may have been introduced. For although this may be thought to be very improbable on account of the distance and the uninhabited state of both regions, which makes the transportation of anything almost impossible, nevertheless it behooves you to be very vigilant to prevent this crime (whether it exists or whether it is planned), and I advise you that any omission that may be made in the execution of this command will constitute

245

a serious charge. You are to send me advices as to the reception of this letter and of what you may do by reason thereof. I pray God to preserve you many years. México, October 23, 1723. To Señor Don Juan Domingo de Bustamante.

In order to make the investigation which is herein ordered, I command my secretary of government and war, Don Miguel Henrríquez, to assemble in this royal palace the inhabitants and soldiers who are the oldest and most experienced in this kingdom, each to say and declare under oath what he may know concerning these things in order to comply fully with what his excellency is pleased to order. In testimony whereof I signed this with the aforesaid secretary, on this ordinary paper, not having any stamped paper in this kingdom. Don Juan Domingo de Bustamante. Before me, Mig^l Enrríquez, secretary of government and war.

Summons. Villa of Santa Fé, the twentieth of the said month of April, 1724, by the above secretary of government and war, by reason of the order of the governor and captain-general, and on account of the above edict, I summoned Lieutenant-General Don Juan Paez Hurtado, Don Francisco Cassados, Captain Ignacio de Roybal, Lieutenant Francisco Montes Vijil, Don Miguel de Coca, Don Diego Arias de Quiros, Manuel Theniente de Alva, Sergeant-Major Don Alphonso Rael de Aguilar, Phelipe de Tamariz, and the captain of the royal forces, Rael de Aguilar (the younger), who having heard the above edict said they would obey it and come. In testimony whereof I signed. Don Miguel Enrríques.

B. Council of War, Santa Fé, April 21–May 4, 1724

1. DECLARATION OF CASSADOS, SANTA FÉ, APRIL 21, 1724

[*Marginal note:* Declaration of Don Francisco Lorenzo de Cassados.] At Santa Fé, April 21, 1724. Before me, Don Juan Dom° de Bustamante, governor and captain-general of this kingdom, Don Francisco Lorenzo de Cassados, to whom I administered the oath, swore by Christ and the holy cross that he would speak the truth so far as he knew it, in answer to all questions. The edict issued by me and the letter of his excellency, the Marqués de Casa Fuerte, viceroy, governor and captain-general of New Spain, having been read and understood by him, the declarant said that he had been in this kingdom since the year ninety-three and in all this time he has never heard of anyone in the kingdom trading or dealing with any Frenchmen, nor has any person reported having seen them or knowing where they live; that

246

it would be a pity if anyone in this region dealt with the aforesaid Frenchmen in these parts, because every year they go to the royal stores at Chiguagua to buy what they need in clothing and other things necessary for their maintenance.

The declarant has only seen some French muskets that some of the native Indians carry, among those who come into this kingdom for peaceful barter, and the declarant also knows that by order of his excellency the Marqués de Valero, former viceroy of New Spain, General Don Antonio de Balverde sent a detachment of soldiers to reconnoiter certain settlements and they reported that there were Frenchmen there, and he does not know nor has he ever heard that the aforesaid Balverde sent any silver or money. All that he saw was a string of mules loaded with provisions for carrying on such a long journey as that on which they were going, because there was no place to supply themselves in that region, seeing that it was inhabited by none but savage tribes and they live chiefly on the flesh of buffalo. This is what he says under oath, which he affirms and verifies. He said he is about fifty-six years old. He signed this, together with myself and my secretary of government and war. Francisco Lorenzo de Cassados. Don Juan Domingo de Bustamante. Before me, Don Miguel Enrriquez, secretary of government and war.

2. DECLARATION OF HURTADO, SANTA FÉ, APRIL 21, 1724

[*Marginal note:* Declaration of Lieutenant-General Don Juan Paez Hurtado.] At Santa Fé on the said day, month, and year appeared before me, Don Juan Domingo de Bustamante, governor and captain-general of this kingdom, Lieutenant-General Don Juan Paez Hurtado, resident of this said town, of whom I administered the oath, which he took in the name of God and the holy cross and promised to speak the truth in all he might known or be asked. The edict issued by me and the letter of his excellency, the Marqués de Casa Fuerte, viceroy, governor and captain-general of New Spain, having been read and understood by him, the declarant said that he has been in this kingdom for thirty-four years; that he does not know nor has he heard of any trade with the French, nor even that any of their merchandise entered into these regions, the proof of which is that the inhabitants of this kingdom go to the royal stores of Chiguagua and Parral to get the goods they need for their use.

The only things he has seen come in are French muskets brought by the friendly Indians who visit this kingdom with deer and other skins for exchange, and according to what they say, the muskets aforesaid were taken from a tribe called the Pananas [Pawnees] when they were at war with them. The Pawnees had them from the French, with whom they are friendly. This declarant also knows that by order of the honorable Marqués de Valero, former viceroy of New Spain, General Antonio de Balverde, then governor of this kingdom, sent a detachment of soldiers to reconnoiter certain settlements and they reported there were Frenchmen in those places. This declarant saw the said order, but he does not know nor has he ever heard that the said Balverde sent any silver for trading with the Frenchmen. All he knows from hearsay is that what he sent was half a piece of baize, some short swords and knives, and some sombreros, as gifts to the friendly Indians who would serve as guides, and thus accomplish what his excellency had commanded. This is all he knows under oath, and he has signed this together with myself and my secretary of government and war. Juan Paez Hurtado. Don Juan Domingo de Bustamante. Before me, Don Miguel Enrríquez, secretary of government and war.

3. DECLARATION OF VIJIL, SANTA FÉ, APRIL 21, 1724

[*Marginal note:* Declaration of Lieutenant Francisco Montes Vijil.] At Santa Fé on April 21, in the year 1724, appeared before me, Don Juan Domingo de Bustamante, governor and captain-general of this kingdom, the retired lieutenant Francisco Montez Vijil, resident of the new town of Santa Cruz, to whom I administered the oath which he took in the name of our Lord and the holy cross. He promised to tell the truth in all that he may know or be asked. The edict issued by me and the letter of his excellency, the Marqués de Casa Fuerte, viceroy, governor and captain-general of New Spain, having been read and he having comprehended its context, the declarant said that he had lived in this kingdom thirty-one years and has never seen nor heard it said that any of the inhabitants of the kingdom have traded with the French; that what he does know is that when he, the declarant, was lieutenant of the garrison of this presidial palace, an order came to the then governor, who was at that time Don Antonio Balverde, from the honorable Marqués de Valero, former viceroy of New Spain, that he or his lieutenant-general should reconnoiter certain French settlements which were said to be in these parts. The said lieutenant-general, who was Don Pedro de Villasur, did as he was ordered and carried with him all that the very long journey required in the way of necessaries. This he declares from having been an assistant and seeing with

248

his own eyes. This is all he knows, under the oath which he affirmed and ratified, and said he is about sixty-four years old. He signed this, together with myself and my secretary of government and war. Francisco Montes Vijil. Don Juan Domingo de Bustamante. Before me, Don Mig¹ Enrríques, secretary of government and war.

4. DECLARATION OF A. AGUILAR, SANTA FÉ, APRIL 21, 1724

[*Marginal note:* Declaration of Sergeant Major Don Alphonso Rael de Ag^{lar}.] At Santa Fé on the said day, month, and year appeared before me, Don Juan Domingo de Bustamante, governor and captain-general of this kingdom, Sergeant-Major Don Alphonso Rael de Aguilar, resident of this villa, to whom I administered the oath, which he took in the name of our Lord and the holy cross. He promised to speak the truth in what may be known or be asked. The edict issued by me and the letter of his excellency, the Marqués de Casa Fuerte, viceroy, governor and captain-general of New Spain, having been read and understood by him, he said that in the forty-one years that he has lived in this kingdom he has neither seen nor heard of any inhabitant or any other person whatsoever having had commerce in this kingdom with the French as referred to in the aforesaid letter, nor with any others.

It is known that General Don Antonio Balverde, former governor of this kingdom, sent a detachment to reconnoiter some settlements of Frenchmen that were said to be in these parts, and this on account of orders from the honorable Marqués de Valero. These orders this declarant saw several times and therein it was required that either he or his lieutenant-general should carry out the command. He did not see that this lieutenant had carried any silver for trading with the Frenchmen. He only took what was needed for maintenance, and a little baize, some knives, and sombreros, to give to the friendly Indians of the region in order to accomplish what his excellency required. This he knows because he saw it all and was present when everything was loaded. This declarant adds that all the silver they took were some platters, cups, spoons, and forks, a candlestick and inkhorn; that this is all he knows under the oath, which he affirmed and ratified. He said he is about sixty-four years old and signed this, together with myself and the undersigned secretary of government and war. Don Alphonso Rael de Aguilar. Don Juan Domingo de Bustamante. Before me, Don Miguel Enrríquez, secretary of government and war.

5. DECLARATION OF A. AGUILAR, JR., SANTA FÉ, APRIL 21, 1724

[*Marginal note:* Declaration of Captain Don Alphonoso Rael de Aguilar (Jr.).] At Santa Fe on the day, month, and year aforesaid appeared before me, Don Juan Domingo de Bustamante, governor and captain-general of this kingdom, Captain Don Alonso Rael de Aguilar, resident of said villa, to whom I administered the oath, which he took in the name of our Lord and the holy cross, and promised to speak the truth in all that he may know or be asked. The edict issued by me and the letter of his excellency, the Marqués de Casa Fuerte, viceroy, governor and captain-general of New Spain, having been read and the context understood by him, the declarant said he has not seen or heard of any inhabitants of this kingdom nor any other persons having had dealings or contacts with the French. He has seen some arms of the aforesaid brought in by the friendly Indians who come with deer and other skins to exchange, and, according to what these savages say, they took them from the Pawnees in their war with them, these being in friendship and communication with the French.

He also knows as an eyewitness, being one of the soldiers who went on the reconnaissance of the French settlements said to be in these parts, by order of his excellency, the Marqués de Valero, in virtue of which they were sent out by Don Antonio de Balverde, under command of Lieutenant-General Don Pedro de Villasur, that there was no silver carried other than some four or six dishes, a candlestick, an inkhorn, a saltcellar and some spoons for their use, and, although they took some other pack mules, these carried provisions for the journey. He also saw a small amount of baize, knives, and sombreros taken, with the idea of distributing them among the friendly Indians of the region to reward them for what they might offer to do, as was done. What they carried was given to the friendly Indians called Carlanas to present to the Indians who served as guides. This is all he knows under the oath which he affirmed and ratified. He said he is about thirty-four years old and signed it together with myself and the undersigned secretary of government and war. Alonsso Rael de Aguilar. Don Juan Domingo de Bustamante. Before me, Don Miguel Enrríquez, secretary of government and war.

6. DECLARATION OF TAMARIZ, SANTA FÉ, APRIL 22, 1724

[*Marginal note:* Declaration of Commander Phelipe Tamaris.] At Santa Fé, on the twenty-second day of the month and year appeared before me, Don Juan Domingo de Bustamante, governor and captain-general of this kingdom, Company Commander Phelipe de Tamaris, soldier of the garrison, to whom I administered the oath which he took in the name of our Lord and the holy cross, on the strength of which he promised to speak the truth in what he might know or be asked. The edict issued by me and the letter of his excellency, the Marqués de Casa Fuerte, viceroy, governor and captain-general of New Spain, having been read and its context understood by him, this declarant said that he has neither seen nor heard it said that the Spaniards of this kingdom have traded or done business with the French nor with any others, as stated in the letter. All that he has seen in this kingdom were some muskets of the Frenchmen, which were brought here by the friendly Indians, who bring in deer and other skins for exchange; and, according to what this declarant has heard from the savages, they took them from the Pawnees, to whom they were given by the French because they have trade and friendship with them.

This witness declares that he was one of those selected to reconnoiter those settlements that were said to be in these parts. They were sent by General Don Antonio de Balverde by reason of orders which he had from the former honorable viceroy, Marqués de Valero, and this declarant did not see that Lieutenant-General Don Pedro de Villasur (who commanded them) carried any silver to trade or do business with the French. Had it been there he would have seen it, since he was charged with helping to load some of the packs, which he carried to the drivers. These were made up of provisions. He also saw they had half a load of tobacco, a little baize, some sombreros, and some short swords and knives, in order to satisfy with them the chiefs of the Carlanas, Jicarillas, and El Cuartelejos, who might serve as guides. This was done among the Carlana tribes, where they opened what they carried and gave baize, knives, sombreros, and tobacco to those who were guides on their route. They marched from this town until they arrived at the place where they had the misfortune to be attacked by the enemy. This declarant does not know whether they were French or some other nation. It took them two months to reach the point where they were attacked and defeated. He also saw that the lieutenant-general carried six silver dishes, and some cups and spoons and candlesticks for his own use; the declarant knows this from having seen them. He declares this to be the truth under oath, all of which he affirmed and ratified, saying that he is about thirty-eight years old. He signed this, together with myself and my secretary of government and war. Phelipe de Tamaris. Don Juan Domingo de Bustamante. Before me, Don Miguel Enrríquez, secretary of government and war.

7. DECLARATION OF VEGA, SANTA FÉ, APRIL 22, 1724

[*Marginal note:* Declaration of Don Miguel de la Vega y Coca.] At Santa Fé on the said day, month and year appeared before me, Don Juan Domingo de Bustamante, governor and captain-general of this kingdom, Don Miguel de la Vega and Coca, resident of this town, to whom I administered the oath which he took in the name of our Lord and the holy cross, by virtue of which he promised to speak the truth in all that he might know or be asked. The edict issued by me, together with the letter of the Señor Marqués de Casa Fuerte, viceroy, governor and captain-general of New Spain, having been read and its context understood by him, the declarant said that he had lived in this kingdom thirty years and has never seen or heard it said that any Spaniards here, or other persons, have held any kind of commerce with the French or others, as charged in the letter. He has seen French muskets brought in by the friendly Indians coming into the country with deer and other skins to exchange, but had there been any trading in the kingdom, neither the declarant nor many others would have to go for supplies to New Vizcaya, more than two hundred leagues distant from here.

He also knows of the dispatch of soldiers by General Don Antonio de Balverde, who was at that time governor of this kingdom, and that this was done under orders from the Señor Marqués de Valero, then viceroy of New Spain, to reconnoiter the settlements that the French were said to have in these parts; but he did not see, nor did he hear it said, that any silver was supplied for bartering with them. All they had, so far as he knows, were some mules loaded with provisions needed for such a long trip as that, since there was no place where they could restock because it was an Indian country. This is under oath all he knows, the which he affirmed and ratified. He said he is about fifty-four years old, and he signed the statement together with myself and my secretary of government and war. Miguel Joseph de la Vega y Coca. Don Juan Domingo de Bustamante. Before me, Don Miguel Enrríquez, secretary of government and war.

8. DECLARATION OF QUIROS, SANTA FÉ, APRIL 23, 1724

[*Marginal note:* Declaration of Don Diego Arias de Quiros.] At Santa Fé, the twenty-third day of the month of April in the year 1724 appeared before me, Don Juan Domingo de Bustamante, governor and captain-general of this kingdom, Don Diego Arias de Quiros, resident of this town, to whom I administered the oath, which he took in the name of God our Saviour and with the sign of the cross, promising to tell the truth in all he might know or be asked. The edict issued by me, with the letter of the Señor Marqués de Casa Fuerte, viceroy, governor and captain-general of New Spain, having been read and its contents understood, this declarant said he has lived in this kingdom for thirty-eight years and has neither seen nor heard that the inhabitants thereof, or any other persons, have traded with the French as the letter affirms, nor with any other people.

He only knows that while Don Antonio de Balverde was governor of the kingdom he sent the above mentioned detachment of forty soldiers, under command of Lieutenant-General Don Pedro de Villasur, to reconnoiter the settlements that the Frenchmen were said to have in these parts, and that this was done by virtue of orders sent by the señor viceroy, the Marqués of Valero. The declarant knows that what the lieutenant took with him was a few mules loaded with provisions for his journey, and he knows that no silver to trade with the Frenchmen was taken. This he avers because he was an eyewitness. He heard it said that they carried some dishes and spoons for their own use. This is the truth under oath, which he affirmed and ratified; he deposed that he is about sixty-four years old and signed the statement together with myself and the undersigned secretary of government and war. Don Diego Arias de Quiros. Don Juan Domingo de Bustamante. Before me, Don Miguel Enrríquez, secretary of government and war.

9. DECLARATION OF ROYVAL, SANTA FÉ, APRIL 23, 1724

[*Marginal note:* Declaration of Don Ignacio de Royval.] At Santa Fé on the said day, month, and year appeared before me, Don Juan Domingo de Bustamante, governor and captain-general of this kingdom, Captain Don Ignacio de Royval, resident of this jurisdiction from the new town of Vera Cruz, to whom I administered the oath in the name of our Lord and with the sign of the cross; he promised to speak the truth in all that he knew or might be asked. The edict issued by me with the letter of the Señor Marqués de Casa Fuerte, viceroy, governor and captain-general of New Spain, having been read and understood by him, this declarant said that he has lived in this kingdom since the year ninety-three and in all that time has neither seen nor heard it said that the inhabitants of this kingdom, or any other persons whatever, had had dealings in trade with the French as asserted in the aforesaid letter.

All he knows is that when General Don Antonio de Balverde was governor of this kingdom he sent out a detachment of soldiers, under Lieutenant-General Don Pedro de Villasur, to reconnoiter certain settlements of the French which were said to be in these parts. This was done under orders received from the Señor Viceroy Marqués de Valero, and he neither knows, nor has heard it said, that the lieutenant carried any silver money to trade with the French. He knows he had some mules loaded with provisions to supply the journey, and he heard that he had some silver dishes for use; this is all he swears under oath, which he affirmed and ratified. He said he is about fifty-two years old. He signed this, together with myself and my secretary of government and war. Ignacio de Royval. Don Juan de Bustamante. Before me, Don Miguel Enrríquez, secretary of government and war.

10. DECLARATION OF ALVA, SANTA FÉ, APRIL 23, 1724

[*Marginal note:* Declaration of Manuel Teniente de Alva.] At Santa Fé on the day, month, and year [aforesaid] appeared before me, Don Juan Domingo de Bustamante, governor and captain-general of this kingdom, the corporal, Manuel Teniente de Alva, resident of this villa, to whom I administered the oath in the name of our Lord and the holy cross, in virtue of which he promised to speak the truth in what he might know or be asked. The edict issued by me, containing the letter from the honorable viceroy, Marqués de Casa Fuerte, viceroy, governor and captain-general of New Spain, having been read and its context understood, this declarant said that he does not know nor has he heard that any commercial trading ever took place between the inhabitants of this kingdom and the Frenchmen, as asserted in the letter, or with any other people.

All that this declarant knows, because of having been one of the soldiers who were sent by General Don Antonio de Balverde (who was then governor of this kingdom) to discover the settlements said to have been made by the French in these parts, under orders from his excellency the viceroy, who was the Marqués de Valero, is that he saw no silver taken to barter with the French, and that all the lieutenant-general, Don Pedro de Villasur (under whose command the troops went) took with him were some mules laden with supplies, a little tobacco, a little baize, and other small things for the purpose of re-

254

warding the friendly Indians of the Jicarilla, Carlana, and El Cuartelejo tribes. This was done when they arrived in the country of the Carlanas, where they opened their stores and gave some to these Indians so that they could let them have guides. They did this and they took them on rafts across a river in the country of the Carlanas. The commander only took with him six silver dishes, a few spoons, and a candlestick for his own use; and, as the declarant was charged on various occasions with assisting the pack-driver who accompanied the lieutenant, he had to be on hand almost every evening and see the packs opened and everything else they carried. He never saw any silver other than what he has mentioned. This is the truth under oath which he affirmed and ratified. He said he is about twenty-six years old; he signed this together with myself and my secretary of government and war. Manuel Then^e de Alva. Don Juan Domingo de Bustamante. Before me, Don Miguel Enrríquez, secretary of government and war.

C. Edict of Bustamante, Santa Fé, May 2, 1724

Edict: Santa Fé, May 2, 1724. Don Juan Domingo de Bustamante, governor and captain-general of this kingdom, having concluded the inquiry which was ordered by his excellency, the Marqués de Casa Fuerte, viceroy and governor and captain-general of New Spain, as to whether the French have had dealings or trade with the inhabitants of this kingdom; and, seeing that no charges have been brought against any person, as appears at length in the affidavits herein, the originals of which I transmit in order that his excellency may do what in his judgment seems best, I order my secretary of government and war to copy the testimony literally and to place it in the archives of this administration which are in his charge. In witness whereof I have signed this with my secretary of government and war. Don Juan Domingo de Bustamante. Before me, Don Miguel Enrríquez, secretary of government and war.

This agrees with the original which was sent to his excellency the viceroy, Marqués de Casa Fuerte, and from which I, the secretary of government and war, transcribed this exactly by order and command of the señor governor and captain-general, Don Juan Domingo de Bustamante. It is a true and accurate copy, covering eleven sheets of ordinary paper because there is none stamped in this region. These witnesses were present to see it compared and corrected. Lieutenant-General Don Juan Paez Hurtado, Sergeant-Major Don Alphonso Rael de Aguilar, and Adjutant Don Joseph Manuel de Giltomey. Done at Santa Fé, on the fourth of May, 1724.

In testimony whereof I affix my accustomed signature and rubric.

MIGUEL ENRRÍQUEZ
[rubric]
Secretary of Government and War.

D. Bustamante to Casa Fuerte, Santa Fé, April 30, 1727[209]

Most Excellent Lord: I have certain information, namely, that the French nation is settled in the direction of the east, distant (according to the report which I have examined) from this kingdom three hundred leagues. My greatest care being to look for security of the realm, I have advised the alcaldes mayores of the frontiers of this jurisdiction always to observe the movements and motives of the savage Indians who enter from those directions to trade and barter the goods which they acquire in their lands, a precaution which has resulted in the alcalde mayor of San Gerónimo de los Thaos remitting me a letter, its date, twenty-first of April of this present year. In this he notifies me that a number of Apache Indians of the nation Xicarilla are in that pueblo. Their territory is that which adjoins that jurisdiction. He advises me likewise according to one of his sentences as follows: "I am notifying your lordship of there having arrived an Apache, who came from the interior, with the same news which I have given to your lordship, of the French who are in El Cuartelejo. The Apache specified there were six who came, and from there five went out with the Apaches in search of the Comanches; the other remained in El Cuartelejo. Likewise, he says that on Chinali[210] the French are already established. The Comanches are in El Almagre[211] or a little farther away. He avers that they are not coming to attack this pueblo; this same statement Joseph, governor of this pueblo, gave me, vouching that another Apache told him so." Of this I advise your lordship in order not to err. The Apaches lie a great deal, but one can neither believe everything nor can he afford to neglect anything. I report this rumor in order not to be guilty of an omission.

It is to be noted, most excellent Sir, that I have previous information from other Indians of this same nation that the French are very close to these settlements. This is the reason why I must set forth to your Excellency that the distance which there is from here to El Cuartelejo is one hundred and sixty leagues with little variance. From the first, I

256

infer that they are coming closer to these territories. During the past year of '26, Brigadier Don Pedro de Rivera being engaged in the inspection of the arms of this presidio, it happened that a group of Apaches of the nations Escalchufines and Palomas brought prisoners[212] who were Comanches. These latter through an intelligent interpreter told in their language that there were white men with the said Indians [Apaches] who captured them; and, according to their narrative and manner of describing them, they were French.

A few days ago there came to this villa an Indian captive, a Commanche woman, who, having been questioned by an interpreter, corroborated that which the alcalde mayor informed me and added that she has seen them. She specifies the manner of their dress, which she says is of white cloth, some wearing red coats, hats with a small band of silver, and having equipment of tents and much provision of arms. Asked the manner which they had of preparing and cooking what was necessary to sustain them, she answered that they carry kettles of copper in which they prepare their fare of meat, and bread, and jugs in which according to our understanding they prepare chocolate. She added that on the above mentioned Río de Chinali, a short distance from El Cuartelejo, is an inlet where they had established and built some walled houses, and that is where there is found the greatest number of them. She says that these white people are stationed outside that place where they protect those who go in and out, for according to the information which she gave, they are colonizing in those regions. Above all, the captive states that it causes the greatest satisfaction to see people so well disposed and likeable.

During the month of September of the year of '26 an Indian chief of the pueblo of this government went out, among others of his nation, to hunt meat and it happened that, having arrived at the land of the above mentioned Jicarilla nation, many Indians of this tribe told him, because he was supposed to be one of themselves, that if he wanted to see a Frenchman, they would take him inside of three days where one was. The latter, either because of his shyness or because he had sufficient affairs to occupy himself, did not wish to comply with that which they asked of him. They indicated to him that the Frenchman was stopping in the vicinity of El Cuartelejo, and that other Frenchmen who came with him had left him there. Those went with a great force of Apaches of the nations Palomas, Cuartelejos, and Sierra Blancas to look for the Comanches (a people widely scattered because of the numerousness of their nation) to see if they could force

257

them to leave these regions. The information which I am giving according to the Jicarilla Indians from the context of their tale is that the French have conquered and won to their devotion the greater part of the infidel Indians who were living on the plains, which they call the buffalo [plains].

These are the considerations which I have investigated up to the present, and there is no doubt that they are not to be despised because always one should suspect greatest dangers, remembering particularly the mishap and casualty which occurred while the most excellent lord, Marqués de Valero, was governing this kingdom. When he commanded my predecessor to dispatch, for the reconnaissance of the French settlements, soldiers from this presidio in sufficient number, the inhabitants of those settlements killed them with firearms. It is also to be remembered that those with whom the French live have long muskets and carbines made in their lands [France] and visit frequently this kingdom, being attracted here by virtue of the union and commerce which they have with the Apaches who bring them to these regions. In case that your Excellency may decide that I should set out to reconnoiter El Cuartelejo and Chinali, I wish to place before the high consideration of your Excellency that there are not sufficient soldiers in this presidio to go and still leave the kingdom in the safety and security which it demands. In this affair your Excellency may be pleased to require the captains of La Vizcaya to detach from their companies the soldiers which appear to your Excellency to be competent to make the reconnaissance which your Excellency may order of me. I shall do it personally, although I must advise that if the order of your Excellency is not here by the month of July, it cannot be accomplished until the coming year because of the roughness of the country and of the snow which falls there. I hope that your Excellency may command me that which I ought to do, which will always be for the best. I trust that I am not erring conjecturing the proper resolution of your Excellency. I am sending a soldier from this presidio so that this information may arrive at the notice of your Excellency quickly and surely in order not to incur expense for the royal treasury. May our Lord protect the most excellent person of your Excellency for many years in His greatest goodness. Villa of Santa Fé of New Mexico. April 30, 1727.

Most Excellent Lord. At the feet of your Excellency.

JUAN DOM^O DE BUSTAMANTE
[rubric]

258

The Most Excellent Lord, Viceroy Marqués de Casa Fuerte.
México, fourteenth of August, 1727
To Señor Don Juan de Oliban
    [*rubric* of Valero]

E. Revolledo to Casa Fuerte, México, August 19, 1727

Most Excellent Lord: With respect to what has happened in the
month of July, in which this governor says it was imperative to have
the order of your Excellency in New Mexico for the entrada to El
Cuartelejo where they say a Frenchman is, and others settled near
there; since the soldier who brought this letter over the great distance
which there is from that to this México, which is six hundred leagues,
has delayed until this August, your Excellency may be pleased to order
that the file of papers be brought concerning the expedition made in
the time of the most excellent lord, Marqués de Balero, which is referred to, and the other made by the brigadier against his predecessor,
Don Antonio Valberde, concerning the loss of soldiers who died on it.
Since the governor, as he believes, cannot go this July, because of the
snows, to carry out the expedition until next year, if your Excellency
so decides, your Excellency may order that advice of the receipt of this
letter be given him and an order that he continue in his care to confirm
these intelligences which he affirms.   México, August 19, 1727.

                                    JUAN DE OLIBAN REVOLLEDO
                                                [*rubric*]
México, August 20, 1727.
    Let these proceedings be looked for immediately and taken to the
lord auditor.
                                    [*rubric of* VALERO]

F. Revolledo to Casa Fuerte, México, November 21, 1727

Most Excellent Lord: In view of this file and of memorandum of
one of the Apaches and of this representation of the governor of New
Mexico, in which he says that through different notices which has had,
he knows that the French are settled in El Cuartelejo and Chinali at
one hundred sixty leagues distant from the villa of Santa Fé, capital
of that kingdom; and that, with the order of your Excellency, he will
go in the coming year if in view of the information which he provides,
your Excellency orders him to reconnoiter those spots, but that the
number of soldiers being insufficient which that presidio has, your
Excellency will be pleased to require the captains of La Vizcaya to
detach those necessary for this expedition.

However, because of the measure which your Excellency was pleased to take on the first of April of this year with the opinion of the auditor concerning the reply of the señor fiscal and report of Brigadier Don Pedro de Rivera, which is in folio ninety-three of the cited num-one file, it was provided what the governor might do because the Apaches of the valley of La Jicarilla were going to settle at the pueblo of Thaos, distant twenty leagues from Santa Fé; the erection of the new presidio was set aside, and the nation was to be congregated at Taos and that kingdom better garrisoned, for the reasons which the brigadier promulgated in his report. When this was understood a dispatch was forwarded on the fifth of April, which this governor would not have received when he wrote this letter on the thirtieth, concerning a recapitulation of the event of the death of more than forty soldiers executed by the French and Pawnees in the other recon-naissance which was made beyond El Cuartelejo in the time of his predecessor, for the purpose of learning whether the French were approaching that neighborhood, since war had then broken out with that nation. Today there is neither danger that they can attack that kingdom for this reason nor does it appear necessary to make this reconnaissance now, to assemble the proposed detachment to carry it out, nor incur the expense which necessarily follows, since the purpose the French have in appearing there is but to trade their goods, muskets, and arms with the savages, as this governor sets forth in his letter, or that of aiding some nation against another, as they are accustomed, especially living among the Pawnees at a distance of two hundred leagues from Santa Fé.

But yet this governor can be advised that he continue the obligation of investigating rumors of the forays which the French make in those distances, seeking to learn their ends by means of the same Indians, their allies and traders, and that he give an account of that which results, and likewise of the receipt of this dispatch. In view of it your Excellency can, with more basis, take measures with regard to the point of his report, or that which your Excellency may esteem best fit. México, November 21, 1727.

JUAN DE OLIVAN REBOLLEDO
[rubric]

México, November 24, 1727.
As it appears to the assessor auditor.

[rubric of Valero]

Date of the dispatch: Twenty-sixth of the said month.

260

EDITORIAL NOTES

[1] Carta del Padre Fray Silvestre Velez de Escalante, en 2 de Abril de 1778 años a R. P. lector Fray Juan Agustín Morfi, in "Relaciones de Nuevo Mexico," *Documentos para la Historia de México* (tercera serie; México, 1856), pp. 115-25, translated in Twitchell, *Spanish Archives of New Mexico,* II, 267-80, item 779.

Escalante refers here to Archuleta's expedition in discussing Teguayo and Quivira, denying the treasures of the latter and stating that only the Pawnees live there, no more civilized than the Moqui. His note that the French are trading with the Pawnees is not unlikely. Perrot mentions the Panys (Pawnees) in his *Mémoire,* between 1666-1669 (Perrot, *Mémoire,* R. G. Thwaites, ed., Collections of the State Historical Society of Wisconsin, XVI, 27). Moreover, by 1672 the Pawnees were known well enough to find a place on Father Marquette's map of that year.

The date of Archuleta's expedition can be approximately determined. As Escalante indicates, the journey took place about the middle of the seventeenth century; absence of any mention of either Archuleta or this El Cuartelejo in the "Informe" of Father Posadas in 1687 concerning the frontiers of New Mexico, leads to the belief that the journey occurred after 1664. Posadas' omission of any reference to this El Cuartelejo is the more significant since he twice uses another El Cuartelejo, in the opposite direction from Santa Fé, as a point of reference. Unquestionably, then, Archuleta made his journey after 1664, the year in which Posadas gave up his custody of New Mexico. Obviously, since the Pueblo Revolt expelled the Spaniards from New Mexico in 1680, the expedition predates that year.

[2] This is the only known reference to the use of copper among the plains Indians in this region in the seventeenth century. The indefiniteness of Quivira itself makes it impossible to state what Indians were the source of this metal.

[3] Don Diego de Vargas, *Journal of Events in the Second Uprising of the Pueblos in 1696,* S.A.N.M., Archive 60, fols. 80-120. Roque de Madrid from the valley of Santa Cruz reported the uprising to Vargas on October 18, 1696 (*ibid.,* fol. 86). The governor spent the next few days ascertaining from spies where the Picuríes had fled. Twitchell, *Leading Facts of New Mexican History,* III, 390-96, n. 249, translates the diary from the twenty-second of October to November 9, 1696, omitting, however, the events of

October 23. The diary is listed in Twitchell, *Spanish Archives of New Mexico,* II, 111, item 60.

[4] Hereafter, this certification which appears at the end of each day's entry is omitted.

[5] That is, east along the stream that flows from the mountains through the Picuríes pueblo.

[6] *Diario y derrotero que hizo el Sarg^{to} Mayor Juan de Ulibarri de la jornada que executó de orden del Sor Govern^{or} y Capit^{n} General de este Rn^{no} Don Franz^{co} Cuerbó y Valdes,* A.G.N., *Provincias Internas,* Tomo 36, Expediente No. 4, fols. 131-40. (MS copy, Bolton Collection, University of California.)

The following extract is an eighteenth-century account of Ulibarri's expedition:

"In the year 6 Captain Juan de Uribarre set out with soldiers, settlers, and Indian allies for the plains of Cibolo. He reached La Jicarilla, which is thirty-seven leagues northeast of the pueblo of Taos. The Apaches who were then living in those regions received the expedition well and conducted it to El Cuartelejo, where had been restored the houses which the fugitive Taos Indians built in the past century, which I spoke of elsewhere. Some families of them were living at this settlement, which had only a hovel or hut. Uribarre called it the great settlement of Santo Domingo and the land that he saw from the summit of the sierra of Taos, the province of San Luís. Flourishing a sword, he took possession of this land in the name of his majesty and returned to Santa Fé with his command" ("Este Cuaderno .... de un Religioso," *op. cit.,* p. 180). The huts mentioned above are referred to in Ulibarri's diary under date of Wednesday, August 4, *supra,* p. 68. For further reference to these constructions see editorial note No. 23.

The date of the flight of the Picuríes to El Cuartelejo is fixed at 1704 by Bandelier (*op. cit.,* p. 182, n. 1). Possibly some Indians did flee from the Picuríes pueblo in that year, but Governor Cuerbó did not mention the fact in his report to the viceroy of Ulibarri's undertaking. Therein he specifically states that Ulibarri went to get Indians there since 1696. See *supra,* p. 77. Cf. Bloom and Donnelly, *New Mexico History and Civics,* pp. 125-26.

[7] Governor Cuerbó ruled New Mexico, March 10, 1706–August 1, 1707. His name is sometimes mistakenly spelled Cuberó. See Bancroft, *Arizona and New Mexico,* p. 227, n. 6. A governor Pedro Rodríguez Cuberó ruled New Mexico 1697-1703.

[8] This is the earliest known direct reference to the Comanches. On their origin, see *supra,* p. 26.

[9] This is the present stream which flows near the pueblo from the Taos Mountains.

[10] This valley is still called La Ciéneguilla.

[11] This stream was probably Rayado or present Cimarron Creek. Ulibarri camped near present Cimarron, New Mexico.

[12] The Río Colorado was the present Canadian River in New Mexico.

[13] These groups, Lemitas and Nementinas, belonged to the Faraon Apache tribe. The Flechas de Palo and Penxayes were possibly Carlana Apaches. Cf. *supra*, p. 64, entry for July 25. The Apache groups in this area then were the Jicarillas in northeastern New Mexico, the Carlanas between the Purgatoire and Arkansas, and the Cuartelejos beyond the Arkansas in present eastern Colorado. The Paloma Apaches evidently lived along the South Platte in northeastern Colorado. Cf. *supra*, p. 132. The Calchufines or Escalchufines also lived with the Cuartelejos and Palomas. See Hodge, *Handbook*, under these names.

[14] This is one of the earliest known references to the Jicarilla. They are, however, indirectly, referred to in a passage which indicates that they were known by that name to the Spaniards in 1696. The reference is to the flight of some Pecos, during the revolt of 1696, to the Jicarillas ("Este Cuaderno .... de un Religioso," *op. cit.*, p. 180). The range of the Jicarilla was from northeastern New Mexico northward an undetermined distance, but apparently not beyond the Platte River in present Colorado; and east to west from present Oklahoma to Arizona. Cf. "Diary of Valverde," *supra*, p. 116; testimony of Gerónimo, *supra*, p. 80, where he states the Jicarilla visited Faraon rancherías along the present Canadian River.

[15] The range separating the headwaters of the Purgatoire and the Canadian rivers was known as the Sierra de la Jicarilla or Sierra Blanca. See *supra*, p. 64, 171, and editorial note No. 143.

[16] This stream is the Purgatoire, which runs northeast. Cf. editorial note No. 68.

[17] *Geologic Atlas of the United States,* Department of the Interior, Pueblo Folio (Washington, 1897), indicates a number of stinking springs in this region.

[18] The Huerfano River. It will be noted that the rough character of the terrain indicated in the diary between the twenty-sixth and twenty-ninth of August indicates clearly that Ulibarri was crossing the foothill region directly north of present Trinidad, Colorado.

[19] The Arkansas River. Ulibarri reached this stream opposite present Pueblo, Colorado. Napestle, or Napeste, was, as Ulibarri indicates, the original Indian name of the river. He is the first known European to describe the stream in this region. The present town of Nepesta, Colorado, preserves the early Indian appellation.

[20] The Río de San Buenaventura was the Spanish name for present Fountain Creek. For further details regarding this stream, see Thomas, *Forgotten Frontiers,* p. 376, n. 36.

[21] Ulibarri now turned eastward from Fountain Creek to the plains in eastern Colorado, his route generally paralleling, some miles to the north, the course of the Arkansas River.

[22] This reference to the Jumanos as enemies of the Cuartelejos in 1706 is intriguing. In 1714, Indians reported in Santa Fé that some French traders, allied with the Jumanos, had attacked El Cuartelejo ("Este Cuaderno .... de un Religioso," *op. cit.*, p. 295). Again, five years later, in 1719, the writer of the diary of Valverde's expedition notes that the Pawnees and Jumanos were allied against the Cuartelejo Apaches. It has not been believed generally that the Jumanos, who ranged in southwestern Texas, ever reached the Arkansas in the early eighteenth century (H. E. Bolton, "The Jumano Indians in Texas," *Texas State Historical Association Quarterly*, XIV, 66-80). Certainly no evidence is known establishing that Cuartelejos ever invaded the Jumano area. On the other hand, Dr. F. W. Hodge (quoted by Bolton, *ibid.*, p. 67) states that an Indian group whom he calls the northern Jumano lived near the Arkansas River in the early eighteenth century and were the enemies of the Apaches.

[23] It is apparent from the diary as traced to this point that El Cuartelejo was located approximately in present Otero or Kiowa County, Colorado. The region Ulibarri reached here was probably the junction of Mustang and Adobe creeks. The diary of Governor Valverde, who followed, thirteen years later, approximately the same route as that of Ulibarri, indicates the Cuartelejos in this locality. The location of El Cuartelejo itself, determined as nearly as possible upon the details of these two diaries and other contemporary sources, is indicated in editorial note No. 79. The houses or little huts (the Spanish reads ".... la ranchería que esta muy cerca a la baxada de dho alto, de cuyos ranchos, o casitas salió Don Lorenzo ....") were undoubtedly those built by the Picuríes in 1696. Escalante states that such constructions were built by these fleeing Pueblos on the plains, a circumstance that gave the name El Cuartelejo to the region and to the Apaches themselves (see *supra*, p. 53). One of the Spaniards with Ulibarri at this time testified thirteen years later that he had seen at El Cuartelejo "some ruins which according to the reports were made a long time ago by the Taos tribe" (*supra*, p. 158). See also editorial note No. 6 for another statement regarding these constructions.

[24] Jean de l'Archévèque, who was with La Salle's ill-fated expedition into Texas, was found there among the Indians by the León expedition in 1689. Taken first to México, he later found his way into New Mexico, where he settled down and became a trader and respected citizen. The sentence (p. 70) beginning with: "They told me ...." and ending here with "his kinsman" is translated in Pichardo's *Treatise on the Limits of Louisiana and Texas* (Charles Wilson Hackett, ed. [Austin, 1931], I, 187). Some difference in the renderings should be noted. Father Pichardo continues to

argue (*ibid.*, pp. 187-88) that this Archévèque, whom he calls Larcheveque, is not the same individual who accompanied La Salle. For definite proof, however, that the two are identical, cf. Bandelier, *op. cit.*, p. 187, n. 4; also his article, "The Betrayer of La Salle," *Nation*, XLVII (August 30, 1888), 166-67. For extensive references to Archévèque, consult the Index to Twitchell, *Spanish Archives of New Mexico*, Vols. I and II, *passim*, and Hackett, *Historical Documents Relating to New Mexico, Nueva Vizcaya and Approaches Thereto, to 1775*, II, 470 ff.

[25] Ulibarri's reference here to the five "large, principal" rivers suggests the five most important in this general region. We are left in no doubt as to three of them. The first, the Río Napestle, was the Arkansas. On the stream farther down dwelt the Quiviras of Coronado and Oñate. The Sitascahe, the dwelling place of the Pawnee, was the Republican or Platte River. It is of interest to note that the Pawnee servant of Captain Serna was named Sistaca (*infra*, p. 136). The Nasatha, of course, was the Mississippi, which meets the Apaches' description of that stream. Possibly the Nisquisandi was the Osage River; and the Daenasgaes, the Missouri.

[26] "Ulibarri to Governor Cuerbó," Río de San Francisco Xavier, August 27, 1706, A.G.N., *Provincias Internas*, Tomo 36, Expediente No. 4, fols. 144-45.

[27] "Franss^{co} Cuerbó y Valdes to Exmo Sor Virrey Duque de Albuquerq^{e}," mi Señor, Sta Fée del nueuo Mex^{co}, Sep^{o} 23 de 1706, A.G.N., *Provincias Internas*, Tomo 36, No. 4, fols. 149-50.

[28] "D^{or} Espinosa, Fiscal, to the Viceroy," Mex^{co}, Diciembre 22, 1706, A.G.N., *Provincias Internas*, Tomo 36, No. 4, fols. 149-50.

[29] *Autos y Junta de Guerra sobre la campaña de los Apaches Chipaynes y faraones o lemitas y ordenes que se dieron p^{ra} ella y diario y derrotero que el Gral. Ju^{n} Paes Hurtado hizo, Año de 1715* (Original MS, Bancroft Library, University of California). Since the essentials of the brief letters concerning the first reports of the Faraon attack are summarized by Mogollón in the documents translated here, they are omitted. For other references to campaigns against the Faraones made to the south and southeast in 1714 and 1715, cf. Bandelier, *op. cit.*, p. 183, n. 2.

[30] Don Juan Ignacio Flores Mogollón was governor of New Mexico from October 5, 1712, to 1715. The Mogollón range in New Mexico is named after him (Bancroft, *Arizona and New Mexico*, p. 231).

[31] The town of Trementina, New Mexico, some miles east of Pecos, may have derived its name from this Apache group.

[32] This is the only known description of such Indian constructions in this part of the plains. Cf. editorial note No. 60.

[33] The visitor-general referred to here was Captain Don Antonio Cobián Bustos. See "Martínez to Valero," *supra*, p. 187.

265

[34] Citing for the most part only the failures, critics have asserted that, if in its theory of Indian affairs the Spanish royal motive was humanitarian, in execution it was oppressive. The specific instruction of Mogollón here that the Indians be treated kindly is a vital expression of the execution of the royal policy. Indeed, the entire collection of documents here presented is far from a record of Spanish oppression of the Indians. Valverde, if his diary be consulted, will be seen receiving the Indians constantly with "his *accustomed* kindness." The impression grows that any sensible view must consider all aspects of Spanish-Indian relations so that sound conclusions may be drawn from data and not from sentiment.

[35] The total number of horses and mules amounted to 275 animals. The personnel totaled: Soldiers, 36; settlers, 52; Indians, 149. In all, 237, including Hurtado.

[36] Vargas followed this same stream to the east. See *supra,* editorial note No. 5.

[37] This is the earliest known reference to present Mora Valley, which Hurtado was following. He called the Mora River here the Río de San Esteban de las Cuevas.

[38] There are several indications in this area east of the mountains of house construction resembling the pueblo type. Cf. editorial note No. 61.

[39] For indication of the agricultural activities of Indians east of the mountains, see map, *supra,* p. 50.

[40] There is today in this vicinity a village called Cueva, i.e., cave.

[41] The command here turned to make its way to the present Canadian River.

[42] The present Canadian River. Throughout the eighteenth century the Canadian was known to the Spaniards as the Río Colorado. The present name "Canadian" probably arose from the use of the river by French traders, though there is no documentary evidence establishing this origin of the name. It is interesting to note that the stream is still called in New Mexico the Río Colorado (Charles N. Gould, *Oklahoma Place Names* [Norman, 1933], pp. 23, 24).

[43] This ranchería was some distance north of the present town of Amarillo, Texas. For evidence of extensive Indian occupation in this region, see W. K. Moorehead, *The Origin and Development of the Pueblo Cliff Dweller Culture* (Andover: Privately printed, 1920).

[44] *Autos y diligencias y se han hecho: en que se les declara la guerra a los Yndios Yutas,* No. 511, fols. 1-19, Año de 1719, Archive No. 301, S. A. N. M., Santa Fé; Twitchell, *op. cit.,* II, 188 (see editorial note No. 8).

[45] Governor Valverde summarizes the essentials of these letters in the statement above of his reasons for calling the council of war. For this reason, the letters are omitted.

[46] A Spanish-American term for a mixed-blood.

[47] A stream emptying into the Río Grande some distance south of the pueblo of Taos.

[48] Admiral Don José Chacón Medina Salazar y Villaseñor, Marqués de la Peñuela, was appointed governor in 1705, but did not rule until 1707-1712 (Bancroft, *Arizona and New Mexico,* p. 229).

[49] This is the earliest known record of a peace made by the Spaniards with the Utes and Comanches. The documents have not yet come to light.

[50] *Diario y derrotero que cujio el Sr General Dⁿ Antonio Balverde Cosio, Govern^{or} General de este Reyno y Govern^r provincias de la nueva Mexico en la campaña que ejecuto contra las naciones Yutas y Cumanches,* 1719 (MS, Bancroft Library, University of California). Some important details not included in the diary appear in Valverde's letter to the viceroy recounting the history of this campaign ("Valverde to Valero," Santa Fé, November 30, 1719, *supra,* pp. 141-45).

Because the last pages of the account of Valverde's expedition have been destroyed, there is no way to determine the diarist. Bancroft, giving no authority, states that the diary was written by Valverde's secretary, Alonso Rael de Aguilar (Bancroft, *Arizona and New Mexico,* p. 236, n. 24). However, according to the certifications at the end of each affidavit in the proceedings of the council of war which provided for this expedition (*supra,* p. 100), Miguel Thenorio de Alba signs as Valverde's secretary of government and war.

[51] Governor Don Antonio Valverde Cosio was born in Villa Presente, in the mountains of Burgos, Castile, in 1671. The circumstances of his coming to the New World are unknown. In 1693, at the age of twenty-one, he entered the royal service and campaigned with Vargas in the Reconquest. In 1696 he was made captain for life of the presidio at El Paso and an officer in the presidio at Santa Fé. In the same year he commanded the presidials in Vargas' expedition in pursuit of the Picuríes who fled to the plains in that year. Apparently, after the Reconquest was over Valverde returned to El Paso, where he developed holdings, cultivating in particular the vine. In 1716 he was given an *ad interim* appointment as governor of New Mexico, which was confirmed by royal title in 1718. He governed the province until 1722, when he was succeeded by his nephew and son-in-law, Governor Bustamante. As governor, Valverde had considerable difficulty with the cabildo at Santa Fé; executed a number of campaigns against the Apaches and Comanches, and made at least one general inspection of the province. In 1726 he was tried for negligence as a result of the massacre of the Villasur expedition in 1720. Though found guilty, he was punished with only a nominal fine. After his term of office had expired, he returned to El Paso, where he was summoned by Visitor Rivera for trial in Santa Fé in 1726. Nothing is known of his later life. The above details are based upon the various documents of this study; Twitchell, *Spanish Archives of New*

Mexico, I, II, *passim;* Bancroft, *Arizona and New Mexico, passim;* and Pichardo, *op. cit.,* I, *passim.*

[52] The proceedings of this council of war are translated, *supra,* pp. 100-10.

[53] Illustrative details of the process of preparing a similar expedition will be found in the Hurtado documents, *supra,* pp. 90-93.

[54] For the total number of Spaniards, Indians, horses, and mules taken, see Historical Introduction, *supra,* p. 28.

[55] Valverde was following the route of Ulibarri up San Fernando Creek to La Ciéneguilla, see *supra,* editorial note No. 10.

[56] If these entries of September 20 and 21 are compared with those of Ulibarri for July 20 and 21, it will be apparent that the two routes were thus far over practically the same ground. The Río de San Francisco at the foot of the mountains is probably the Río de San Joseph of Valverde.

[57] Regarding these adobe houses and like structures of the Apaches, see editorial note No. 60. For agricultural activities, see map, *supra,* p. 50.

[58] Ulibarri mentions the Flecha de Palo Indians in this region (*supra,* pp. 17, 63).

[59] This stream, Cimarron Creek or Rayado Creek, Ulibarri called Río de Santa Magdalena. See *supra,* p. 63, entry of Wednesday, twenty-first.

[60] The reference here in Valverde's diary (*supra,* p. 114), and in Valverde's letter to the viceroy (*supra,* p. 142), to flat-roofed adobe houses in this part of New Mexico may be of considerable significance in association with other known data concerning house construction east of the Pueblo area. Oñate refers to Apaches living in pueblos, one of which had fifteen plazas (Bolton, *Spanish Exploration in the Southwest,* p. 218). As noted in several sources, some pueblo constructions, built by fugitives from New Mexico in the late seventeenth century, existed at El Cuartelejo in present eastern Colorado (*supra,* p. 53, and editorial note No. 6). Of greater antiquity are other pueblo remains in Scott County, Kansas (S. W. Williston and H. T. Martin, "Some Pueblo Ruins in Scott County, Kansas," *Kansas Historical Society Collections,* VIII, 126-27). Don Lorenzo, the lieutenant-governor of the Picuríes pueblo, referred in 1715 to Faraon Apaches who lived in thirty wooden houses whose sides were plastered with mud, ten days' journey east of Santa Fé (*supra,* p. 82). In 1696, Vargas, on his expedition in pursuit of the Picuríes, reported the walls of a ruined "rancho" on the eastern slope of the mountains directly east of the Picuríes pueblo. In 1715, Hurtado, pursuing Apaches over the same route, noted the existence of an old house with adobe walls in present Mora Valley, close to the Vargas location (*supra,* p. 94).

[61] The Sierra Blanca and Sierra Jicarilla were the same. These names referred to the eastward-running spur of the Rockies that separates the headwaters of the Canadian and Purgatoire rivers. See "Declaration of Martínez," *supra,* p. 171.

268

[62] The exact location of the Sierra Blanca Indians cannot be determined beyond the fact that they evidently lived in the Sierra Blanca itself. How far they extended beyond is unknown.

[63] No further information is available regarding the identity of this chief or of his Apaches.

[64] Either this is flattery or the Apache memories were too short to recall Ulibarri.

[65] For other evidence of Jicarilla relations with the Navajo, see editorial note No. 14.

[66] See editorial note No. 60, *supra*.

[67] The present Canadian River. Lack of water at this time of the year probably accounts for Valverde calling the stream an arroyo. Between this point and the stream called Nuestra Señora del Rosario (the Cimarron or Rayado), Valverde left the route of Ulibarri. Ulibarri went almost directly north, while Valverde holds to the northeast to reach, as he says, the Río Colorado. Ulibarri does not mention this stream. Valverde reached it near present Dillon, New Mexico.

[68] Río de las Animas. This naming of the present Purgatoire River by Valverde may be the manner in which this stream received its Spanish name. At some time later, apparently, the word "Perdidas" was added, whence we get the French "Purgatoire." In the mouths of the Anglo-Saxon pioneers, Purgatoire became "Picketwire" as it still is locally called. Ulibarri called the stream the Río de Santa Ana, being, so far as known, the first European to name it.

[69] This is an important indication that Valverde, like Ulibarri, was crossing the foothill region directly north of Trinidad of today, towards the Arkansas.

[70] This is evidence that the Carlana or Sierra Blanca Apaches inhabited the region between the Purgatoire and the Arkansas. It will be recalled that Ulibarri found Penxaya Apaches in this region in 1706.

[71] This is one of the many proofs of Comanche intrusion into this area.

[72] Ulibarri compared the Arkansas to the Río Grande, that is, the Chiopo or San Antonio of Valverde. The Chiopo is not the Arkansas, called the Napestle by the Indians and not Chiopo. Likewise, Valverde's subsequent movements exclude the possibility of its being the Arkansas.

[73] Where this road was, it is, of course, impossible to state. But it is interesting to note that the expedition was then in the neighborhood of the old Indian trails along the Huerfano that later came to be routes used by early nineteenth-century fur traders between the Arkansas River and the New Mexican towns. For a contemporary description of these routes in the early years of that century see *An Anonymous Description of New Mexico, 1818;* "Melgares Report," Alfred B. Thomas, ed., *Southwestern Historical Quarterly*, XXXIII, 50-74.

269

[74] This statement precludes the possibility of the Río de San Francisco's being the Arkansas. This stream named here may have been the Huerfano.

[75] The command was apparently close to the eastern slope of the Wet Mountains, somewhat south of present Pueblo, Colorado.

[76] Apparently on this day, the sixth, Valverde crossed the Arkansas River somewhat east of present Pueblo, Colorado. It is strange that the crossing is not mentioned in the diary. This interpretation of his movements at this point is, to the writer, the only possible one in order to reconcile his route with the details given before and after this date and with Valverde's later statement to the viceroy that he went beyond the Napestle and reached it later lower down (*supra*, p. 143). It will be noted, for example, that on or before the sixth the writer of the diary refers almost daily to the wooded mountains on the left, their steady *northward route*, mountain lions, bears, and the rough character of the terrain. After this date, absence of wood and water, the presence of buffalo and the plains-like character of the terrain are evident. Likewise, on the seventh, and from the eleventh to the fourteenth, the route is not north but always east and down the river. The Arkansas River is the only stream that flows eastward in this region. Finally, on the sixteenth, it is stated the command marched ten leagues (about twenty-five miles) and reached the Napestle (Arkansas River). This statement is explainable by the fact that the command has been moving along the north side after the sixth and had cut across the plain on the fifteenth to avoid following the bend in the river where it dips sharply towards present La Junta. Thus, this ten-league march brought the expedition to the Arkansas again (as Valverde later stated to the viceroy as "lower down"). The command accordingly, was at that point some distance east of present La Junta.

[77] The five-league turn southward on the eighth to follow the enemy trail is now compensated for by six leagues northward on this date, the tenth.

[78] The command was now encamped in the vicinity of present Rocky-ford, Colorado.

[79] The location of El Cuartelejo was in present eastern Colorado. The evidence establishing the fact is the "Diary of Ulibarri" (*supra*, pp. 59-77). The route followed by Ulibarri from Santa Fé to El Cuartelejo was a zigzag one. From Taos he went over the mountains east, approximately to the present site of Cimarron, New Mexico ("Diary of Ulibarri," *supra*, pp. 59-63). Turning northward, he marched along the foothills until he reached the Arkansas River, near present Pueblo ("Diary of Ulibarri," *supra*, pp. 63-66). Turning east again, he traveled seven days for a total recorded distance of twenty-two leagues, about fifty or sixty miles ("Diary," *supra*, pp. 66-69). This distance, measured from Pueblo, places El Cuartelejo in

either southern Lincoln or western Kiowa County, Colorado, of today. The diary of Valverde's expedition confirms this location. His command, it will be noted, followed Ulibarri's trail from Taos eastward to present Cimarron ("Diary of Valverde," *supra,* pp. 111-16). Thence, continuing north somewhat to the east of Ulibarri's route, Valverde crossed the Sierra de Jicarilla directly north of present Dillon, New Mexico, and came upon the Purgatoire River. From there he continued northward across the foothills and came upon the Arkansas somewhat east of present Pueblo ("Diary," *supra,* pp. 116-24). Next turning eastward on October 7, he went down the Arkansas River for a recorded distance of thirty-eight leagues, some ninety miles, where he met the Indians from El Cuartelejo. In 1706, over the winding route he followed, Ulibarri recorded 142 leagues. Over a route more or less parallel, Valverde's expedition marched a total of 149 leagues, to the point at which he encountered the Cuartelejo Apaches in 1719. Other independent sources of the period likewise place El Cuartelejo at approximately 150 leagues from Santa Fé. In 1720, Captain Felix Martínez, a former governor of New Mexico, stated that he had journeyed on one occasion to the Arkansas and that he estimated El Cuartelejo to be 155 leagues northeast of Santa Fé ("Declaration of Martínez," *supra,* pp. 70-71). In 1727, Governor Bustamante reported to the viceroy that the distance from Santa Fé to El Cuartelejo was "160 leagues, with little variance" (*supra,* p. 256).

Until the discovery of the Ulibarri documents by Professor Herbert E. Bolton, who first concluded that El Cuartelejo was in eastern Colorado, it was believed that this settlement was in Scott County, Kansas (Bolton and Marshall, *Colonization of North America,* p. 291). This belief rested upon: first, the discovery in 1896 of some Pueblo ruins in that country; and, secondly, upon the assumption that the ruins were the remains of the buildings constructed there by the Pueblo Indians whom Escalante stated fled from New Mexico in the middle of the seventeenth century and fortified themselves in a spot called El Cuartelejo (S. W. Williston and H. T. Martin, "Some Pueblo Ruins in Scott County, Kansas," *Kansas Historical Society Collections,* VIII, 126-27; Hodge, *Handbook,* Pt. II, "El Cuartelejo"; Benavides, *Memorial,* p. 245, n. 33). However it is clear that Scott County, Kansas, is too far east, since Ulibarri's diary establishes that El Cuartelejo was some fifty to sixty miles east of Pueblo, but halfway to the Colorado boundary line, and one-third of the way to Scott County.

[80] The expedition reached the Arkansas east of Las Animas. It will be noted that this is the first mention of the Napestle in the diary.

[81] Valverde mentions elsewhere the orders given him by the viceroy for this purpose (*supra,* p. 138, paragraph 2).

[82] This statement would place the Paloma rancherías apparently in northeastern Colorado, presumably along the South Platte River.

[83] Regarding this statement of Pawnee-Jumano relations, see editorial note No. 22.

[84] This remark definitely indicates the retreat of the Palomas. See editorial note No. 85.

[85] That is, the Napestle. This statement seems to establish the beginning of the withdrawal of the Cuartelejo Apaches from their ancient lands in the face of Pawnee attack. It should be recalled also, that they were subject to Ute and Comanche raids emanating from the west. Some fifty years later this area is occupied by the Comanches, when Governor Anza campaigned against the latter in 1779 (Thomas, *Forgotten Frontiers,* pp. 129-36).

[86] The great river is the Mississippi, whence supplies were taken to the Pawnee along the Platte.

[87] The final pages of the diary giving, doubtless, the return route are torn off. As to the probable route back, see Historical Introduction, *supra,* p. 32. For Valverde's report of the expedition to the viceroy, see *supra,* pp. 141-45. For an interpretation of this undertaking by an enemy of Valverde, see "Martínez to Valero," *supra,* pp. 181-82.

[88] Don Pedro de Villasur was a native of Castile. Before coming to Santa Fé, he was sublieutenant at El Paso, alcalde mayor and a captain of war in Santa Barbara, New Vizcaya, visitor of Rosario with its jurisdiction, for Don José de Neira y Quiroga, alcalde mayor and captain of war of Chihuahua and the villa and mines of Cosaguriachi. In 1719, as lieutenant-general, Valverde left him in charge of New Mexico while he campaigned in the fall of that year northeast of New Mexico. In 1720, selected as commander of the expedition to reconnoiter the French northeast of Santa Fé, he lost his life in the undertaking ("Confession of Valverde,"*supra,* pp. 230-34; "Diary of Valverde," *supra,* p. 130).

[89] Le Baron Marc de Villiers, "Le Massacre de l'expédition espagnole du Missouri (11 août 1720)," *Journal de la Société des Américanistes de Paris* (Nouvelle série), Tome XIII (1921), 246-49. The fragment of Villasur's diary, translated in this study from the above, was first rendered into English by A. E. Sheldon, "The Battle at the Forks of the Loup and the Platte, August 11, 1720," in *Nebraska History,* Vol. VI, No. 1 (1923), pp. 13-19. Of the two, Mr. Sheldon's is the more reliable because of his expert knowledge of the local area. However, both writers had at their disposal only the contemporary and later French versions of the battle as reported some time afterwards by Indians, or possibly French voyageurs. Some of these accounts are so unreliable that they report fifteen hundred men, women, and children in Villasur's expedition! Both Villiers and Sheldon put the date of the massacre on August 11. However, the Spanish sources establish that the event occurred on August 13 (See "Declaration of Tamariz," an eyewitness, *supra,* p. 174). As to the location of the battle, see

272

editorial note No. 152. Citing the same sources as Villiers and Sheldon, Mrs. N. M. Miller Surrey lists the two translations of the fragments, made from Spanish into French, in her *Calendar of MSS in Paris Archives ....* *and Libraries Relating to the History of the Mississippi Valley, to 1803,* I, 274, 352. She gives no indication, however, that the two are separate copies or that they had been published in both English and French.

90 The command had reached at this point the South Platte River, which was called the Río Jesús María (see entry for the seventh). They were encamped some distance west of the north and south forks. The Río Jesús María was named by Naranjo, who states he reached it on one of the four entradas he made to the country of the El Cuartelejo Apaches ("Opinion of Naranjo," *supra*, p. 144).

91 The correct names of these individuals are: Tomás Olguín, Adjutant Joseph Domínguez, Bernardo Casillas, Miguel Thenorio de Alva, Alonzo Rael de Aguilar, Pedro Lujan, Corporal José Griego, Lorenzo Rodríguez, Captain Cristóbal de la Serna, Juan de Archévèque. Cf. list of those killed, *supra*, pp. 186-87.

92 Captain Joseph Naranjo; also spelled in this fragment "Narrans."

93 This was the North Platte River, which they named the San Lorenzo (see entry for Friday the ninth). Apparently the advance guard crossed this stream, but the command itself had to march along it for three leagues to find a ford.

94 This statement indicates that the command, now across the North Platte, was encamped on the north side near the junction.

95 This statement clearly indicates that a Pawnee village existed in 1720 on the south side of the Platte River, apparently some twenty miles east of the junction of the two forks.

96 The fragment of the diary ends here. The documentary record of the expedition is continued in Valverde's report of the subsequent massacre and in the testimony of two of the soldiers who escaped (*supra*, pp. 226-28, and 228-30).

97 *Autos sobre lo consultado por los Governadores del Parral y Nueva Mexico en razon de los designos de los Franceses de internarse en aquellos Paises,* A.G.N., *Historia,* Tomo 394, Documento XX, 1719-1727. (MS copy, Bolton Collection.)

98 The father refers here to the Jicarillas. For an account of the abbess, see Joseph Ximénez Samaniego, *Relación de la Vida de la Venerable Madre Son María de Jesús, Abadesa, que fué del Conuento de la Purisima Concepción de la Villa de Agreda* (Madrid, 1727), pp. 27 ff., "Maravillosa Conversion de Infieles en Nuevo Mexico."

99 There were some undertakings which were carried out at the personal expense of the governor in accordance with his contract for that office. Matters involving general defense of the frontier, however, were borne by the central government.

[100] For a statement of French interest in Texas during this period, see "Projected Attacks upon the Northeastern Frontier of New Spain, 1719-1721," C. C. Shelby, ed., *Hispanic American Historical Review*, XIII (November, 1933), 457-72; cf. also, editorial note No. 115.

[101] The proceedings of this council of war are translated *supra*, pp.99-110.

[102] The route Valverde followed has already been commented upon, so that note here will be taken only of the new material he adds and of data that varies from the diary of his expedition.

[103] In Valverde's diary the Chiopo is compared to the Río Grande. However, Valverde's movements before and after leaving the Chiopo exclude that stream as a possibility of being the Arkansas ("Diary of Valverde," *supra*, pp. 116-24, and editorial notes Nos. 72-74).

[104] The diary shows that an eastward direction was followed between the seventh and the fourteenth (*supra*, pp. 124-29).

[105] The Indian said in fact that his people had fought the French united with the Pawnees and Jumanos (*supra*, p. 132). The Canceres were the Kansa Indians (Hodge, *Handbook*, "Kansa"; also see "Declaration of Martínez," *supra*, p. 171. With reference to the marginalia which frequently appear hereinafter in this document, see editorial note No. 132.

[106] The record of this expedition by Naranjo has not come to light, though he mentions on one occasion that he reached the Río Jesús María. See editorial note No. 118.

[107] See "Life of Villasur," editorial note No. 86.

[108] Paragraph 9 of this document is partially translated in Pichardo, *op. cit.*, p. 186. Pichardo mistakenly gives the date as November 3.

In paragraph 12 the auditor of war states the letter was dated November 30 as it is here. Pichardo apparently took his material from this source, as he refers to this Document XX and to this paragraph 9.

[109] Reference is made to the Manila Galleon. See W. L. Schurz, "The Manila Galleon and California," *Southwestern Historical Quarterly*, XXI, 107-26.

[110] Pichardo, *op. cit.*, p. 259, has five quartas.

[111] *Ibid.*, p. 259, writes lieutenants here for captains.

[112] *Ibid.*, pp. 259-60, wherein this paragraph is translated.

[113] This was Valverde's messenger taking the report in 5-9, *supra*, to the viceroy.

[114] The Cadodoches were on the Red River (H. E. Bolton, *Texas in the Middle Eighteenth Century*, p. 2).

[115] Regarding defensive activities in Texas in this period, cf. editorial note No. 138.

[116] This cape is at the southern end of Lower California. The island was on the route to Acapulco, southeast of the cape (Schurz, *op. cit.*, p. 111).

[117] Bandelier, *op. cit.*, p. 183, n. 1, refers to the original MS of this council of war. In *ibid.*, p. 184, nn. 1, 2; p. 185, n. 2; p. 186, nn. 2, 3; and p. 187, n. 1, he presents excerpts from this MS, parts of the covering letter reproduced here in paragraph 20 *supra,* and parts of paragraphs 22-26. A copy of this council of war is also listed in Twitchell, *Spanish Archives of New Mexico,* II, 189, item 308.

[118] Three of the four entradas made by Naranjo are: 1717, with Ulibarri to El Cuartelejo; in 1715 there was an order for him to take a letter to El Cuartelejo ("Duque de Linares [?] a Governor de la Nueva Mexico," Julio de 1715, S.A.N.M., Archive 126); 1719, with Valverde; the fourth, unknown, is possibly that which Naranjo mentions here which took him to the Río Jesús María or South Platte.

[119] For Alcedo's description of the Panis, see editorial note No. 147. With regard to this marginal note itself, see editorial note No. 132.

[120] However, cf. Ulibarri's description of the fertility of the land, *supra,* p. 72-73.

[121] This reference to a settlement by Spaniards at El Cuartelejo in former times is interesting but has no foundation in fact. Cf. "Declaration of Naranjo" (*supra,* p. 157), who had been on this frontier since the Reconquest. Father Posadas, a missionary in New Mexico for some years before 1660, wrote an extensive description of the regions adjoining the province in 1687. Therein, he did not mention either this El Cuartelejo or any other settlement in the northeast. The record of Archuleta's expedition likewise precludes such a possibility. See editorial note No. 1.

[122] Garduño was with Ulibarri in 1706.

[123] This statement undoubtedly refers to the constructions made by the Taos mentioned by Escalante. See editorial notes Nos. 1 and 23.

[124] This phrase and the preceding sentence are to be seriously considered with the details of Valverde's diary in any analysis of his route. Also, see editorial note No. 104.

[125] It is clear from the diary of Valverde's expedition that the governor went little beyond the Arkansas.

[126] This statement illuminates tribal locations and relationships northeast of New Mexico in the early eighteenth century.

[127] Considering the lack of gold mines in this region, this statement seems strangely out of line with the traditional motive assigned for Spanish expansion.

[128] This would put Valverde's entry into the royal service in 1693, when he was 21 years old, since he stated (*supra,* p. 231) in 1726 that he was 55 years old.

[129] This paragraph to this point is translated in Pichardo, *op. cit.,* p. 195.

[130] Valverde's account of the massacre of Villasur's expedition is to be read with the fragment of Villasur's diary, *supra,* pp. 133-37; the proceed-

ings of the trial of Governor Valverde, *supra,* pp. 219-45; and the various documents included in paragraphs 35-56. This letter of Valverde in paragraphs 29-34 is translated in Pichardo, *op. cit.,* I, 195-99.

[131] Pichardo, *op. cit.,* I, 195, has the fifteenth as the date.

[132] This note in parentheses seems to establish that the copyist was either Fray Melchor de Talamantes or Father Doctor José Antonio Pichardo, who were successively instructed to comply with a royal order of May 20, 1805, the purpose of which was to prepare a brief for the Spanish side of the Louisiana boundary question. The statement of this order by the Señor Civil Fiscal Don Ambrosio Sagarzurieta is in Pichardo, *op. cit.,* p. 5. For further explanation regarding this work of Father Pichardo see *ibid.,* Preface, and Editor's Introduction, by Professor C. W. Hackett. It may probably be concluded also that the rest of the notes in parentheses, and possibly those in the margin throughout this document, are those of the copyist. On the other hand there is a possibility, of course, that some of the marginal references are the notes of the fiscal or auditor who considered this material in reporting to the various councils of war held between 1720 and 1727. The reference, however, to Alcedo's *Diccionario* in paragraph 22 must be that of the later copyist, since this work was published between 1786 and 1790.

[133] Pichardo, *op. cit.,* I, 196, has here "a banner of fine linen."

[134] These figures total forty-four. Pichardo, *op. cit.,* I, 197, giving the same details, has forty-five; while the list of the dead in paragraph 55 (*supra,* p. 186-87) amount to forty-six. Here (paragraph 33) Naranjo is not to be included with the Indians as he is listed with the soldiers in paragraph 55. The names of those who escaped, including himself, as given by Alonzo Rael de Aguilar amount to twelve. However, he failed to include Montes Vigil and Diego Arias de Quiroga who, according to their own testimony, also escaped. Thus fourteen Spaniards escaped. Finally, since forty-nine of the sixty Indians who left New Mexico returned, the total number of soldiers and Indians escaping was sixty-three; those killed thus amounted to fifty-seven.

[135] These details establish that the French had constructed buildings, doubtless trading posts, on the Platte River some twenty miles east of the junction of the north and south forks. See editorial note Nos. 87-95 and 152. Also see "Declaration of Martínez," wherein he states that Pawnees in New Mexico told him of these French establishments, *supra,* p. 171.

[136] This was Phelipe Tamariz, see *supra,* paragraph 40, p. 171. For an interpretation of this expedition by an enemy of Valverde, see "Martínez to Valero," México, undated, *supra,* pp. 180-82.

[137] Some years later Commander-General Croix made an interesting characterization of the three classes of soldiers serving on the northern

276

frontier of New Spain (A.G.I. Aud. de Guadalajara, 275, "Croix to Galvez," No. 293, Chihuahua, October 23, 1778, fols. 22-25).

[138] The Marqués was preparing an expedition in Coahuila for the defense of Texas. For the result of this undertaking, see E. Buckley, "The Aguayo Expedition into Texas and Louisiana, 1721-1722," *Texas State Historical Association Quarterly*, XV, 1-65. Bancroft, *Arizona and New Mexico*, I, 629, says that the expenses must have considerably exceeded the $250,000 granted by the viceroy. See also C. C. Shelby, "Projected Attacks upon the Northeastern Frontier of New Spain, 1719-1721," *Hispanic American Historical Review*, XIII, 1933.

[139] The Palizada as is indicated here was a seventeenth-century name for the Mississippi River. W. E. Dunn, *Spanish and French Rivalry in the Gulf Region of the United States, 1678-1702* (Austin, 1917), p. 162.

[140] Don Felix Martínez held the office of governor of New Mexico from October 20, 1715, to January 20, 1717. For details of his life, see Bancroft, *Arizona and New Mexico*, pp. 233-35; and *supra*, pp. 170-72, 177-93.

[141] This statement, 205 leagues, should be compared with that of Villasur, who recorded he had marched three hundred leagues and was then on the Río Jesús María. Martínez's estimate of 155 leagues is accurate as to the distance from El Cuartelejo (see editorial note No. 87). The weakness of his statement is his estimate of fifty leagues for the distance from El Cuartelejo to the site of the battle on the South Platte. Measurement on the map indicates that from El Cuartelejo (i.e., from the junction of present Adobe and Mustang creeks) to the junction of the North and South Platte is fully two hundred miles on an air line. Allowing for additional leagues necessary to cover this distance marching, Villasur's statement is to be taken as correct regarding the distance between Santa Fé and the site of the battle. The Editor has seen no other account than the one here of Martínez's expedition to the Arkansas. Bancroft, *Arizona and New Mexico*, p. 234, n. 20, says Martínez became captain for life of the presidio at Santa Fé in Peñuela's time, 1707-1712. He was captain under Mogollón (*supra*, p. 83) until he took the office of governor in 1715.

[142] Cf. editorial note No. 135.

[143] Besides establishing that the Sierra Blanca was then the range which divided the headwaters of the Canadian River from those of the Purgatoire, this statement and that of Garduño's, which follows (pp. 170-74), clearly indicate the location of the Kansa and Sierra Blanca Indians in the early eighteenth century. See Hodge, *Handbook*, "Kansa."

[144] Martínez is undoubtedly correct in his statement that the horse had not reached the Pawnee by 1720.

[145] This remark indicates the Julimes Indians were in rebellion in 1720. Bancroft intimates that they did not rebel until about 1725 (*North Mexican States and Texas*, I, 591-93).

277

[146] Martínez had a lapse of memory here, as he has just explained the intervening location of the Sierra de la Jicarilla.

[147] Alcedo's description is as follows: "*Panis*, Pueblo de Indios de la nación de esta nombre en la Provincia y Gobierno de la Luisiana y America Septentrional donde tenian los Franceses un establicimiento defendido con un fuerte, y rodeado de doce Pueblicillos ó ranchos a orilla del río de su nombre.

"Otro Pueblo hay del mismo en esta Provincia, a orilla del río Misouri, donde tambien tienan los Franceses un fuerte y establecimiento, y al rededor de el hay mas de quarenta pueblicillos de Indios. El río referido corre al E. y entra en el Misouri" (*Diccionario Geográfico-Histórico de las Indias Occidentales ó America* . . . . Escrito por el Coronel Don Antonio de Alcedo, Capitan de Reales Guardias Españoles, de la Real Academia de la Historia, Tomo 4 [Con Licencia: Madrid: en al Imprenta de Manuel Gonzales, MDCCLXXXVIII]. Alcedo's complete work consisted of five volumes published in Madrid between 1786-1790).

[148] It was fourteen years previously, in fact, that Garduño went with Ulibarri (1706).

[149] These statements indicate the interesting mixture of Spanish and French cultural elements among the Cuartelejos.

[150] This estimate of the Sierra Blanca at seventy leagues from Santa Fé is a little high; Martínez's estimate of fifty-seven leagues is about right. See editorial note No. 143.

[151] It is a fragment of this diary that is translated herein, *supra*, pp. 133-37. The second composed by Tamariz has not yet come to light.

[152] The site of the battle from the documents in this study appears clearly to have been on the south side of the North Platte River near the town of North Platte, Nebraska. Several scholars have proposed the junction of the Loup River and the Platte as the site of the attack. This region was first suggested by Baron Marc de Villiers, who discovered the fragment of Villasur's diary in the French archives. Neglecting Spanish sources, the Baron relied entirely on French accounts, which in turn were based on Indian reports of the massacre at the time (Villiers, *op. cit.*, pp. 239 ff.). In his conclusion he has been followed by Monsigneur M. A. Shine ("The Platte-Loup Site," *Nebraska History*, VII, 83-87), and by Mr. A. E. Sheldon ("A New Chapter in Nebraska History," *Nebraska History*, VI, 13-18). Opposed to this interpretation is the opinion of all students who have studied part or all of the Spanish documents available herein. Moreover, these investigators concur in placing the site near the junction of the Platte. A. F. A. Bandelier, who first investigated the question, believed the massacre to have occurred in the region of Platte City, not far from the junction, on the South Platte (Bandelier, *op. cit.*, p. 198, n. 1); R. E. Twitchell likewise concludes the action occurred on the South Platte (*Spanish Archives*

278

of New Mexico, II, 190); W. E. Dunn, following Bandelier, and utilizing in addition some of the documents in this study, places the massacre on the South Platte near the junction ("Spanish Reaction against the French Advance toward New Mexico, 1717-1727," *Mississippi Valley Historical Review,* II, 348-62). The present writer, employing for the first time, in conjunction with the Spanish documents translated above, the fragment of Villasur's diary, has concluded that the site of the battle was, as stated, near the present town of North Platte. On August 6, according to Villasur's diary, the expedition was on a stream the Spanish called the Río Jesús María, which divided "the tribe of the Cuartelejo Apache, our allies, from the Pawnee" (*supra,* p. 163). This contemporary statement of Apache boundaries on the north eliminates the Loup, since Apachería certainly at this time did not reach that far into eastern Nebraska. Moreover, Villasur himself states that on August 6 the expedition had journeyed three hundred leagues, about 750 miles. This distance corresponds roughly to that between Santa Fé and the union of the North and South Platte, recalling that intervening mountains and the route followed by Ulibarri and Valverde placed El Cuartelejo about halfway between, that is, 150 leagues. (See editorial note No. 79.) Particularly significant in establishing that the expedition was near the junction is the note in Villasur's diary that on the ninth of August the Spaniards discovered that the Río Jesús María united with another stream "in such a manner that if we had not crossed already, it would be impossible." Finally, a glance at the map of Nebraska shows that the Loup is altogether too far away, some six hundred miles on an airline from Santa Fé, and (excepting that stream) there is no other joining the Platte on the north side except the North Platte itself. (See also, Alfred B. Thomas, "Massacre of the Villasur Expedition," *Nebraska History,* VII [1924], 68-81.)

[153] This reference is to the site of the presidio proposed by Valverde (*supra,* pp. 155-56). The idea was eventually given up (*supra,* pp. 212-16).

[154] The Zumas (Sumas) Indians were located near El Paso (Thomas, *Forgotten Frontiers,* p. 109).

[155] Cf. editorial note No. 140.

[156] Don Juan Flores Mogollón is referred to here.

[157] Some material bearing on this quarrel between Martínez, Mogollón, and Valverde is listed in Twitchell, *Spanish Archives of New Mexico,* II, 178-88. Bancroft, *Arizona and New Mexico,* pp. 235-36, has a sketch of the struggle. These materials are interesting as they reflect an aspect of the Creole-Peninsular conflict in New Mexico. Martínez was American born while both Valverde and Mogollón came directly from Spain to assume office in New Mexico. The fact that the latter were Peninsulars doubtless explains the favor they met with at the viceroy's court and, conversely, the difficulties Martínez had in presenting his side of the case.

[158] Cuerbó was governor of New Mexico from 1705-1707 (see editorial note No. 7).

[159] The Manza Indians were in mission near El Paso (Thomas, *Forgotten Frontiers*, p. 109).

[160] Valverde, as a matter of fact, stated he had another order from the viceroy ("Confession of Valverde," *supra*, p. 233). Elsewhere, he stated specifically that he went on a campaign against some Apaches as far as the Seven Rivers (Pichardo, *op. cit.*, I, 210). On the other hand Twitchell (*Spanish Archives of New Mexico*, II, 190, item 309), lists an account of a visita of Valverde during the months of July-September, 1720. Martínez also stated that Valverde went on an inspection of the province (*supra*, p. 184).

[161] Valverde placed the blame for the massacre on this officer, Tomás Olguín (*supra*, p. 223).

[162] The list referred to here by Martínez is incorporated in the body of the documents translated herein, paragraph 55, *supra*, pp. 186-87.

[163] It is impossible to check the truth of this statement, considering the ill feeling between Martínez and Valverde. However, it must be remembered that Martínez undoubtedly talked in Mexico City with Tamariz, an eyewitness, and had also received letters from New Mexico. Without a doubt, he incorporated herein data that are important but indistinguishable. One feels that Olguín was unjustly blamed by Valverde, as he was an experienced frontiersman and not likely to expose himself as Villasur did the command to attack in high grass.

[164] Obviously, Martínez is trying to raise in the viceroy's mind the specter of another Pueblo revolt.

[165] One wonders how frequently such a rise from the status of a common soldier to that of governor of a province occurred in colonial Spanish America. Another case was that of Juan Bautista de Anza, the son of a frontier captain, who became governor of New Mexico in 1777.

[166] This list appears in Pichardo, *op. cit.*, I, 199.

[167] The Duke of Linares ruled from January 15, 1711, to August 16, 1717 (Nicolas León, *Compendio de la Historia General de México* [México, 1919], pp. 309-10).

[168] Bancroft, *Arizona and New Mexico*, p. 234, n. 20, says that neither he (Mogollón) nor his property could be found after the conclusion of the trial in Santa Fé in 1721.

[169] After this point, the documents in this file bear primarily upon the question of founding a presidio among the Jicarilla Indians in northeastern New Mexico.

[170] What stream the Río de Guadaloupe was is not determinable. It is likely present Rayado Creek or Cimarron Creek along one or the other; both Ulibarri in 1706 and Valverde in 1719 found these same Apaches.

[171] Bustamante records but nine leagues (twenty-two or twenty-three miles) after reaching the Río de Guadalupe, so that he probably went no farther than the vicinity of the present town of Rayado, New Mexico.

[172] The proceedings of this council of war and the order of Viceroy Valero to found the presidio are translated within (supra, pp. 234-39).

[173] Conchos presidio was at the junction of the Río Grande and the Conchos River. Casas Grande, also called Janos, was far to the west, in northern New Vizcaya.

[174] Bancroft, Arizona and New Mexico, pp. 161-62, citing a royal order of May 19, 1631, states that the Commissary-General Sosa made the recommendation for a bishopric.

[175] For further references to Jicarilla-Navajo relations, see editorial note No. 14 and "Diary of Valverde," supra, p. 115.

[176] This is the first official step in the policy which eventually resulted in the transfer of the Jicarilla to the settlements of New Mexico.

[177] Rivera was about to leave Mexico on an inspection of the frontier posts of New Spain. He began his tour on July 24, 1724, but did not reach Santa Fé until June 26, 1726. His policy was one of retrenchment, which doubtless influenced his decision in this case of the Jicarilla post. For materials on Rivera's inspection, see H. E. Bolton, Guide to the Materials for the History of the United States in the Principal Archives of Mexico (Washington, 1913), pp. 50, 56, 93; A.G.I. Guadalajara, 144, Superior Govierno, Año de 1725; Pichardo, op. cit., I, 199-207.

[178] Visitor Rivera's excellent statement of the Jicarilla problem here is a typical portrayal of the influence of frontier Indian groups on the process of Spanish expansion. For an almost identical situation, cf. the details regarding the Jumano, who, seeking protection from the Apaches in Southwest Texas, attempted to secure a mission and presidio (Bolton, Spanish Exploration, pp. 313-19).

[179] This statement of Visitor Rivera is, so far as known, the only early eighteenth-century account of the origin of the Comanches. Rivera gleaned his details here, as he just stated, from his personal investigations in Santa Fé at the moment. His remarks, accordingly, incorporate what the Spaniards knew of the Comanches, who were then recent arrivals on this frontier. Except the accounts of Comanche attack on New Mexico, these notes are the only known ones which bridge the gap between Rivera and Posadas, who wrote of Teguayo in 1687. The dissertation referred to in the commentator's note is that in Pichardo, op. cit., Vol II, chap. xxv.

[180] That is, 1724, not 1722.

[181] The location of the Natagées was in the region of the present Organ Mountains and Seven Rivers, New Mexico.

[182] Carrizal and Ojo Caliente are about one hundred miles south of El Paso.

[183] Los Adaes was in eastern Texas west of the Red River and opposite present Natchitoches, Louisiana.

[184] That is, at the junction of the Río Grande and Conchos rivers.

[185] The value of Rivera's general survey here of conditions on this part of New Spain's frontier is doubly enhanced by the fact that he was fresh from a reconnaissance of the entire area. His report is a distinct contribution to the understanding of the problems confronting the Spaniards in this "southwestern" area in the early eighteenth century. However, for a criticism of his decision in this particular case of the Jicarillas, see Historical Introduction, *supra,* p. 45.

[186] Whether the Jicarillas settled here as the result of this particular recommendation is not known. The fact remains, however, that six years later they were settled north of Taos and near Pecos pueblo. (See Historical Introduction, *supra,* p. 46.)

[187] This is a statement of Spain's characteristic policy of caring for Indians during the first year of their reduction to the mission.

[188] *Autos echos p^r el Brigadier D^n Pedro de Rivera en razón de la pesquisa contra d^n Antt^o Valberde, Gov^or que fué de la nueba Mex^co de haver confiado el reconozim^to del Río Jesús María y Poblazión de los Yndios Pananas Confederados con frances y no haver ydo a ella como se le ordenó p^r el Sor Marqués de Casafuerte,* A.G.I., *Provincias Internas,* Tomo 37, Expediente No. 1 (MS copy, Bolton Collection).

[189] A copyist error. Viceroy Valero commanded Valverde to make the reconnaissance.

[190] Apparently the "Interrogatory" mentioned by Valverde is that translated in Pichardo, *op. cit.,* pp. 208-10. Pichardo therein states Valverde presented nine witnesses in his behalf, but their testimonies have not yet come to light.

[191] From this point to the end of this writ, it is possible that Pichardo (*op. cit.,* I, 201) got the quotation he presents there.

[192] From this point to the fourth sentence from the end, this material appears in Pichardo, *op. cit.,* I, 201-03.

[193] Only part of the entire testimony of José Santiesteban is known (see Pichardo, *op. cit.,* I, 203-04).

[194] This confession, without its title, is in Pichardo, *op. cit.,* I, 204-07.

[195] Pichardo, *op. cit.,* I, 204, has p. 189.

[196] Pichardo, *op. cit.,* I, 205, has Valverde governor until the accession of Viceroy Casafuerte and not that of Governor Bustamante.

[197] Pichardo, *op. cit.,* I, 205, has a sentence, not in this copy, stating that the viceroy agreed to the postponement. The council of war held September 26 in Mexico City certainly gave Valverde authority to send Villasur (see *supra,* pp. 238-39). However, Valverde did not in point of fact have this authority, as the council of war was held on September 26, over three

282

months after Villasur had left. The fiscal, however, concluded that Valverde could not, therefore, have been advised that he personally should conduct the reconnaissance (*supra,* pp. 240-41).

[198] Pichardo, *op. cit.,* I, 205, is in error when he states the expedition went northwest. See "Diary of Valverde," *supra,* pp. 110-33, *passim.*

[199] This river is not mentioned in Valverde's diary. Pichardo, *op. cit.,* I, 206, has Cances River.

[200] Pichardo, *op. cit.,* I, 206, has seventy,. evidently a mis-copy. See "Martínez to Valero," *supra,* p. 182.

[201] *Autos echos por .... Rivera .... contra Valverde,* fols. 53-60. This document, the proceedings of a council of war held on September 26, 1720, in Mexico City, was evidently submitted to Rivera by Valverde to establish his authority to send his lieutenant-general, Villasur, in place of going himself.

[202] *Mandamiento* of Viceroy Marqués de Casa Fuerte, Mexico, May 29, 1727, S.A.N.M., Archive 346. This document closes the body of materials bearing upon the Villasur expedition originating just ten years before. The document is incomplete, lacking the usual signatures and rubrics.

[203] Bandelier, *op. cit.,* p. 198, n. 1, gives a short excerpt from the original of this document.

[204] *Ibid.,* p. 200, n. 1, includes an excerpt from the original of these six points.

[205] *Ibid.,* p. 202, n. 1, gives additional details taken from the original sources.

[206] Juan Domingo Bustamante, April 22, May 2, 1724. "Interrogatories taken by Governor Bustamante relative to illegal commerce with the Louisiana French," S.A.N.M., Archive 327. Bandelier, *op. cit.,* p. 191, n. 2, and p. 192, n. 1, refers to parts of the testimony of Alphonso Rael de Aguilar and that of Alonzo Rael de Aguilar translated herein.

[207] Bustamante was governor of New Mexico from 1722 to 1731 (Bancroft, *Arizona and New Mexico,* p. 238).

[208] Casa Fuerte was viceroy of México from October 15, 1722, to October 15, 1734 (León, *op. cit.,* p. 311).

[209] *Autos echos por .... Rivera .... contra Valverde,* fols. 74-76.

[210] No information regarding this river has been found. Possibly it was the Arkansas.

[211] El Almagre was a Spanish name applied to the front range of the Rocky Mountains in present Colorado. Cf. Thomas, *Forgotten Frontiers,* p. 129. Also "An Anonymous Description of New Mexico, 1818," Alfred B. Thomas, ed., *Southwestern Historical Quarterly,* XXXIII (July, 1929), 50-74, for a description of the various approaches to El Almagre.

[212] Rivera mentions the fact *supra,* p. 257.

BIBLIOGRAPHY

The following abbreviations have been used in citing the manuscript materials:

A.G.I.—Archivo General de Indias, Seville, Spain.
A.G.N.—Archivo General y Público de la Nación, Mexico.
S.A.N.M.—Spanish Archives of New Mexico, Santa Fé, New Mexico.

Manuscript Materials

"Reconquista del Reyno de la Nuebo Mexico, por d^n Diego de Vargas Zapata, Año de 1694, Reconquista de la Nuevo Mexico," MS copy, Bolton Collection, University of California, Berkeley. Original in "Journal of Events in Second Uprising of the Pueblos in 1696," S.A.N.M., Archive 60. Listed in R. E. Twitchell, *Spanish Archives of New Mexico,* II, III.

"Diario y derrotero que hico el Sarg^{to} mayor Juan de Ulibarri de la Jornada que executtó de Orden del Sor Gouern^{or} y Capit^n General de este R^{no} Don Franz^{co} Cuerbó y Valdes. Cau^o del Orden de Santiago á la tierra Yncognita; de los llanos al rrescate de los Yndios Xptianos de la nazion de los Picuríes: y descubrimy^{to} de la nueua Prouincia de San Luís y gran Población de Santo Domingo. del quartelejo hauitada de Ynnumerables naciones de Yndios Ynfideles q^e quedan pazificadas Y á la Obedienz^a de S. M. &^{a}. con los testimonios, y Zertificaziones de esta empresa. Año de 1706," MS copy in Bolton Collection. Original in A.G.N., *Provincias Internas,* Tomo 36, No. 4.

"Autos y Junta de Guerra sobre la Campaña de los Apaches Chipaynes y Faraones ó limitas y ordenes que se dieron p^{ra} ella y diario y derrotero que el Gral. Ju^n Páez Hurtado hizo. Año de 1715," MS in Bancroft Library, University of California.

"Autos y diligencias q se han hecho: en q se les declara la guerra á los Yndios Barbaros Gentiles yuta, por las muertes, y robos q han executado, en este Rey^{no} para cuyo efecto y rresoluz^n el s^r Genl d^n Antonio Balue Cosio hizo y formó junta de guerra; de los ofiz^s de este Castillo Presidial y con los Vez^{nos} Practicos y may^s experienzios &^{a} Año de 1719," S. A. N. M., Archive 301. Listed in R. E. Twitchell, *Spanish Archives,* II, 188.

"Diario y derrotero que cujio el Sr General D^n Antonio Balverde Cosio, Govern^{or} General de este Reyno y Govern^r de las provincias de la nueva Mexico en la campaña que ejecutó contra las naciones Yutas y Cumanches. 1719," MS in Bancroft Library, University of California.

"Juan de Ulibarri to Sr Gou^{or} y Capp^n Genl D^n Franss^{co} Cueruó y Valdes mi Señor, S^n franss^{co} Xauier, Agosto 27 de 1706," A.G.N., *Provincias Internas,* Tomo 36, No. 4, fols. 144-45.

"Franss^{co} Cuerbó y Valdes to Exmo Sor Vierry Duque de Albuquerq^e mi Sor Sta Fée del nueuo mex^{co}, Sep^o 23 de 1706," A.G.N., *Provincias Internas,* Tomo 36, No. 4, fols. 149-50.

D^{or} Espinosa, Fiscal to the Viceroy, México, December 22, 1706, in A.G.N. *Provincias Internas,* Tomo 36, No. 34, fols. 149-50.

"Duque de Linares (?) Para que el Gou^{or} de la Nueua Mex^{co} de las prouidencias resueltas en la Junta Gral Ynserta á fin de que el Cap^n Naranjo Vaia al quartelejo á entregar la carta que en ella se preuinene, como se expresa. México y Jullio Onze de 1715," S.A.N.M., Archive 226. Listed in R. E. Twitchell, *Spanish Archives,* II, 178.

"Junta de Guerra," Felix Martínez, August 20–October 14, 1716. Proceedings and edicts of a council of war relative to an offensive campaign led by Captain de la Serna against the Utes and Comanches. S.A.N.M., Archive No. 279. Listed in R. E. Twitchell, *Spanish Archives,* II, 184.

"Autos sobre lo consultado por los Governadores del Parral y Nueva Mexico en razón de los designos de los Franceses de internarse en aquellos Paises," MS copy in Bolton Collection. MS in A.G.N., *Historia,* Tomo 394, Documento XX, 1719-1727.

Juan Domingo Bustamante, Interrogatories taken by Governor Bustamante relative to illegal commerce with the Louisiana French, April 22–May 2, 1724. S.A.N.M., Archive 327. Listed in R. E. Twitchell, *Spanish Archives,* II, 193.

"Autos echos p^r el Brigadier D^n Pedro de Rivera en razón de la pesquisa contra d^n Antt^o Valberde, Gov^{or} que fué de la nueba Mex^{co} de haver Confiado el reconozim^{to} del Río Jesús María y Poblazión de los Yndios Pananas Confederados con franses. y no haver yro á ella como se le ordenó p^r el Sor Marqués de Casafuerte" (1726), MS copy, Bolton Collection. Original in A.G.N., *Provincias Internas,* Tomo 37, No. 1.

"Mandamiento" of Casa Fuerte, México, May 29, 1727, ordering Antonio de Valverde Cosio to pay two hundred pesos. S.A.N.M., Archive 346. Listed in R. E. Twitchell, *Spanish Archives,* II, 195.

Juan Domingo de Bustamante (?) November 26, 1727, blotter of a letter to the viceroy concerning the Jicarilla Apaches and a journey thither. S.A.N.M., Archive 347. Listed in R. E. Twitchell, *Spanish Archives, II*, 196.

"Da cuenta de las resultas que tuvieron las paces pretendidas por los Apaches del Gila; de la infructuosa campaña que se les hizo; de la que se queda practicando, y expone causas que inutilizan las operaciones de las Tropas, y las dificultades de remediarles y en much tiempo," A.G.I., Guadalajara 275, Teodoro de Croix to José de Gálvez, Chihuahua, October 23, 1778, No. 293, fols. 20-27.

List of Printed Materials

Antonio de Alcedo, *Diccionario Geográfico-Histórico de las Indias Occidentales ó América,* Tomo IV (Madrid, 1788).

Hubert Howe Bancroft, *History of Arizona and New Mexico 1530-1888,* Vol. XVII (San Francisco, 1889).

Fray Alonso de Benavides, *The Memorial of Fray Alonso de Benavides 1630,* trans. by Mrs. Edward E. Ayer, annotated by Frederick Webb Hodge and Charles Fletcher Lummis (Chicago, 1916).

Lansing B. Bloom and Thomas C. Donnelly, *New Mexico History and Civics* (Albuquerque, 1933).

Herbert Eugene Bolton and Thomas Maitland Marshall, *The Colonization of North America 1492-1783* (New York, 1920).

Herbert Eugene Bolton, *Guide to Materials for the History of the United States in the Principal Archives of México* (Washington, 1913).

—— *The Spanish Borderlands* (New Haven, 1921).

—— *Spanish Exploration in the Southwest 1542-1706* (New York, 1916).

Cesáreo Fernández Duro, *Don Diego de Peñalosa y su Descubrimiento del Reino de Quivira* (Madrid, 1882).

William Edward Dunn, *Spanish and French Rivalry in the Gulf Region of the United States, 1678-1702* (Austin, 1917).

Fray Silvestre Velez de Escalante, "Carta del padre Escalante escrita en 2 abril de 1778 anos a R. P. lector Fray Juan Agustín Morfi." in "Relaciones de Nuevo-Mexico," pp. 115-26, in *Documentos para la Historia de México* (Tercera serie; México, 1856).

"Este Cuaderno se cree ser obra de un Religioso de la Provincia del Santo Evangelio," in "Relaciones de Nuevo-Mexico," pp. 126-208, *Documentos para la Historia de México,* (Tercera serie; Mexico, 1856).

Charles Wilson Hackett, *Historical Documents relating to New Mexico, Nueva Vizcaya, and Approaches Thereto, to 1773,* collected by Adolph F. A. and Fanny R. Bandelier, 2 vols. (Washington, 1923-26).

—— *Pichardo's Treatise on the Limits of Louisiana and Texas,* Vols. I and II (Austin, 1931 and 1934).

George Peter Hammond, *Juan de Oñate and the Founding of New Mexico* (Santa Fé, 1927).

—— and Agapito Rey, *Expedition into New Mexico made by Antonio de Espejo, 1582-1583, as revealed in the Journal of Diego Pérez de Luxán,* Quivira Society Publication (Los Angeles, 1929).

—— *The Rodríguez Expedition, Gallegos' Relación* (Santa Fé, 1927).
Frederick Webb Hodge, *Handbook of American Indians,* 2 vols. (Washingington, 1907-10).

——, ed., *The Narrative of the Expedition of Coronado by Pedro de Castañeda* (New York, 1907).

Nicolás León, *Compendio de la Historia General de México* (México, 1919).

Mrs. N. M. Miller Surrey, ed., *Calendar of Manuscripts in Paris Archives and Libraries Relating to the History of the Mississippi Valley to 1803,* 2 vols (Washington: Privately printed, 1926), Vol. I, 1581-1739.

Padre Juan Amando Niel, "Apuntamientos que á las Memorias del Padre Fray Gerónimo de Zarate hizo, no tan solo estando practico del terreno que se cita, si no es que llevaba en la mano las memorias para cotejarlas con el," "Relaciones de Nuevo-México," pp. 59-112, in *Documentos para la Historia de México* (Tercera serie; México, 1856).

Nicolás Perrot, "Mémoire," *Wisconsin Historical Society Collections,* Vol. XVI (Madison, 1902).

Pedro de Rivera, *Diario y Derrotero de lo caminado, visto, y observado en el discurso de la visita general de Precidios, situados en las Provincias Ynternas de Nueva España* (Guatemala, 1736).

Joseph Ximénez Samaniego, *Relación de la vida de la Venerable madre Sor María de Jesús, Abadesa, que fué del convento de la Purisima Concepción de la Villa de Agreda* (Madrid, 1727).

Henry Morse Stephens and Herbert Eugene Bolton, eds., *The Pacific Ocean in History* (New York, 1917).

Alfred Barnaby Thomas, *Forgotten Frontierss A Study of the Spanish Indian Policy of Don Juan Bautista de Anza, Governor of New Mexico, 1777-1787* (Norman, 1932).

Ralph Emerson Twitchell, *Leading Facts of New Mexican History,* 5 vols. (Cedar Rapids, 1911-17).

———— *Spanish Archives of New Mexico,* 2 vols. (Cedar Rapids, 1914).

Joseph Antonio de Villa-Señor, *Teatro Americano, Descripción General de los Reynos y Provincias de la Nueva España y sus Jurisdicciones,* Segunda parte (México, 1748).

George Parker Winship, "The Coronado Expedition, 1540-1542," Bureau of Ethnology, *Fourteenth Annual Report,* Pt. I (Washington, 1896).

Special Studies

A. F. A. Bandelier, *Contributions to the History of the Southwestern Portion of the United States* (Cambridge, 1890).

———— "Report on the Ruins of the Pueblo of Pecos," in *Papers of the Archæological Institute of America* (American ser. I; Boston, 1883).

———— "The Betrayer of La Salle," *Nation,* XLVII (August 30, 1883), 166-67.

J. N. Baskett, "A Study of the Route of Coronado," Kansas State Historical Society Collections, Vol. XII (1911-12), No. 6.

Herbert Eugene Bolton, "French Intrusions into New Mexico, 1749-1752," in *The Pacific Ocean in History,* ed. by H. Morse Stephens and Herbert E. Bolton (New York, 1917).

———— "The Jumano Indians in Texas, 1650-1771," *Texas State Historical Association Quarterly,* Vol XV (1911-12), No. 1.

———— "Spanish Occupation of Texas, 1519-1690," *Texas State Historical Association Quarterly,* Vol. XVI (1912-13), No. 1.

E. Buckley, "The Aguayo Expedition into Texas and Louisiana, 1721-1722," *Texas State Historical Association Quarterly,* Vol. XVI (1912-13), No. 1.

Amado Chaves, "The Defeat of the Comanches in 1716," No. 8 of the *Publications of the Historical Society of New Mexico.*

Joaquín de Codallos y Rabal, "Opinion," trans. by Charles Fletcher Lummis in *Land of Sunshine,* Vol. VIII (1894), No. 1.

William E. Dunn, "Spanish Reaction against the French Advance toward New Mexico, 1717-1727," *Mississippi Valley Historical Review,* Vol. II (1915-16), No. 3.

Robert Carlton Clark, *The Beginnings of Texas, 1684-1718,* Bulletin of the University of Texas, No. 98 (Austin, 1907).

Charles Wilson Hackett, "New Light on Don Diego de Peñalosa: Proof That He Never Made an Expedition from Santa Fé to Quivira and the Mississippi River in 1662," *Mississippi Valley Historical Review,* Vol. VI (1919), No. 3.

—— "Causes for the Failure of Otermín's Attempt to Reconquer New Mexico, 1681-1682," *The Pacific Ocean in History,* ed. by H. Morse Stephens and Herbert E. Bolton (New York, 1917).

—— "Otermín's Attempt to Reconquer New Mexico, 1681-1682," *Old Santa Fé* (1917), Vol. IV.

—— "Revolt of the Pueblo Indians of New Mexico in 1680," *Texas State Historical Association Quarterly,* Vol. XV (1911-12), No. 2.

Frederick Webb Hodge, "French Intrusion toward New Mexico," *New Mexico Historical Review,* Vol. IV (1929), No. 1.

Dorothy Hull, "Sosa's Expedition," *Old Santa Fé* (1916), Vol. III.

Irving A. Leonard, "DonÁndres de Arriola and the Occupation of Pensacola Bay," in *New Spain and the Anglo-American West,* Vol. I (Los Angeles, 1932).

Anna Lewis, "Du Tisné's Expedition into Oklahoma, 1719," *Chronicles of Oklahoma,* Vol. III (1925), No. 4.

—— "La Harpe's First Expedition in Oklahoma, 1718-1719," *Chronicles of Oklahoma,* Vol. II (1924), No. 4.

J. Lloyd Mecham, "Antonio de Espejo and His Journey to New Mexico," *Southwestern Historical Quarterly,* Vol. XXX (1926), No. 2.

—— "The Second Spanish Expedition to New Mexico, an Account of the Chamuscado-Rodriguez Entrada, 1581-1582," *New Mexico Historical Review,* Vol. I (1926), No. 1.

W. K. Moorehead, "Recent Explorations in Northwest Texas," *American Anthropologist* (New ser.), Vol. XXIII (1921), No. 1.

—— "The Origin and Development of the Pueblo Cliff Dweller Culture" (Andover: privately printed, 1920).

Fray Alonso de Posadas, "Informe á S. M. sobre las tierras de Nuevo Méjico, Quivira y Teguayo," in Cesáreo Fernández Duro, *Don Diego de Peñalosa y su Descubrimiento del Reino de Quivira* (Madrid, 1882).

W. L. Schurz, "The Manila Galleon and California," *Southwestern Historical Quarterly,* Vol. XXI (1917), No. 2.

C. C. Shelby, "Projected Attacks upon the Northeastern Frontier of New Spain, 1719-1721," *Hispanic-American Historical Review,* Vol. XIII (1933), No. 4.

Addison E. Sheldon, "Translation of a Leaf from a Journal in Spanish, Found at the Defeat of a Detachment of That Nation by the Otoptata," in *Nebraska History and Record of Pioneer Days,"* Vol. VI (1923), No. 1.

Rt. Rev. Monsignor M. A. Shine, "In Favor of Loup Site," *Nebraska History,* Vol. VII (1924; issued November, 1925), No. 3.

Alfred B. Thomas, "An Eighteenth-Century Comanche Document," *American Anthropologist* (New ser.), Vol. XXXI (1929), No. 2.

——— "An Anonymous Description of New Mexico, 1818," *Southwestern Historical Quarterly,* Vol. XXXIII (1929), No. 1.

——— "The Massacre of the Villasur Expedition at the Forks of the Platte River, August 12, 1720," *Nebraska History,* Vol. VII (1924; issued November, 1925), No. 3.

——— "Spanish Expeditions into Colorado," *Colorado Magazine,* Vol. I (1924), No. 7.

——— "Spanish Exploration of Oklahoma, 1599-1792," *Chronicles of Oklahoma,* Vol. VI (1928), No. 2.

Le Baron Marc de Villiers, "Le Massacre de l'expédition espagnole du Missouri (11 août 1720)," *Journal de la Société des Américanistes de Paris* (Nouvelle série), Tome XIII (1921).

S. W. Williston and H. T. Martin, "Some Pueblo Ruins in Scott County, Kansas," *Kansas Historical Society Collections,* VIII (1897-1900).

Gerónimo de Zarate-Salmerón, "Relación," trans. by Charles F. Lummis in *Land of Sunshine,* XI-XII (1897-98), *passim.*

Maps

Herbert Eugene Bolton, *Explorations on the Northern Frontier of New Spain,* University of California Map Series, No. 1, Berkeley, 1916.

Geologic Atlas of the United States, Department of the Interior, Pueblo Folio (Washington, 1897).

291

INDEX

Ácoma, 59

Acansa, French name of Arkansas, 142

Adidasde, ranchería of El Cuartelejo, 20, 71

Administration: see Bustamante, Casafuerte, Church, Cobían Bustos, Council of war, Cuerbó, Expeditions, French, Hurtado, Indians, Irrigation, License, Martínez, Militia, Missionaries, Missions, Mogollón, New Mexico, Palacios, Pay, Presents, Pueblo Indians, Regidors, Revolledo, Rivera, Sainz, Salaries, Settlers, Spanish policy, Trade, Troops, Valero, Valverde, Vargas, Villasur, Weapons

Agreda, Madre sor. María Jesús de, 138

Agriculture: see Crops, Food, Irrigation, La Jicarilla; map, 50; Faraon corn, 81; of Penxayes, 64; proposed development in La Jicarilla, 207

Aguayo, Marqués de, warned of French, 176-77

Aguilar, Alphonso Rael de: declaration regarding French, 249; opinion of, 108-09; sergeant-major of kingdom, 108; testimony in Valverde trial, 226-28; with Vargas, 59

Aguilar, Alonzo, 83; opinion of, 158; with Valverde, 118

Aguilar, Alejandro Rael de, with Valverde, 121

Albuquerque, raided by Faraones, 208; settlers of, 91

Alcedo y Bexarano, Antonio de, *Dictionary* of, 156

Alva, Manuel Teniente de, declaration regarding French, 254-55

Anaya, Salvador de, with Valverde, 118

Andadores, sell Cuartelejo captives, 73

Anian, Strait of, 2, 7

Animals: see Bear, Buffalo, Deer, Dogs, Ewes, Oxen; hunted by Valverde, 28

Antonio, Don, Indian governor, 57

Anza, Juan Bauptiza de, policy of, 47

Apaches: see Calchufines, Carlanas, Chi-

paynes, Conejeros, Cuartelejos, Escalchufines, Faraones, Flechas de Palo, Jicarillas, Julimes, Jumanos, Limitas, Mansos, Natagées, Navajos, Nementinas, Ochos, Palomas, Penxayes, Querechos, Quinias, Qusutas, Río Colorados, Sejines, Sierra Blancas, Trementinas, Vaqueros; mentioned, 1, 8, 19-20, 150-60, 176, 193; alliance ordered with, 35; attack El Paso, 185; fear of Comanches, 142; flee with Picuríes, 56-57; French with, 257; friendly to French, 257-58; groups in northeastern New Mexico, 17; met by Ulibarri, 63; lodges of, 15; kindness of, 165; plazas of, 7; in Spanish plans, 138-39; plans for conversion, 34; propose war on Pawnees and French, 166; search for Comanches, 257; war on, 47; women captives of French, 166; *see* n. 13, p. 263

Apodaca, Antonio de, campaign equipment of, 92; with Hurtado, 89

Apostates, among Jicarillas, 43; among Cuartelejos, 21

Aranz, Chaplain, with Ulibarri, 61

Archévèque, Juan de: campaign equipment of, 92; death of, 38; life of, 16; opinion of, 106-07; opinion regarding El Cuartelejo, 158; with Hurtado, 88; writes French, 163; with Ulibarri, 70; Valverde reports on, 145; with Villasur, 36, 37, note; *see* n. 24, pp. 264-65

Archuleta, Diego de: campaign equipment of, 92; with Hurtado, 89; *see* n. 1, p. 261

Archuleta, Juan de, expedition to El Cuartelejo, 11-12, 53

Archuleta, Juan Joseph de, with Hurtado, 88

Arebalo, Chaplain, with Hurtado, 94

Arias, Diego de, opinion of, 108

Arkansas River: see Río Napestle, 5, 6, 8; described by Ulibarri, 18; French on,

293

36; names and descriptions of, 65-66; Valverde near, 30; Villasur crosses, 37; see n. 18, p. 263

Armenta, Antonio de, escapes Pawnees, 228

Armigo, Bisente de, campaign equipment of, 92; with Hurtado, 88

Avalos, Christoval Moreno, attorney for Martínez, 189

Aviles, Antonio de, declaration of, 190; difficulties with Martínez, 188

Ayjaos, 8

Baca, Alonzo, expedition of, 11, n. 22

Baca, Simón, campaign equipment of, 93; with Hurtado, 89

Barreda, Domingo de la, Vargas' secretary, 54

Barrios, Juan Antonio, escapes Pawnees, 228

Beans, 29

Bear, 123; near Purgatoire, 28

Benavides, Javier, with Hurtado, 88

Bernalillo, 58

Blankets, 13, 61

Bishopric, proposed for New Mexico, 207-08

Brandy, made at El Paso, 122; with Valverde, 28

Buena Vista, Pass of, 64

Bueno y Bohorques, Francisco, opinion of, 106

Buffalo, 31, 125, 126-27, 129

Bustamante, Juan Domingo de: 42, 245-56, 258; diary of, 197-201; edict regarding French, 255; expedition to La Jicarilla, 43, 46; investigates French trade, 245-56; measures against French, 256; measures for La Jicarilla, 193; opinion in council of war, 197; part in Valverde's punishment, 42; prepares campaign, 166; proposes expedition against French, 258; reports to Casafuerte, 200-03; reports French, 46, 256-58; suggests expedition, 47; takes possession of La Jicarilla, 43; writes viceroy, 208

Cabrera, Miguel Enríquez, 200

Cadadachos, 196; French among, 36, 143

Calchufines, same as Escalchufines; near Arkansas River, 31; visit Valverde, 130

Californias, 214

Camargo, Father (Comargo), proctor of custody, 197; with Bustamante, 43

Campaigns, see Expeditions

Canadian River: see Río Colorado, 8; French at mouth of, 36; Hurtado on, 25-26; identified with Río Colorado, 25; named, 116; see n. 42, p. 266

Canal, Domingo de la, patron of Valverde, 179, 188

Canceres: 169, 177, 196, 205, 211; attack Apaches, 143; location of, 40, 171, 174; united with French, 143

Candelaría, Juan de, campaign equipment of, 93

Candelaría, Sierra of, Zumas in, 215

Carrizal, 45, 214

Carlanas: 40, 142, 255; chief appeals to Bustamante, 194; chief of Sierra Blancas, 114; Jicarilla chief of, 29; join Valverde, 30, 117; location of, 142, 170-71; meet Bustamante, 197; meet Ulibarri, 63; rancherías of, 30, 119

Casados, Francisco Lorenzo: campaign equipment of, 92; declaration regarding French, 246-47; opinion of, 107; with Hurtado, 88; with Valverde, 118

Casafuerte, Viceroy: 46, 220, 245-56; Bustamante reports to, 43; orders regarding French, 260; orders aid to Jicarillas, 219; orders investigation of French, 245-46; orders investigation of La Jicarilla, 209; orders trial of Valverde, 220; plans regarding Jicarillas, 44

Casas Grandes (alias Janos), 215-17

Case River (also Casse), 211; habitation of Comanches, 232

Casillas, Bernardo: campaign equipment of, 91; opinion of, 104; with Hurtado, 88; with Valverde, 112

Castillo, Diego de, expedition of, 11, n. 22

Cavendish, 7

Caypa, occupied by Oñate, 7

Chama, 83

Charles III, Indian policy of, 47

Chavarría, Chaplain, with Vargas, 57

Chavez, Pedro de, campaign equipment of, 90; with Hurtado, 88

Chihuahua, 45; distance to El Paso, 213; New Mexican trade with, 247

Chile, English plans against, 33, 140

Chimayó, Faraones rob, 82

Chinali, river of, 47

Chiopo, river of: Indian name for Huerfano River, 34; Valverde on, 121
Chipaynes: 26; identified as Faraones, 80; ranchería of, 26, 96-98; attack Picuríes, 13
Chocolate, supply with Valverde, 28
Church: see Missions, Missionaries, Religion; Apaches inclined to, 72; Jicarillas appeal for, 194-95; Jicarilla interest in, 112-13, 198-200; preachers of, 195
Churlique, Chief, meets Bustamante, 43, 198
Cíbola, Pueblo flight to, 11
Ciéneguilla Creek, Ulibarri on, 17
Cimarron (New Mexico), site of Ulibarri camp, 17; Valverde near, 29
Cimarron Creek, identified with Río de Guadaloupe, 43
Clarinero, Antonio de la, with Hurtado, 88
Clothing, of French, 143; leather jackets, 28
Coahuila, boundary of, 151
Coasts, defense of, 152
Cobián Bustos, Antonio de: reports of visit, 187; visit in New Mexico, 187, 225; visitor, 41, 220
Coca, Miguel de la Vega y, opinion of, 105; with Hurtado, 88
Cochití, 28, 59, 102; Ute attack near, 99
Codallos, Governor, report on La Jicarilla, 46; on Jicarilla location, 46
Cojo, Chief, see El Coxo
Comanches: 18, 21, 43-46, 169, 205, 211; attack La Flecha, 116; attack Palomas and Escalchufines, 46; attack Jicarillas, 112, 194; attack Taos and Cochití, 27; camp near Arkansas River, 30; campaign against by Valverde,, 26-33, 231; captured, 257; council of war against, 99-110; description of, 211; destroy Jicarillas, 46; Jicarillas join, 46; outrages on Jicarillas, 42; origin of, 4, 26, n. 179, p. 281; plan attack on Taos, 16; raid Jicarillas, 201; Serna expedition against, 27; sold in New Vizcaya, 27; steal animals, 103-09; summary of raids of, 27; war on Ute, 47; with French, 257; with Utes in New Mexico, 26-27; see nn. 44-87, pp. 266-72
Conchos, 176, 206, 215
Conchos, river of, 170
Conchos, presidio of, importance of, 216

Conejeros, group meets Ulibarri, 17; report of destruction of, 13
Copala, identified with Teguayo, 10; lagoon of located, 10
Copper, use of on plains, 261
Córdova, Simón de, campaign equipment of, 91; with Hurtado, 88
Corn, 29
Corncobs, valley of, 94
Coronado, journey on plains, 5
Council of War: against Comanches, 28; against Faraones, 24, 80-86; against Utes and Comanches, 99-110; in México, 234-35; members of, 110, 134; opinions in, 195-97; order for, 154, 193; ordering presidio at La Jicarilla, 34, 35, 234-39; regarding French, 168; Valverde calls, 30-31, 127-28, 156-60; Villasur calls, 33, 37-38, 133-34
Coxo, El, Jicarilla chief, 115; meets Bustamante, 43, 199
Crops: see Agriculture, El Cuartelejo, Foods, Indians, La Jicarilla; at El Cuartelejo, 21, 73, 156-60; map of, 50; in Mora valley, 94; of Faraones, 81, 84; of Jicarillas, 73, 112-15, 142, 156-60, 207; of Palomas, 132; of Penxayes, 17; Valverde notes on Jicarilla, 29
Cruz, Father Juan de la, at Taos, 27, 99, 130
Cruz, Manuel Juan de la, governor of New Vizcaya, 33; reports French, 33; writes Valero, 137-38, 145-48, 150-54
Cuartelejo Indians: 19-20, 40, 47, 205, 212, 229, 255, 257; allies of Spaniards, 163; boundary with Pawnees, 163; crops of, 72-73; description, 72-73; flight from Pawnees and French, 71; friendship for Spaniards, 69; kindness of, 39; murder French man and woman, 20; number of, 129, 131; receive Ulibarri, 19; relations with French and Pawnees, 14, 70; sell Pawnees to Spaniards, 74; Pawnee spoil among, 173; trade at Taos, 143; trade with French, 12; Valverde seeks friendship of, 131; visit Valverde on Arkansas, 31; war with Jumanos, 21, 72; with Pawnees, 20-21
Cuberó, Governor Pedro R., expedition against Navajos, 22
Cuerbó y Valdéz, Governor Francisco; 22, 59-61, 158; holds council of war, 16; litigation with soldiers, 179; provides

295

Ulibarri expedition, 78; reports Ulibarri expedition, 77-78; writes Valero, 77; Ulibarri reports to, 22; see n. 7, p. 262.

Culebras, river of, 170

Custodia, see Lepiane, Francisco de, 195

Customs and habits of Faraon Indians, 23

Dabichildildixe, Cuartelejo chief, 75

Daenasgas, Apache name of river, 73

Deer, 12; near Purgatoire River, 30

Defense, against French and English, 140-41; of New Vizcaya, 153

Domínguez, Joseph: campaign equipment of, 90; opinion of, 105, 158; opinion of Faraones, 24; with Hurtado, 87

Domínguez, Juan, opinion of, 85

Dillon (New Mexico, Valverde near, 30

Dogs, Apache use of, 131

Drake, Sir Francis, 7

Durán, Miguel Fernández, writes Valero regarding French, 139

Durán, Miguel, campaign equipment of, 91; with Hurtado, 88

Durango, 45, 214

Du Rivage, on Red River, 36

Du Tisné, among Osage, 36

El Almagre, Comanches in, 256

El Coxo, Chief, rancherías of, 76

El Cuartelejo: location of, n. 79, pp. 270-71; mentioned, 17-19, 40, 45, 59, 160, 182, 212, 259, 260; Escalante on Archuleta at, n. 1, p. 261; Apaches of visit Valverde, 129; Archuleta at, 53; Archuleta expedition to, 12; being abandoned, 144; distance from Santa Fé, 155, 171, 173, 256; French at, 46-47, 256-58; French attack, 36; not a Spanish settlement, 157-58, n. 121, p. 275; opinions regarding, 156-60; plans for presidio at, 34, 150; presidio ordered for, 235; rancherías of, 71; ruins at, 158; Spanish ceremony of possession of, 69; survivors of Villasur expedition at, 38; trade with New Mexico, 107; tribes near, 73; Ulibarri at, 68-75; Valverde near, 30, 142; Valverde opinion of, 159; Villasur at, 37; see n. 23, p. 264

El Embudo, Ute attack, 99

El Paso: 166, 221, 231; distance to Chihuahua, 213; Rivera at, 220; Valverde at, 155, 235; Valverde's provisioning of, 178

English: declare war on Spain, 12; designs of, 151; order to seize, 139; plan attacks in America, 140; ships threaten Spanish, 33

Enríquez, Miguel, secretary to Bustamante, 198

Escalante, Silvestre Velez de, account of Archuleta expedition, 12

Escalchufines, see Calchufines; arrive in New Mexico, 46; bring Comanches to New Mexico, 257

Escanjaques, met by Oñate, 8

Espejo, Antonio de, expedition of, 6

Expeditions: see Routes, Archuleta, Bustamante, Hurtado, Madrid, Serna, Ulibarri, Vargas, Valverde, Villasur; against Faraones, 23; Bustamante to La Jicarilla, 43, 197-203; Cuerbó reports Ulibarri's, 77-78; east of El Paso, 12, n. 24; effect of Villasur massacre, 39; food on, 28; Hurtado's equipment, 90-93; Hurtado summarized, 22; marching order of, 28; organization of, 23-24; Serna against Comanches, 26; southeast of Santa Fé, 11, n. 22; Ulibarri: effect of, 22, fiscal summarizes, 79, Garduño summarizes, 173, return from El Cuartelejo, 21-22; Valverde: against Ute and Comanches, 26-33, 110-33, importance of, 33, route of, 123, summary of, 181-82; Villasur: seeks French, 33, 36-39, origin of, 182-83

Explorations, see Expeditions

Ewes, 54

Faraones: 43, 45, 194, 201; bury corn, 81; council of war against, 80-86; cultivate corn, 81; distance to rancherías of, 82; expedition against, 14; joined by Pecos, 81; location of rancherías, 26, 80; methods of attack, 80; plunder Albuquerque, 208; raid Pueblos, 23; relations with Spaniards, 23; trade at Pecos, 26; various names for, 24; see nn. 27-43, pp. 265-66

Fez, Martin, with Hurtado, 89

Firearms, see Weapons

Fish, Ulibarri notes, 67

Flaco, chief of Sierra Blancas, 114

Flechas de Palo, meet Ulibarri, 17

Foods: see Agriculture, Crops, Fruits, Indians; of Apaches, 64; of Cuartelejos, 19-21, 68; of French, 47

Fountain Creek (Colorado), identified with Río de San Buenaventura, 18; n. 20, p. 263

French: *see* Archévèque, Bustamante, Casafuerte, Clothing, Houses, Indians, New Mexico, Revolledo, Valero, Valverde, Villasur, Weapons; mentioned, 21, 27, 40, 42, 45-46, 68, 82, 137, 149, 169, 177, 181, 183, 196, 203, 205, 220, 223, 226, 229, 235, 260; among Cadadoches, 143; alliance with England and Savoy, 139; allied with Pawnees and Jumanos, 144; apparel of, 47; attack Palomas, 31; attack Cuartelejos, 31; buy Apache Captives, 74; description of, 173; defense against, 215; designs of, 151; dress of, 257; Duke Regent declares war, 33; equipment of, 67; expansion toward New Mexico, 13; fear of, 4; houses of, 132, 232; houses among Pawnees, 31; intrusions, 47; investigation of trade of, 245-56; in Villasur defeat, 174, 242; items taken by Cuartelejo Apaches, 20; join Cuartelejos against Comanches, 256; killed by Apaches, 67; location of, 176; manner of living of, 166; orders against, 168; on Red River, 36; ordered reconnoitered, 155; order to seize, 139; plans against, 34, 237; plans regarding, 176; policy of Spanish toward, 259-60; precautions against, 149; reach Rockies, 21; reconnaissance of, 162-67; relations with Canceres, Texas and Pawnee Indians, 143; reports of, 14, 46, 147; settlements of, 132, 166; on Río de Jesús María, 144; threaten Spanish ports, 33; sought by Villasur, 134; summary of expansion of, 35; threaten New Mexico, 33; trading activities among Indians, 256-60; trade among Indians, 247-55; trading customs among Indians, 260; Ulibarri hears of, 67; united with Pawnees, 70; Valverde hears of, 131; weapons and clothing of, 143; with Apaches, 47; with Comanches, 257; with license, 139

Fresqui, Ambrosio, with Ulibarri, 67

Fruits, *see* Plums

Gallegos, Juan, campaign equipment of, 90; with Hurtado, 88

Gallegos, Nicolas, campaign equipment of, 90

Gambling, prohibited on campaign, 87

Garcitas River, 3

Garduño, Bartolomé de, 40; declaration of, 172-74

Garzía, Alonzo, campaign equipment of, 90; with Hurtado, 88

Garzía, Luís, campaign equipment of, 91; with Hurtado, 88; with Valverde, 117

Gerónimo, Don, explains Faraon habits, 23; lieutenant-governor of Taos, 80; with Valverde, 112

Giravalle, Santiago de, escapes Pawnees, 38

Goats, 54

Gran Quivira, 53

Granillo, Luis, reports French in Cíbola, 13

Griego, Joseph, campaign equipment of, 91; with Hurtado, 88

Griego, Nicolas, campaign equipment of, 92, with Hurtado, 88

Guadalajara, Diego de, expedition of, 11, n. 22

Guadalupe, island of, 152

Guerro, Father Jose Antonio, guardian of convent at Santa Fé, 195

Gutiérrez, Alejo, with Hurtado, 88

Habits, of Faraones, 81

Hennepin, Father, reference to map of, 13

(H)errera, Antonio de, campaign equipment of, 91; with Hurtado, 88

Holguin, *see* Olguín, Thomas

Holland, boundary of, 168

Horses: *see* Horses and mules, Mules, Hurtado, Valverde; mentioned, 54, 56; among Apaches, 122, 129; French trade in Spanish, 36; given Jicarillas, 200; given settlers, 111; herds kept apart, 28; left at El Cuartelejo, 74; number with Hurtado, 91-93; not among Pawnees, 172; Picuríes flee with, 15; raided by Faraones, 24, 83; stolen by Utes, 99-110; traded at El Cuartelejo, 20; Vargas loses, 58

Horses and mules: *see* Horses, Mules; among Faraones, 24, 81; number with Valverde, 28, 117; summary of with Hurtado, 25; taken by Archévèque, 37, n. 97

Horse Creek (Colorado), site of El Cuartelejo, 19

Houses: *see* French, El Cuartelejo, Indians, La Jicarilla; adobe, 94; of Apaches,

297

112; of Faraones, 82; of French, 47, 166, 232, 257; of Jicarillas, 46, 114, 141-42; terraced by Jicarillas, 29, 115; plazas of Indians, 7; proposed for La Jicarilla, 203; of Pueblos at El Cuartelejo, 12, 19, 54, 68; *see* n. 23, p. 264 and n. 60, p. 268

Huerfano River (Colorado), called Chiopo, 34; named San Antonio by Valverde, 30; Valverde on, 30

Huguenots, blamed for Villasur defeat, 39, 164

Humaña, expedition to Quivira, 6

Hurtado, Juan Páez: 24, 25, 82, 87; appointed for Faraon campaign, 86; campaign against Faraones, 80-98; declaration regarding French trade, 247-48; diary of, 94-98; orders Pueblos for campaign, 86; orders to, 86-87

Indatiyuhe, chief of Cuartelejos, 21

Indians: *see* Agriculture, Crops, Foods, French, Houses, Irrigation, Presents, Spanish policy, Trade, Weapons; Ayjaos, Cadadachos, Calchufines, Canceres, Carlanas, Chipaynes, Comanches, Conejeros, Cuartelejos, Escalchufines, Faraones, Flechas de Palo, Jémes (also Xémes), Jicarillas, Julimes, Jumanos, Limitas, Natagées, Navajos, Nementinas, Ochos, Osage, Palomas, Panis (also Pawnees), Pawnees, Pecos, Pelones, Penxayes, Pueblo Indians, Querechos, Queres, Quinias, Quiviras, Qusutas, Río Colorados, San Juan Nambé, San Ildefonso, Santa Clara, Sejines, Shoshone, Sierra Blancas, Tanas, Taos, Teguayo, Tejas, Tiguas, Toucaras, Trementinas, Utes, Utes and Comanches, Vaqueros; French trade among, 73, 246-55, 256-60; habitation around New Mexico, 166; houses of, 8; number estimated, 30; Spanish trade with, 247-55; statement of Spanish policy toward, 79; stone circles of, 8, n. 9; with pierced ears, 171; with Ulibarri, 60; women and children protected, 87

Irrigation, use of by Jicarillas, 29, 115, 142

Isdelpain, Cuartelejo chief, 20

Ivy poison, 116, 118

Jacona, 58

Janos, *see* Casas Grandes; 217

Jediondo, Ojo de, 65

Jémes (Xémes), 59

Jicarillas: mentioned, 21, 40, 42-44, 47, 64, 137, 155, 205, 255; appeal to Bustamante, 208; appeal to Cruz, 138; ask for Christianity and Spanish rule, 43, 194; attack of Utes and Comanches on, 29; bulwark to New Mexico, 196; expedition among, 43; council of war regarding, 193-97; crops of, 207; Faraones attack, 24, 80; keep peace at Taos, 80; life of described, 29; move near Taos and Pecos, 46; offered land at Taos, 218-19; Faraon enemies, 81; flee Comanches, 27; friendly with Spaniards, 29; groups met by Ulibarri, 17; join Comanches, 46; join Valverde, 29; plans for land for, 44; ask for aid, 193; proposals regarding lands of, 199; proposal for pueblos for, 198; propose joining Navajos, 44, 208; reasons for desiring conversion, 211-12; reports at Taos of French, 256; report horses among Faraones, 81; report news of French, 257; seek protection at Taos, 27; summary of problem of, 209-17; supplies for, 218; Valverde meets, 29; visit Navajos, 115; with Hurtado, 25; *see* n. 14, p. 263

Jirón, Dimás, campaign equipment of, 91; with Hurtado, 88

Josephe, guide of Humaña, 6

Julimes, 176; rebellion of, 40

Jumanos: 7, 53; allied with French, 36; attack Palomas, 31; Cuartelejo enmity for, 68; French attack, 14; French and Pawnees allied with, 132, 134; in eastern Colorado region, 31; relations with French, 31; war with Cuartelejos, 21; *see* n. 22, p. 264

King of Spain, fund for ransoming children, 13

Kino, Father, 2

Kiowa County (Colorado), site of Cuartelejo Apache ranchería, 19

La Cañada, 24, 60, 104; Faraones raid, 80; settlers from, 192

La Ciéneguilla, location of, 62; Valverde on, 29, 111

La Flecha River, named Nuestra Señora del Rosario, 113; Valverde on, 113

La Fuente, Joseph de, with Valverde, 131

La Harpe, on Red River, 36
La Jicarilla: mentioned, 25, 40, 43, 45-46, 141, 160, 213, 256, 260; Apache groups of, 63; Archévêque opinion of, 158; Bustamante at, 197-201; boundary of, 197; description of, 200; distance from Santa Fé, 162; distance from Taos, 170, 212; fiscal reply regarding, 204; French near, 47; government and missionaries proposed for, 204; Naranjo's opinion of, 157; Tenorio's opinion of, 158; order for presidio for, 234-39; possession taken of, 200; presidio proposed for, 34, 176, 204-07; ridge of, 64; same as Sierra Blanca, 111; summary of projects regarding, 205; Valverde opinion of, 159-60
La Junta (Colorado), Valverde near present site of, 31
La Junta de los Ríos, 214-17; Valverde pays for ornaments for, 244
La Palotado, canyon of, 62
La Salle, 3, 12, 13
León, Nuevo, boundary of, 151
Lepiane, Francisco de, custodian of New Mexican custody, 195
Ladrones, Sierra de, lair of Faraones, 23, note
Leyva de Bonilla, journey to Quivira, 6
Limitas, Apache group, 17; identified as Faraones, 24, 80
License, of French in Spanish colonies, 151-52
Linares, Duke of, 101; appoints Martínez governor of New Mexico, 186
Lincoln County (Colorado), site of Cuartelejo ranchería, 19
Lovato, Blas, campaign equipment of, 91; with Hurtado, 88
López, Antonio, campaign equipment of, 91; with Hurtado, 88
López, Juan, campaign equipment of, 93
López, Luys, campaign equipment of, 92; with Hurtado, 89
Lorencito Canyon, identified with Canyon of Ulibarri, 18
Lorenzo, Don: testimony regarding Faraones, 82; mentioned, 20; chief of Picuríes, 16; enslaved at El Cuartelejo, 16, 69; explains Faraon habits, 23; flight of, 54, 57; petitions Cuerbó, 61; receives Ulibarri, 19; sends messenger to Cuerbó, 16

Los Adaes, 45, 214
Louisiana, reported trade with New Mexico, 245-56
Luján, Joseph, campaign equipment of, 92; with Hurtado, 89
Luján, Juan, campaign equipment of, 91; with Hurtado, 88
Luján, Mattias, with Vargas, 54-55
Luján, Pedro, campaign equipment of, 90; opinion of, 103; with Hurtado, 98

Madrid Matheas, escapes Pawnees, 228
Madrid, Roque de, campaign against Navajos, 22-23; with Hurtado, 87
Mánquez, Diego, opinion of, 101
Mansos, tribe of Indians, 9
Manila Galleon, plans to protect, 33
Manza, revolt of, 179
Mares, Joseph, escapes Pawnees, 228
Marqués de la Peñuela, Ute-Comanche invasion during rule of, 27; see n. 48, p. 267
Marqués de San Miguel, ordered to seize Pawnees, 40; to form Apache alliance, 34, 169
Marqués, Diego, campaign equipment of, 92; with Hurtado, 88
Martín, Alejo de, opinion of, 102
Martín, Antonio, campaign equipment of, 93
Martín, Diego, with Hurtado, 89
Martín, Francisco, campaign equipment of, 93; with Hurtado, 89
Martín, Hernán, expedition of, 11, n. 22
Martín, Jazinto, with Hurtado, 89
Martín, Marzial, with Hurtado, 89
Martín, Sebastián, opinion of, 103
Martínez, Diego, with Hurtado, 88
Martínez, Felix: 170; alcalde mayor of Taos, 61; appeals to Valero, 187-89; appointed governor, 186; declaration of, 170-72; demands affidavits of removal, 188-89; difficulties with Mogollón, 187-88; file of papers regarding, 187-93; knowledge of La Jicarilla, 207; loses office of governor, 178-79; opinion of, 84; opinion on Indians and geography, 40; opinion regarding Faraones, 24; residence in Santa Fé, 172; review of petition of, 189-90; summary of difficulties in New Mexico, 177-86; writes Valero, 177-86, 188-89; see n. 140, p. 277, and n. 157, p. 279

Martínez Dios, Juan de, campaign equipment of, 90
Massacre: see Villasur; of Spaniards by Pawnees, 38; effect in Mexico, 39; Revolledo's analysis of causes of, 42; location of, see n. 152, pp. 278-79; see nn. 90-96, p. 273, and n. 141, p. 277
Matha, Chaplain, with Ulibarri, 60-61
Melons, preserves with Valverde, 28
Mendoza, Juan Domínguez de, expedition of, 12, note
Metals, at El Cuartelejo, 53
Mexico City: 41; plans to guard coast, 33; council of war regarding Villasur defeat, 239-45; members of council of war in, 234-35
Militia, asked for New Mexico, 169; for coast defense, 151-52; with Hurtado, 86
Mínguez, Father Juan, with Villasur, 36; death of, 38
Missionaries: see Church, Missions, Religion; Aranz, Arebalo, Camargo, Cruz, Escalante, Guerro, Lepiane, Matha, Mínguez, Muñoz, Peña, Perea, Pino, Salas, Ximénez, Zarate Salmerón; Jicarillas ask for, 201; north of New Mexico, 9; proposed for Jicarilla, 204
Missions: see Church, Missionaries, Religion; Jicarilla mission, 46; ornaments for La Junta de los Ríos, 42
Mississippi River; 150, 176, 196; French on, 168
Missouri River, 15, 176, 211; French on, 36
Mittas, Juan de, opinion of, 101-02
Mizquia, Alonzo, secretary of Bustamante, 197
Mogollón, Juan Ignacio de: 25, 82-87; arranges Faraon campaign, 24-25; calls council of war, 23-24, 80; escort of visitor, 85; expedition against Faraones, 23; Martínez's difficulties with, 177-86, 187-88; opinion on Faraon campaign, 85; orders campaign, 86; orders to Hurtado, 25; reports to regarding Faraones; see n. 30, p. 265
Montoya, Andrés, campaign equipment of, 92; with Hurtado, 88
Montaño, Joseph, campaign equipment of, 90; with Hurtado, 88
Monterrey, 151
Moquis, 213

Mora River, Hurtado on, 25, 94; route to Faraones, 82
Mulattos of Mazatlan, 151
Mules: see Horses, Horses and mules, Hurtado, Mogollón, Valverde; with Hurtado, 91-93; with Villasur, 247-56
Muñoz, Francisco, missionary, 9

Nambé: see San Juan Nambé
Nanahe, ranchería of El Cuartelejo, 20, 71
Naranjo, José de: scout, 28, 30; commands Pueblos, 25, 89; death of, 38; gathers Picuríes, 71; on Río Jesús María, 144; opinion of, 101; opinion of El Cuartelejo, 156-57; scout with Ulibarri, 15, 67; with Hurtado, 89; with Valverde, 112; with Vargas, 16
Nasatha, Apache name for river, 73
Natagées, 213
Navajos: 22, 45, 209; Jicarillas propose to join, 208; behead children, 13; campaign against, 22, 23; Jicarillas visit, 115; journeys to Quivira, 13-14; Pawnee spoil traded at New Mexico, 14; Spanish alliance with, 47
Nechas River, 3
Nemantinas, Apache group, 17
New Mexico: see Bustamante, Casafuerte, Church, Cobián Bustos, Cuerbó, French, Indians, Martínez, Mogollón, Presidios, Pueblo Indians, Pueblos and towns, Rivera, Trade, Valero, Vargas, Valverde, Villasur, Weapons; mentioned, 1-3, 5-6, 26, 45, 137, 150, 187; Valverde appointed governor of, 231; conditions of weapons in, 145; depopulated condition of, 213-14; effect of Villasur massacre on, 166-67; French interest in mines of, 35; Indian policy in, 47; Indians arrive at, 168; difficulties of provisioning presidios, 189-90; lack of munitions in, 236; viceregal order regarding Jicarillas at Taos, 219; personal difficulties of governors of, 177-86; plans for defense of, 40-41; soldiers and artisans for, 238; summary of Comanche raids on, 27; trade with El Cuartelejo, 107; troops recommended for, 175; visita of Cobián Bustos, 187
New Vizcaya: 6, 206, 220, 259; Comanches sold in, 27; Cruz, governor of, 33; inadequacy of defense of, 153; New

Mexico trade with, 252; number of soldiers of, 147-48; troops and pay asked for, 146-48
New Spain, 3
Neyra y Quiroga, Joseph de, 223
Nisquisandi, Apache name for river, 73
North Platte River, identified with Río de San Lorenzo, 37
Nueces River (Texas), expeditions to, 11, n. 22
Nuestra Señora del Buen Suceso, El Ojo de, Ulibarri names, 66
Nuestra Señora de Guadalupe, ranchería of El Cuartelejo, 71
Nuestra Señora de los Angeles de Porciuncula, named by Ulibarri, 19, 68; ranchería of El Cuartelejo, 68, 71

Ochos, Apache group meets Ulibarri, 17
Olguín, Thomas: 229, 233; opinion of, 107, 158; opposes Villasur, 184; Valverde blames for loss of Villasur, 223
Ojo de Jediondo, Ulibarri on, 18
Ojo Caliente (New Mexico), 45, 214
Ojo de Naranjo, location of Apaches of El Coxo, 17
Ojo de Santa Rita, named by Ulibarri, 19
Oñate, Juan de: colonizes New Mexico, 7; expedition east of New Mexico, 7-8; expedition to Colorado River, 9; interest in Teguayo, 9
Ornaments, religious, among Apaches, 72
Ortis, Luís, campaign equipment of, 91; with Hurtado, 88
Ortiz, Nicolas, opinion of, 101
Osage, French among, 36; French traders among, 13, 36
Oxen, 54

Pacheco, Don Juan, governor at Taos, 61
Palacios, fiscal: exonerates Valverde, 240-41; recommends land for Jicarillas, 209; reply concerning La Jicarilla, 217; reply to Casafuerte, 203
Palizada, river of, same as Mississippi, 168
Palomas: 47, 143, 229, 252; arrive in New Mexico, 46; attacked by French, 31; capture Comanches, 257; location of, 31; near Arkansas, 31; wounded by French and Pawnees, 132
Panis (Pawnees), river of, 156

Parral (Mexico), 170, 235; Cruz at, 148; New Mexican trade with, 247; order to governor of, 140-41
Pawnees: mentioned, 20, 40, 42, 69, 135, 137, 163, 169, 170, 196, 205, 223, 226, 229, 260; allied with French, 4, 70, 163; attack Palomas, 31; allied with French and Jumanos, 132; boundary of, 159; boundary with Cuartelejos, 163; communication with Villasur, 38, 163-64, 226-27; Cuartelejo enmity for, 68; estimated location of, 173; French guns among, 248; in New Mexico, 14, note; on Arkansas, 36; on Hennepin's map, 13; raids in eastern Colorado region, 4; ransomed captives of, 4; relations with El Cuartelejo, 20, 70; relations with French, 31; sell Apaches to French, 74; settlements of, 171, 183; village of, 37; see n. 147, p. 278
Pay, asked for New Vizcaya troops, 147-48
Pecos: 5, 7, 24, 46; Faraones at, 26, 80; Jicarillas live near, 46; missionary at, 110; Vargas at, 58
Pecos Indians: 24, 54, 86; friendly with Faraones, 24; lose horses, 15; relations with Faraones, 81; with Hurtado, 89, 93
Pelones, 74
Peña, Manuel de la, father at Cochití, 99
Peñalosa, Governor, false claim of, 11, note
Peñuela, Marqués de la, Ute-Comanche invasion during rule, 27; Ute-Comanche peace, 105
Penxayes, Apache group, location, 17; meet Ulibarri, 17, 64-65
Perea, Fray Estevan de, expedition of, 9
Perea, Jacinto, escapes Pawnees, 228
Peru, English plans to attack, 33, 140
Philippine Galleon, attack planned on, 140; protection of, 151-52
Picuríes: 21, 24-25, 60-61, 82-84, 103, 157; aid to, 83; assembly point of campaign, 86; attacked by Faraones, 23-24; Chipaynes at, 13; Faraones enemies of, 81; few Indians at, 60; Hurtado at, 89, 94; Ulibarri at, 60, 76; Vargas at, 53
Picuríes Indians: 21, 24, 40, 54, 55, 60, 85-86, 156-58, 236; at El Cuartelejo, 68, 69, 73, 74; captives of El Cuartelejo, 20; n. 6, p. 262; delivered to Ulibarri, 73; flight of, 14; number returned by Ulibarri, 74, 77; pursue Faraones on Canadian River, 26; see Don Lorenzo,

chief; with Hurtado, 89, 93; with Valverde, 126
Pino, Father, missionary at Pecos, 110; with Valverde, 110
Pineda, Juan de, opinion of, 102
Pinole, taken by Valverde, 28
Pintto, Roque, secretary to Mogollón, 81
Platte River, 4, 6; Apache name of, Sitascahe, 73
Plum trees, 30
Popé, chief, 20
Posadas, Alonzo de, identifies Escanjaques with Aijados, 8
Presents: for Apaches, 63, 246-56; for Cuartelejos, 71; for Indians, 37; for Jicarillas, 17, 43, 113; given Penxayes, 18; Villasur sends to Pawnees, 137
Presidio: see Councils of war, El Cuartelejo, French, La Jicarilla, Naranjo, New Mexico, Rivera, Troops, Valero, Bustamante: arguments for establishing, 214; Bustamante recommends, for La Jicarilla, 43-44, 202-03; condemned for La Jicarilla, 45, 212-16; difficulties regarding provisioning of, 189-90; for La Jicarilla, 204-07; 234-39; lawsuits over provisioning of, 177-80; ordered for El Cuartelejo, 155; plans for El Cuartelejo, 34; urged by Codallos, 46; Valverde recommends for La Jicarilla, 34
Provinces, jurisdictions of, 151
Pueblo (Colorado), Ulibarri near site of, 30
Pueblo Indians: see Jémez (Xémes), Pecos, Queres, San Juan Nambé, San Ildefonso, Santa Clara, Tanas, Taos, Tiguas; mentioned, 1; list of with Hurtado, 89, 93; revolt of, 11, 12, 14-15; with Hurtado, 86; with Valverde, 111, 141
Pueblos and towns: see Ácoma, Bernalillo, Caypa, Chama, Chimayó, Cochití, Jacona, La Cañada, Moquis, Nambé, Ojo Caliente, Pecos, Pujuaque, Queres, Río Arriba, San Felipe, San Ildefonso, San Juan Nambé, Santa Clara, Santa Cruz, Santo Domingo, Santa Fé, Socorro, Taos, Tezuque, Vera Cruz, Zía
Pujuaque, 25, 101, 104
Pujuaque Indians, with Hurtado, 89, 93
Purgatoire River, identified with Río de las Animas, 30

Quazula, province of, 10
Querechos, 5

Queres, 84, 102
Queres Indians, friendly to Faraones, 81
Quima, Captain, see Quinias; lands of, 9
Quinias, Apaches north of New Mexico, 9, note
Quiros, Diego Arias de, declaration regarding French, 252-53
Quiviras: 5, 8, 9-10, 12, 53; description of, 15; visited by Pueblos and Cuartelejos, 12; identified with Wichitas, 8
Qusutas, possibly Utes, 10

Ramon, Diego de, in Texas, 231
Real, Alonzo, campaign equipment of, 90; with Hurtado, 88
Real, Eusebio, campaign equipment of, 90; with Hurtado, 88
Recopilación de Indias, cited, 204
Red River, French on, 36
Regidores, imprisoned by Valverde, 180
Religion, Cuartelejo idea of Christianity, 20
Revolledo, Juan de Olivan: advises presidio for La Jicarilla, 44; reports on Cruz and Valverde, 149; convicts Valverde of incompetence, 41-42, 240-44; examines Martínez, 170; interviews regarding Villasur defeat, 171-75; investigates Villasur massacre, 40; opinion on presidio, 150; recommendations regarding Villasur massacre, 40; requests information on French and Indians, 170; reports to Valero, 149, 169-70; report regarding Jicarillas, 218-19; reviews Martínez's petition, 189-90; summarizes evidence regarding Villasur defeat, 175-77; writes Casafuerte, 191-92; writes Casafuerte regarding French, 259-60; writes Valero regarding La Jicarilla, 205-07; writes Valero regarding Villasur defeat, 175-77
Ribera, Juan Phelipe de, campaign equipment of, 91
Río Arriba, 103; Faraones rob, 82
Río Colorados, Apache group meets Ulibarri, 17
Río Colorado (New Mexico): see Canadian River; Hurtado on, 95-98; identified with Canadian River, 25; Valverde on, 30, 116
Río de las Animas, identified with Purgatoire River, 30; see n. 68, p. 269
Río de Chinali, French houses on, 257; French on, 46-47, 256

Río de Guadaloupe, identified with Cimarron Creek, 43; in La Jicarilla, 197
Río de Jesús María: 40, 65, 135-36, 170, 187, 219, 228, 239; distance from El Cuartelejo, 171, 173; French on, 31, 144; identified with South Platte, 37; named by Naranjo, 144; Naranjo reaches, 156; Villasur on, 134
Río de Napestle (Napeste, Nepeste): 40, 170, 211, 226, 229; distance from Santa Fé, 171; French call Acansa, 142; identified with Arkansas River, 18; near El Cuartelejo, 73; Ulibarri on, 65; Valverde on, 30, 129, 133, 143; Valverde reaches, 142
Río de las Piletas, 65
Río de Penas, at El Cuartelejo, 19, 71
Río de los Picuríes, 94
Río de San Pantaléon, 94
Río de San Buenaventura, identified with Fountain Creek, 18; Ulibarri on, 66
Río de San Blas, Ulibarri names, 63
Río de San Christobál, 64
Río de San Estebán of the Caves, Hurtado on, 94
Río de San Francisco de Xavier, Ulibarri names, 62
Río de San Ignacio, 67
Río de San Joseph, Valverde on, 112
Río de San Juan de Bauptista, 65
Río de San Lorenzo, 38, 227, 229; identified with the North Platte, 37; Valverde on, 121; Villasur camp on, 223
Río de San Raymunda, nonnato, Hurtado on, 95
Río de Santa Ana, identified with the Purgatoire River, 18; Ulibarri on, 17, 64
Río de Santa María Magdalena, Ulibarri names, 63; 17
Río de Santiago, Ulibarri on, 17
Río de la Santíssima Cruz, Ulibarri names, 63
Río Grande de San Francisco, Ulibarri's name for Arkansas River, 65
Río Grande del Norte: 3, 6, 40; crossing of, 169; fear French on, 168; St. Denis on, 36
Rivera, Pedro de: visitor, 225, 228, 234, 239, 260; at Santa Fé, 41; authority for visit, 220; criticism of Jicarilla action, 45; Escalchufines and Palomas bring Comanches to, 257; holds trial of Valverde, 219-34; investigates Jicarillas, 44-

45; to investigate La Jicarilla, 209; investigates Villasur defeat, 41; with Hurtado, 88; writ of, 224; writ of Valverde trial, 220; writes Casafuerte regarding New Mexico, 209-17; see n. 177, p. 281, and nn. 178-202, pp. 281-83
Rodarte, Cristobál, campaign equipment of, 93; with Valverde, 120
Rodríguez, Juan Antonio, campaign equipment of, 92; with Hurtado, 88
Rodríguez, Agustin, missionary on expedition, 6
Rodríguez, Lorenzo, campaign equipment of, 91; with Hurtado, 88
Rodríguez, Melchior, escapes Pawnees, 228
Rroxas, Pedro de, campaign equipment of, 91; with Hurtado, 88
Rojas, Juan Rico de, campaign equipment of, 90; with Hurtado, 88
Romero, Domingo, campaign equipment of, 91; with Hurtado, 88
Romero, Fray Bartolomé, 9
Rosales, Francisco Antonio, attorney, 187; writes Casafuerte, 192
Routes:see Expeditions; of Valverde, 111, 118, 123-24, 127, 133; of Villasur, 226; to El Cuartelejo, 173
Royval, Ignacio, declaration of regarding French, 253-54; opinion of, 106
Ruins, at El Cuartelejo, 158
Ruíz, Juan, with Vargas, 54

Sainz, Master, opinion on Villasur defeat, 167-69
Salaries, for fathers, 207
Salas, Fray Juan de, expedition of, 11. n. 22
Salas, Joseph de, campaign equipment of, 90; with Hurtado, 88
Saldívar Mendoza, Vicente de, expedition of, 7
Sanasesli, ranchería of El Cuartelejo, 20, 71
San Antonio, river of, Chiopo named, 121
San Agustín, ranchería of El Cuartelejo, 71
San Carlos (Colorado), river of, Valverde on, 30
San Felipe, attack by Apaches, 185
San Fernando, river of, Ulibarri on, 17; Valverde on, 29; mentioned, 62
San Francisco, river of, Valverde on, 122
San Ildefonse, 6, 25, 58
San Juan, Miguel de, campaign equipment of, 91; with Hurtado, 88

303

San Juan Bautista, presidio of, St. Denis at, 36

San Juan Nambé, 25, 58

San Juan Nambé Indians, with Hurtado, 89, 93

San Lucas, Cape of, 152

San Miguel, river of, Valverde on, 117

San Ofre, river of, Valverde on, 123

Sánchez, Bartolomé, with Ulibarri, 63

Sánchez, Joachín, campaign equipment of, 91; escapes Pawnees, 228; with Hurtado, 88

Sandía, Sierra of, fruit trees at, 213; habitat of Faraones, 23

Sandoval, Miguel de, campaign equipment of, 92

Santa Ana, Francisco Sánchez de, secretary of Rivera, 221

Santa Clara, 25

Santa Clara Indians, captives among Cuartelejos, 20, 72; with Hurtado, 89, 93

Santa Cruz, 101-04; alcalde of, 104; Naranjo from, 101

Santa Fé: mentioned, 21, 24-26, 40, 43-45, 58, 60, 100-01, 147, 150, 198, 228, 230, 235, 239; alcalde mayor of, 106; councils of war at, 90, 99-110, 156, 195-96; distance from Villasur massacre, 170; Jicarillas at, 42; members of council of war at, 246; Rivera at, 41, 224; seat of Valverde trial, 220-45; settlers of, 92; Ulibarri at, 76; Ulibarri organizes expedition at, 16; Vargas returns Pueblos to, 16; Valverde leaves, 110; Valverde returns to, 32; Ulibarri leaves, 163

Santiestevan, Joseph de, escapes Pawnees, 228

Santiestevan, Salvador de, opinion of, 84, 106; with Hurtado, 87

Santo Domingo, 89, 184

Santo Domingo, principal ranchería of El Cuartelejo, 60, 69-71

Santo Domingo, river of, Valverde on, 120

Sejines, Taos for Chipaynes or Limitas or Faraones, 24

Serna, Xptoval de la, death of, 38; interpreter of, 163; opinion of, 105

Settlers, list of, with Hurtado, 88-89; number with Hurtado, 91-93; number with Valverde, 111, 141

Sheep, taken by Valverde, 28

Shoshone, relations with Comanches, 26

Sierra Blanca: distance from El Cuartelejo, 173; location of Carlanas, 142, 171; see n. 15, p. 263

Sierra Blanca Indians, 40, 47, 155, 205, 257; meet Valverde, 114

Siete Ríos, fertility of, 213

Silva, Manuel, campaign equipment of, 90; with Hurtado, 88

Silver: see Villasur, personal possession of

Sistaca, François, Pawnee interpreter, 136

Sitascahe, Apache name for Pawnee river, 73

Six Missions, rebellion of Indians of, 170

Slaves, sold by Cuartelejo Apaches; by Pawnees, 20

Socorro, 213

Sopesta, Manuel de, missionary, 107

South Platte River, identified with Río de Jesús María, 37; Villasur on, 37

South Sea, English voyage to, 140

Spaniards: activities north and east of Santa Fé, summarized, 22; reasons for expansion of, 2-4; relations with Cuartelejos, 21

Spanish Indian Policy: of Hurtado, 87; proposed for La Jicarilla, 203, 207, 218-19; toward French, 259-60; toward Indians, 177

Squash, 29

St. Denis, on Red River, 36; on Río Grande, 36

Sylvia, Governor Francisco de, 9

Tachichichi, Cuartelejo ranchería, 67

Tafoya, Antonio, campaign equipment of, 91; with Hurtado, 88

Tafoya, Christobál, opinion of, 103; with Valverde, 126

Tafoya, Diego, escapes Pawnees, 226

Tagle Villegas, Captain Joseph de, at presidio of Santa Fé, 109; opinion of, 108; with Valverde, 115

Tamariz, Francisco, campaign equipment of, 90; with Hurtado, 88; declaration of, 174-75

Tamariz, Phelipe: declaration regarding French, 250-52; escapes Pawnees, 228; eyewitness of Villasur massacre, 39; reports Villasur's defeat, 174; reports concerning Villasur diary, 40; testimony in Valverde trial, 228-30

Tano, 54

Tanos Indians: captives of Cuartelejos, 73